CORRECTIONS IN CANADA

Social Reactions to Crime

CORRECTIONS IN CANADA

Social Reactions to Crime

John A. Winterdyk
Mount Royal College

Toronto

To my loved ones, whose support and understanding
can be measured only by what the heart can feel

—J.A.W.

Canadian Cataloguing in Publication Data

Main entry under title:

Corrections in Canada: Social reactions to crime

Includes index
ISBN 0-13-084425-X

1. Corrections in Canada. I. Winterdyk, John.

HV9507.C67 2001   324.6'0971   C00-930907-1

ISBN 0-13-084425-X

Vice President, Editorial Director: Michael Young
Executive Editor: David Stover
Marketing Manager: Sophia Fortier
Signing Representative: Colleen Henderson
Developmental Editor: Lisa Philips
Production Editor: Avivah Wargon
Copy Editor: Madeline Koch
Production Coordinator: Wendy Moran
Page Layout: Heidi Palfrey
Art Director: Mary Opper
Cover Design: Dave McKay
Cover Image: PhotoDisc

1 2 3 4 5   05 04 03 02 01

Printed and bound in Canada

Statistics Canada information is used with the permission of the Minister of Industry, as Minister responsible for Statistics Canada. Information on the availability of the wide range of data from Statistics Canada can be obtained from Statistics Canada's Regional Offices, its World Wide Web site at **http://www.statcan.ca**, and its toll-free access number 1-800-263-1136.

Brief Contents

Contents

Chapter 3: Corrections in Canada: Public Knowledge and Public Opinion   *Julian V. Roberts*   49

Chapter 6: Incarceration in Canada: Past and Present
Michael G. Young 102

Chapter 7: Prison Life and Daily Experiences
Shivu Ishwaran and *Robynne Neugebauer* 129

Chapter 8: Limiting the State's Right to Punish
Kelly Hannah-Moffat   151

Chapter 9: Special Populations within Corrections
D.A. Andrews, Craig Dowden, and
L. Jill Rettinger   170

PART 5: COMMUNITY CORRECTIONS AND THE FUTURE OF CORRECTIONS

Chapter 13: Community-Based Corrections Livy Visano   296

Preface

The history of corrections is one that has been marked by constant change. These changes have, in part, been influenced by the evolving economic, social, and political nature that characterizes Canadian society. Since 1867, when Canada acquired nationhood status, we have been witness to numerous dramatic shifts in correctional practices. Ironically, many of these practices have gone largely unnoticed by Canadians until more recent times. Being the final formal link in the criminal justice system, corrections is sometimes euphemistically referred to as the "hidden element" of the system.

Today, in large part due to mass media, public awareness and opinion range across the spectrum from liberalism to conservatism. A growing awareness about crime and, in particular, about violence, has spurred public intolerance towards criminals and increased calls for more punitive sanctions. We have seen the prison population steadily grow over the past few decades. This growth has placed a significant burden on the resources of the criminal justice system. Increasing financial constraints, as well as a growing number of women and older individuals entering the correctional system, have further compounded the dilemma. To counter these trends, a variety of alternative programs and practices, both formal and informal in nature, have been introduced, and in some cases reintroduced.

Collectively, the correctional changes and challenges have prompted a new level of interest by criminologists and criminal justice practitioners and administrators. There is an urgent need to better understand and evaluate the needs of society and how corrections can play an effective and efficient role in protecting society.

To this end, the primary goals of this book are to:

1. Provide students with a comprehensive and up-to-date overview of the development and current status of corrections in Canada;

2. Provide an overview of the major elements and issues confronting the different aspects of correctional practices in Canada;

3. Show how economic, social, and political issues have helped to forge current correctional practices ranging from incarceration to community-based corrections;

4. Provide an overview of current policy and administrative practices that affect the different aspects of corrections today;

5. Provide insight and identify possible issues and directions for correctional practices in the future.

Although this book was intended as an introductory text for corrections, each chapter bridges descriptive information with thought-provoking issues to help students both understand and critically examine the diversity of corrections.

ORGANIZATION OF THE TEXT

This textbook is composed of 14 chapters written by individuals who have both academic and practical knowledge of their subject area. This approach ensures that students not only are presented with a sound overview but also benefit from the most current and relevant information in regards to policy and administrative issues, as well as being provided with practical insights. In addition to reviewing the "facts," each chapter provides provocative questions about the various aspects of corrections. Overall, the intention of the text is to stimulate discussion and encourage the reader to explore issues beyond the scope of this book so as to facilitate an enriched understanding of, and appreciation for, the complex and dynamic nature of corrections in Canada.

For the most part, the order of the chapters reflects a chronological and practical approach in corrections. We begin in Chapter 1 with a discussion of the concept of corrections followed by a historical overview of correctional practices in Canada in Chapter 2. Chapter 3 explores how public perceptions can influence correctional policy; drawing on his own findings, Julian Roberts also shows those areas in which the public is ill informed about correctional issues raising interesting questions about how the public obtains its information and role of the media. In Chapter 4, Laurence Motiuk provides a concise yet comprehensive review of the administration and management of corrections in Canada. Here the reader will learn that corrections involves much more than incarceration.

Beginning with Chapter 5, the book moves into the concrete aspects of the correctional system in a logical and practical manner. John Anderson deals with the most common form of community-based sentences—probation. In addition to describing the purpose of probation, he also addresses some of the key administrative issues confronting probation officers. In Chapter 6, Michael Young provides a comprehensive overview of the Canadian prison system. In addition to providing a historical context, he identifies some of the current issues Canadian prisons are facing. Shivu Ishwaran and Robynne Neugebauer present a concise summary of a wide range of issues confronting the management of prisoners in Chapter 7. They begin by clarifying the concept of "total institutions" and then discuss issues such as inmates entering prisons, the relation of prison riots to overcrowding, and inmate codes. The issue of prisoners rights is presented in Chapter 8 by Kelly Hannah-Moffat, who covers the evolution of prisoners' rights and considers the offender grievance system, correctional investigation procedures, among other contemporary issues. In Chapter 9, D.A. Andrews, Craig Dowden, and Jill Rettinger address the issue of special offender populations in the correctional system. They begin by reviewing the different philosophical approaches to corrections and go on to discuss such groups as young offenders, the aging inmate population, Aboriginal offenders, and sex offenders. In Chapter 10, Helen Bortich focuses exclusively on the female offender and discusses a wide range of issues, such as cross-gender staffing, female offender profiles, types of facilities available for female prisoners, and the controversial array of programs and services available to female prisoners. In Chapter 11, Paul Gendreau, Paula Smith, and Claire Goggin shift the focus to treatment-related issues. Rather than simply discuss specific programs that can be found within the broad spectrum of corrections, the authors draw on their knowledge of meta-analysis to review what types of programs work and what types do not. This chapter provides numerous opportunities to explore the role and purpose of correctional practices and philosophy.

The final three chapters deal with post-incarceration and future directions and issues in corrections. Chapter 12 focuses on conditional release. Tim Segger and Darryl Plecas use the most current data to provide a thorough overview of conditional release. They cover all the major elements involving conditional release from types, to conditions, victim involvement, the role of Aboriginal culture, to how an offender can obtain a pardon. In Chapter 13, Livy Visano offers a stimulating discussion on community-based corrections. Visano encourages the student to examine some of the fundamental assertions of community-based corrections. In the final chapter, J. Oliver Doyle presents a cogent and pragmatic approach to the future of corrections by dividing the issues into internal and external factors and carefully and realistically exploring their implications.

SPECIAL FEATURES OF THIS TEXT

In addition to this text consisting of original contributions from experts in their respective fields, it offers the following elements to help students and instructors:

- Box inserts
- Web links
- Study and discussion questions
- Key terms and concepts

ACKNOWLEDGMENTS

This text would not have been possible without the contributions of the exceptional cross-section of contributors. Each has offered a level of expertise that could not have been provided by the editor alone. Although it is always a challenge to produce an edited text with a consistent style and level of writing, each contributor has worked diligently to ensure that his or her chapter was student-friendly and covered common pedagogical elements.

I would like to thank the reviewers from across Canada who provided some very helpful and insightful feedback: J. Oliver Doyle (Sir Sanford Fleming College), Desmond Ellis (York University), Colin Goff (University of Winnipeg), John Jones (Sir Sanford Fleming College), David Osborne (Langara College), Robert Ritchie (Centennial College), Oliver Stoetzer (Fanshawe College), and Rebecca Volk (Algonquin College). Reviewers are often the unsung heroes of any textbook. Their dedication to reviewing and helping to draw attention to both the strengths and weaknesses of a textbook can go a long way in ensuring that the final product reflects what is in the best interests of the students.

I am once again indebted to Rosemary Buck for her continued support and encouragement. In addition to being a significant part of my life, Rosemary played a major role in preparing the Instructors Testbank and providing helpful feedback on many of the chapters. With regards to my colleagues Roland LaHaye, Doug King, and Sandie McBrien, I appreciate the time they took out of their busy schedules to share their views and offer their insights on certain aspects of the book. To my research assistants Nikki Thompson and Andrea Moormann, I am indebted to them for their level of dedication.

Last, but not least of all, a big thank you to the "gang" at Pearson Education. In particular, I would like to thank David Stover, Acquisitions Editor, for his continued support and friendship, and to Lisa Phillips, Developmental Editor, whose uplifting approach and professionalism helped to ensure that all the major elements of the book were able to come together. Finally, but not least of all, I am grateful for the incredible quality of work and support provided by Madeline Koch, the copy editor.

Notes on Contributors

John Anderson is the Chair of the Criminology Department at Malaspina University-College on Vancouver Island, B.C. His professional career includes working with young offenders in residential treatment, adult corrections in a maximum security remand centre, and working on various research projects in corrections and policing. He is currently conducting research into the process by which offenders leave criminal lifestyles. He has also been largely responsible for setting up a helpful criminology Web page that, among other links, includes correctional links (see web.mala.bc.ca/crim/).

D.A. Andrews received his Ph.D. in psychology from Queen's University at Kingston, Ontario. He is a professor of psychology at Carleton University, Ottawa, Ontario. His research interests include a variety of assessment, intervention, evaluation, and theoretical issues in juvenile and criminal justice, corrections, and other human service agencies. He is co-developer of risk/need assessment instruments in wide-scale use with young offenders and adult offenders. Recent consultation and training efforts have involved the U.S. National Institute of Corrections, National Parole Board of Canada, Ontario Ministry of Community and Social Services, Ontario Ministry Correctional Services, and the states of Vermont, Ohio, and Colorado. The first edition of his book, *The Psychology of Criminal Conduct,* was nominated for the Hindelang Award of the American Society of Criminology. His research and theoretical contributions to correctional policy and practice were recognized by the American Probation and Parole Association through the University of Cincinnati award in 1997. In addition, he received the Margaret Mead Award for contributions to social justice and humanitarian advancement from the International Community Corrections Association.

Helen Boritch is an associate professor of sociology at the University of Alberta. Her research interests centre on women and crime, and she is the author of *Fallen Women: Female Crime and Criminal Justice in Canada.* In addition, she is continuing her historical research into crime, criminality, and criminal justice institutions in the 19th and early 20th centuries.

Craig Dowden is a doctoral candidate in the Department of Psychology at Carleton University, Ottawa, Ontario, and a Research Assistant in the Research Branch of the Correctional Service of Canada. His current research interests include the assessment of attitudes of correctional staff, organizational behaviour, and issues relating to the efficacy and evaluation of correctional interventions for offenders.

J. Oliver Doyle spent a short time in farm management after graduating from the State Agricultural College in Ireland. He then embarked on a career in the insurance industry, working in Ireland, England, and Canada. He changed careers and enjoyed a successful 15 years in corrections before joining the Centre for Law and Justice at Sir Sandford Fleming College in Peterborough, Ontario. He teaches future correctional workers and police officers, specializing in management of disturbed behaviour, crisis prevention, conflict management, and mediation. He has completed undergraduate and graduate degrees at Queen's University, Kingston, Ontario, plus a host of training programs in England, Canada, and the U.S.

Alan Erdahl has taught as a sessional instructor in the criminology program at Mount Royal College in Calgary, Alberta, for the past 16 years. He also teaches in the Academic Foundations Department at Bow Valley College in Calgary. He has a master's degree in social work from the University of Manitoba and has extensive experience in social work and corrections in both community and institutions in Alberta and Saskatchewan. He worked as a Probation Officer/Supervisor, Group Home Director, Deputy Director at Calgary Remand Centre, and Deputy Director in both adult and young offender centres. He is currently a board member for the Calgary John Howard Society and a member of the Parole Citizens Advisory Committee.

Paul Gendreau is the Director at the Centre for Criminal Justice Studies at the University of New Brunswick in Saint John. He has conducted extensive research in a wide range of correctional issues with a special interest in effective offender treatment, the effects of deterrence, the effects of prison life, and developing rational correctional policies. His research has appeared in numerous books and journals.

Claire Goggin is Associate Director at the Centre for Criminal Justice Studies at the University of New Brunswick in Saint John. Her research interests include studying the effects of intensive probation/parole treatment, assessment and classification in criminal justice and mental health, program evaluation, actuarial versus clinical assessment, and meta-analysis.

Kelly Hannah-Moffat is Assistant Professor in the Department of Sociology at Erindale College, University of Toronto. She worked as a Research and Policy Advisor for the Commission of Inquiry into Certain Events at the Prison for Women (the Arbour Commission) and is a past president of the Toronto Elizabeth Fry Society. Her areas of research include women's imprisonment, penal reform, sociology of punishment, parole, risk theory, feminist theory, governmentality, and Foucaudian theory.

Shivu Ishwaran is an independent researcher and plans to defend his Ph.D. dissertation at Leiden University in the Netherlands. He is the editor of the *International Journal of Comparative Sociology,* the *Journal of Asian and African Studies,* and the *Journal of Developing Societies*. His research focuses on comparative criminology, criminal justice, corrections, and cultural values and international models of crime.

Laurence L. Motiuk received his Ph.D. in psychology from Carleton University, Ottawa, Ontario, and is currently the Director General of the Research Branch at Correctional Service of Canada. He began his correctional career in the psychology department at the maximum security Ottawa-Carlton Detention Centre in 1979 and was an employee of the Ontario Ministry of Correctional Services until 1988. Dr. Motiuk is now an adjunct professor in the Psychology Department at Carleton University. He is also editor of *Forum on Corrections Research*, and he has chapters to *What Works in Corrections: A Blueprint for Action* and a co-written chapter in *Adult Correctional Treatment*. Recent journal articles include "Situating Risk within a Reintegration Potential Framework" and "Using Dynamic Factors to Better Predict Post-Release Outcome." Current research interests include offenders assessment, population profiling, and reintegration potential.

Robynne Neugebauer is Assistant Professor in Sociology at York University. Her research and teaching focus on policing, inequality and criminal justice, penology, wife assault, and aging. Her books include *Criminal Injustice: Racism in the Criminal Justice System, Aging and Inequality: Cultural Constructions of Differences,* and *Police-Community Relations* (forthcoming).

Darryl Plecas was one of the first graduates of the master's program at Simon Fraser University in Vancouver, B.C. He went on to complete his doctoral work in education at the University of British Columbia, also in Vancouver. While attending school he taught at Fraser Valley Community College (now the University College of Fraser Valley in

Abbotsford, B.C., where he was Chair of the Department of Criminology and Criminal Justice. He has conducted extensive research in addressing a wide range of corrections and law enforcement issues.

L. Jill Rettinger is a research consultant who specializes in criminal justice system research, including program and legislation implementation evaluation. Jill received her Ph.D. in psychology from Carleton University in Ottawa, Ontario, in 1998. Her dissertation involved a long-term recidivism follow-up of community-based and institutionalized adult female offenders in a provincial correctional system, with an emphasis on the determination of risk and need for female offenders. Recently, she has participated in the evaluation of an adult pre-trial diversion project, a domestic violence courts project, and the implementation of the Child Support Guidelines Initiative.

Julian V. Roberts is a professor of criminology at the University of Ottawa. He holds a Ph.D. in psychology from the University of Toronto. Since 1992 he has served as the editor of the *Canadian Journal of Criminology*. His research interests include sentencing, parole, public attitudes to crime, and criminal justice, with a particular emphasis on sentencing and parole. Recent books include *Public Opinion, Crime, and Criminal Justice* and *Making Sense of Sentencing*. He is currently working on an international study of public opinion, with co-authors in several other countries.

Tim Segger is a former parole officer. In 1980, he joined Fraser Valley College, now known as University College of the Fraser Valley, in Abbotsford, B.C. He is currently Chair of the Department of Criminology and Criminal Justice. His areas of research interest include the socioeconomic impact assessment of prisons on surrounding communities, correctional program design and evaluation, criminal justice policy, and criminal justice in the media.

Paula Smith is a research assistant at the Centre for Criminal Justice Studies at the University of New Brunswick. Her research interests include developmental issues, comparative utility of actuarial assessment measures, evaluating the quality of correctional programming, and meta-analytic methodologies.

Livy Visano is currently Associate Professor in Sociology at Atkinson College, York University, in Toronto, Ontario. His publications include a forthcoming book *Teaching Controversy*, and *Crime and Culture, This Idle Trade, Canadian Penology: Advanced Perspectives and Research, Understanding Policing*, and *Deviant Designations: Crime, Law and Deviance in Canada*. In addition, he has published dozens of book chapters and journal articles. He brings to his research and teaching his various experiences as a former Dean of Atkinson College, parole officer with Corrections Canada, chair of a citizens' advisory committee, to name only a few.

John Winterdyk is a graduate from the School of Criminology at Simon Fraser University in Vancouver, B.C. His areas of interest and research include young offenders, comparative criminology, research methods, and a range of issues related to criminal justice. In addition to his list of published articles, he is the author or co-author of *Canadian Criminology, Issues and Perspectives on Young Offenders in Canada, Canadian Criminal Justice Today, Diversity and Justice in Canada*, and *Juvenile Justice Systems: International Perspectives* (forthcoming).

Michael G. Young holds a B.A. and M.A. in criminology and is a doctoral candidate at the University of Victoria in Victoria, B.C. He is currently an instructor in the Criminal Justice Program at Camosun College in Victoria. He has research experience in provincial and federal corrections and with young and adult offenders, and has worked in adult community-based corrections.

CORRECTIONS AND THE CRIMINAL JUSTICE SYSTEM

John Winterdyk
Department of Criminology
Mount Royal College
Calgary, Alberta

LEARNING OBJECTIVES

After reading this chapter, you should be able to:

- Describe the complex nature of corrections;
- Define corrections in terms of its evolving nature;
- Explain corrections as a political and social concept;
- Describe the mandate and principles of adult corrections;
- Explain the different practical and philosophical orientations of corrections; and
- Describe the role of corrections within the criminal justice system.

Just punishment and chastisements do indeed spring from a good principle, but they are good only because we cannot do without them—it would be better that neither individuals nor states should need anything of the sort.

—Aristotle, *Politics VII*, 13 (c. 384–346 BC).

Crime is an integral part of our social fabric. As Karl Menninger (1968, 6) observed, "crime is *everybody's* temptation. It is easy to look with proud disdain upon 'those people' who get caught . . . But who does not get nervous when a police car follows closely?" [emphasis added]. Therefore, if we are all capable of transgression, how do we justify responding to those who get caught?

Although we have witnessed a general decline in the crime rate throughout most of the 1990s, crime rates are still considerably higher than they were when the current Uniform Crime Reporting system for reporting crime was introduced in the early 1960s. Despite a recent decline in the crime rate, there has been a steady increase in the crime rate since the 1960s. The rise and decline raise a number of questions about whether any of the measures taken by the different elements of the Canadian criminal justice system might account for the change. Pertinent to this text, one of the questions could be what role, if any, does corrections play? While this is arguably a cynical statement, corrections has still not managed to contradict Robert Martinson's (1974) unwelcome declaration that "nothing works" in corrections (see Chapter 11). Even though most academics would agree that the assertion is overstated, penological theory continues to be shrouded in an air of skepticism and public support is waning.

Most people have an intuitive sense of what crime is. They tend to view it as some kind of violation of the values and norms of society that undermine their sense of order. As the father of American sociology, Charles H. Cooley, proposed at the turn of the 20th century, all humanity shares a common core of "values and rules on how to act" (cited in Christie 1996, 179). Yet our compliance can be neutralized by various economic, individual, political, and social circumstances. Hence social scientists try to define the concept of crime in more precise terms. In so doing, their frame of reference influences the various factors of criminal behaviour a criminologist will focus on. And although there is a variety of definitions and explanations (e.g., biological, economic, psychological, and sociological—see, generally, Winterdyk 2000a), given the context of this textbook we will use the legal definition. Accordingly, then, **crime** is defined as an act or omission that violates the criminal law and is subject to a legal response that is sanctioned by the state. **Criminal law** is the formal means by which society attempts to protect the public and define guidelines for public order and stability based on "how close the law is the core of common human experience" (Christie 1996, 181). Imposing **sanctions**[1] on convicted offenders provides four rationales for protecting society. They include *deterrence, incapacitation, rehabilitation,* and *retribution* (see below). When these rationales for intervention are officially applied to the convicted offenders through the judicial process, they are collectively referred to as **corrections**. The forum in which the rationales are applied in contemporary society include probation, parole, incarceration, fines, fine option programs, restitution orders, conditional release, conditional sentences, and a variety of other alternatives that have evolved over the years. However, as reflected in Box 1.1, different societies apply different informal and formal measures to prevent people committing crimes or disrupting social order.

Although it represents a diverse collection of options, Canadian corrections has been under fire throughout most of the 1900s as the public tends to perceive that corrections does not properly carry out the sanctions of the courts. In addition, as reflected in these samples of dramatic media stories below, correctional practices also seem to violate the public's sense of justice.

- "Prisoners Suits against Ottawa on the Rise" (*Calgary Herald* 1999a). As a result of a prison riot in January 1997 at the Drumheller Institution in Alberta, nine inmates are suing the government because they claim to have been innocent bystanders who were injured by staff trying to suppress the rampage.

BOX 1.1	The Many Faces of Social Order

Crime and social order share a universal concern, but they mean different things in different cultures. Hence, different societies use different response mechanisms to attain and maintain social order. How different cultures achieve social order tends to reflect variations in their social, economic, political, and historical characteristics.

How countries respond to crime can in part be described by examining their incarceration rates (see Table 1.1). The United States, which has the highest incarceration rates in the world, emphasizes penalization as the appropriate response to maintaining social order. On the other hand, Japan has a very low incarceration rate. Corrections in Japan relies on social conformity and prefers informal sanctioning (e.g., public shaming), while Poland, which has a comparatively high incarceration rate, is characterized "by appealing to each person's sense of civic obligation" (Reichel 1994, 266).

Meanwhile, even within countries there can be noticeable differences in incarceration rates. Queensland has a significantly higher rate of incarceration than all the other Australian states. Texas executes more death-row inmates than any other American state, and Quebec is considered to be more liberal in its handling of young offenders than most other provinces in Canada.

While most countries (and their states or provinces) share similar justifications and goals for punishment, there is considerable variability in their justifications. For example, even though more than 40 percent of all nations had abolished the death penalty by the end of the 1980s, it is still used in such countries as Iran, Iraq, China, South Africa, Japan, and the United States. Of these, only Japan and the United States employ protracted processes in the execution of offenders (Fairchild 1993). Nevertheless, contrary to pleas from the signatories to the United Nations' Universal Declaration of Human Rights, they still practice the death penalty. In fact, the United States is among the few countries that still use the death penalty as a "corrective" measure for certain types of crimes committed by young persons.

Using a **comparative analysis** of different correctional systems, one can observe how the concept of social control varies and how different systems achieve their goals of control. Comparative studies allow researchers to explore such questions as to which model works best, under what conditions do they work best, how and why do they vary, etc. This, in turn, makes us ask questions: Given the diverse nature of social control, should we strive for universal concepts of social control? What challenges (i.e., economic, social, or political) might such efforts pose?

- "Corrections Canada Probes Thatcher Horse Play" (*Calgary Herald* 1999c). Colin Thatcher, a former Saskatchewan Cabinet minister, is serving a 25-year prison term for killing his wife in the early 1980s. In late 1998, he was moved from a maximum-security facility to a minimum-security one. After being moved Thatcher requested that his horse be moved to the prison. The request attracted an outcry from the Reform Party and numerous citizens questioning the justification of such a request and expenditure of taxpayers' money.

TABLE 1.1	International Incarceration Rates		

Country	Incarceration rates (per 100,000 population)	Country	Incarceration rates (per 100,000 population)
Northern Africa		Canada	115
Sudan	115	Greenland	140
Tunisia	250	United States	645
Southern Africa		South America	
Lesotho	235	Chile	375
South Africa	320	Guyana	200
Europe		Paraguay	60
Belarus	505	Asia	
Cyprus	35	Hong Kong	190
France	90	India	25
Greece	55	Japan	40
Iceland	40	Kazakhstan	495
Netherlands	85	Saudi Arabia	45
Poland	145	Singapore	465
Russia	685		
United Kingdom	125	Oceania	
North America		Australia	95
Bermuda	360	Guam	320
		New Zealand	145

SOURCE: Adapted from Walmsley 1999.

- "Prison Break Blamed on Boredom, Booze" (Weber 1999). A 1998 federal inquiry into a series of escapes at the minimum-security prison in Drumheller, Alberta, revealed that the escapes were in part attributable to "boredom, lack of on-site employment and (meaningful) leisure time activities . . ."

- "Lock-'em-up Favoured in Alberta, But There Must Be a Better Way" (*Calgary Herald* 1999b). In a poignant editorial, news columnist Don Martin pointed out that a three-day justice summit held in Calgary would focus on correctional alternatives that would not (and did not) include incarceration as the primary objective of corrections. Yet Martin used the results of an Alberta poll that showed that these alternatives did not resonate with those surveyed. If the criminal justice system is to command public support, can they—or should they—balance public interests with policy?

- "Ontario Set to Take Ottawa to Court over Parole Quotas" (Blackwell 1999). Calgary columnist Tom Blackwell accused the federal government of making a "farce" of the correctional system by intending to release as many offenders on parole as are in prison. Currently, the ratio of inmates to those on parole is about two to one. In Ontario alone, such a decision could mean freeing an additional 1,600 inmates.

- "Murders, Suicides on the Rise in Canadian Prisons" (Bailey 1999). A report cited in the *Calgary Herald* describes the increase in suicides and murders as "significant." Escapes in 1998/99 were the highest in five years. While the report focuses on problems within federal institutions, Dennis Finlay, a spokesperson for the Correctional Service of Canada points out "what you don't see are how many we stop."

- "Audit Reveals Security a Problem in Prisons" (Bronskill 2000). An article in the *Calgary Herald* discusses how an internal audit by the Correctional Service of Canada revealed that confidential file management is so poor in some Canadian prisons that information about victims may be falling into the hands of their attackers. Of the seven institutions audited, it was found that misfiling and lack of file security was common.

As illustrated by these headlines, much of the current dissatisfaction focuses on the "leniency" and lack of constructive programming and apparent confusion over the objective and mandate of corrections. These issues represent serious concerns that deserve closer scrutiny. Hence, throughout this text we will examine the diverse nature of correctional practices, policy, and issues in Canada. In addition, the text will provide information to help the reader assess whether the various forms of corrections are either too lenient or too harsh. Finally, by offering a comprehensive overview of corrections, we hope the reader will gain a richer understanding and appreciation of the diversity and complexity of corrections in Canada, and apply that understanding to creating constructive social policy and educative options.

In *Corrections in Canada: Policy and Practice*, one of the first Canadian textbooks exclusively devoted to corrections in Canada, Ekstedt and Griffiths (1984, vii) argued that the need for a textbook on the subject was based on the "expansion of criminal justice and correctional courses . . . and the development of staff training programs for correctional personnel." Twenty years later, the general rationale still applies, but the scope has evolved in its depth and mandate. For example, until fairly recently, corrections in Canada was synonymous with incarceration (see Chapter 6) and concept of community-based corrections (see Chapter 13) did not really emerge until the early 1990s. In addition, other factors, such as the impact of the media and public perceptions (Chapter 3), victims of crime, conditional sentencing, restorative justice, a return to privatization, the use of after-care services, among other community-based options, have all become part of the correctional enterprise. For example, while the public tends to view corrections as the practice of incarceration (as reflected in the media reports above), in the 1990s less than 7 percent of all offenders sentenced experienced custody. Yet, as the Norwegian criminologist Nils Christie observes in the preface to the second edition of *Crime Control as Industry* (1996), "the growth in prison populations within major industrialized nations has only accelerated" (see Chapter 6).[2]

With the 50th anniversary of the Universal Declaration on Human Rights in 1998, the efforts of Amnesty International, and the Canadian Charter of Rights and Freedoms (enacted in 1982), the mandate to maintain the delicate balance between individual freedom and social order has a higher national profile than ever before. For many, this profile is a negative image. And when one takes into account that corrections and the law (i.e., legal system) symbolize the failure of the criminal justice process to deter potential offenders, the negative profile and general skepticism bear an additional burden for Canadian society.

Let us now turn to the current meaning of corrections. Then we will consider the concepts of punishment and intervention that largely define operational principles of corrections. From here, we will describe the scope of corrections in Canada before offering an overview of some of the practical elements of corrections in Canada. Then we will explore the various justifications for punishment before examining some of the political, social, and legal aspects of corrections. This chapter will conclude with a general overview of corrections within the criminal justice system.

DEFINING CORRECTIONS: MORE THAN PENOLOGY

Since antiquity, all societies have considered certain behaviour, or acts, as unacceptable in accordance with their sense of social harmony and social order. These acts are referred to as *proscribed* behaviour. Conversely, societies have encouraged, or *prescribed*, other behaviour such as marriage, working for a living, respecting the person and property of others. Hence, all behaviour can be placed along a continuum of unacceptable to acceptable behaviour. The Canadian sociologist John Hagan (1984) used a pyramid to illustrate this continuum as it relates to perceived deviance in societies. At the top of the pyramid are the *consensus* acts of crime or deviance that are uniformly sanctioned and at the bottom are the vast range of behaviour that he describes as social diversions for which there is no uniform agreement whether they constitute any social harm and whether there should be any formal response (e.g., neglecting to bathe, wearing "outrageous" clothing, etc.).

Historically, corrections focused on punishment and imprisonment. In fact, it was not until mid 1900s that the term penology became a part of corrections. **Penology** is derived from a Latin word meaning punishment. Hence, penologists, as social scientists, study the relative effectiveness of different punishments that in turn are translated into policy.

In the past, punishment was the primary mode of righting wrongs. It is only the method by which punishment is administered that has changed. Although some of these methods can still be found in some parts of the world today, most societies have evolved from self-help justice through blood feuds between families to the state assuming responsibility for administering punishment. After the state assumed the role of administering punishment, prisons were introduced to serve as remand or detention centres until an appropriate punishment could be delivered. Hence, the role prisons played in early times, when prisons and institutional experiences were a *punitive* and *retributive* response to wrongdoing, served no corrective function. Therefore, as a social science, penology represents a narrow focus but one that has not been completely neglected. As will be illustrated throughout this textbook, those interested in the study of penal reform continue to explore various rationales for justifying the punishment of certain types of offenders.

Meanwhile, corrections embraces three elements: punishment, treatment, and prevention. Some critics, such as Michel Foucault (1977), suggest that modern corrections does little more than engage in surveillance, control, and management. Nevertheless, the concept of corrections covers the broader range of responses and programs, as well as alternatives that are available to deal with convicted offenders. When the term and concept of corrections replaced penology in the late 1800s, it reflected the variety of facilities, programs, and services that deal with convicted criminals. Much of the impetus for change originated at the first International Prison Congress in 1872, held in London, England, where the ideas of rehabilitation and humane treatment were highlighted. This transition and its implications for corrections in Canada are explored in Chapter 2.

Regardless of the name change from penology to corrections, our historical review of corrections in Canada reveals that our correctional system still emphasizes punishment over other objectives. It is, in part, Canada's long history of relying on punitive strategies that poses challenges for correctional reforms today. In addition, the process of administering corrections is also complicated by the complex relationship of corrections to the rest of the criminal justice system. For example, the police are often seen as the "gatekeepers" of the criminal justice system. Under certain circumstances, the police are able to decide whether formal actions should be taken against an offender. Meanwhile, the courts can exercise a certain degree of discretion over which and how many offenders enter the correctional system. Corrections has become the last one out there that can provide hope and resources for dealing with those who cannot be deterred from committing a crime and from whom society (and the criminal justice system) feels legally obliged to protect itself from further harm. However, competing correctional objectives (i.e., punishment versus treatment and rehabilitation versus maintenance of the offender—see below) have seldom made good partners. In fact, one of the most enduring questions in corrections is "Can you punish and treat someone at the same time?"

In addition to the philosophical issues, correctional services in Canada must also contend with a range of practical issues. For example, corrections is administered by all levels of government, namely federal, provincial, and municipal. There are also private and voluntary agencies and groups that provide services such as supervision, reintegration, employment advocacy, social services, and a host of other services, which have been privatized in some provinces. These levels of delivery and variations in services provide numerous administrative and practical challenges in the delivery of corrections.

The Evolving Nature of Corrections

As described in Chapter 2, the meaning and nature of corrections have evolved throughout Canadian history. However, it can generally be said that while the practice of corrections involved the use of punishment as the measure of enforcing social order, the process of applying corrections has varied. For example, as noted above, less than 7 percent of convicted adult offenders served time in a custodial institution in the late 1990s as compared to the frontier days of Canada. Today's prisoners have rights (see Chapter 8) and opportunities (see Chapter 7) that were unknown to prisoners in earlier times. Before Confederation, for example, correction practices such as branding, flogging, hanging, being placed in the stocks or the pillory were used; people's ears were even cut off for certain crimes (Carrigan 1991).

The early Canadian "prisons" were initially modelled after the British Elizabethan **bridewells** (see Box 1.2), which were workhouses used to accommodate everyone from the poor, the sick, and the insane to petty criminals. However, as the bridewells fell out of favour in England, Canadian prisons were then modelled after the Pennsylvania and Auburn prison systems. Keeping with the social and political mindset of the day, little concern was given to the well-being of the inhabitants of these correctional facilities.

BOX 1.2   **Bridewells**

Bridewells, or workhouses, emerged during the 1500s in Europe as a measure for providing employment training and housing for vagrants. These facilities controlled the masses of poor who congregated in urban centres. Only men were confined to these "houses of correction," which were based on a work ethic. They quickly gained popularity throughout the continent. However, by the end of the century many had fallen into serious decay.

Despite our glimpse into the evolving nature of corrections in Canada, before we can begin to examine any issues surrounding corrections, we must define corrections as a subject of investigation. Its meaning and scope, as suggested by Ekstedt and Griffiths (1984), are influenced by such factors as the social and political elements underlying corrections and the legal relation of corrections to the criminal justice system, as well as its relative conceptual diversity.

To place the correctional process into its diverse conceptual framework, let us examine the meaning of corrections from these perspectives.

CORRECTIONS AS A POLITICAL AND SOCIAL CONCEPT

As is the case with all concepts unique to the study of crime and criminal justice, the term corrections is both *relative* and *evolving* (see Box 1.3). As others have noted, corrections is a term that neither is well understood nor engenders universal agreement on its objective.

This general level of confusion has its roots in the context of who is defining corrections and the period in which it is being defined. During Canada's frontier days, criminals had a social status no better than an animal. Criminals were considered incorrigible and deserving of punishment. Hence, the notion of corrections developed into the practice of *retribution* and *just deserts* (see below). Corrections involved punishment that we would consider inhumane by today's standards. Yet at the time, given the understanding of who and what a criminal was, these practices were seldom questioned—other than perhaps by the prisoners themselves! However, this political and social concept of corrections prevailed until the Age of Enlightenment (c. 1700s), when a number of scholars began to express concern for the rights of humanity.

A variety of intellectual scholars during this period began to apply a scientific and rational approach to understanding their society. Among some of the more notable scholars were Charles Montesquieu, François Marie Arouet Voltaire, and Jean Jacques Rousseau of France; Jeremy Bentham, John Howard, David Hume, and Adam Smith in England; and Cesare Beccaria in Italy. These and other scholars argued that regardless of class, occupation, or race, all people are equal and deserve to be treated as such. For example, in his early writings, Rousseau (1712–1778) argued that it was the growth of civilization that corrupted the natural goodness and increased inequality within society. Along these lines, he also targeted private ownership of land as a causative factor of crime and corruption. In his epical *The Social Contract*, published in 1762, Rousseau lashed out against the political status quo and called for equity, fraternity, and liberty for all. In fact, these words became the battle cry of the French Revolution in 1812. In the book, he also wrote of **natural law** and the concept of natural rights (e.g., freedom of speech, equality before the law, freedom of persons). Collectively, these ideas helped to redefine the social and political notion of justice and corrections.[3]

Another intellectual who had a profound influence of the concept of justice, and indirectly on corrections, was Beccaria (1738–1794), who published his treatise *On Crimes and Punishment* in 1764.[4] Complementing the ideas of Rousseau, Beccaria called for equality of all, liberty for all, humanitarian treatment of all people regardless of the type of crimes they commit, and a utilitarian approach to justice. That is, it is better to prevent a crime than to punish it. However, if someone has done harm, then punishment should be certain, severe (i.e., in measured proportion to the offence), and swift. And should someone do harm, then the state has no right to use torture prior to the determination of guilt.

BOX 1.3 — The History and Evolution of Corrections

Antiquity to 1700 AD:

- *Self-help justice:* People took justice into their own hands.

- *Retaliation and vengeance:* Blood feuds (i.e., vendettas) were a common practice in early times.

- *Retribution:* The Sumarian codes (1850 BC) were often associated with the legal principle *lex talionis*—"an eye for an eye and a tooth for a tooth"—but limited the degree of retaliation allowed. Even so, punishments were harsh and often administered by the injured party. Some people point out that today's victim-impact statements are a "civilized" form of vengeance.

- *Capital punishment:* The code of Hammurabi (1750 BC) is the first codified law that legislated social interactions. A sentence of death was a common disposition for many offences.

- *Measured justice:* The Justinian code (600 AD) during the Roman Empire attempted to match the punishment to the perceived gravity of the crime. The concept of proportionality was introduced (e.g., "scales of justice").

- *Wergeld:* Also known as *lex scalia,* this form of retaliation involved payment to the victim. This practice is still evident in a number of Middle Eastern and Far Eastern countries. Payment is proportionate to the injured party's position in society.

- *Friedensgeld:* During the Middle Ages (c. 1200 AD), as the state and church gained in power, wergeld was replaced by friedensgeld. The administration of punishment became the responsibility of the state. Hence, payment was no longer made to the victim but to the state, which also addressed collective wrongs.

The works of Rousseau, Beccaria, and other Enlightenment scholars were instrumental in forging penal and correctional reform at a social and political level. Bentham (1748–1832), for example, called for the reform of criminals through the use of education and adequate provisions upon release. He also outlined a set of criteria by which punishment could be precisely calculated. Meanwhile, John Howard (1726–1790) devoted his life to the introduction of humane conditions and handling for all prisoners (see Box 1.4).

BOX 1.4 — John Howard

John Howard, a Quaker by faith and a high sheriff of Bedfordshire, England, by profession, became a strong advocate for prison reform after he was himself incarcerated. His pivotal work on reform appeared in 1777; entitled *The State of the Prisons in England and Wales,* it exposed the squalour and deplorable treatment of prisoners. It prompted Parliament to amend many of its abusive prison practices in 1779.

In summary, the social and political notions of corrections have influenced our understanding of corrections and will continue to do so. Our thoughts and political agendas combined with scientific findings will influence future correctional policy and practices. In this light, it becomes ever more important to understand corrections in this context so that the process of corrections can continue to strive towards a balance of respecting individual freedoms and protecting society.

Corrections as a Legal and Criminal Justice Subsystem

Corrections and the criminal justice system, in general, have their own social structure. The structure is made up of the social values in society, the various statuses found in corrections (e.g., inmates, offenders, guards, living units officers), and the norms specific to or of concern to corrections (see Chapter 7).

In terms of the latter component, the law gives corrections its specific meaning. The law defines the programs and agencies that have legal authority over the custody or supervision of those who have been convicted of a criminal offence and sentenced by the court.

In Canada, the mandate of correctional services has been influenced by a number of major legislative acts. The *British North America Act* of 1867 defined the distribution of power between provincial and federal governments. Specifically, section 91(27) of the Act granted the federal government exclusive jurisdiction to make criminal law and to define procedural matters. Section 92(14), meanwhile, granted the provinces the power to administer matters pertaining to justice. Hence, the Act gave the federal government control over the serious crimes while the provinces became responsible for administering justice over the less serious offences. Today, the responsibility for corrections continues to be shared among federal, provincial, and municipal levels of government. However, as defined in the Constitution, the federal and provincial correctional agents are the most important.[5] The Act underwent a number of major amendments until 1982 when, under the stewardship of Prime Minister Pierre Elliott Trudeau, it was integrated into the new *Constitution Act*.

Further clarification of correctional jurisdiction is defined by the legal system—in particular the Criminal Code. When first passed in 1892, the Criminal Code transported many of the British common law traditions to a Canadian context. However, over the years, amendments slowly eliminated the common law crimes (e.g., felonies and misdemeanours) and replaced them with indictable and summary offences. *Indictable offences* are defined as serious offences punishable to a sentence of two years or more. Sentences are served in federal institutions. *Summary offences* are considered less serious and generally do not exceed six-month sentences of incarceration or fines up to $2,000, or both. Summary conviction offences are tried by a provincial court judge, and terms of incarceration are served in provincial or territorial correctional facilities.

Mandate and Principles of Adult Corrections

In Canada, the handling of young offenders is legislated under the *Young Offenders Act* (see Box 1.5). However, since this text focuses on the adult offender, we will not discuss youth corrections.[6]

As noted earlier, corrections is faced with the challenge of trying to "maintain the delicate balance between individual freedom and social control" (Canadian Criminal Justice Association 1998). As reported by the Canadian Criminal Justice Association, some of the

BOX 1.5	Youth Criminal Justice Act

Proposed in early 1998, the *Youth Criminal Justice Act* was to be tabled by late 1998. However, due to provincial disputes over funding, jurisdictional autonomy, and various elements of the Act, Bill C-68 did not receive first reading until March 11th, 1999, by Justice Minister Anne McLellan. In March 2000, the Bill (now called Bill C-3) received its second reading and meetings were held across the country to inform criminal justice personnel about the intentions of the Act (Winterdyk 2000b).

guiding principles have been universally defined under the United Nations Covenant on Civil and Political Rights, to which Canada became a signatory in 1978.

More specifically, however, the principles governing corrections and the other elements of the criminal justice system can be found in the Canadian Charter of Rights and Freedoms, the Criminal Code, the *Corrections and Conditional Release Act* (1992), and relevant provincial legislation.

According to the Canadian Criminal Justice Association (1998), the primary principles of corrections in Canada include the following elements:

- Throughout the correctional process, the rights and dignity of the offender must be respected.
- While a convicted person's liberty and mobility are restricted, correctional services cannot impose further punishment that exceeds those defined under the court disposition.
- In accordance with the *Corrections and Conditional Release Act,* correctional services must adhere to the guidelines and standards established to ensure the fair treatment and handling of all offenders.
- Inmates must be treated with dignity. Hence, they must, within reason, be granted the opportunity to maintain positive family relations and other supportive relationships. Corrections also has an obligation to offer a wide range of programs that allow offenders to seek assistance and improve their odds of reform and rehabilitation.
- Correctional agencies must be accountable and subject to regular independent and public assessment.
- The ultimate goal is the reintegration of offenders into society and the protection of society from harm.

THE SCOPE OF CORRECTIONS

As is evident throughout this textbook, correctional practices involve more than the incarceration and institutionalization of offenders. Until recently, probation has been the most common disposition for provincially charged offenders and, depending on the province, many other offenders are placed into community-based programs such as conditional sentencing. As a result of the evolution that has occurred in corrections, today the correctional process includes:

- Absolute and conditional discharges (Chapter 12);
- Fines and fine option programs (Chapter 5 and 12);

- Conditional sentencing (Chapter 12);
- Probation (Chapter 5);
- Incarceration (Chapters 6–11);
- Conditional release/parole (Chapter 12); and
- Community residential centres (Chapter 13).

These broad classifications can be further divided into municipally, provincially, and federally based programs. The range of programs are presented in greater detail in subsequent chapters. For an illustration of how the system works, refer to Figure 1.1.

Although there is a degree of variability in how the different levels of jurisdiction operate, they share some common denominators. For example, all jurisdictional levels include public and private correctional programs.

In recent years, there has been a concerted effort at all levels of corrections, and with regard to the criminal justice system in general (in particular the courts), to move towards greater use of alternative measures for both adult and young offenders. What is less clear is who drives the operational realities of correctional programming. Is it social, political, or economic factors, or some intricate combination?

FIGURE 1.1   An Overview of Events in the Adult Correctional System

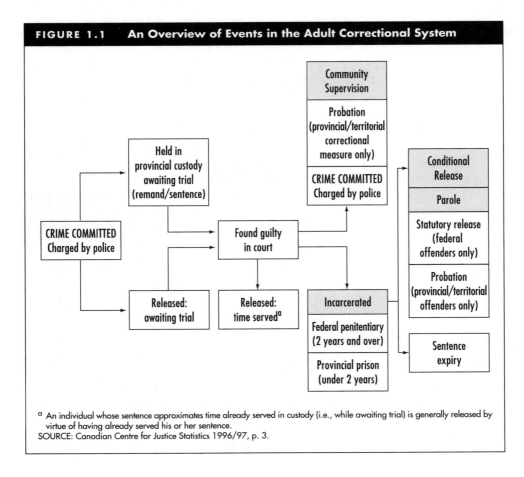

[a] An individual whose sentence approximates time already served in custody (i.e., while awaiting trial) is generally released by virtue of having already served his or her sentence.
SOURCE: Canadian Centre for Justice Statistics 1996/97, p. 3.

Today, the options of alternative measures are commonly referred to as *restorative justice, circle sentencing,* or more recently as *transformative justice.* These programs have been embraced in subtly different ways at all levels of the system, both by the public and private sectors. While in actuality not a new concept, the idea was popularized by John Braithwaite in *Crime, Shame and Reintegration,* published in 1989. Braithwaite advocates "reintegrative shaming" as a more humane and utilitarian way of dealing with offenders. The concept of shaming as a correctional strategy will be explored in Chapter 13.

Ekstedt and Griffiths (1984, 7), among others, have noted that the range of correctional programs have an impact on the "style of management and organization within correctional programs." Regardless of the type of program, all must subscribe to the mandate and principles of corrections (see above). However, the different levels of corrections tend to subscribe to different correctional ideologies. Nevertheless, collectively they reflect the shifting philosophies and ideologies that have characterized the history of corrections.

The Changing Face of Correctional Ideologies

In order to understand the complexity of corrections today, its issues and concerns, as well as its future direction, it is helpful to examine the varying ideologies. An **ideology** is a frame of reference that we rely upon to explain and understand some aspect of our culture—past or present. As is commonly suggested, there are three broad ideologies that apply to correctional practices: punishment, treatment, and prevention. They are not mutually exclusive and may overlap, depending on the level and type of correctional program. Nevertheless, the divisions are useful in understanding the ideologies.

Punishment

The oldest form of societal response to a wrongdoer is **punishment**. It usually fell into one of two categories: death or a wide array of **corporal punishments** (any act that, when

---

BOX 1.6 **Should We Bring Back Capital Punishment?**

Stan Faulder, Clifford Olson, Paul Bernardo—should we be allowed to execute them? How might Canadians have reacted prior to the abolition of capital punishment in 1976? With respect to Stan Faulder, would Canadians have been as concerned about the legal technicalities surrounding his last-minute stay of execution in January of 1999? (After numerous appeals he was executed on June 17, 1999, in Huntsville, Texas. He became the first Canadian to be executed in nearly 50 years.)

Although there are numerous Internet sites pertaining to the issue of capital punishment, you might be interested in visiting the Mennonite homepage at www.mennonite.ca. It takes an anti-capital punishment stance. For a compelling and thought-provoking movie on the subject, consider viewing *Dead Man Walking.* It is based on the true-life story of Sister Helen Prejean from New Orleans who provides spiritual counsel to inmates on death row in Louisiana.

inflicted, produces physical pain short of death). Although some countries still practice these methods, corporal punishment involves such practices as mutilation, flogging, branding, torture, among other activities now considered outdated. In addition to the physical pain inflicted on the offender, one of the most significant aspects of corporal punishment was their public nature. Many of the punishments were administered in public to add humiliation, set an example for others, and provide an opportunity for public retaliation; hence "adding insult to injury." Compared to the past, there has been a gradual reduction in the current level of severity of punishment. Today, rationales for punishment are couched in specialized terminology and scientifically grounded approaches.

There are three general rationales used to justify the use of punishment: retribution, deterrence, and incapacitation. **Retribution** dates back to very early times when an offender was considered a threat and an enemy of society who deserved to be punished, put to death, or banished. In earlier times, the administration of such justice, although often swift, did little to deter people from committing similar (or other) crimes. We refer again to the observation made by Menninger at the beginning of this chapter—is not retribution both a crime against the individual and against ourselves?

It is interesting to note that in 1976 the Canadian Law Reform Commission essentially embraced a non-utilitarian version of punishment. The Commission observed: "Organizing the future . . . is not the major function of the criminal law. Even if we cannot control the future, this does not mean we must ignore the present and the past. We still need to do something about wrongful act . . ." (cited in Walker 1991, 29). Surely, this raises some questions about the purpose of punishment. If punishment does not deter crime, or rehabilitate offenders, is it acceptable to justify it simply as a measure of **just deserts** (individual responsibility where imprisonment is seen as an appropriate consequence and one that is deserved)? In many respects, this notion represents a return to the more basic rationale for incapacitation—punishment. Citing a number of concrete examples, Schmalleger (1999) makes a sound argument for the assertion that in the late 1990s prisons in the United States have moved away from any notion of rehabilitation, prevention, or treatment to simple warehousing and managing prisoners. Similar opinions are expressed by the Canadian David Cayley (1998) in *The Expanding Prison*. To offset the growing problems of overcrowding, such practices as selective incapacitation and other community-based programs have been introduced. Yet, as Menninger (1968) noted, the concept of just deserts is little more than an illusion that offers the offender and the victim little, if any, opportunity for reparation of the harm done.

Based on the principles of the **classical school, deterrence** is based on the notion that we are capable of free will and, should the threat or risk of punishment be sufficient, we are less inclined to offend. The concept also assumes that someone who is punished is less likely to re-offend because deterrence implies premeditation (Cayley 1998). This is referred to as *primary deterrence,* while the deterrence of others is referred to as *secondary deterrence.* When Ben Johnson was caught using illegal drug performance enhancing products in the 1988 summer Olympics, it deterred neither him nor other athletes from using similar drugs. More recently, in 1998, the Alberta and Manitoba governments proposed an amendment to the Criminal Code that would create a mandatory minimum two-year sentence for "repeat offenders who commit a second offence of break and enter within two years of expiry of their last sentence" (Roberts 1999). Yet, as research has shown, mandatory sentences and overpunishment, let alone expected severity of punishment, are ineffective—hence, there is no deterrent effect (Cayley 1998; Roberts 1999).[7] For example, did your first speeding ticket stop you from ever speeding again? Did getting caught telling a white lie when you were a child stop you from telling another one?

Walker (1991), among others, argues that the deterrent concept is only marginally effective provided the offender does not have a long history of prior convictions. However, to what extent is the rationale of deterrence simply used as a cloak for vengeance? According to philosopher Immanuel Kant (1724–1804), the purpose of punishment is not to deter but to make the offender suffer as part of a higher moral order. Nevertheless, some criminologists continue to explore new variations of the concept. John Braithwaite's (1989) concept of *shaming* is a recent example. Representing an extension of Frank Tannenbaum's idea of labelling, put forth in the 1930s, shaming is based on the notion that people prefer not to be negatively labelled (see Williams and McShane 1998 for a general review of the labelling theory). However, it remains unclear to what extent factors such as the offenders' social, personal, cognitive, and even spiritual circumstances play in determining whether any orientation designed to serve as a deterrent works. Based on the voluminous amount of research involving the labelling theory, the findings show that while most ex-offenders are aware of the stigma they carry, it is less clear how they process, or how or why the label of ex-offender has a lasting negative or positive influence (see Box 1.7). Therefore, any notion of deterrence is based on a subjectively distorted understanding of norms that cannot be predicted or quantified.

BOX 1.7	Section 718.1 of the Criminal Code

Section 718.1 of the Criminal Code states: "a sentence must be proportionate to the gravity of the offence and the degree of responsibility of the offender." How could a mandatory sentence be justified under such conditions?

The third reason for punishing an offender is **incapacitation**. The intention is to prevent the offender from committing any further offence by incarcerating him or her. While at one time offenders were simply placed into prisons for the duration of their sentence, it has only been in the last 200 years that incapacitation has been used in conjunction with one or more of the other forms of punishment. Today, incarceration is seen as the standard response by which justice is seen to be done—in spite of a growing body of evidence that questions its effectiveness. The law is not well structured to enable the courts or correctional officials to predict future risk. Furthermore, the notion of justice being served is a subjective term. As Menninger (1968) comments, depending on the context, justice offers help to some and pain to others. So what justice is there in incarcerating someone? In a more concrete sense, Christie (1996) has observed that the more serious and frightening the crimes, the poorer our ability to predict the risk of recidivism.

Treatment

Tracing its history back to the Enlightenment and the Positivist School of Criminology, the **treatment** approach reflects a more humane ideological approach to responding to criminal behaviour. The positivist approach maintains that human behaviour, including criminality, is physiologically based. It may be either inherited or environmentally influenced. Hence, offenders are thought to have some ailment or "sickness" that, as with a medical model, is assumed treatable. Like the medical model, treatment modalities, or therapies, attempt to "remove" criminal behaviour using a wide variety of approaches. They range from community-based programs or minimal security settings that provide offenders with an opportunity to "heal" their anger, frustration, or other "ills" to physical or chemical interventions, or both (e.g., lobotomies and chemical castration for chronic sex offenders).

The treatment ideology can be divided into four subcategories. They include:

1. *Medical model:* In the early part of the 20th century, at the same time that psychology emerged as a discipline, corrections officials embraced the notion that the problem of criminality was somehow associated with the constitutional makeup of the individual. The solution was to develop diagnostic tools to diagnose the "ailment" and then to apply the appropriate treatment program. The "patient" would be considered well if he or she would be considered "cured" or rehabilitated, and either returned to the community or placed on probation or parole (see Chapters 5 and 12 for the difference between probation and parole).

2. *Reformatory model:* Rooted in Quaker and Calvinistic doctrines, offenders were considered to be culturally, educationally, or socially disadvantaged in some way. Introduced during the late 1800s, the reformatory approach attempted to use education to provide basic vocational and occupational skills within a regime of strict discipline. The goal was to reform criminal tendencies by offering offenders more socially acceptable responsive outlets.

3. *Reintegration model:* Although the reintegrative concept can be traced back to ancient times (see Winterdyk 1998), it did not emerge until the late 1960s as a formal correctional option. The basic premise is a mutually acceptable resolution between the offender and the victim(s) so that harmony (emotional, mental, physical, and spiritual) could be restored. Unlike the other models, the causes of crime are thought to be community related. That is, crime is the byproduct of a lack of legitimate opportunity (e.g., poverty, being unskilled, insufficient education, urban decay) to attain socially prescribed goals (e.g., home, decent paying job, safe community).

   A recent variation of the reintegration model, which emerged in the mid 1990s, is the concept of transformative justice. Briefly, it involves a process of resolving conflict, whether between individuals, in social settings, throughout the justice system, in workplaces, or in any other communities (Transformative Justice Australia, 1999).[8] We will explore this concept and other aspects of the reintegrative and transformative models in Chapter 13.

   Since the late 1980s, the variety of reintegrative approaches has burgeoned. Some of the more common programs include community service orders, fines, fine option programs, probation, and electronic surveillance. All are designed to enable the offender to remain in the community and demonstrate a desire to remain a part of the community. Correctional personnel act as brokers for services. Relying on established criteria, correctional personnel must apply the doctrines of *proportionality* (i.e., the perceived level of risk the offender poses to themselves and the community) and *parsimony* (i.e., how much freedom can the offender be afforded).

4. *Treatment model:* The treatment model uses indeterminate sentences so the system can detain an offender until he or she is deemed "reformed" or rehabilitated. Based on the medical model, intervention is deemed to be in the best interest of the offender. Canadian prisons and correctional initiatives include programs such as anger management and other cognitive-behavioural programs, educational and vocational programs, life skills workshops, addiction management courses, family intervention initiatives, and multimodal programs.

Researchers have not been able to agree on the effectiveness of the treatment modality. Yet, as Gottfredson (1979) and Lab and Whitehead (1988, 90) have observed, the skeptics tend to apply overly rigorous methodological standards that make even positive results seem questionable. For example, after an extensive review of the literature, American criminologist Ted Palmer (1992, 76) concludes that based on the large numbers of positive outcomes "that have been found in the past three decades with studies whose designs and analysis were at least adequate [there is] little doubt that many programs work, and not just with one or two types of offenders and programs." However, he indicates that a multiple-intervention strategy works best, rather than any single type of program.[9] This observation supports some of the emerging integrated and interdisciplinary theories of crime (see Barak 1998; Winterdyk 2000a).

Aside from methodological issues, the notion of rehabilitation implies a return to a former condition or competence, but as several critics have observed, how can someone return to a former state that has never been experienced?

Prevention

The final correctional ideology is prevention. Since there are few exceptions that enable the correctional system to detain someone for the remainder of his or her life, there is a real risk of overcrowding. Incarceration is an expensive option; it is physically (and morally) impractical to incarcerate all offenders; prevention offers another option. Furthermore, without an offender there is no crime; therefore the criminal justice enterprise can either attempt to prevent crimes from ever occurring or utilize strategies to prevent convicted offenders from re-offending. Given the rather variable success rate of current correctional program in Canada, the public and the justice system have been turning to more crime prevention initiatives as possible solutions.

Theoretically, **prevention** is intended to divert potential offenders away from criminal or delinquent activity. Prevention initiatives operate on the principle of being able to identify cues (e.g., environmental, social, and economic) that can trigger criminal behaviour or to identify the signs of criminal propensity (e.g., victim of abuse or neglect, and family or personal difficulties). Unfortunately, the literature is replete with examples illustrating the difficulty and complexity of the process of predicting. Crime prevention programs either target factors in the individual's life (e.g., self-defence programs, safe-walk programs, educational programs) or they target environmental and social factors designed to reduce criminal opportunity (e.g., alarm system, door locks, street lighting, and window bars).

In partial response to the questionable effectiveness of treatment and punishment initiatives, there has recently been a shift back to prevention initiatives. In earlier times, people and communities took steps to protect their person and environment. Beccaria ([1764] 1963, 93, 98) observed that, "it is better to prevent crimes than to punish them" and, among other points, he suggested, "perfecting education" and involvement in constructive change.[10] Today, prevention initiatives reflect the broad spectrum of ideas put forth by Beccaria and others of his time. Prevention strategies fall into three major categories.

- *Primary prevention* is aimed at factors within the physical or social environment that are believed to contribute to criminal behaviour. An example of a physical change is using security alarms; a social change might involve reducing poverty, population density, and gender inequality.

- *Secondary prevention* works on the assertion that the seeds of criminal and delinquent activity are sown early in life. Hence, secondary prevention strategies focus on development factors such as providing early intervention programs for high-risk families and individuals, providing opportunities for those who are economically or socially deprived, and expanding resources for such groups as abused children and women.
- *Tertiary prevention* tends to be criminal justice initiatives. Since research has revealed the limited effectiveness of imposing criminal sanctions such as imprisonment, advocates focus on such projects as community-based corrections, making prisons more community friendly, repealing those crimes that have no deterrent effect (e.g., certain drug offence laws, the death penalty).

In this section we have examined the major ideologies that relate to corrections. The corrective orientation is influenced by a variety of factors ranging from traditional beliefs and folkways to political and economic factors. Hence, contemporary influences play a significant role in directing corrections and the contextualization of social order. As McCormick and Visano (1992, x) noted, the study of corrections is not "independent of social life but emerges out of complex interactive processes." However, as we will see in Chapter 3, the media continue to offer up dramatized unrepresentative vignettes of that confound the direction corrections takes.

Finally, it is worth noting the origin of punishment and pain and how these two elements have been woven into the fabric of corrections. The word "punish" comes from the Latin word *punire*—"to see to it that the duty of *poena* is fulfilled." *Poena* is Latin meaning "the compensation value to be paid in order to resolve a criminal conflict" (Cayley 1998, 124). These concepts are imbedded in the correctional rationales. For example, rather than ask what is to be done, corrections takes the stance (under the direction of the courts) of asking how much punishment a person deserves. Whether it is punishment, treatment, or prevention, they all share an element of compensation to the state and (usually indirectly) to the victim. Until recently, this has been reflected in the practice of compensating the state, while the rights and pains of the victim have been largely overlooked. Although by the late 1990s this orientation appears to have shifted somewhat, we will see later in this textbook that this orientation is also fraught with various issues.

Society's response to crime resembles an unbalanced pendulum. While correctional practices swing back and forth from retribution to treatment to management, criminological and penological theories introduce variations on the otherwise rhythmic swing. Hence, the "proper" corrective response is not so much a question of crime control or what works but a question of the extent to which the correctional response is based on cultural values. As a number of academics and scholars have observed, justice must be seen to be done. But, as Jeffery Reiman (1995) remarked, if we wanted to design a criminal justice system (i.e., correctional system) that would fail, it would look very similar to the one we have. Menninger noted in *The Crime of Punishment* (1968) that society gets the crime and criminals it deserves! However, inside such gloomy observations, there may be a silver lining. Menninger suggested that it is our increased level of awareness about the plight of the criminal justice system that will enable us to devise more effective crime prevention and crime control remedies.

CORRECTIONS WITHIN THE CRIMINAL JUSTICE SYSTEM

The major elements of the criminal justice system consist of law enforcement, prosecution, courts, and corrections. In addition, there is the hidden element known as the public. While it is beyond the scope of this textbook to discuss the nuances of the meaning of "system," a brief comment is warranted at this point (see Cox and Wade 1985 for a more detailed discussion).[11] For our purposes, let us assume that based upon the operational (i.e., legislational and jurisdictional), interdependent, and interrelated links of corrections to the criminal justice system, corrections fulfills the basic mandate of processing those persons "who have been screened through one or more of the system's other components" (Ekstedt and Griffiths 1984, 9).

As part of its link to the criminal justice system, corrections is responsible for the accused and convicted. Therefore, in the final section of this chapter, we will take a brief look at the characteristics of the correctional population and how fiscal resources are deployed to deal with this segment of society.

Correctional Population

As we noted earlier, corrections in Canada is diverse and involves four major categories of the offender population. Throughout most of the 1990s, approximately two thirds of all adult provincial court cases resulted in a conviction. As the *Juristat* report (Canadian Centre for Justice Statistics 1997/98a, 4) indicates, "on any given day in 1997/98 an average of 157,766 adult offenders were in prison or under community supervision." Between 1996 and 1997, there was a dramatic shift from probation (approximately 65 percent) to remand custody in 1997/98 (33 percent), followed by provincial/territorial or federal facilities (31 percent), then probation (21 percent), conditional sentences (approximately 5 percent), conditional releases[12] (approximately 4 percent), and, finally, remand custody (approximately 4 percent).

Figure 1.2 illustrates that the majority of offenders are *not* incarcerated. Rather, most offenders serve their sentences in the community. For example, in 1997/98 32 percent of federal and provincial sentenced offenders were serving their sentence under some form of community supervision. It should be noted, however, that there is considerable variation among the provinces and territories; explanations for these trends will be explored elsewhere in the book. In addition, the percentage of life terms of imprisonment increased from 3 percent in 1992/93 to 4.6 percent by 1996/97 (N=173 to 210 respectively) but declined to 4.3 percent in 1997/98. Issues of gender, race, ethnicity, a "greying" population, and other related characteristics will also be discussed in subsequent chapters.

Even though public opinion reflects the general notion that the correctional system has gotten "soft" on offenders, the distribution of offenders has remained fairly consistent since the early 1980s. For example, in 1979 there were 9,200 offenders incarcerated in federal institutions (i.e., 15.2 percent minimum, 53 percent medium, and 31.8 percent maximum security). The incarceration rate of adult female offenders to adult male offenders in the mid 1970s was 1 to 20 (Griffiths, Klein, and Verdun-Jones 1980).

Comparing provincial level dispositions is more difficult to articulate because of the wide variability in the type of services available at the provincial level. For example, in 1977/78 British Columbia had services in all 12 areas of community services identified at the time, while Newfoundland only had two community-based services (i.e., probation and temporary absence) (Griffiths, Klein, and Verdun-Jones 1980, 207). By 1997/98, the list of services had expanded; however, as a recent *Juristat* report (Canadian Centre for Justice Statistics 1997/98a) points out, because of inconsistent data collecting and coding of conditional sentences, it is not possible to provide an accurate picture of how community-based services are being used across Canada.

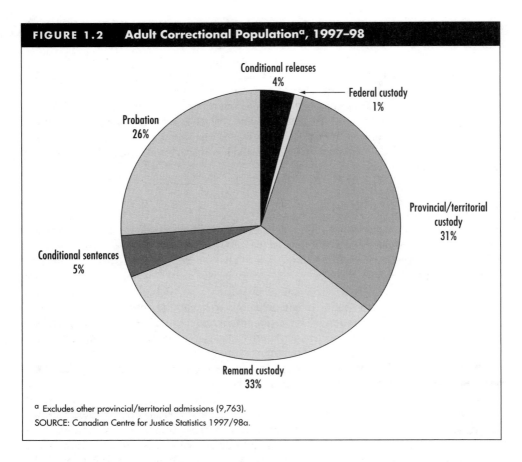

FIGURE 1.2   Adult Correctional Population[a], 1997–98

Conditional releases
4%

Federal custody
1%

Probation
26%

Provincial/territorial
custody
31%

Conditional sentences
5%

Remand custody
33%

[a] Excludes other provincial/territorial admissions (9,763).

SOURCE: Canadian Centre for Justice Statistics 1997/98a.

Nevertheless, general data are available on community service use. For example, in 1997/98, 108,828 offenders were given a community sentence—a 0.3 percent decrease over the previous year. However, since 1995/96, admissions to prisons have declined while the number of offenders serving their sentences in the community has increased (see Chapter 13).

The Cost of Corrections

Increasingly we hear about the rising cost of administering the criminal justice. In 1977/78, adult correctional services accounted for 21.1 percent of the total justice service budget. This converts to $551 million or $23.62 per capita (Griffiths, Klein, and Verdun-Jones 1980, 4). The total criminal justice budget for 1977/78 was around $2.5 billion. Griffiths, Klein and Verdun-Jones predicted that the budget would soar to "between $5 and $7.5 billion annually by 1986" (p. 3). Nearly 20 years later, in 1997/98, the correctional budget reached $2.08 billion, an increase of 11 percent since 1993/94. This converts to a per capita cost of $128.35 to house an inmate in custody. However, the provincial and territorial costs vary dramatically: the per capita inmate cost for Newfoundland was $146 while it was only $83 per person in Alberta (Canadian Centre for Justice Statistics 1998/99a) (see Table 1.2).

TABLE 1.2	Correctional Budget and Employees: Various Years

	Employees			Expenditure		
	1977/78[a]	1994/95[d]	1997/98	1977/78	1994/95	1997/98
Police	63,000[b]	55,865	74,398	$1,631 M	$5.8 B	$5.9 B
Crown counsel	1,600[c]	3,198	3,130[e]	51 M	258 M	N/A
Legal aid	1,900[d]	3,028	2,878	84 M	646 M	455 M
Courts	10,400	11,954	11,914[e]	248 M	835 M	857 M[e]
Adult corrections	21,900	27,103	27,475	552 M	1.9 B	2.1 B

[a] Adapted from Ekstedt and Griffiths 1984,10.
[b] Includes private security.
[c] Excludes use of private practice legal professions—approximately 2,300.
[d] Canadian Centre for Justice Statistics 1994, 1997, 1997/98b.
[e] Denotes data from 1996/97 as no data for 1997/98 was available at the time.
Note: M = million, B = billion

	1994/95	1996/97	1997/98
Federal institutions	$946 M	$970 M (+13%[f])	$1.03 B (17%)
Provincial institutions	970 M	998 M (−2%)	1.05 B (−0.4%)
Total budget	1.88 B	1.97 B	2.08 B

[f] The percentage score represents the percentage of change in the budget from five years earlier after adjusting for inflation.
SOURCES: Ekstedt and Griffiths 1984; Canadian Centre for Justice Statistics 1994, 1994/95, 1995, 1996/97, 1997/98a.

Although we began this chapter by commenting on the general level of public dissatisfaction with corrections (i.e., the "lenient treatment" of convicted criminals), we must remember that the mandate of corrections is dictated by the overriding orientation of the criminal justice system. In particular, the type of disposition received by a convicted offender is administered by the courts. In Canada, judges are independent agents of the criminal justice system and are not politically or publicly accountable. Hence, we might want to ask to what extent are correctional practices a true reflection of public or political will. Furthermore, as has already been mentioned and as will be discussed in greater detail throughout this text, the breadth of corrections is much greater than the public realizes. In fact, much of corrections is hidden from public view. Its success only attracts public attention when problems arise (e.g., a re-offender, escape, a riot, or some other dramatic incident—refer back to the media headlines at the beginning of this chapter). And, as we will see, many of today's problems have a long history that is rooted, in part, in public fear, misconception, and the societal conditions in which those problems occurred. However, corrections continues to evolve, making it an interesting and exciting topic for study and research.

Since human behaviour is inextricably linked to societal issues and trends, how we respond to wrongdoers can only be understood in a historical context. Therefore, in the next chapter we will trace the historical roots of corrections in Canada in order to appreciate how historical antecedents have forged contemporary correctional practices.

SUMMARY

We began this chapter by observing that crime is an integral part of our social fabric and that corrections plays a pivotal role in our formal response to it. Our notions and practices of how to "correct" transgressors of the law have been dominated by a punitive approach—revenge and just deserts. In fact, the term penology was used until fairly recently to represent the nature and study of how to address offenders. Yet research has repeatedly shown that such measures, however contrived, seldom produce the desired results of abating or deterring offenders.

Next, we briefly examined the dynamic and evolving nature of corrections. We explored the impact of politics and various social forces on corrections. Then we looked at the influence of the legal system on corrections. From here, we considered the complexity of corrections and how corrections continues to evolve in its practice and ideology.

In the final section, a brief summary of some of the practical elements (e.g., correctional population, budgetary matters, and the process behind corrections) were presented.

KEY TERMS AND CONCEPTS

bridewell	criminal law	penology
classical school	deterrence	prevention
comparative analysis	ideology	punishment
corporal punishment	incapacitation	retribution
corrections	just deserts	sanctions
crime	natural law	treatment

STUDY AND DISCUSSION QUESTIONS

1. The concept of corrections has a long history. How has it evolved throughout the ages? Do you agree with the current orientation of corrections?

2. The costs of delivering corrections (and criminal justice in general) have increased dramatically since the late 1970s. What correctional approach might help to reduce such costs?

3. Recently, there has been a noticeable shift towards community-based programs such as conditional release. What possible pitfalls might such programs represent for corrections?

4. Corrections is a dynamic and evolving aspect of the criminal justice system. What direction should programs and services take? What role do politics, public opinion, jurisdictional boundaries, etc., play in forging such initiatives?

NOTES

1. A sanction is generally defined as a "consequence or punishment for violation of accepted norms of social conduct" (Gifis 1975, 186). Sanctions can be used to redress either civil injuries or criminal offences.

2. Canadian incarceration rates rose from 100 per 100,000 in 1979 to 111 in 1989, and to 125 by 1993. This compares to 230 to 426, and then to 532, for our neighbours to the

south, and in Spain from 37 to 80 to 117, for the same periods. Even for the Netherlands, once recognized for its restraint, the imprisonment rate rose from 23 to 44 to 52 for the same periods (Christie 1996, 192). Mandel (1992) draws a similar conclusion. Referring to the 1980s as "the great repression," he used historical data to show that by that time Canada's incarceration rate had nearly doubled since the late 1860s.

3. It is somewhat ironic to note that Rousseau's personal life was less than exemplary. He was abandoned at age ten and wandered the countryside of France for most of his life. He sired five children, whom he later gave to an orphanage, with a servant girl (Rousseau [1766] 1968).

4. Graeme Newman and Pietro Marongiu (1990) have questioned whether Beccaria actually wrote this work. Drawing on Beccaria's academic and professional track record, they suggest that some of his colleagues may have helped. Regardless, the work stands as the cornerstone to the classical school of criminological thought.

5. Municipal correctional facilities are police lock-ups, intended for short-term detention only.

6. See Winterdyk (2000b) for an overview of the issues pertaining to young offenders in Canada.

7. Part of the irony of this proposed legislation is that the current incarceration rate for break and enter is currently higher than for most violent crimes including assaults and sex-related assaults (Roberts 1999).

8. One of the first Web sites to be established on the subject is hosted by Transformative Justice Australia at www.tja.com.au.

9. Palmer (1992, ix–x) found that "25 percent to 35 percent of all reasonably evaluated experimental treatment programs do in fact work." Intervention programs demonstrating the greatest promise are those based on a developmental model.

10. Note these are elements shared by those who advocate the reintegrative, restorative, and transformative approaches.

11. Cox and Wade (1985, 5) suggest that the best way to view the criminal justice system is "as a network of interrelated, but independent individuals who are subject to many internal and external pressures . . ."

12. When Bill C-41 became law in September 1996, it created a new type of community-based alternative to incarceration referred to as *conditional sentences*—see Chapter 12.

WEBLINKS

Correction Service of Canada (wide range of links to current correctional issues, research reports, and correctional links): **www.csc-scc.gc.ca**

Juristat reports, Statistics Canada: **dsp-psd.pwgsc.gc.ca/dsp-psd/pilot/statcan/85-002-XIE/85-002-XIE.html** (if your school has access to online Juristat)

REFERENCES

Bailey, I. 1999. Murders, Suicides on the Rise in Canadian Prisons. *Calgary Herald,* 6 July, A11.

Barak, G. 1989. *Integrating Criminologies.* Boston: Allyn and Bacon.

Beccaria, C. [1764] 1963. *On Crimes and Punishments* (translated by Henry Paolucci). Indianapolis: Bobbs-Merrill.

Blackwell, T. 1999. Ontario Set to Take Ottawa to Court over Parole Quotas. *Calgary Herald,* 27 March, A20.

Braithwaite, J. 1989. *Crime, Same and Reintegration.* Cambridge: Cambridge University Press.

Bronskill, J. 2000. Audit Reveals Security a Problem in Prison. *Calgary Herald,* 10 February, A6.

Calgary Herald. 1999a. Prisoners Suits against Ottawa on the Rise. 11 January, A4.

———. 1999b. Lock-'em-up Favoured in Alberta, But There Must Be a Better Way. 26 January, A17.

———. 1999c. Corrections Canada Probes Thatcher Horse Play. 6 February, A12.

Canadian Criminal Justice Association. 1998. Mandate and Principles of Adult Corrections in Canada. home.istar.ca/~ccja/angl/mandatan.html (April 2000).

Carrigan, D.O. 1991. *Crime and Punishment in Canada: A History.* Toronto: McClelland and Stewart.

Cayley, D. 1998. *The Expanding Prison.* Toronto: House of Anansi Press.

Canadian Centre for Justice Statistics (Statistics Canada, Catalogue No. 85-002). 1994. Police Personnel and Expenditure in Canada. *Juristat* 16(1).

———. 1994/95. Adult Correctional Services in Canada. *Juristat* 17(4).

———. 1995. Justice Spending in Canada. *Juristat* 17(3).

———. 1997. The Justice Data Factfinder. *Juristat* 17(13).

———. 1996/97. Adult Correctional Services in Canada. *Juristat* 18(3): 3.

———. 1997/98a. Adult Correctional Services in Canada. *Juristat* 19(4).

———. 1997/98b. Justice Spending in Canada. *Juristat* 19(12).

Christie, N. 1996. *Crime Control as Industry* (2nd ed.). London: Routledge.

Cox, S.M., and **J.E. Wade.** 1985. *The Criminal Justice Network: An Introduction.* Dubuque, IA: W.C. Brown.

Ekstedt, J., and **C.T. Griffiths.** 1984. *Corrections in Canada: Policy and Practice.* Toronto: Butterworths.

Fairchild, E. 1993. *Comparative Criminal Justice Systems.* Belmont, CA: Wadsworth.

Foucault, M. 1977. *Discipline and Punish: The Birth of the Prison.* London: Penguin.

Gifis, S.H. 1975. *Law Dictionary.* Woodbury, NY: Barron's Educational Series.

Gottfredson, M.R. 1979. Treatment Destruction Techniques. *Journal of Research in Crime and Delinquency* 16: 39–54.

Griffiths, C.T., J.F. Klein, and **S.N. Verdun-Jones, S.N.** 1980. *Criminal Justice in Canada: An Introductory Text.* Toronto: Butterworths.

Hagan, J. 1984. *Disreputable Pleasures: Crime and Deviance in Canada* (2nd ed.). Toronto: McGraw-Hill.

Lab, S.P., and **J.T. Whitehead.** 1988. An Analysis of Juvenile Correctional Treatment. *Crime and Delinquency* 34: 60–85.

———. 1990. From "Nothing Works" to "The Appropriate Works": The Latest Stop on the Search for the Secular Grail. *Criminology,* 28: 405–418.

Mandel, M. 1992. The Great Repression: Criminal Punishment in the Nineteen-Eighties. In K.R.E. McCormick and L.A. Visano (Eds.), *Canadian Penology.* Toronto: Canadian Scholars Press.

Martinson, R. 1974. What Works? Questions and Answers about Prison Reform. *The Public Interest* 35: 22–54.

McCormick, K.R.E., and **L.A. Visano** (Eds.). 1992. *Canadian Penology: Advanced Perspectives and Research.* Toronto: Canadian Scholars Press.

Menninger, K. 1968. *The Crime of Punishment.* New York: Viking Press.

Newman, G., and **P. Marongiu**. 1990. "Penological Reform and the Myth of Beccaria." *Criminology* 28: 325–46.

Palmer, T. 1992. *The Re-emergence of Correctional Intervention.* Newbury Park, CA: Sage.

Reichel, P.L. 1994. *Comparative Criminal Justice Systems: A Topical Approach.* Englewood Cliffs, NJ: Prentice-Hall.

Reiman, J. 1995. *The Rich Get Richer and The Poor Get Prison* (4th ed.). Boston: Allyn and Bacon.

Roberts, J.V. 1999. Mandatory Sentencing Rides Again. *Juristat* 19(1): 1, 3.

Rousseau, J.J. [1766] 1968. *The Social Contract* (translated by Maurice Cranston). Baltimore: Penguin.

Schmalleger, F. 1999. *Criminal Justice Today: An Introductory Text for the 21st Century* (5th ed.). Upper Saddle River, NJ: Prentice-Hall.

Transformative Justice Australia. 2000. *Welcome to Transformative Justice Australia.* www.tja.com.au/welcome.htm (April 2000).

Walker, N. 1991. *Why Punish?* Oxford: Oxford University Press.

Walmsley, R. 1999. World Prison Populations: An Attempt at a Complete List. In D. van Zyl Smit and F. Dünkel (Eds.), *Imprisonment Today and Tomorrow* (2nd ed.). Deventer: Kluwer.

Weber, B. 1999. Prison Breaks Blamed on Boredom, Booze. *Calgary Herald,* 6 February, A3.

Williams III, F.P., and **M.D. McShane**. 1998. *Criminological Theory* (3rd ed.). Upper Saddle River, NJ: Prentice-Hall.

Winterdyk, J. 1998. It's Time, It's Time . . . Is It Time for Restorative Justice? *Law Now* (April/May) 20–22.

———. 2000a. *Canadian Criminology.* Scarborough: Pearson Education.

———. 2000b. *Young Offenders in Canada: Issues and Perspectives* (2nd ed.). Toronto: Harcourt Brace.

HISTORY OF CORRECTIONS IN CANADA

Alan Erdahl
Department of Criminology
Mount Royal College
Calgary, Alberta

LEARNING OBJECTIVES

After reading this chapter, you should be able to:

- Review early corrections history that led to the Kingston era in Canada;
- Understand how penitentiaries came into existence;
- Describe the problems with using prisons for rehabilitation and punishment;
- Be familiar with correction inquiries and prison commissions and how they contributed to the change in corrections philosophy;
- Explain emergence of a new "kind" of corrections—community corrections; and
- "Understand the effect of the 1996 Arbour Commission on Canadian corrections.

The mood and temper of the public with regard to the treatment of crime and criminals is one of the most unfailing tests of the civilization of any country.

—Winston Churchill

THE EVOLVING NATURE OF CORRECTIONS

This chapter reviews the development of corrections in Canada from a historical perspective, highlighting the events, personalities, legislation, and reports that have influenced present-day Canadian correctional philosophy. Particular emphasis has been placed on royal commissions and other government reports, such as the 1996 Arbour Report, to illustrate their role. Indeed, corrections in Canada is a dynamic process, ever changing in nature, and continues to "correct" itself and adapt to its environment even as this is being written.

The origin of Canadian correctional history dates back to a much different world from the one we know today. As noted in Chapter 1, during antiquity corrections was severe and harsh with an emphasis on punishment. Life was cheap and authorities believed that punishment was a swift, fair, and sure deterrent. Our oldest surviving criminal code, the laws of Hammurabi of Babylon (1750 BC), prescribed death sentences for almost everything, and no one questioned the state's right to take a life. The community had the right to defend and protect itself. If the means of **retaliation** were out of all proportion to the offence, so be it. At least it would serve as a warning to others.

The Hebrews were more restrained than the early Babylonians. There were only 15 capital offences in the early Mosaic Code, including murder, bestiality, blasphemy, cursing parents, adultery, and practicing witchcraft.

Under subsequent Roman law, death sentences were carried out for treason, adultery, sodomy, murder, forgery by slaves, corruption, kidnapping, and seduction and rape. (The term capital punishment originates with the Latin word *caput,* meaning head; thus decapitation was the most common method of execution, long before hanging.)

By 13th-century England, the death penalty was imposed for all felonies except mayhem and petty larceny. Most of the crimes were religious in nature. In fact, by 1870, England's **Bloody Code** contained more than 350 offences punishable by death. In medieval Europe, the methods of execution were limited only by the tools at hand and the morbid imagination of the judiciary. Condemned criminals were flayed, impaled, exposed to insects and animals, drowned, stoned, crucified, burned, drawn and quartered, beheaded, strangled, buried alive, pressed to death, boiled, broken on the wheel, shot, starved, blown out of the mouth of a cannon, or, in later years, hanged.

In New France (the territory claimed by France before Confederation), there were some 11 legal methods of execution including the wheel, head crushing, shooting, and hanging. Of the 67 Europeans executed in New France, 54 were hanged. This was consistent with the rest of Europe at the time, as hanging was by far the most popular method of "corrections." It was a festive occasion for the whole family and a gala celebration by the state. (In the 38-year reign of Henry VIII, there were more than 78,000 hangings in England alone—an average of 2,050 per year) (Carrigan 1991).

By the late 18th century, authorities in both Europe and North America began to realize that these wholesale executions were not reducing the crime rate. In fact, they accomplished little except to reduce the world's precarious population, already ravaged by plagues and wars. Pickpockets and thieves plied their trades in the very shadows of the noose!

As discussed in Chapter 1 (see Corrections as a Political and Social Concept), a variety of intellectual scholars during the Age of Enlightenment (c. 1700s) began to ask what good is a death penalty if it does not deter. The basis for this argument was that capital punishment for even minor offences was not just cruel—it also appeared to be useless. By 1810, only 10 percent of those condemned to death in England were, in fact, hanged. The rest were either imprisoned (a new form of corrections) or "transported" to other lands (see Chapter 6).

Several different streams of thought contributed to this push for correctional reform. The new philosophy of liberty and equality emphasized human dignity and the rights of the individual (see the discussion about Cesare Beccaria in Chapter 1). It inspired a growing sensitivity to physical torture and cruelty, and capital and corporal punishment began to look barbaric. Quakers and evangelicals revived the idea of spiritual reform through solitude, penitence, and strict discipline (the basic correctional philosophy of the future penitentiary system). They believed that prisons should "improve" people.

Pioneers of Correctional Reform: John Howard and Elizabeth Fry

The real watershed in modern corrections occurred in 1777 when **John Howard** (1726–1790) published his historic *The State of the Prisons in England and Wales* (see Box 2.1). The book was an account of his exhaustive investigations of jails across England and Europe (see Chapter 1 for further details).

Howard was one of the first reformers to apply scientific methods to social research. His conclusions jarred the complacency of polite English society and forced the English government to act.

Howard proposed a new prison system that he believed would be both fair and humane. This model prison would be quiet, clean, and orderly. The "keepers" would be paid civil servants who were held accountable to the government. There would be no corporal punishment. The inmates would be isolated in their cells and "protected" from all corrupting influences.

BOX 2.1 John Howard's Ideas on Prison Reform

In order to redress this hardship, I applied to the justices of the country for a salary for the gaoler in lieu of his fees. The bench was properly affected with the grievance, and willing to grant the relief desired: but they wanted a precedent for charging the country with the expense. I therefore rode into several neighbouring counties in search of a precedent; but I soon learned that the same injustice was practised in them; and looking into the prisons, I beheld scenes of calamity, which I grew daily more and more anxious to alleviate. In order therefore to gain a more perfect knowledge of the particulars and extent of it, by various and accurate observations, I visited most of the Country Gaols in England.

Seeing in two or three of them some poor creatures whose aspect was singularly deplorable, and asking the cause of it, I was answered, "they were lately brought from the *Bridewells.*" This started a fresh subject of inquiry. I resolved to inspect the Bridewells; and for that purpose I travelled again into the counties where I had been; and, indeed, into all the rest; examining *Houses of Correction, City and Town-Gaols.* I beheld in many of them, as well as in the *County-Gaols,* a complication of distress: but my attention was principally fixed by the *gaol-sever,* and the *smallpox,* which I saw prevailing to the destruction of multitudes, not only of *felons* in their dungeons, but of *debtors* also.

SOURCE: *The State of the Prison in England and Wales,* John Howard, 1777.

The British *Penitentiary Act* of 1778 was born from Howard's recommendations. It provided for several major reforms, including safe and sanitary buildings, regular prison inspections, abolition of the "fee system" (illegal payments to the jailers) and a reformatory program inside the prison walls. Unfortunately, many years passed before these ideals were put into practice.

In 1790, the father of prison reform died, ironically, of jail fever contracted in Russia. Howard had lived to see the abolition of most tortures and the building of the first penitentiary, at Wymondham in Norfolk, England, in 1785. But he never knew that the regime he had fought so hard for—the system of solitary confinement—would come to be feared as the cruellest punishment of all.[1]

Elizabeth Fry (1780–1845) was a wealthy Quaker matron who was active in various 19th-century English philanthropies. In 1812/13 she visited the female prisoners at New Gate Prison in London and was horrified by what she saw: a horde of filthy, ragged, drunken women stacked on top of each other. (It was "almost like a slave ship," she later told the English House of Commons.) The women's quarters had no heat and babies lay unclothed and "blue with cold." The women survived by daily begging and prostituting (Dobash, Dobash, and Gutteridge 1986, 61).

Fry's visit to New Gate marked the beginning of a lifelong commitment to prison reform. Like her male counterpart John Howard, she inspected prisons all over Britain, including convict ships before they sailed off to foreign lands (the "transportation" of convicts). Fry insisted that the female inmates be kept separate from the men and that they be supervised by other females. She wanted the jails to rehabilitate women convicts through education and job training. In 1822, she helped to open the first halfway house for female ex-convicts (in London, England).

Fry's influence was very evident in the *British Prison Act of 1823*, which ordered jailers to separate men and women and hire female guards for female prisoners. At the time, society believed that women offenders must be innately corrupt and abnormal and could not be reformed. A criminal woman was considered evil and a "monster"! Fry was one of the very few people who subscribed, at the time, to the theory of **social determinism**: she believed that women broke the law because they were in needy and desperate circumstances.

The reform movement for female offenders continues to this day, with the Elizabeth Fry Society carrying on her legacy to bring an element of humanity and hope to incarcerated females and their families.

EMERGENCE OF THE PENITENTIARY, 1800s

The prison reformers, following Howard, were sure they could change men's minds by regulating their bodies. They even dared to hope that the penitentiary would become the model of order and morality for the rest of the community. Now crime was viewed as a kind of moral disease; the carriers must be quarantined (Melossi and Pararini 1981).

Although the idea of the penitentiary originated in Europe, it was the Americans who became its early enthusiasts. In fact even in colonial times, the Americans had resisted the British system of corporal and capital punishment. As early as 1682, the Quaker leader William Penn had established a penal code for whipping or mutilation. Capital punishment was retained for the crime of murder only.

In 1787, William Bradford, Benjamin Rush, and Caleb Lownes formed the Philadelphia Society for Alleviating the Miseries of the Public Prisons. In 1790, they persuaded the state legislature to create the first true correctional institution in North America, in a wing of the **Walnut Street Jail**.

In this penitentiary, most inmates were still housed together in large rooms but hardened criminals were put in solitary confinement. The disciplinary regime of the Walnut Street Jail became known as the **Pennsylvania system** (also known as the **separate system**).

The most drastic experiment with solitary confinement took place in 1821 at the Auburn Penitentiary in New York State. A group of prisoners were shut up in their cells with absolutely no distractions—not even labour. So many of the subjects (more than half) committed suicide (shades of Alcatraz in the near future) that the project had to be stopped two years later. The French criminologists Alexis de Tocqueville and Gustave de Beaumont condemned this extremism: "it does not reform, it kills" (Anderson 1960).

The regime at Auburn was subsequently modified to permit prisoners to work in silence during the day, returning to solitary confinement only at night. This became known as the Auburn system (sometimes referred to as the congregate system, or the silent associated system—see Chapter 6).

In Pennsylvania, prison authorities were still committed to the principle of total isolation and giving criminals their just deserts (see Chapter 1). The showplace of the Pennsylvania system was the huge Eastern State Penitentiary at **Cherry Hill**, built in 1829, where all prisoners were kept in solitary confinement 24 hours a day. They were permitted no visitors and worked alone in their cells. Their only human contact was with their keeper, who checked on them three times a day.

"Solitary confinement, first conceived as a humane and redemptive discipline, became the dreaded 'Hole'—immeasurably worse than any torture of the body," wrote Charles Dickens, who later toured Cherry Hill in the 1840s (Baehre 1977).

In 1849, members of Canada's Brown Commission visited this infamous prison and found that "the prisoners as a group have a shallow, worn-out appearance: the eyes are deeply sunk . . . and the eyeballs glare with a mad look and feverish brightness" (Baehre 1977, 32). The prison authorities reluctantly admitted that at least 50 of their 300 prisoners were, in fact, mad.

John Howard himself had not advocated total separation. He thought prisoners should be allowed to work and exercise together. Unbroken solitude, he warned, might lead to "insensibility or despair."

Despite its drawbacks, the Pennsylvania system was eventually adopted in most parts of Europe. The Auburn system prevailed in the U.S. and Canada. (During the 19th century in Canada, only the Prison of Isolation at Kingston Penitentiary in Ontario was based on the Pennsylvania model.) Regardless of the system used, the 19th-century penchant for silence and segregation continued. By the late 1880s, overcrowding in the penitentiaries had made traditional discipline irrelevant. Silence and segregation could hardly be enforced when cells had to be shared. Solitary confinement ceased to be a reformatory method and soon evolved into pure punishment and revenge. The dungeon, or "hole," became the prison-within-a-prison.

The penitentiary, as Howard had conceived it, had failed. Yet, the system continued to thrive long after its original practices and rationale had been abandoned.

Corrections in Early Canada, 1830–1867

"There is one thing which can hardly fail to strike an emigrant from the old country, on his arrival in Canada. It is this—the feelings of complete security which he enjoys . . . he sees no fear—

he need see none. This is a country where the inhabitants are essentially honest—here you may sleep with your door unbarred for years" (Catherine Parr Traill, cited in Carrigan 1991, 15).

Canada was hardly this idyllic in 1857 (nor is it today as we begin a new millennium). Crime in the form of robbery, assault, and murder has always existed in Canada and can be traced back to the very earliest days of exploration and settlement.

Canada had more than its fair share of lawbreaking in New France, the Maritimes, and Upper and Lower Canada, and, of course, in the "Wild West" (Coles 1979). Out of this situation developed the need for a corrections system, a system that ideally would both correct and rehabilitate.

This system would effectively begin with the passing of the **British North America Act** (BNA Act) on July 1, 1867. Our legal system would be based on England's common law system and our correctional system would be divided forever—parole and penitentiaries to Ottawa and the rest to the provinces (see Chapter 1).

But prior to the BNA Act, there was little interest in jailing Canadians. In the early 1800s in Canada, jails were not viewed as a common punishment for criminals and there was little interest in reform and even less interest in "rehabilitation programs."

In 1800, a Canadian could be hanged for stealing a shirt. Robbery was one of several dozen offences that carried the death penalty (see Cayley 1998 for a detailed account). For less serious offences, sanctions included branding, banishment, transportation, and whipping. The people of Upper and Lower Canada had inherited Britain's Bloody Code.

Writing as an editor of the Toronto *Globe* in 1846, George Brown expressed early Canadian sentiments about whipping and punishment in the jail system[2] (cited in Beattie 1977, 148) (see Box 2.2).

Any early correctional reforms in Canada were along the lines of basic improved medical treatment, better food, and more sanitary accommodations. An early advanced idea was the notion of giving inmates a limited opportunity to practice their trade, as was done in 1830 at a Hamilton jail. A further modern idea was to allow prisoners to work outside together during the day and return to jail at night, a practice common today in minimum-security Canadian prisons. This early idea received no support at all.

BOX 2.2	Lash!—Lash!!—Lash!!!

The Globe, 4 November 1846, Kingston Penitentiary—It appears from statements which are not contradicted, that from 200 to 300 punishments are inflicted on the prisoners of the Penitentiary every month. Supposing these average to 20 lashes, it follows that 1300 lashes are given in a month, and 50,000 in a year, a far greater amount we are sure than the whole British Army and Navy undergo. A hundred and fifty lashes must be given in this den of brutality every day the sun rises. Who can calculate the amount of pain and agony, that must be imposed in this pendemonium [sic]. Who can tell the amount of evil passions, of revenge, and of malice, that must be engendered by such treatment? A penitentiary is a place where the prisoner should reflect on the past, and be placed under such a system of moral training as may fit him for becoming a better member of society. Will the lash do that? Did it ever do anything but harden the person whose body was torn by its infliction?

SOURCE: Ekstedt and Griffiths 1988, 37.

Western Canada had no need for jails in the early 1800s, as the population was sparse and crime was dealt with "instantly and on the spot." As in Britain, hangings were frequent enough to begin to cause widespread revulsion. By 1833, the number of capital crimes in Canada had been reduced to 12 from more than 300—including murder, rape, robbery, burglary, and arson. By 1841, only murder and treason were punishable by death.

As described in Chapter 6, the first real correctional facility was opened at **Upper Fort Garry** (in what is now Winnipeg, Manitoba) in 1835—a simple courthouse and a two-cell jail. Prisoners had to provide their own food and other amenities. For those who could not afford this, the state provided a daily ration of 1 pound of pemmican (at public expense, of course) and water.

The first quarter of the 19th century saw a fairly well-defined correctional philosophy in this country. While there was a strong belief in punishment both as the wages of sin and as a deterrent, there was also a growing belief that criminals could be reformed as law-abiding citizens. To achieve this, prisoners began to be placed in separate cells, and classified according to their crimes and past records. This included hard labour, strict discipline, and silence. The major program was religious instruction, given by the prison chaplain. This system was known as moral reformation.

Thus, the Christian church influence in both French and English Canada was the predominant penal philosophy. Our correctional philosophy was one of spiritual change through penitence—later known as the **reform model**. Unfortunately, however, for early Canadian reformers, the conditions in most early Canadian jails were not conducive to penance, discipline, or reform.

In those early years, few Canadian communities could afford to build any jails, let alone spend money on lavish jail items like food, staff, repairs. Reform was not a high priority. Most jails, like the Fort Garry one, were small and isolated, with a single, poorly paid keeper.

In the first part of the 19th century, a large wave of immigrants from Europe significantly increased Canada's population. This fit the natural formula for crime increase, resulting in the more frequent use of jail as a punishment and a deterrent. The existing small jails could not accommodate this increase in inmates and an alarmed public began to worry about recidivism rates, inmate behaviour, and terrible jail conditions. The overcrowding, as Young notes in Chapter 6, led the newspapers of the day to describe Canadian jails as being schools for crime.

Birth of the Kingston Penitentiary

As the crimes punishable by death decreased, an alternative form of punishment was growing by leaps and bounds—hard labour in a penitentiary. Canada's first penitentiary, in Kingston, opened on June 1, 1835.

In the common Canadian jails of the 1830s, one could still find most of the abuses that John Howard had condemned in the British prisons of the 1770s. They were filthy, disease ridden, and chaotic. Until 1836, prisoners in the Toronto jail received only a pound and a half of dry bread a day. They had no work and no exercise, and many were kept in chains.

At the time, Canadian lawmakers were greatly interested in the American penal experiments. The respective strengths and weaknesses of the Auburn and Pennsylvania systems were hotly debated in Parliament. Finally, in 1831, a select committee of the House of Assembly of Upper Canada called for the building of a penitentiary near Kingston. A board of commissioners settled on the Auburn system, or the silent associated system, as the most productive penal philosophy. Moral re-education had been born in Canada!

The first Canadian *Penitentiary Act* was passed in 1834. It set out the new objectives for the Kingston jail. It would provide "the means . . . not only of deterring others from the commission of like crimes, but also of reforming the individuals and inuring them to habits of industry" (Carrigan 1991). Thus, moral re-education was to replace intimidation. Lofty ideals indeed!

Brown Commission, 1848–1849

The actual experience of the early years was quite different from what the legislators had envisioned. Whereas Kingston was conceived as a humane alternative to the cruelty of the Bloody Code, the first warden, **Henry Smith** (1794–1862) had in fact instituted his own "reign of terror," all in the name of reform.

Shoom (1966, 215) notes that any violation of prison rules was met by a punishment of a "swift and often brutal nature." It involved flogging with the cat-o'-nine-tails and rawhide, as well as the use of irons, solitary confinement, and rations of bread and water. Table 2.1 offers a sample of entries from the Kingston Punishment Book for 1843.

Smith was finally removed in 1849, after an investigation by a special government commission headed by the Honourable Adam Ferguson and chaired by its secretary, George Brown, editor of the Toronto *Globe* and soon-to-be-elected Reform member of the legislature in Upper Canada.

In its first report, issued in 1848 (cited in Beattie 1977), the Brown Commission condemned the use of corporal punishment but not the structure or regimen imposed on the inmates. It criticized the way Kingston operated and recommended the removal of the warden. In its second report, in 1849, the Commission recommended that:

* Its major objective should be reformation;
* The operation of the jail should be run more efficiently;
* Moral suasion should replace physical force;
* Chaplains should be regularly employed; and
* Government penitentiary inspectors should be employed to inspect prisons regularly.

Beattie (1977, 28–29) argues that "what was really on trial was the system itself, the silent or congregate system under which Kingston was established . . . Ultimately, the Commission

TABLE 2.1	Sample Entries from the Kingston Punishment Book, 1843
Offence	**Punishment**
Laughing and talking	6 lashes; cat-o'-nine-tails
Talking in wash-house	6 lashes; rawhide
Threatening to knock convicts' brains out	24 lashes; cat-o'-nine-tails
Talking to keepers on matters not relating to their work	6 lashes; cat-o'-nine tails
Finding fault with rations when desired by guard to sit down	6 lashes; rawhide, and bread and water
Staring about and inattentive at breakfast table	bread and water
Leaving work and other convict there	36 hours in dark cell, and bread and water

SOURCE: Shoom 1966, 16. © Canadian Criminal Justice Association.

concluded that the silent system was fine—it was the warden who had failed to get the most out of it!"

The Commission, which was made up of Brown and five commissioners, toured the U.S. and concluded that the Auburn system should be retained and modified to provide for the best parts of the Pennsylvania system. Some of the modifications would include:

- Maximum of six months in solitary confinement;
- Separate facilities for young offenders;
- A separate asylum for criminally insane offenders;
- Improved small local jails;
- Education programs; and
- The creation of private prison societies to help offenders re-enter into the community.

The Brown Commission concluded that the primary purpose of a penitentiary was "simply the prevention of crime and that aim demanded the reclamation of prisoners whenever possible through using the minimal amount of force, making every attempt at rehabilitation" (cited in Bellomo 1972, 22).

The two reports by the Brown Commission were the first formal inquiries into Kingston's operation, and also the first in a long line of royal commission investigations into the running of Canada's penitentiary system.

While there is still debate to this day about the real impact of the Brown Commission on correctional reform, one thing is certain. In the years following its release, several pieces of legislation were passed that implemented many of the Commission's recommendations:

- The *Penitentiary Act* of 1851 provided for the construction of new cells, reduced corporal punishment, appointed two jail inspectors, and removed the mentally ill offenders; and
- The *Prison Inspection Act* of 1857 allowed the transfer of insane convicts and young offenders to separate, newly built facilities.

Subsequent legislation in 1859 established a system of regular prison inspection. By the 1860s, government penitentiary inspectors were characterizing the Canadian system as "one of rigid repression, of uncompromising coercion, one which admits no change or improvement in the condition of the convict as a consequence of good conduct" (Ouimet 1969). They advocated the adoption of a progressive system like the one used in Ireland, making use of a mark system for graduated, early release on account of good behaviour.

British North America Act, 1867

According to the Irish system, or Crofton system, convicts could gradually work their way back to freedom. They would begin their sentences in solitary confinement (Pennsylvania system) and then move on to working together by day (Auburn system). During this second phase, a convict could earn marks or chips for good behaviour, and these could, in turn, bring privileges such as a ticket of leave, or early release (i.e., parole).

At Confederation in 1867, the prisons themselves were deteriorating. Thus the federal government, in accordance with the BNA Act, assumed responsibility for the provincial penitentiaries at Kingston, Halifax, Nova Scotia, and Saint John, New Brunswick. This came under the legislative authority of Parliament, with the passing of the revised *Penitentiary Act* of 1868.

Conditions did not noticeably improve in the jails, but Canada at last had a federal penitentiary system. Additional penitentiaries were constructed in Montreal (1837), Quebec (1873), Stony Mountain, Manitoba (1876), New Westminster, British Columbia (1878), and Prince Albert, Saskatchewan (1911) (see Box 2.3).

Most of these prisons are still in operation today, with the most notable improvement being the five new decentralized prisons for women. In 1997, the prison for women at Kingston was finally closed. In addition to the existing provincial and federal facilities (fewer than 10), the federal government agreed to build five cottage-style, small prison centres across the five federal regions in Canada (Goff 1999, 251; see Chapter 10).

The BNA Act laid the very foundation for our present federal correctional system in Canada. And as reflected in Box 2.3, we see that after the initial construction of federal prisons, it was not until the 1960s and finally the 1980s that additional prisons were built.

THE EMERGENCE OF CANADIAN PENITENTIARIES

The penitentiaries constructed in Canada between 1873 and 1882 helped to ease inmate overcrowding and relieve the pressure, but the alarming frequency of prison riots—both in

---

BOX 2.3 — **Federal Prison Construction Prior to 1990***

Before the 1940s

Kingston Penitentiary—1832
Laval Penitentiary—1837, closed in 1989
Dorchester Penitentiary—1880
Saskatchewan Penitentiary—1911
B.C. Penitentiary—closed in 1976
Stony Mountain Institution—1920s and 1930s
Collins Bay Institution—1930s
Prison for Women—1930s

The 1950s

Federal Training Centre
Leclerc Institution
Joyceville Institution

The 1960s

Springhill Institution
Correctional Development Centre (Quebec)
Archambault Institution
Cowansville Institution

Millhaven Institution
Warkworth Institution
Drumheller Institution
Matsqui Institution

The 1970s

Regional Reception Centre (Quebec)
Regional Psychiatric Centre (Prairies)
Edmonton Institution
Kent Institution
Mission Institution

The 1980s

Atlantic Institution
Drummond Institution
Donnacon Institution
Port-Cartier Institution
Special Handling Units
La Macaza Institution
Bowden Institution

* Penitentiaries were later referred to as institutions and centres.

SOURCE: Posner 1991.

Canada and in the U.S.—made it clear that the system itself was fundamentally flawed. The deprivation of liberty, in itself, did not reform anymore. Better methods had to be found.

Like the reformers of the 18th century, the 19th-century Victorian prison reformers were part of a larger progressive social movement. But now, there was an increasing emphasis on professionalism. Prison reformers in Canada and the U.S. strove to make criminology a respectable science. National and international organizations were formed and Canadians participated in the first penal congresses held in Boston and New York in the latter part of the 19th century. At this same time, groups such as the Prisoners' Aid Association of Toronto were formed in 1874 to help ex-convicts.

The old religious explanations for crime were no longer accepted, but there was still no general consensus about what caused crime or what could cure it. With ever spiralling recidivism rates, penal reformers began to explore other correctional philosophies.

Biological explanations were popular. This was the heyday of phrenology (analysis of head bumps) and the theory of the "born criminal." Cesare Lombroso (1835–1909), for example, called himself a criminal anthropologist when he wrote *L'Uomo Delinquente* in 1889. He claimed that criminals were evolutionary throwbacks who could thus be identified by their "sloping foreheads, extra-long arms and prominent ears" (Travis, Schwartz, and Clear 1983). As late as 1930, most Canadians still believed that crime was hereditary and that habitual offenders should be sterilized. J.G. Moylan, Inspector of Penitentiaries from 1875 to 1895, remarked that "convicts are excellent subjects for experiment; for they are not allowed to have any will of their own . . . the interior of our prisons is a grand theatre for the trial of all new plans in hygiene, education, physical, and moral reform" (Baehre 1977, 112). Our correctional system in Canada was about to enter the medical arena.

By the turn of the century, the new theme was the criminal is sick and needed to be treated and hopefully cured. The recommendations of royal commissions began to reflect this new theme in corrections. In 1914, for example, a royal commission was called to investigate the state and management of Kingston Penitentiary. It found that "many of the guards are not qualified by education or character for the jobs they fill . . . when they carry on illicit traffic . . . and rob convicts . . . they cannot help to make prisoners honest men. Their influence must have an evil effect which nothing can overcome" (Carrigan 1991). They concluded by calling for "a careful and scientific study of the individual . . . prisons can no longer be run like factories, processing human material into interchangeable units" (p. 88). There was, of course, a great gap between theory and practice in the Canadian correctional system. Fluctuations in the crime rate, financial constraints, shifting political priorities, and countless administrative problems interfered with the implementation of desirable programs. Penal reformers and correctional authorities did not always see eye to eye. The reformers' first concern was in assisting the offender while the wardens' priority was with keeping institutional order.

In 1924, the Superintendent of Penitentiaries, W.S. Hughes, commented in his *Report on Prison Affairs* that "the treatment of inmates in a penitentiary continues to be a subject of debate, and many people who know little of crime and nothing of criminals still continue to offer suggestions . . . for the treatment of offenders. It is most fortunate for the convicted ones that the suggestions of these inexperienced ones are seldom tried" (see Box 2.4) (Archambault 1938).

Change came very slowly, but by the late 1920s, there were the beginnings of inmate classification, special juvenile facilities, a system of industrial prison farms, and legislation for earned remission and parole.

During the Depression there was a surge of economic crimes, especially among unemployed men. In 1929, there were 2,769 offenders in Canadian penitentiaries. In 1933, there

---

BOX 2.4   **What is Prison Reform?**

In 1924, Thomas Matt Osborne, a former warden of three large prisons (including Auburn and Sing Sing prisons), published the following basic tenets of prison reform:

1. Prisoners are human beings; for the most part remarkably like the rest of us;

2. They can be clubbed into submission—with occasional outbreaks; but they cannot be reformed by that process;

3. Neither can they be reformed by bribery in the shape of privilege; special favours or tolerant treatment;

4. They will not respond to sentimentality; they do not like gush;

5. They appreciate a "square deal" when they get one;

6. There are not many of them mental defectives; on the contrary, they majority are embarrassing clever;

7. All of these facts must be taken into consideration, if we want prisons which will protect society. Unless they are taken into consideration, our correctional institutions will continue to be what they have been in the past—costly schools of crime—monuments of wasted effort, of misguided service; and

8. To date, all forms of severity, all forms of kindly mental and moral pauperizing, have been tried; and all have failed and will continue to fail.

SOURCE: Osborne 1924, 7–8.

---

were 4,587, an increase of 66 percent in just four years. As discussed in Chapter 1, this continued to escalate right up to 1997, when Canada was listed as the third leading nation in the western world in terms of incarceration rates—256 per 100,000 population—a very dubious honour (Solicitor General 1997).

The Canadian authorities were beginning to take a hard line on crime and criminals. Reform was once again subordinated to repression. During General D.M. Ormond's militaristic regime as superintendent of prisons (1928–1938), there were 20 riots and disturbances. All seven penitentiaries at the time were beset by disturbances including strikes, fires, and fatal shootings.

A Watershed Report: The Archambault Commission, 1936–1938

The violence in Canadian prisons stirred public and media attention and certainly served as a catalyst for the **Archambault Commission** of 1938. Its report and subsequent recommendations formed the turning point for modern Canadian correctional reform. The report's 88 recommendations covered almost every aspect of the system and still serve for much of today's 20th-century penal philosophy in Canada.

The main thrust of the report was that change could not be effected by punishment. The overall goals of the correctional system ought to be:

1. To prevent crime;
2. To rehabilitate offenders; and
3. To deter other habitual criminals.

Under the direction of Justice Joseph Archambault, this royal commission held its first meeting in 1936. The Commission toured most federal penitentiaries before releasing its final report in 1939. What it found was disheartening:

- An almost complete lack of rehabilitation programs;
- A prison system completely focused on punishment and cruelty;
- Inmates locked up in their cells for over 16 hours per day;
- Filthy living conditions;
- No granting of privileges; and
- No education programs or instructors.

Most alarming of all, the Commission found a very high recidivism rate amongst inmates—in 1936/37 alone, it was more that 70 percent. Thus, it was not surprising that the Commission's report was highly critical of the existing Canadian federal correctional system. Some of its major recommendations for change were as follows:

- Improvements in prison education, recreation, and work programs;
- Better conditions for female prisoners;
- Reforms to the probation and parole systems;
- Better aftercare services;
- Reorganized administration;
- Improved inmate classification;
- The combination of the provincial and federal systems under Ottawa;
- Retraining of existing staff and hiring of new, more qualified staff; and
- Improved medical and psychiatric services.

Post–World War II and Treatment

The Second World War diminished further public interest in prison reform and the full implementation of Justice Archambault's recommendations was temporarily shelved. Only a few inmate liberties such as earned remission, easier visiting hours, and increased recreation were granted the offenders.

Perhaps the real start of modern penal change in Canada came about in 1946 when Ottawa created the new job of commissioner of penitentiaries. Major-General Ralph B. Gibson became the first Commissioner of Penitentiaries for Canada and Joseph McCulley was appointed Deputy-Commissioner (McGrath 1976). With their appointment they were given the power to review and influence change through recommendations on the system. By 1950, the Commissioner was able to report that Canada had implemented a prisoner classification system and completed a social history for each inmate (Solicitor General of Canada 1950). He had conducted psychological testing for all the inmates and improved the educational and vocational programs. Canada had finally entered the modern age of corrections and was using a rehabilitative approach.

In 1953, Ottawa appointed a Committee of Inquiry to study remission services. Chaired by Justice Joseph Fauteux, this committee concluded that the main purpose of the correctional system was the rehabilitation of the offender. The goal was to retrain, not punish the offender.

Carrigan (1991, 374) maintains that it was this committee that truly adopted the word "corrections" in Canada, a term it explained as ". . . the total process by which society attempts to correct the anti-social attitudes or behaviours of the individual."

The result was the development of specialized aftercare programs for addicts, sex offenders, and psychopaths. Other benefits included:

- The construction of new medium security jails;
- Liberalization of probation and parole;
- Mandatory review of parole;
- Increased use of pre-sentence reports; and
- Creation of a new national federal board.

In short, the **Fauteux Report** accomplished what many previous committees did not—a Canadian correctional system based on the rehabilitation of the inmate as its guiding philosophy. Canada had entered, albeit late, the Age of the Medical Model in corrections.

From 1946 to 1960, the correctional system was led by Major-General Ralph Gibson. During his leadership, the number of federal jails increased from 7 to 15. Gibson implemented many of Archambault's and Fauteux's suggestions. Psychological services (1947), a full-time psychiatrist (1958), and a new staff training college in Kingston were just three of the many changes under his leadership.

For almost 30 years after the Archambault Report, the penitentiary system continued to come under scrutiny by royal commissions, government committees, and private-sector organizations. These reports rarely questioned the original penitentiary goal: to reform. They steadfastly maintained that most inmates could be rehabilitated while in prison. However, in time the rehabilitation philosophy began to "crack," and opponents criticized it as oppressive, too lenient, and anti-humanitarian. For example, in the **Ouimet Report** the commissioners concluded that most "reformable convicts would probably do better outside the prison walls" (Ouimet 1969). This report advocated the idea that offender change "might be more profitably pursued within a community setting than inside correctional institutions." Generally described as the start of the **reintegration era** of corrections in Canada, this second philosophy moved away from institutionalization and "experts" and the medical model towards decentralized, community-run models with open institutions that respected prisoner rights.

The Report of the Task Force on Community-Based Residential Centres (Outerbridge 1972) spelled out the means to be used in this new model:

- Divert persons entirely from jail (jail is a last resort);
- Divert persons from the criminal justice system;
- Shorten sentences by the court;
- Shorten actual incarceration; and
- Provide temporary relief from jail.

The 1970s saw many changes implemented in the Canadian correctional system. Prisoners began to be called by their names; they could grow beards, and even had a say in prison conditions through their inmate committee representatives. The psychiatric period and medical model in Canadian penitentiaries were at an end. Almost every conceivable form of therapy had been tried, including various forms of psychotropic drug treatments, electroshock, behaviour modification, sensory deprivation, weekend marathons—even nude encounter groups.

In the 1970s, there was an attempt to humanize some aspects of daily life in jail. There was even an attempt to give prisoners a limited degree of self-government, through their inmate committees. In 1971, the **Mohr Committee** suggested that inmates could be rehabilitated better in a small-group setting. Living units were created so that inmates and staff members could reside in family-like groups (Ekstedt and Griffiths 1988).

In 1973, the Solicitor General's Perspectives paper recommended diversion for non-violent offenders. According to its authors, prison must be regarded as the sanction of last resort. During this period, community service orders began to replace prison sentences and there were also some successful experiments with restitution (see Chapter 13). More and more offenders were being given the opportunities to leave the penitentiary on a work or educational release program.

In the mid 1970s, a report published by the Law Reform Commission of Canada said that "prisons had failed both as deterrents and rehabilitators." It declared that offenders could "not be re-educated for life in society while separated from it" (Gosselin 1982).

Reparation in the 1980s

By 1980, the British Columbia Penitentiary at New Westminster had shut down for good. The old fortress had stood for more than a century. Its closing signalled the beginning of the end for Canada's Victorian prisons and the philosophy they represented.

Throughout the 1980s, Ottawa continued to be interested in the concept of community corrections and sanctions. Bill C-19 (*Criminal Law Reform Act* of 1984) proposed that sentencing policy in Canada focus on community alternatives to prison. According to this proposal, emphasis would be given to non-custodial sanctions, with imprisonment reserved for cases where such non-custodial sanctions are appropriate. However, despite these suggestions, there was a gradual shift towards a more "get tough" approach with correctional policies. This shift involved a change from a service approach to one that emphasized the risk that offenders posed to the community. As Michael Young points out in Chapter 6, this resulted in increased prison construction, longer sentences, prison overcrowding, and accompanying prison violence and riots, and expansion of probation and parole.

The 1980s punishment objective was actually based on the theory of **reparation**, which meant an "emphasis on offender responsibility for rehabilitation" (Ekstedt and Griffiths 1988, 70).

Carson Report, 1984

On July 27, 1984, the Advisory Committee to the Solicitor General of Canada on the Management of Correctional Institutions (**Carson Committee**) was formed. Its mandate was to review and report on the management of the Correctional Service of Canada in response to earlier concerns and studies on suicide and violence in the system. The Committee's report was submitted on November 30, 1984.

One of its major findings was that Canadian prison wardens had little autonomy and, because of the excessive centralization of control by the Correctional Service of Canada, they were often reduced to "paper-shuffling" bureaucrats (Carson 1984). The Committee also raised serious concerns about the viability of the existing seven-level security system and the practice of "cascading" inmates (moving them to progressively lower levels of security over the course of their confinement). Concern was also expressed about the "over-classification" of inmates in maximum security prisons. The Committee noted that:

> . . . since the overcrowding is particularly serious in medium security institutions, there are a large number of inmates presently in maximum security who would, under normal conditions, be in medium security. The difficulties associated with the proper classification of offenders and the fact that such a process is often subjective rather than premised on established predictive guidelines must be a major consideration in any discussion of correctional treatment (Ekstedt and Griffiths 1988, 194).

The concerns raised in the Carson Report continue to this very day. A major concern of the correctional system since 1998 has been a process known as accelerated review or the extensive review of inmates in penitentiaries who are serving their first term of imprisonment for non-violent offences. The hope is to release them on full parole after they have served one third of their sentence. In 1999, there was a controversy because of a leaked federal government memo and related rumours about a 50-50 formula for federal release; that is, a plan by the correctional system to release as many as 50 percent of federal inmates back into the community after one third of their sentence was served (*The Globe and Mail,* 17 February 1999). Naturally enough, this spawned a backlash by many citizens and government representatives. At the time of writing this chapter, the issue has not been resolved and continues to be widely debated.

Emergence of the "Opportunities Model," 1980s

In the 1980s, corrections continued to be practiced in Canadian prisons and communities in much the same fashion as in the 1970s—punishment "dressed up" as reparation. A new name emerged to present this corrections philosophy to the Canadian public: "the program **opportunities model**" (Subcommittee on the Penitentiary System in Canada 1977). This model is based on the idea that "the offender is ultimately responsible for his behaviour . . . he is convicted and sentenced on the basis of his criminal behaviour, not on the basis of some underlying personality disorder or deprived socio-economic condition" (p. 71).

In using the opportunities model, corrections shifted total responsibility for reformation onto the offender. The system did, however, retain responsibility for making basic and essential programs and services available to prisoners, should they choose to participate.

Corrections in the 1990s

As the 1990s neared, correctional philosophy was a "mixture of the program opportunities model, with a strong emphasis on control of offenders, and perhaps a dash of what remains of the rehabilitation model of the 1960's" (Griffiths and Verdun-Jones 1994, 288).

The Solicitor General of Canada (1991, 4) describes it best in its *Mission of the Correctional Service of Canada*:

> The Correctional Service of Canada, as part of the Criminal Justice System, contributes to the protection of society by actively encouraging and assisting offenders to become law-abiding citizens, while exercising reasonable, safe, secure and humane control.

Obviously the goal is to balance the concepts of assistance and control: "our aim is to assist and encourage to the extent that is possible and to control to the extent that is necessary" (Solicitor General of Canada 1991, 6).

This age-old dilemma is still unresolved in the 1990s. Its philosophy is now contained in the *Corrections and Conditional Release Act* (1992), which states that the main purpose of the federal correctional system is twofold:

1. Carry out sentences imposed by the courts through the safe and humane custody and supervision of offenders; and

2. Assist the rehabilitation of offenders and their reintegration into law-abiding citizens through the provision of programs in penitentiaries and in the community.

Section 10 of this act goes on to state that the service should "use the least restrictive measures consistent with the protection of the public, staff members and offenders." More recently, the Task Force on Reintegration of Offenders (1997) states that:

- Low-risk offenders will receive more of their programming in the community; and

- Program referrals will be monitored more closely to ensure that only offenders who require specific programs are referred. These points reflect the risk/needs model of justice supported throughout much of the 1990s.

Arbour Commission, 1996

In 1994, a series of events occurred in the Prison for Women (P4W) in Kingston that would go on to define the new "face" of corrections in Canada. It is ironic that the smallest group of inmates in Canada's federal correctional system (in 1996 there were 320 female inmates in total, 142 in Kingston) would help to redesign a system that was, at the time, "hopelessly afloat in a sea of chaos and confusion" (Commission of Inquiry into Certain Events at the Prison for Women in Kingston 1996, 91).

On April 10, 1995, a commission chaired by Justice Louise Arbour was appointed to "investigate and report on . . . the incidents which occurred at the Prison for Women in Kingston . . . beginning on April 22, 1994, and further to make recommendations to the policies and practices of the Correctional Service of Canada" (Commission of Inquiry 1996, ix). What were the events that caused such a major crisis in Canadian corrections?

- On April 22, 1994, at P4W, a "brief but violent physical confrontation" took place between six female inmates and a number of correctional staff.

- The inmates were placed in segregation and charged.

- In subsequent days, with tension running very high, various inmates "slashed, took a hostage and attempted suicide."

- On April 26, correctional staff demonstrated outside the prison to demand the transfer of the inmates;

- The same day, the warden ordered in an emergency response team to remove the prisoners from their cells and strip-search them. This was captured on videotape. The eight female inmates were then left in restraints and leg irons in empty segregation cells, wearing nothing but paper gowns.

- On April 27, seven of the eight inmates were subjected to body-cavity searches by male officers.
- Ultimately most of the women were transferred to a psychiatric treatment centre and then returned again to segregation.
- On December 22, the women pleaded guilty to related criminal charges. In January 1995, they were released from segregation and returned to the general population.

As Justice Arbour stated in her report, ". . . the incidents that gave rise to this inquiry could have gone largely unnoticed" (Commission of Inquiry 1996, xi). The public viewing of the videotape and the release of a special report by a correctional investigator in 1995 helped to shed light on the current state of the correctional system; otherwise the Correctional Service of Canada had essentially "closed the book" on these events.

But the Arbour Commission reopened the book with what was probably the most exhaustive and thorough royal commission inquiry in the history of Canadian federal correctional practices. The process took place in two phases:

- Phase I: Judicial public hearings were held for 43 days and heard 21 witnesses.
- Phase II: Policy discussions held over nine days with staff from the Correctional Service of Canada, inmates, and correctional experts from across Canada and abroad.

In total, the Commission interviewed more than 130 people and took evidence from 21 witnesses. In addition, Justice Arbour visited correctional facilities across Canada and met with staff in Kingston as well as staff in several other federal penitentiaries. The Arbour Commission Report was released on March 28, 1996.

It made 14 wide-sweeping major recommendations, including:

1. Male members of emergency response teams should not be employed in women's institutions, nor should they be allowed to strip-search and cavity-search female prisoners.
2. A position of Deputy Commissioner for Women should be created with all the powers necessary to implement appropriate changes.
3. Special training programs should be implemented to allow more sensitive responses.
4. Segregation should only be used in compliance with the law.
5. Input from other criminal justice agencies and staff should be included and used in such future situations.
6. The Correctional Service should improve its accessibility at all levels.

The Prison for Women was closed in 1997. All female inmates were transferred to their respective five regional prisons in Canada (see Chapter 6).

There is no doubt that the Arbour Commission and its report helped to hasten the slow process of change within Canadian corrections. As Justice Arbour noted, ". . . they were part of a prison culture which did not value individual rights." Many of the report's recommendations have since had an impact on the way the Correctional Service of Canada now treats all of its federal prisoners. Male inmates have also received better, accelerated reviews of their cases with respect to their needs, rights, and ultimate review for release.

The present risk/needs model is intended to provide a fair assessment for both public protection and inmate release into the community. It can be improved with increased and better staff training, improved prediction models, and, finally, more correctional research into crime and offender behaviour.

CONCLUSION

The evolution of corrections in Canada, although influenced by American trends, is tied directly to Canadian royal commission inquiries throughout the 20th century. The current *Federal Corrections and Conditional Release Act* (1992) still supports reintegration ideology. Hence Canada has moved from a just deserts approach towards a more reintegrative one. These changes have not always met with public or political support; however, they reflect the dynamic nature and the role that social, economic, and political interests play in the administration of criminal justice and, in this case, corrections.

Of all the above "treatments," restorative justice offers the most promise. Private prisons and increased use of modern technology such as electronic monitoring and home confinement are also worth considering. Whatever the final direction, Canadian corrections has taken some unique and very positive steps forward since 1835. Unlike our American counterparts, Canada has decided to tackle problems of prison violence and overcrowding with healing programs as opposed to constructing more jails and executing more offenders.

Canadian correctional philosophy has discarded the traditional deterrent sentencing model and adopted a risk/needs model. By employing trained staff who assess an individual offender's risks and needs, we should be better able to determine our program and service direction. And while the treatment may be far different than what our predecessors plotted in the early part of this century, they were correct on one count. The environment required to carry out these new treatments and programs will be the community—the "hidden element" of the criminal justice system. Only in the community do we have a fighting chance to battle and control crime. Only in the community can we have any future long-term successes, with the reintegration of offenders, assistance to victims, and protection of the public.

As Justice Louise Arbour stated in her report, ". . . the history of women and crime is spotted with opportunities most of which have been missed. We hope that history will not dictate our future" (Commission of Inquiry 1996). (Justice Arbour went on to chair the United Nations War Crimes Tribunal and in 1999 was appointed to the Supreme Court of Canada.)

The past and present history of our federal correctional system practices does not necessarily accurately reflect the views of average Canadians. But it is important to note that the problem is much broader than a an issue of Native rights or female inmates. If it is a social ill to jail too many people for too long, then we desperately need new alternatives in the community, alongside increased and expanded existing resources.

Judges, as a body, are now finally realizing that as a long-term solution jail is not the answer. As so many past royal commissions have recognized in Canada, jail should be nothing more than a "last resort." In their attempts to explain why this should be obvious to us, these same judges stress that jail only removes offenders from our midst temporarily. Arbour further notes that imprisonment has thus far failed to satisfy a basic function of the Canadian judicial system, which is to protect society from crime in a manner commanding public support while avoiding needless injury to the offender (Commission of Inquiry 1996).

SUMMARY

This chapter provides a historical overview of corrections in Canada. This history can be characterized as one of punishment. Although punishment has dominated correctional practices in Canada, the royal commissions and various government reports have been instrumental in forging significant changes to how the concept of corrections is implemented. For example, we no longer hang people, we no longer flog offenders, and we classify offenders according to type of offence and risk to society;, more recently, the reports have helped to improve prison conditions and offender rights. In terms of prison architecture and correctional operations, the various commissions and reports have also had a dramatic impact. During pre-Confederation days, Canada's correctional system was based on the Auburn (congregate or silent association) system of penitentiaries—a combination of punishment and penitence. It became the dominant model for our early prisons across Canada, including our first penitentiary, the Kingston Provincial Penitentiary.

This approach lasted throughout the 1800s, and for most of the 19th century. It was not until the medical model of corrections was adopted in the 20th century that ideologies such as rehabilitation, deterrence, reintegration (1980s and 1990s), and, finally, restorative justice (from the 1990s on) emerged.

The history of corrections in Canada has not been static. In fact, it is very dynamic as correctional decision-makers have relied on the various royal commissions and government reports to ensure that the future direction of corrections in Canada continues to be humane and just. And as will be seen in the other contributions in this text, there is almost no area within the correctional arena that is not experiencing some type of reform.

KEY TERMS AND CONCEPTS

Archambault Commission	John Howard	reintegration era
Bloody Code	Mohr Committee	reparation
British North America Act	opportunities model	retaliation
Carson Committee	Ouimet Report	social determinism
Cherry Hill	Pennsylvania system	Henry Smith
Fauteux Report	(separate system)	Upper Fort Garry
Elisabeth Fry	reform model	Walnut Street Jail

STUDY AND DISCUSSION QUESTIONS

1. What role did John Howard and Elizabeth Fry play as early correctional reformers? What major contributions were made by each?

2. How did Canadian jails come into existence? What role did Kingston Penitentiary play?

3. What impact did the Brown Commission have upon Canadian penitentiaries?

4. Contrast the Archambault Commission (1938) with the Carson Report (1984). What are the similarities and/or differences?

5. Why was the Arbour Commission (1996) necessary? How did it affect the correctional philosophy of the 1990s?

 WEBLINK

Correctional Service of Canada: **www.csc-scc.gc.ca**.

NOTES

1. Actually, the San Michele House of Corrections in Rome was the first jail to use Howard's ideas and methods. This reformatory for delinquent boys, opened in 1704, used the principles of isolation, work, silence, and prayer to reform their "wayward inmates" (Cayley 1998).
2. Two years later George Brown would chair the Brown Commission of Inquiry into Kingston Prison practices.

REFERENCES

Anderson, F.W. 1960. Prisons and Prison Reforms in the Old Canadian West. *Canadian Journal of Corrections.*

Archambault, J. (Chairman). 1938. *Report of the Royal Commission to Investigate the Penal System of Canada.* Ottawa: King's Printer.

Baehre, R. 1977. Origins of the Penitentiary in Upper Canada. *Ontario History* 59.

Beattie, J.M. 1977. *Attitudes Towards Crime and Punishment in Upper Canada, 1830–1850.* Toronto: Centre of Criminology, University of Toronto.

Bellomo, J.J. 1972. Upper Canadian Attitudes towards Crime and Punishment. *Ontario History* 64: 11–26.

Carrigan, D.O. 1991. *Crime and Punishment in Canada: A History.* Toronto: McClelland and Stewart.

Carson, J. (Chairman). 1984. *Report of the Advisory Committee to the Solicitor General on Management of Correctional Institutions (Carson Report).* Ottawa: Ministry of Supply and Services.

Cayley, D. 1998. *The Expanding Prison.* Toronto: House of Anansi Press.

Coles, D. 1979. *Nova Scotia Corrections: An Historical Perspective.* Halifax: Corrections Service Division.

Commission of Inquiry into Certain Events at the Prison for Women in Kingston. 1996. *The Prison for Women in Kingston: A Commission of Inquiry into Certain Events (Arbour Commission Report).* Ottawa: Canada Communication Group. www.sgc.gc.ca/epub/corr/e199681/e199681.htm (April 2000).

Dobash, R., R. Dobash and S. Gutteridge. 1986. *The Imprisonment of Women.* New York: B. Blackwell Publishers.

Ekstedt, J.W., and C.T. Griffiths. 1988. *Corrections in Canada: Policy and Practice* (2nd ed.). Toronto: Butterworths.

Goff, C. 1999. *Corrections in Canada.* Cincinnati: Anderson.

Gosselin, L. 1982. *Prisons in Canada.* Montreal: Black Rose Books.

Griffiths, C.T., and S.N. Verdun-Jones. 1994. *Canadian Criminal Justice.* Toronto: Harcourt Brace.

McGrath, W.T. (Ed.). 1976. *Crime and Its Treatment in Canada* (2nd ed.). Toronto: Macmillan.

Melossi, D., and M. Pararini. 1981. *The Prison and the Factory: Origins of the Penitentiary System.* Totowa, NJ: Barnes and Noble.

Osborne, M.T. 1924. *Prisons and Common Sense.* Philadelphia: J.B. Lippincott.

Ouimet, R. (Chairman). 1969. *Report of the Canadian Committee on Corrections—Towards Unity: Criminal Justice and Corrections.* Ottawa: Information Canada.

Outerbridge, W.R. 1972. *Report of the Task Force on Community-Based Residential Centres.* Ottawa: Information Canada.

Posner, C. 1991. An Historical Overview of the Construction of Canada's Federal Prisons. *Forum on Correctional Research* 3(2): 4.

Shoom, S. 1966. Kingston Penitentiary: The Early Decades. *Canadian Journal of Corrections*, July, 215–220.

Solicitor General of Canada. 1950. *Annual Report of the Commissioner of Penitentiaries, 1949.* Ottawa: King's Printer.

———. 1973. *Criminal in Canadian Society: A Perspective.* Ottawa: Supply and Services Canada.

———. 1991. *Mission of the Correctional Service of Canada.* Ottawa: Supply and Services of Canada.

———. 1997. *Basic Facts about Corrections in Canada.* Ottawa: Public Works and Government Services Canada.

Subcommittee on the Penitentiary System in Canada. 1977. *Report to Parliament by the Subcommittee on the Penitentiary System in Canada.* Ottawa: Supply and Services Canada.

Task Force on Reintegration of Offenders. 1997. Ottawa: Corrections Branch, Solicitor General of Canada.

Travis, L.F., **M.D. Schwartz**, and **T.R. Clear**. 1983. *Corrections: An Issues Approach* (2nd ed.). Cincinnati: Anderson.

CORRECTIONS IN CANADA: PUBLIC KNOWLEDGE AND PUBLIC OPINION

3

Julian V. Roberts
Department of Criminology
University of Ottawa
Ottawa, Ontario

LEARNING OBJECTIVES

After reading this chapter, you should be able to:

- Have an idea of how well informed you are about the correctional system in Canada;
- Have an idea of whether you are more or less well informed than the average member of the public;
- Describe the critical issues of public opinion with respect to the correctional system;
- Describe the nature of public attitudes with respect to the correctional system; and
- Understand the role the news media play in informing the public and influencing public opinion about corrections in Canada.

We are all pilgrims on the same journey—but some pilgrims have better maps.

—Nelson De Mille

Winston Churchill once famously wrote that a society should be judged by the way in which it treats its offenders. Most Canadians would respond that Canada treats its offenders well, perhaps too well. It is probably true that prisoners in this country are treated better than prisoners in many others parts of the world. Nevertheless, prison conditions are not as rosy as many people believe. This chapter will explore **public knowledge** of the correctional system, including prison and parole.

Although the criminal justice system is a complex bureaucratic machine with its own "checks and balances" that are intended to "respond to a wide diversity of human behaviours" (Roberts 2000, 3), it does not operate independently of the society that it is designed to serve and protect. Members of that society frequently have strong views on many issues related to criminal justice, and these views can sometimes affect the nature and functioning of the criminal justice system.

In some respects, as one of the defining features of a democratic society, the public plays a direct role: community-based corrections cannot proceed without the support of the public, whose members sometimes oppose the establishment of halfway houses for offenders. This is sometimes referred to as the NIMBY ("not in my backyard") syndrome.

The traditional public response to crime has involved the use of imprisonment, with long-term imprisonment for the offenders convicted of the most serious offences. This public response has put pressure on judges and correctional officials such as parole board members, who may in fact realize that imprisonment has important limitations as a response to crime.

Public opinion can have direct and indirect effects upon criminal justice policy-making, including correctional policy. An example of an indirect effect could involve the decisions of parole boards. These boards may become more conservative in their releasing decisions (for instance, releasing fewer inmates on parole, or releasing inmates later in their sentences) as a result of public pressure. When an inmate serving a sentence on parole in the community is convicted of a serious crime, there is often a strident public reaction, and this may affect parole boards. In the same way, public pressure (particularly following a high-profile crime committed by a parolee) may affect politicians and policy-makers, who will feel pressured to introduce legislation to restrict the parole eligibility dates for certain offenders. For example, in 1988, following a tragic case of murder committed by a parolee, the Solicitor General introduced legislation that would have abolished parole except for inmates serving sentences for non-violent crimes. (The proposal was strongly opposed by professionals working in the correctional system, and was subsequently dropped.)

As has been noted elsewhere (e.g., Roberts 1992), the public in Canada (and elsewhere) is often quite uninformed about the nature and functioning of the criminal justice system, including the correctional system. There are several reasons for this lack of knowledge.

First, criminal justice is just one of many important social issues that members of the public are concerned about. Public knowledge of the economy is probably just as poor; there are simply too many issues crowding the newspapers for us all to be experts in every subject. Second, the criminal justice system is quite complex; it has to be, in order to respond appropriately to a complex phenomenon like crime.

Third, media coverage of crime and criminal justice tends to be rather poor, and presents a distorted image of the system. As we all know, news coverage often sensationalizes crime and criminal justice. In addition, the media are apt to oversimplify complex issues. A complex issue such as sentencing is reduced to a simple equation of crime on one side and time (in prison) on the other. This is true of the media in Canada (e.g., Roberts 1995), as well as other nations such as Germany (Boers and Sessar 1991) and the U.S. (e.g., Barkan and Cohn 1994).

For some inmates in Canada, such as life prisoners, the public is critical to the correctional experience. Almost all life prisoners are entitled, according to section 745.6 of the Criminal Code, to a review of their parole eligibility dates.[1] Here is how such a review works. Consider a prisoner convicted of first-degree murder and serving a life sentence with no possibility of parole until he or she has served 25 years in prison. After 15 years in prison, this prisoner can apply for a review of the parole eligibility date. If a judge believes that there is a reasonable chance of success, the inmate will make a case before a jury, which will hear evidence of the prisoner's activities while in prison, his or her plans if granted parole, and so forth. The jury has the power to reduce the number of years that the prisoner must serve in prison before becoming eligible for parole from 25 down to 15. The jury can also choose an amount in between these limits. (For the results of parole eligibility reviews to date, see Roberts and Cole 1999.)

In 1999, Colin Thatcher applied to a jury for a review of his parole eligibility date. Fifteen years earlier Thatcher had been convicted of first-degree murder in the slaying of his wife. The case attracted a great deal of media attention at the time, and was eventually made into a movie. Once Thatcher's application for a parole review was made public (in the summer of 1999), the media attention returned, and the application galvanized the community. Many people argued that Thatcher should not be eligible for a review (and should have to serve the full 25 years before becoming eligible for parole), since he has steadfastly refused to admit his responsibility for the killing (even though he has exhausted all appeals against his sentence). The jury is still hearing evidence in the Thatcher application as this book goes to press.

So the public is important to the correctional system in general, and also to the lives of specific individual prisoners. In this chapter we will review the research on public opinion with respect to corrections in Canada. Before getting to the opinion data, however, it is necessary to understand the nature of public knowledge regarding this critical component of the criminal justice system. Where possible, we shall discuss the findings from Canadian research in light of research conducted in other countries. We will also consider the consequences of allowing public opinion on a complex topic such as corrections to influence policy development.

First, however, let us look at Box 3.1, which contains a number of questions about various aspects of the correctional system in Canada. See how many you get right. As the chapter progresses, we shall see how accurate people were when they were asked some of these questions.

CORRECTIONAL POLICY AND PRACTICE AND THE VIEWS OF THE PUBLIC

One of the thorniest problems relating to the criminal justice system concerns the extent to which policy-makers and politicians should heed the views of the public. Some people argue that it is inappropriate for the correctional system (or the sentencing process) to be affected by the public's reaction, particularly since (as we shall see in this chapter), the public is often misinformed about how the system functions. A good example is the use of imprisonment. Many people believe that prison serves as a good deterrent to offending, and that long prison sentences act as a better deterrent than short terms of custody. Correctional professionals now know (from systematic research on the subject) that prison is not a particularly good

BOX 3.1	Corrections Knowledge Quiz: Check Your Knowledge of the Canadian Correctional System

Prison Population Statistics

Question: How many offenders were in prison on the average day in 1997/98 in Canada?

Answer: There were an average of 32,970 inmates were housed in custody per day.

Question: What percentage of offenders admitted to federal penitentiaries were serving sentences for crimes of violence in 1997/98?

Answer: 60 percent.

Question: What category of crime accounts for the highest percentage of admissions to custody in the provincial prison system?

Answer: Crimes against property.

Question: How many prisoners in Canada served life sentences in 1997/98?

Answer: 2,191.

Question: How many years must an offender convicted of first-degree murder spend in prison before becoming eligible for release on parole?

Answer: 25 years.

Question: How many years must an offender sentenced to life imprisonment for second-degree murder spend in prison before becoming eligible for parole?

Answer: Between 10 and 25 years, depending upon the sentencing judge.

Question: What was the average daily cost of housing an inmate in custody in 1997/98?

Answer: $128.

Question: Aboriginal people made up what percentage of admissions to federal penitentiaries in 1997/98?

Answer: 17 percent of federal admissions were Aboriginal people.

Question: Aboriginal people made up what percentage of admissions to provincial prisons in 1997/98?

Answer: It varied from 1 percent in Quebec to 72 percent in Saskatchewan.

Question: What is the average length of stay in a provincial correctional facility?

Answer: 24 days.

Parole and Temporary Release Trends

Question: In 1997/98, what percentage of federal inmates were granted release on parole?

Answer: About 40 percent of applicants were granted release.

Question: Has the parole rate increased over the past few years?

Answer: No, the parole grant rate has declined.

Question: What percentage of offenders released on parole commit another offence before their period of parole has elapsed?

Answer: Approximately 1 in 10.

Question: What percentage of prisoners released on an escorted temporary absence fail to return to prison?

Answer: Less than 1 percent. In 1997/98, all but 11 of 47,625 escorted absences were completed successfully.

Question: What percentage of prisoners released on an unescorted temporary absence fail to return to prison?

Answer: Less than 1 percent. In 1997/98, all but 26 of 6,154 unescorted absences were completed successfully.

SOURCES: Reed and Roberts (1999), adapted from *Juristat* 19(4), Catalogue No. 85-002; and Solicitor General of Canada (1998), reproduced with the permission of the Minister of Public Works and Government Services Canada, 2000.

deterrent, or is no more effective at deterring offenders than intensive probation. As for long terms of custody, there may be other reasons for putting people in prison for long periods of time, but a ten-year sentence is not going to deter offenders any more effectively than a five-year sentence. So if judges and correctional authorities were to favour the use of imprisonment, particularly long-term imprisonment because that is the what the public wants, this policy would be inconsistent with the results of careful research in the field of corrections.

Another perspective argues that the sentencing and correctional systems should be sensitive to the views of the public. This view is based upon the position that in a democracy, public institutions such as the government and its constituent departments (including the prison system) should reflect the "will of the people." In addition, independent of the democratic argument, it is sometimes suggested that if the criminal justice system drifts too far away from public sentiment, people will resort to their own individual means of responding to crime. This will result in them pursuing revenge rather than justice.

The Canadian correctional system attempts to incorporate both these perspectives. Judges and parole boards do not allow their decisions with respect to specific individuals to be influenced by petitions and the like. On the other hand, the government engages in extensive public consultation (using surveys, focus groups, and "town hall" meetings) before it introduces reform in any area of criminal justice. The only neglected area, as we shall see over the next few pages, involves public legal education. The government spends much more time consulting and surveying the public than educating people about the reality of the correctional system. The public is therefore forced to rely on the media for information about crime and justice in Canada.

News Media Coverage of Correctional Issues

Many say that as far as the media are concerned, bad news is good news. This means that if something goes wrong, it is newsworthy. Nowhere is this more true than with respect to criminal justice and in particular corrections. A sentence of five years for the crime of sexual assault is not newsworthy, because that is what most people think that offenders convicted of that crime should receive. But if a judge imposes a sentence of 90 days to be served on weekends for the crime of sexual assault, that sentence will create headlines.

This tendency to cover the worst-case scenarios (and to ignore the system when it is functioning appropriately) is most apparent with respect to prisons and parole. When the parole system makes headlines, it is almost always because an offender on parole has committed a serious crime of violence. How often do you read a story in which a man convicted of a very serious crime completes his sentence in the community, and then, with the help of his parole officer, turns his life around and becomes a law-abiding citizen? Thankfully, such stories exist, and they happen far more often than most people believe. We just do not hear about them from the news media.

As noted, Colin Thatcher's parole review application attracted a lot of media coverage, mostly negative. But there are other life prisoners who obtain release on parole after 15 years and make a success of their lives. One individual who had been convicted of first-degree murder applied for a jury review of his application after 15 years. The jury heard how he had completed two university degrees while in prison, got married, started a program for young offenders, and took a number of other steps towards his rehabilitation. The jury granted him the right to make an early parole application after 15 years, and the National

Parole Board subsequently granted him release on full parole. He is now leading a productive and law-abiding existence, and has been doing so for several years. But when people talk about parole for life prisoners, they think about Clifford Olson and Colin Thatcher, and for that the media must be held responsible. If the media covered some of these "good news" stories once in a while, Canadians would have a more balanced perspective on the criminal justice system.

It is not just the nature of the offender population that is misrepresented by the media. Media coverage of prison life also focuses on stories that will shock or scandalize the public. Bad news again. We only hear about life in correctional institutions when something goes wrong, such as when there is a riot or a disturbance of some kind.

Again, the Thatcher case provides a good example. Colin Thatcher was in the news long before he made his controversial application to have a jury review of his parole eligibility date. While serving his time in prison, Thatcher had been allowed to have occasional access to his horse. This fact was widely cited as an example of the "easy" life that prisoners in Canada lead. No mention of the pains of imprisonment was ever made.

Another good illustration of the power of the media to determine public knowledge of correctional issues comes from the U.S. A survey was conducted of the general public in Florida. Respondents were asked to identify the most important problem facing the state's correctional system. The problem identified by most people was prison overcrowding. Coincidentally (or not), a content analysis of news media stories about corrections in Florida found that the most frequent subject was prison overcrowding. The irony is that at the time that this survey and content analysis were conducted, there was no problem of overcrowding in Florida's prisons. The news media had created public concern about a correctional "problem" that simply did not exist (see Bryant and Morris 1998).

The reliance of the Canadian public on the media has been documented in numerous surveys. For example, in 1986, a representative sample of the Canadian public was asked to name their source of information about sentencing and parole. Fully 95 percent of the sample cited the news media, with television being the most frequently cited medium (Canadian Sentencing Commission 1987).

Public Knowledge of Corrections

Few Canadians have ever been inside a correctional facility. This does not prevent us from having an opinion about **institutional life**, and the manner in which prisoners should be treated. This reality (which is true for other countries as well) represents an obstacle to correctional reform: public opinion about corrections, and in particular prison, is based upon second-hand knowledge and indirect experience (usually through the media). This knowledge is frequently inaccurate. The views that Canadians have of prison life are frequently strongly held.

Many people appear to believe that prisoners should endure a harsh life and should be denied some of the basic comforts that most of us take for granted. Take television as an example. Watching television is a feature of daily life for almost all Canadians. In the early 1990s, Alberta's Minister of Justice advocated the removal of colour television from provincial correctional institutions. Should prisoners be allowed to have a television set in their cells? Many people are surprised to learn that prisoners are allowed to purchase a set. Inmates are also allowed to purchase and use their own computers. To deny offenders access to learning tools such as computers would be self-defeating on the part of the correctional system.

After all, as the name implies, the system is about correction, not simply punishment. If offenders are denied the necessary educational tools to change their behaviour, then they will come out of prison worse off than when they were admitted. This will probably mean that they will get in trouble again and wind up back in prison. So computers are necessary for this reason; they are not just an aspect of a "soft" life. This perspective is seldom brought to the attention of the public, because most people receive information from the media without direct experience of institutional life (Chermak 1995).

Nature of Prison Conditions

Without direct experience of the prison, people are not really in a position to know what prison life is like. One consequence of this is that the public loses sight of the principal pain of imprisonment: the lack of personal freedom that comes from being held in custody. Comparisons are sometimes made between life in some of the newer correctional centres and the life of a university student in residence. But even if prisoners had all the same facilities available to students (gyms, libraries, television, etc.), there can be no comparison between the lifestyles of the two populations. Being deprived of one's personal freedom and forced to live in the company of frequently uncongenial strangers is a very aversive experience. One consequence of overlooking the unpleasantness of losing one's liberty is that the public frequently calls for longer prison sentences, in part because "just six months in prison" is not so bad.

Such views are consistent with the conservative crime control model that is particularly popular with Americans, but that also appeals to many Canadians. For example, an important influence on our federal government has been the get-tough perspective of the public. Two examples involve the *Young Offenders Act* (YOA) and the provision for parole for lifers, which we have already discussed. In 2000, the federal government will introduce a new *Youth Criminal Justice Act* to replace the YOA. One reason for this reform was public outcry over the apparently lenient treatment of young offenders by the old Act (see Roberts 1999). In reality, compared to many other countries, young offenders have been treated more harshly in Canada. This reaction has in part been prompted by such sensationalized stories such as the Ryan Garrioch case of 1992, the 1995 incident in Montreal that involved the killing of a priest and his wife by two young people, the 1997 killing of Reena Virk by a gang of young females and males, and the 1998 case involving the murder of Clayton McGloan, who was killed by some youths while trying to break up a party at his parents' home (Winterdyk 2000). These incidents not only drew national media attention but also spawned several petitions calling for harsher punishment for violent young offenders.

In addition to the changes to the YOA, the parole-for-lifers provision was also amended as a result of a great deal of public pressure. As a result of the reforms introduced in 1996, it is now much harder for life prisoners to obtain permission to apply for parole at the 15-year mark.

Research has shown that people who think that prisons are "easy" also tend to favour longer terms of custody (see Brillon 1984). However, six months in prison can be very bad, even if a person gets out early on parole. In the interim, the inmate may well have lost his or her job, residence, and, in a high number of cases, spouse or partner as well. These are what we might call the **collateral pains** of imprisonment: they are not part of the original sentence, but are nevertheless a common indirect consequence of incarceration.

Finally, the public tends to lose sight of what we might term the "after effects" of imprisonment. When the warrant of the court expires after, say a three-year sentence, the individual is no longer under the control of the criminal justice system. However, that person still carries the stigma of the association with prison. It is obviously hard to find employment when you have a three-year hole in your C.V., and when potential employers know that you have spent time in a penitentiary. The problems that ex-inmates face after their sentences expire are frequently a cause of further offending.

It is important to add that these perceptions of prison life are not restricted to Canadians. Surveys in other countries have shown similar results. For example, Doble (1995) conducted research on Americans' knowledge of the correctional system and found that two thirds of his sample believed (erroneously) that most prison inmates are idle all day instead of working productively at a job. This view was a major source of dissatisfaction with the criminal justice system in that country.

Threat to Inmates' Health and Safety in Prison

Most people unaware of the high rates of assault, homicide, and suicide in correctional institutions (e.g., Roberts and Jackson 1991; also see Chapters 7–9). One national survey conducted in 1991 found that half the sample felt that conditions in prisons were "too soft," although fewer than 5 percent of the respondents reported having first-hand experience of a correctional institution. This perception that prison life is easy may account for some of the fairly hard-line attitudes of members of the public. For example, many people believe that prisoners should not have the right to vote. Others believe that inmates should not have the right to apply for temporary absences from prison for humanitarian purposes (such as funerals of family members).

Use of Imprisonment

Many commissions of inquiry (e.g., Canadian Sentencing Commission 1987) have noted that Canada employs imprisonment as a sanction to a greater extent than most other western nations. Is the public aware of this? It would appear not. A survey conducted for the Solicitor General Canada in 1998 asked Canadians about the rate of incarceration in Canada "compared to other countries." The correct answer to this question is that the imprisonment rate in Canada is somewhat or much higher in Canada (depending on the specific country to which comparison is made). However, only 15 percent of respondents gave this response. The most common answer, in fact, was that the incarceration rate was somewhat *lower* in this country (see Chapter 1 for a breakdown of international incarceration rates). Almost one respondent in five believed that the incarceration rate was much lower in Canada (Roberts, Nuffield, and Hann 1999). Somewhat ironically, Canadian sociologist Robert Silverman (1988, 209) observed that "it is likely that in one week of prime-time television drama one will see more homicides than will occur in Canada in the course of a year." Hence, given the growing amount of media exposure of crime, it might not be surprising to observe that Canadians feel that incarceration rates in Canada are lower than in other countries.

Over-incarceration of Aboriginal Offenders in Prison Populations

Another correctional issue that has received a lot of attention from commissions of inquiry concerns the over-representation of Aboriginal offenders in Canada's prison population.

Although Aboriginal Canadians represent under 4 percent of the general population, as of 1997/98, they represented 17 percent of the federal prison population (Reed and Roberts 1999; also see Chapter 9). In some provincial prison populations, the over-representation is even more striking. Aboriginal inmates represent 68 percent of the Saskatchewan prison population, and 49 percent of the Manitoba prison population.

Interestingly, this appears to be the one important prison-related issue of which the public are aware. Canadians were asked in 1998 to estimate the percentage of the federal prison population that was Aboriginal. The median estimate was 15 percent, which is very close to the correct answer. It seems likely that the considerable media attention paid to the plight of Aboriginal Canadians has sensitized the public to this correctional issue. This would appear to be the one example of that attention having a beneficial effect: most Canadians are aware of the extent of the problem.

Structure of Parole

What do people know about the structure of corrections? As this text makes clear, there are several programs that permit prisoners to leave prison to spend time in the community (see Chapter 13). The best known of these is parole or conditional release (Chapter 12). However, even parole is poorly understood by the public. In the mid 1980s, a national sample of the public was given a multiple-choice question with four options, one of which clearly defined parole. Only 15 percent of the public chose the correct answer, showing that people were confused about release programs (Roberts 1988).

Knowledge of Parole Rates

A frequent complaint about the parole system is that too many prisoners are released too early into their sentences. Surveys conducted in 1982 and 1998 asked the public to estimate the percentage of prisoners released on parole. On both occasions, the public overestimated the parole grant rate by a considerable margin. For example, the grant rate in 1997 was 42 percent. If we accept as accurate anyone providing an estimate between 30 and 49 percent, only 14 percent of the polled public in 1998 were accurate. Over half the sample overestimated the parole grant rate to be higher; they assumed that the system was more lenient than it in fact is.

Edward Zamble and Kevin Kalm (1990) found that almost 90 percent of the public thought that the number of violent offenders released on parole was too high. Another survey conducted in 1987 found that 70 percent of the public supported the view that "parole boards release too many offenders on parole." It is ironic that so many people have such a definite opinion about the issue when so few have a realistic idea of how many violent offenders are actually released. As noted earlier, misinformed opinions present unique problems in light of the fact that "justice must be seen to be done"—in whose eyes?

It is true that under the provisions of the *Corrections and Conditional Release Act,* some inmates are released from prison after serving a relatively small fraction of their custodial sentences. Here, too, the public tends to have inaccurate opinions: people assume that prisoners get out of prison earlier than is in fact the case. Therefore, policy-makers and authorities should be careful to make sure they rely on accurate information in the appropriate context and not rely on the generalized observations that get published in the general media.

Perceptions of Risk of Re-offending

People who oppose parole usually cite the danger to the public as a reason for their opposition. But only a very small percentage of offenders pose a threat to public safety. Once again we can turn to the results of systematic surveys that have asked members of the public to estimate the percentage of inmates released on parole who subsequently commit another offence.

In 1997, 8 percent of prisoners released on full parole had their parole terminated and were returned to prison as a result of fresh criminal charges. However, only 6 percent of the public were accurate in estimating this statistic. Fully 85 percent of the sample overestimated the recidivism rate of parolees, most by a considerable margin (see Roberts, Nuffield, and Hann 1999). These trends are consistent with earlier polls conducted in Canada, and surveys conducted in other countries (see Roberts and Stalans 1997, for a review). However, it is important to note that the extent of misperception with respect to the issue of re-offending is getting worse: the percentage of the Canadian public who overestimate the recidivism rate of parolees has grown over the past decade. Such conservative views pose a threat to some of the liberal-oriented policies being advocated (e.g., reintegration, restorative justice, and community-based corrections).

Finally, there is another element of the debate on dangerousness that escapes the public. People read about a parolee who commits a serious crime a year after leaving prison and six months before his or her period of parole (and sentence) expires. This leads to calls for the abolition of parole (see below), the reasoning being that if the individual had been detained to the end of the sentence, the crime would have been prevented. People also fail to appreciate that the experience of being on parole can lessen the likelihood of relapse into criminality. At least when an offender is on parole, that person can be (indeed should be) monitored carefully, and when warning signs appear (such as associating with other offenders or consuming alcohol) the parole authorities can return the offender to the institution for having violated a condition of parole.

Costs of Supervising Offenders in the Community

Serving part of a sentence in the community obviously benefits the offender, who can maintain family ties, continue to work or go to school, and so on. But there are also benefits to the community: supervising an offender in the community costs much less than incarceration. How much less? Parole costs about one fifth the cost of prison. The public, which is sensitive to the costs of public services (including criminal justice), is unaware of this. When asked to estimate the cost of community supervision in surveys, members of the public failed to appreciate just how much cheaper community supervision is than prison. For example, it cost approximately $123 per capita per day to incarcerate an inmate in a provincial institution, compared to $61,000 per inmate annually in a federal institution during 1998/99 (i.e., approximately $167 per day; for more discussion on the cost of incarceration, see Chapter 1).[2]

Misperceptions regarding prison and prison life are important. Their existence suggests that there would be far less support for imprisonment in Canada (and perhaps, less imprisonment) if the public was fully aware of the costs of incarceration and the effectiveness of alternative sanctions.

Summary of Public Knowledge Findings

We can summarize public knowledge of corrections in the following way. Most Canadians know little about the correctional system, including parole. What little the public does know tends to be negative. For example, people remember the high-profile cases in which a prisoner on parole commits a serious crime; they are unaware of the literally thousands of individuals serving their sentences in the community on parole without violating their parole conditions. When thinking about institutions, people recall prison riots and this contributes to their perception of inmates as dangerous trouble-makers. Members of the public also assume that most offenders will re-offend; many people subscribe to a "once an offender, always an offender" myth, when, in fact, most people convicted of a crime do not commit further offences.

These findings should be borne in mind as we review public attitudes to a number of correctional issues. It is also worth adding that these trends of misperception are not specific to Canadians: surveys in other countries such as the United Kingdom, the United States, and Australia show a similar pattern. Public knowledge of criminal justice (and in particular corrections) appears to be poor in many countries (see Roberts and Stalans 1997 for additional discussion of this material). At this point we turn to the results of surveys that have examined public opinion with respect to a number of correctional issues.

Public Opinion Regarding Correctional Issues

The Purpose of Corrections

Perhaps the most basic question in the field of corrections concerns the purpose of the correctional system. Is it to punish offenders for their crimes or to rehabilitate them and help reintegrate them into society? Our correctional system attempts to do both: prisoners are punished by the deprivation of liberty, and at the same time given opportunities in prison and outside on parole to aid their reintegration. What does the public think the purpose should be?

The most recent national survey of public attitudes towards corrections in Canada posed a direct question about the purpose of corrections (see Box 3.2). Respondents were given a choice between "helping offenders rehabilitate themselves to become law-abiding citizens" and "punishing offenders for their crimes." The answers to this question may surprise some people, including some politicians and criminal justice policy-makers. Rehabilitation was preferred by 58 percent of the respondents, while 42 percent chose punishment. It would appear, then, that although there is substantial support for punishment, most Canadians endorse rehabilitation as the purpose of corrections.

The question in that survey asked respondents their view of the purpose of corrections without identifying any specific kind of offender. The problem with this approach is that most people have the worst kind of offender in mind when they respond to such questions. For

BOX 3.2	Support for Rehabilitation Greater in Canada

Comparing the responses of Canadians to similar surveys in other countries shows that there is more support for rehabilitation in Canada. For example, a survey conducted in the U.S. posed a similar question and found that more than half the respondents favoured punishment and deterrence over rehabilitation (Maguire and Pastore 1998).

example, in 1987 the Canadian Criminal Justice Association asked Canadians about parole and found that 70 percent of respondents supported the view that "parole boards release too many offenders on parole" (Canadian Criminal Justice Association 1987). People in the same survey were then asked what kinds of offenders they had in mind when answering the previous question about parole. It turned out that more than half the sample were thinking exclusively of violent offenders.

The same logic applies to the issue of the purpose of corrections. When asked about this issue, most people were probably thinking of the purpose with respect to violent offenders. If people had been asked to distinguish the purpose of corrections for violent and non-violent offenders, there would likely have been very strong support for rehabilitation for the latter. This is important because property crimes account for the highest percentage of admissions at the provincial level, and non-violent offenders account for more than 40 percent of admissions at the federal level (Reed and Roberts 1999).

Parole

Parole has been under attack for many years in Canada. In 1987, the Canadian Sentencing Commission recommended the abolition of full parole for all inmates except life prisoners. That recommendation was never implemented, but other critics have subsequently called for the abolition of conditional release. In 1998, Eddy Greenspan, the most prominent defence lawyer in the country, became the latest high-profile criminal justice professional to call for the abolition of parole (see Greenspan, Matheson, and Davis 1998). What does the public think? Thanks to a number of recent polls, we have a good idea of the nature of public attitudes towards parole, and in particular to the specific proposal to abolish conditional release.

Until 1999, the most systematic analysis of Canadians' attitudes to parole was a decade old (Roberts 1988). In the mid 1980s, it was clear that Canadians favoured the existence of conditional release from prison. A nationwide survey conducted at that time found that two thirds of the public favoured the existence of a parole system "for certain offenders." The most recent attempt to gauge the views of the public posed a more direct question.

Respondents to a survey in 1998 were given a choice between two clear policy options. They were asked whether they preferred a system that "keeps inmates in prison right to the end of their sentences" (a no-parole system) or a system that releases some prisoners into the community under supervision before their sentence ends (the current system). Results showed that the public supported a parole system over the no-parole option by a margin of three to one (Roberts, Nuffield, and Hann 1999). So it seems clear that although they may frequently be critical of the parole system, Canadians do not support abolishing parole. In this respect, little has changed; the survey published in 1988 found that only one quarter of respondents at that time favoured the abolition of parole.

General Opinions versus Decisions in Actual Cases

A second way of demonstrating public support for parole involves comparing the responses of one group of people who are asked to make a general judgement about parole with the responses of another group who is asked to make a decision with respect to a specific parole application. Cumberland and Zamble (1992) conducted research along these lines. They found that four out of five participants in their research were dissatisfied with the parole system, a finding consistent with the results of nation-wide surveys. However, when a comparable group of people was asked to make decisions in individual cases, a substantial majority supported endorsed release on parole, even for a prisoner with a lengthy record and serving time for a crime of violence.

Where the public and the system appear to disagree is with respect to the kinds of offenders who should be granted parole and the point in the sentence at which parole is granted. Although the public tends to overestimate the percentage of a sentence that must be served in prison (see above), most people would probably still favour a somewhat later parole eligibility date than one third, particularly for prisoners serving time for crimes of violence.

As with other issues, the attitudes of Canadians with respect to parole are similar to those of members of the public in other nations. In a recent review of American attitudes to parole, Cullen, Fisher, and Applegate (forthcoming) reported that support for parole is strong, particularly for inmates who have taken steps towards rehabilitation while in prison. Not surprisingly, perhaps, public support for rehabilitation diminishes—and support for punishment grows—when the question involves offenders convicted of serious crimes of violence, and who have long criminal histories (see Flanagan 1996 for further discussion of American attitudes towards correctional issues).

CONCLUSION

What lessons can we draw from these findings on public knowledge and opinion in the area of corrections? First, although public knowledge of corrections tends to be poor and biased towards a negative view of the system, a strong bedrock of support exists for the concept of rehabilitation. This support includes conditional release on parole. Second, although polls show that public confidence in the correctional system tends to be lower than other branches of the justice system, this reflects, at least in part, lack of awareness of the statistical reality of the correctional system.

To return to one of the questions posed at the beginning of this chapter, what lessons should politicians and policy-makers draw from the public opinion research? One obvious lesson would be to exercise caution in adopting a policy or changing a law solely or primarily to appease the public. The public may well have misunderstood the issue, or may have been manipulated by politicians seeking electoral advantage. Before accepting that policies should change because the public is dissatisfied, policy-makers should conduct careful research to ensure that the public has the facts about the issue and that the question has been put to the public in an appropriate way. As we have seen in this chapter, when people are asked a general, simple question about some correctional issue, they tend to respond with a punitive "top of the head" response. When given more information (for example, when asked about a specific case in some detail), people respond differently.

Finally, an important step for the correctional system in Canada would involve educating the public about offenders (particularly inmates and parolees), prison life and correctional trends. Many Canadians will still be critical of the correctional system, but at least this criticism would be informed by accurate information. A more educated public would permit a more reasoned debate about the future of corrections in this country.

SUMMARY

This chapter examined the level of public knowledge and public opinion about corrections in Canada. It was generally observed that the public is quite naive about the operations of corrections. The public's general lack of understanding about the complex nature of corrections is largely influenced by the role the media takes in reporting correctional issues. Given that media coverage tends to be rather poor, the public can hardly be faulted for general naiveté about prisons, probation, or parole.

Unfortunately for correctional policy-makers, an ill-informed public presents unique challenges when trying to implement positive reforms. Currently, the public leans towards conservative attitudes towards offenders, while correctional philosophy has shifted towards community-based options for offenders (see Chapter 13) and improved methods of assessing the risk and needs of offenders (see Chapter 9).

Corrections personnel must take a more proactive role in disseminating information about what they do and they must work more closely with the media to ensure that the facts are presented in a more balanced and informative manner. These points were recognized and reinforced at the 1999 Canadian Congress on Criminal Justice held in Edmonton, Alberta.

KEY TERMS AND CONCEPTS

collateral pains   institutional life   public knowledge

STUDY AND DISCUSSION QUESTIONS

1. Some researchers suggest that the media play an important role in influencing the political consciousness. What you think about this observation and what are its implications?
2. How well do you think the media inform the public about the correctional issues?
3. Do the media provide enough information about the correctional system? Explain, using media examples to illustrate your point(s).
4. What are the critical issues of public opinion with respect to the correctional system?
5. Compare three or more media articles about a correctional issue (e.g., Nova Scotia maximum security and Bowden medium security lock-downs in January 2000). How do the sources compare in their coverage about the case? How objective or subjective do the articles appear? What kinds of details do they focus on? How fair or realistic is the coverage?

 ## WEBLINKS

There are no specific weblinks for this subject. However, readers are encouraged to refer to local and international news sources to collect stories that reflect the role the media plays in informing the public about correctional-based issues.

NOTES

1. Inmates serving life terms for multiple homicides and those who have been sentenced to life imprisonment without parole for less than 15 years are not eligible to apply for this review.
2. During 1998/99, it cost, on average, $13,000 to supervise an offender on parole or statutory release.

REFERENCES

Barkan, S.E., and **S.F. Cohn**. 1994. Racial Prejudice and Support for the Death Penalty by Whites. *Journal of Research in Crime and Delinquency* 31: 202–209.

Boers, K., and **K. Sessar**. 1991. Do People Really Want Punishment? On the Relationship between Acceptance of Restitution, Need for Punishment, and Fear of Crime. In K. Sessar and H.-J. Kerner (Eds.), *Developments in Crime and Crime Control Research*. New York: Springer-Verlag.

Brillon, Y. 1984. Les attitudes punitives dans la population canadienne. *Canadian Journal of Criminology* 26: 293–311.

Bryant, P., and **E. Morris**. 1998. What Does the Public Really Think? *Corrections Today* February, 26–79.

Canadian Criminal Justice Association. 1987. *Attitudes towards Parole*. Ottawa: Canadian Criminal Justice Association.

Canadian Sentencing Commission. 1987. *Sentencing Reform: A Canadian Approach*. Ottawa: Supply and Services Canada.

Chermak, S.M. 1995. *Victims in the News: Crime and the American News Media*. Boulder, CO: Westview Press.

Cullen, F., **B. Fisher**, and **B. Applegate**. Forthcoming. Public Opinion about Punishment and Corrections. In M. Tonry (Ed.), *Crime and Justice: A Review of Research*. Chicago: University of Chicago Press.

Cumberland, J., and **E. Zamble**. 1992. General and Specific Measures of Attitudes towards Early Release of Criminal Offenders. *Canadian Journal of Behavioural Science* 24: 442–455.

Doble, J. 1995. *Crime and Corrections: The Views of the People of North Carolina*. Englewood Cliffs, NJ: John Doble Research Associates Inc.

Flanagan, T. 1996. Reform or Punish: Americans' Views of the Correctional System. In T. Flanagan and D. Longmire (Eds.). *Americans View Crime and Justice: A National Opinion Survey*. Thousand Oaks, CA: Sage.

Greenspan, E., **A. Matheson**, and **R. Davis**. 1998. Discipline and Parole. *Queen's Quarterly* 105: 9–28.

Maguire, K., and **A. Pastore** (Eds.). 1997. *Sourcebook of Criminal Justice Statistics, 1997*. U.S. Department of Justice, Bureau of Justice Statistics, Washington, DC: USGPO, 1998.

Reed, M., and **J.V. Roberts**. 1999. Adult Correctional Services in Canada, 1997/98. *Juristat* 19(4).

Roberts, J.V. 1988. Early Release from Prison: What do the Canadian Public Really Think? *Canadian Journal of Criminology* 30: 231–249.

———. 1992. Public Opinion, Crime, and Criminal Justice. In M. Tonry (Ed.), *Crime and Justice: An Annual Review of Research*. Chicago: University of Chicago Press.

———. 1995. Sentencing, Public Opinion, and the News Media. *Revue générale de droit* 26: 115–125.

———. 1999. Juvenile Justice Reform in Canada. *Federal Sentencing Reporter* 11: 255–259.

———. (Ed.). 2000. *Criminal Justice in Canada*. Toronto: Harcourt Brace.

Roberts, J.V., and **D.P. Cole**. 1999. Sentencing and Early Release Arrangements for Offenders Convicted of Murder. In J.V. Roberts and D.P. Cole (Eds.), *Making Sense of Sentencing*. Toronto: University of Toronto Press.

Roberts, J.V., and M. Jackson. 1991. Boats Against the Current: A Note on the Effects of Imprisonment. *Law and Human Behavior* 15: 557–562.

Roberts, J.V., and L.S. Stalans. 1997. *Public Opinion, Crime, and Criminal Justice*. Boulder, CO: Westview Press.

Roberts, J.V., J. Nuffield, and R. Hann. 1999. *Parole and the Public: Attitudinal and Behavioural Responses*. Ottawa: University of Ottawa.

Silverman, R. 1988. Interpersonal Criminal Violence. In V.F. Sacis (Ed.). *Deviance: Conformity and Control in Canadian Society*. Scarborough: Prentice-Hall.

Solicitor General of Canada. 1998. *Basic Facts about Corrections in Canada*. Ottawa: Correctional Service of Canada.

Winterdyk, J. (Ed.). 2000. *Issues and Perspectives on Young Offenders in Canada* (2nd ed.). Toronto: Harcourt Brace.

Zamble, E., and K. Kalm. 1990. General and Specific Measures of Public Attitudes Toward Sentencing. *Canadian Journal of Behavioural Science* 22: 327–337.

PUBLIC ADMINISTRATION AND MANAGEMENT OF ADULT CORRECTIONAL SERVICES IN CANADA

C h a p t e r

4

Laurence L. Motiuk[1]
Director General
Research Branch at
Correctional Service of Canada
Ottawa, Ontario

LEARNING OBJECTIVES

After reading this chapter, you should be able to:

- Have basic information about adult correctional services in Canada;
- Be able to identify the relationship between public sector administration and government;
- Be able to identify the key elements of well-performing correctional organizations; and
- Be able to apply an organizational structure to various management and administrative tasks at the executive level.

The protection of society is the paramount consideration in the corrections process.

—Solicitor General Canada

The administration of criminal justice involves the management of people from an initial charge by law enforcement, through conviction and sentencing in the courts, to administration of the penalty by corrections (e.g., probation, prison, conditional release by authorities such as temporary absence, parole, or statutory release) as well as community supervision (see Table 4.1 on page 70–71). While society expects that correctional organizations will contribute to public protection, it is important to recognize that Canadian corrections is a service of government and is therefore structured according to the principles of public administration and management (Archambeault and Archambeault 1982). In keeping with other government agencies, there is a general accountability for public service expenditures. However, one aspect is unique to correctional organizations: the task of reducing the likelihood of criminal futures by effectively and efficiently managing offender populations.

Today, as Wright (1994) has noted for the United States, most correctional organizations are faced with unprecedented challenges, as offender populations continue to expand, federal and provincial budgets are constrained, and scrutiny by the media and other non-government organizations remains intense. In some areas, strong correctional unions demand significant changes in the workplace. Other pressures include high turnover of management and staff, and the expense and complexity of implementing new technologies (see Chapter 11); furthermore, the offender population is becoming increasingly diversified. Historically, to meet such challenges, organizations look to the area of management theory and practice for help. Very often, too, management practice is criticized, as the problems seem ever present. However, as Hammer and Champy (1993, 25) have found:

> Some people blame corporate problems on management deficiencies. If companies were only managed better or differently, they would thrive. But none of the management fads of the last twenty years—not Management by Objectives (MBO), diversification, Theory Z, zero-based budgeting, value chain analysis, decentralization, Quality Circles, "excellence", restructuring, portfolio management, management by walking around, matrix management, intrapreneuring, or one-minute managing—has reversed the deterioration of America's corporate competitive performance. They have only distracted managers from the real task at hand.

In the case of corrections, the Canadian public is concerned primarily with how corrections agencies are managed because they are perceived as being responsible for public safety. In keeping with this important task, Motiuk (1995, 24) notes:

> Faced with the fact that most offenders eventually return to the community, the best way to serve the public is to recognize the risk presented by an individual, and to then put to good use the tools, the training and our fundamental understanding of what it really means to manage offender risk.
>
> Effective risk management implies that decisions impacting on the organization are made using the best procedures available, and are in keeping with the overall goals of the system.

Effective and efficient correctional service has always been about people, not just numbers. State-of-the-art tools, up-to-date risk management procedures, and revisions of policy and practice guidelines are necessary, but unless an organization's people, at all levels, are committed to and support new initiatives, correctional agencies will be limited in their ability to move forward.

THE ADMINISTRATION OF CORRECTIONS IN CANADA

In Canada, federal, provincial, and territorial governments share responsibility for the administration of custodial and non-custodial sentences. Provincial and territorial governments are responsible for offenders remanded into custody pending trial or sentencing, inmates serving custodial sentences of less than two years, and supervision of offenders who have been released on parole. They also have exclusive responsibility for offenders sentenced to probation, as well as for young offenders.

The federal government of Canada is responsible for administering sentences to imprisonment for two years or more (see Chapter 6). This responsibility includes the management of sentenced inmates in correctional institutions and the supervision of offenders who have been conditionally released on parole or those on statutory release.

Throughout the 1990s, the adult correctional population increased as a result of Canadian crime control practices. This dramatic growth is the result of changes in the Criminal Code, in the way crime is reported, and in court processing, and in the policy and practice of sentencing and conditional release.

Four major factors account for the size of the adult offender population: crime rates, sanctioning (e.g., probation and/or incarceration rates), sentence lengths, and release policy and practice (see Figure 4.1).

According to Statistics Canada (1998), in 1997/98 adult correctional services accommodated 32,970 inmates in institutions, and supervised 105,861 probationers and another 12,157 offenders on conditional release (2,507 on provincial parole and the remainder under federal supervision).[2] Taken together, a total of 150,988 adult offenders were under correctional supervision in 1998 (see Box 4.1). Figure 4.2, which illustrates the distribution of Canadian custodial and non-custodial supervision caseloads, reveals that the majority of offenders are being managed in the community.

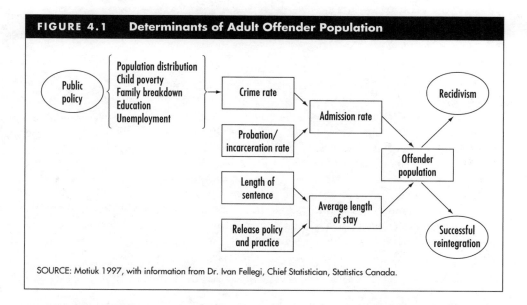

FIGURE 4.1   Determinants of Adult Offender Population

SOURCE: Motiuk 1997, with information from Dr. Ivan Fellegi, Chief Statistician, Statistics Canada.

BOX 4.1   Few Offenders Incarcerated

There are about 250,000 convictions in adult provincial courts each year. About a third of these offences result in a custodial sentence. Less than 3.5 percent of those convicted receive a federal sentence.

SOURCE: Correctional Service of Canada 1999a.

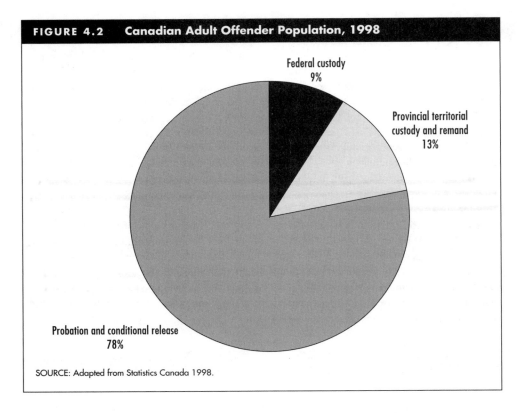

FIGURE 4.2   Canadian Adult Offender Population, 1998

Federal custody
9%

Provincial territorial
custody and remand
13%

Probation and conditional release
78%

SOURCE: Adapted from Statistics Canada 1998.

If we compare these figures to the data for 1990 in *Adult Correctional Services in Canada 1989/90* (Statistics Canada 1990), we can see that there has been an overall increase of 31 percent in offenders (114,014 in 1990) under correctional supervision. More specifically, there has been a 32 percent increase in inmates (29,555 in 1990), 45 percent in probationers (73,044 in 1990), and 7 percent for offenders on conditional release (11,415 in 1990: 2,627 provincial parolees and the remainder under federal supervision). More than two thirds of those under correctional supervision are on probation (growing at a rate of nearly 5 percent per year).

To serve the correctional population in 1997/98, federal corrections employed over 10,701 staff (including 4,918 correctional officers and 575 parole officers), and provincial/territorial corrections had 14,653 (including 4,380 correctional officers and 626 probation/parole officers). As of March 31, 1999, there were 11,386 employees with nearly 2,700 support staff (Correctional Service of Canada 1999a). In the fiscal year 1998/99, federal expenditures for adult correctional services in Canada were $1.3 billion.[3]

PUBLIC ADMINISTRATION

The importance of **public sector administration** and its relation to politics is articulated in the *Report of the Auditor General of Canada to the House of Commons* (1997). Essentially, the role of Canadian federal government's departments is to provide services and apply policy. Mitchell and Sutherland (1999, 21) note:

Ministerial responsibility is the defining principle of our system of parliamentary and cabinet government, a system that is generally known as *Westminster* government. Ministerial responsibility ensures the democratic accountability of ministers to the elected legislature. It also has the core democratic virtue of making the bureaucracy subservient to the elected direction and, through the government, subordinate to the electorate.

Clearly, political forces can shape the management environment and the recruitment of senior administrators. Westmacott and Mellon (1999, 1) find they are linked by

> the institutions of government, the budget setting process, the practice of policy/program evaluation and the sources of policy advice to which a government subscribes.

Archambeault and Archambeault (1982, 41) consider all correctional organizations to be **public service organizations**, which therefore must operate according to the principles of public administration. Ekstedt and Griffiths (1984) also contend that not only must the principles of public administration be reflected in the administration and management of corrections, but so too must the unique characteristics of the corrections process. They note:

> it is common to define "administration" as the overall process used both to organize and to manage the delivery system that brings the services of the organization to the client or consumer. When administration is defined in this way, it can be seen as a process that includes all of the specific tasks and responsibilities associated with the continuing maintenance of the agency.
>
> "Management", on the other hand, can be defined as a task within the administrative process (148).

Public Management

While much has been written about how to achieve success in private sector management, less is known about well-performing government departments or public service agencies. Ingstrup and Crookall (1998a, 8) examined survey research on 40 top public service agencies in 14 countries and found three pillars and some key elements therein that support success in well-performing agencies. They are:

1. *Aim:* The top agencies know clearly the direction they are headed in. Their mission is deeply ingrained in the daily actions and long-term planning of the organization rather than simply relegated to a piece of paper hanging on the wall in the reception area. A long-time leader often exemplifies the mission and everyone is held accountable to it.

2. *Character:* Successful agencies have a strong sense of what they are and what is important. That organizational character, fuelled by a high degree of trust, is communicated internally and externally through activities that are driven by strong principles. The people in the agency and the agency itself exude a sense of integrity, trust, caring, openness, and, crucially, a desire to learn.

3. *Execution:* These organizations get things done, achieving their aim and demonstrating their character through the use of a broad array of management tools. They innovate in an era of never-ending change, realizing that the tools and techniques they employ are a means to an end, not ends in themselves. Teamwork is an essential element: their staff know how to roll up their sleeves, work together, and implement effectively.

The "Three Pillars of Public Management" model should apply equally to **strategic management** in corrections as well. Ingstrup and Crookall (1998b) recommend the following:

> Have your mission speak to the prerequisites of good corrections: safe, secure facilities, respect for the rule of law and due process, and safe reintegration. The outcome of a safer society can then be better achieved.

Boin (1998) also posits a theory of **administrative integration** for correctional organizations whereby "an institution binds its members to a common purpose and a specialized way of working." The adoption of mission, mandate, or vision statements is a good illustration of how Canadian correctional agencies all across the country have responded to national crime control policies.

A mission statement specifies the business that corrections is in, sets the **strategic objectives** of the organization, and establishes major strategies for achieving those objectives. By regularly reviewing its strategic objectives and progress, an organization can focus on the critical areas requiring attention. Strategic objectives are the basis for setting priorities and determining annual **corporate objectives**. Corporate objectives are short- and medium-term goals. For example, one corporate objective for Correctional Service of Canada in 1999/2000 is to:

> Implement security standards and practices that will provide a safe environment for staff/offender interaction and for reintegration efforts.

As Table 4.1 shows, correctional agencies at the federal, provincial, and territorial levels across Canada share a common aim or purpose. "Contributing to public protection" is well entrenched in the daily activities of these organizations and in the minds of their staff.

TABLE 4.1	Missions, Mandates, and Visions of Canadian Correctional Agencies
Jurisdiction	**Statement**
Federal	
Correctional Service of Canada	The Correctional Service of Canada, as part of the criminal justice system and respecting the rule of law, contributes to the protection of society by actively encouraging and assisting offenders to become law-abiding citizens, while exercising reasonable, safe, secure, and humane control.
Provincial	
British Columbia	To protect the community through offender management, offender control, and conflict resolution.
Alberta	Alberta Correctional Services is committed to managing with openness and integrity while being accountable to the people of Alberta; constructive change through initiative and innovation; a climate that promotes professionalism, respect in the workplace and excellence in correctional practices; attaining a safe environment for all resident of Alberta; respecting the dignity of individuals, their cultural differences and the rights of all members of society; providing offenders with assistance and opportunities to become law-abiding citizens; and the right of victims and the community to participate in the justice process.
Saskatchewan	The Corrections Division promotes safe communities by providing a range of controls and reintegration opportunities for offenders.

TABLE 4.1	Missions, Mandates, and Visions of Canadian Correctional Agencies (continued)
Manitoba	Corrections, as part of the Manitoba justice system, contributes to the protection of society by effective administration of sentences imposed by the courts, by the humane care, control, and reintegration of offenders into society and by encouraging active community participation in achieving these objectives.
Ontario	The Correctional Services Division contributes to the protection of public safety through effective supervision of adult and young offenders in community and institutional settings.
Quebec	The Correctional Services Branch works in close cooperation with its partners in the community. It assists the players in the judicial process by providing information that will allow for the most appropriate sentence or other measure when someone has been found guilty of a crime; it administers court decisions and responds to requests from other key players in the judicial process, encouraging those in its charge to take the responsibility for their acts while respecting their rights; and it works actively for the reintegration of offenders.
New Brunswick	The Department of the Solicitor General is the province's principal agency responsible for and providing leadership in the areas of public order and community safety. As part of the justice system, it works in partnership with the community to prevent crime; to create opportunities for offenders to change; and to assist victims. All of these activities contribute to the well-being and quality of life for the people of New Brunswick.
Nova Scotia	Correctional Services contributes to the maintenance of a just, peaceful, and safe society by providing services to assist the courts in remanding and sentencing processes; administering custody and community-based dispositions of the courts; providing safe custody, direction, and control of the accused and the convicted offender; and encouraging the offender's participation, whether in the community or in a correctional institution to aid in successful integration into the community.
Prince Edward Island	Community and Correctional Services is an essential part of the criminal justice system in protecting the public and contributes to the rehabilitation of youth and adult offenders by providing community and custody programs. It provides support services to the courts and victims of crime, and also contributes to new initiatives involving victim issues, crime prevention, public education, research, and policy and program development.
Newfoundland	As a partner in the criminal justice system, the Adult Corrections Division strives for a safer society by encouraging and assisting offenders to become law-abiding citizens. It strives to ensure that victims are able to participate meaningfully in the criminal justice process. It strives to provide access to programs and services necessary for the offender's safe reintegration into the community. It strives to provide access to programs and services necessary for the healing and recovery of victims. It strives to exercise fair, just, and humane measures of custody, supervision, and control.

Territorial

Yukon	Under development
Northwest Territories	The Corrections Division, as part of the criminal justice system, manages offenders in the least restrictive manner required to protect society and assists offenders through restorative justice and culturally relevant programs to become healthy, law-abiding members of the community.
Nunavut	Under development

Strategic Planning and Policy Frameworks

Generally speaking, the Correctional Service of Canada's **strategic planning** and policy framework illustrates very well the relationship between the law (Criminal Code of Canada, the *Corrections and Conditional Release Act*), mission statement, core values, guiding principles, strategic objectives, planning, reporting and accountability structure, and corporate objectives. Figure 4.3 illustrates this framework as well as some of its products, which are the following: planning, reporting accountability structure, reports on plans and priorities, accountability contracts, national capital and accommodation plans, and the departmental performance report.

Organizational Structure

In all correctional agencies, the organizational structure reflects the approaches taken to address the various management and administrative tasks. The Correctional Service of Canada is a federal agency of the Department of the Solicitor General. The Department also includes the National Parole Board (NPB), the Royal Canadian Mounted Police (RCMP), the Canadian Security Intelligence Service (CSIS), the Office of the Correctional Investigator, the Department Secretariat, the RCMP Public Complaints Commission, and the RCMP External Review Committee.

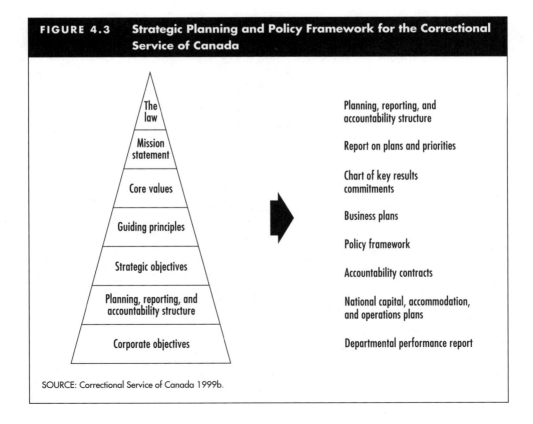

FIGURE 4.3   Strategic Planning and Policy Framework for the Correctional Service of Canada

The law
Mission statement
Core values
Guiding principles
Strategic objectives
Planning, reporting, and accountability structure
Corporate objectives

Planning, reporting, and accountability structure

Report on plans and priorities

Chart of key results commitments

Business plans

Policy framework

Accountability contracts

National capital, accommodation, and operations plans

Departmental performance report

SOURCE: Correctional Service of Canada 1999b.

TABLE 4.2	Organization of the Executive Committee of the Correctional Service of Canada			
		Commissioner		
Regional Deputy Commissioner(s)	**Senior Deputy Commissioner**	**Assistant Commissioner(s)**	**Deputy Commissioner**	**Director General, Counsel**
Atlantic	National headquarters	Communications	Women offender services	Legal services
Quebec		Corporate development		
Ontario				
Prairie		Corporate services		
Pacific		Correctional operation and programs		
		Executive services		
		Performance assurance		
		Personnel and training		

The categories of management and administrative responsibilities for the executive committee of the Correctional Service of Canada are set out in Table 4.2.

The national headquarters of the Correctional Service of Canada is located in Ottawa. The national headquarters is responsible for the Service's overall organization, administration, and management. The country is divided into five regions, and the regional offices are responsible for administering the operations of correctional institutions and supervising offenders in those regions. The regions and their headquarters are as follows:

- Pacific Region (British Columbia and Yukon Territory)—Abbotsford;
- Prairie Region (Alberta, Saskatchewan, Manitoba, and Northwest Territories)—Saskatoon;
- Ontario Region (also covers Nunavut)—Kingston;
- Quebec Region—Laval;
- Atlantic Region (New Brunswick, Nova Scotia, Prince Edward Island, and Newfoundland)—Moncton.

In 1999, the Correctional Service of Canada managed 52 penitentiaries, 17 community correctional centres, 71 parole offices, and 19 district offices (Correctional Service of Canada 1999b).[4] Because there are agreements to exchange services with the provinces, federal offenders can serve sentences in provincial institutions and offenders under provincial jurisdiction can serve their sentences in federal institutions. Agreements also exist for the exchange of supervision services.

Executive Administration

The national headquarters of the Correctional Service of Canada is organized into the Offices of the Commissioner and the Senior Deputy Commissioner, an Executive Secretariat, and a

Legal Services Branch. Other divisions include Communications, Corporate Development, Corporate Services, Correctional Operation and Programs, Performance Assurance, Personnel and Training, and Women Offender Services.

The Commissioner, as the senior executive officer of the Correctional Service of Canada and a deputy minister in the Public Service of Canada, is accountable to the Solicitor General for managing and guiding the policies and programs of the Service. The office of the Senior Deputy Commissioner supports the Commissioner in the management and direction of the Service. The Executive Secretariat is responsible for the daily liaison with the Office of the Solicitor General and for coordinating and preparing executive correspondence to the Commissioner, the Prime Minister's Office, and other members of Parliament and legislative assemblies. The Legal Services Branch, headed by a Director General Counsel from the Department of Justice, provides a variety of in-house legal services to the Commissioner and staff of the Correctional Service, especially with regard to operations, and provides interpretations of related policies, directives, and guidelines.

Each of the following divisions is headed by an Assistant Commissioner (also known as an Assistant Deputy Minister in the federal public service). *Communications* is responsible for the daily liaison with the media, for publications (see Box 4.2), exhibits, and periodicals and for providing expert communication tools to support regions and sectors of the Correctional Service.

BOX 4.2   **Communications**

Correctional Service of Canada Publications

- Let's Talk
- Basic Facts

- Corporate Objectives
- Departmental Performance Report
- Forum on Corrections Research

SOURCE: Correctional Service of Canada.

Corporate Development is responsible for strategic planning and policy, research, operational planning, intergovernmental affairs, and offender affairs. Specific responsibilities include the legislative agenda (e.g., *Corrections and Conditional Release Act* and Regulations), policy development, strategic and corporate objectives, operational and programming research, the National Accommodation and Capital Plan, federal/provincial/territorial projects, international development and visits, restorative justice, and issues relating to human rights, inmate affairs, the Office of the Correctional Investigator, and the *Access to Information* and *Privacy Acts*.

Corporate Services is responsible for contracting and material services, financial management, information management systems, technological support, technical services, construction, finance, and material management. In addition, this division provides all goods and services (i.e., food, clothing, housing, engineering and maintenance services, and capital program management services) to support correctional facilities and activities.

Correctional Operation and Programs is responsible for community and institutional operations and for improving the delivery of correctional services. Specifically this division is responsible for Aboriginal issues such as cultural and spiritual needs, chaplaincy, health services, offender reintegration, institutional operations, operational support, correctional programs (programs for sex offenders, literacy and cognitive skills training, substance abuse, living skills, LifeLine (a program to help relocate long-term offenders), family violence programs, among others), security, and CORCAN (a special operating agency that runs prison industries).

Performance Assurance is responsible for auditing, investigating, evaluating, and reporting on correctional performance. It is also provides performance measurement tools and advice for the regions and other divisions of the Correctional Service of Canada. It focuses on analyzing, monitoring, and measuring results (see Box 4.3).

Personnel and Training is responsible for the identification, resolution, and implementation of human resource activities and interprets related policies, directives, and guidelines. This division is organized into Corporate Classification and Staffing, Staff Relations, Personnel Services, Recruiting and Career Management, Training and Development, Employee Assistance, and Safety and Health.

Women Offender Services is responsible for the effective development of programs and policies for female offenders and the implementation, monitoring, and evaluation of those programs.

BOX 4.3	Performance Assurance Goals for the Correctional Service of Canada	
	Business Line	**Key Results**
Care	To meet the physical and mental health needs of offenders in accordance with all legal requirements.	Significant strides were made in 1997/98 to address the issues surrounding infectious diseases, including HIV/AIDS, hepatitis B, hepatitis C, and tuberculosis.
Custody	To provide reasonable, safe, secure, and humane control of offenders.	Offenders are maintained in the appropriate level of security consistent with the least restrictive measures required for the protection of the public, staff members and offenders.
Reintegration	To actively encourage and assist offenders in becoming law-abiding citizens.	Key criminogenic factors and intervention strategies are identified in intake assessments.
Corporate services	To ensure that corporate policies and services exist to govern programs and activities in the Service and that these are consistent with its stated mission.	Relationships and partnerships are strengthened to contribute to public safety.

SOURCE: Correctional Service of Canada 1998b.

The five regional headquarters are staffed to support the field-level operations of the Correctional Service and interact with the national headquarters. The office of the Regional Deputy Commissioner is located at the regional headquarters and supported by Assistant Deputy Commissioners (Operations and Corporate Services) and various Regional Administrators (e.g., Policy and Planning, Correctional Programs). The regional management committee structure also consists of Wardens (institutions) and District Directors (parole officers).

SUMMARY

This chapter presents an overview of the administration and management of adult correctional services in Canada. In order to administer and manage a credible and efficient correctional system, one can use applied research related to public administration and well-performing public sector management. Clearly, by using a strategic planning and policy framework, a correctional organization can gain the confidence of its minister, the government, other parts of public administration, criminal justice colleagues, and the public.

Throughout the chapter it was shown that for most correctional agencies, contributing to positive change is the primary way of contributing to public safety. The task is more than making programs available; it is to actively encourage and assist offenders to participate in them. Consequently, as reflected in the mission, mandates, and visions of correctional organizations, agencies try to ensure they have the best programs at their disposal. These programs typically concentrate on criminal recidivism and on the causes of criminal behaviour and what can be done to affect it.

A good "strategic management" approach serves to instruct correctional organizations on their corporate direction and helps them take charge of their destiny, have a vision, and stay focused on doing good corrections. There is ample research to guide corrections in delivering programs that work.

KEY TERMS AND CONCEPTS

administrative integration	public service organization	strategic objectives
corporate objectives	strategic management	strategic planning
public sector administration		

STUDY AND DISCUSSION QUESTIONS

1. Using your knowledge of the determinants of the adult offender population, explain the size of the prison population relative to the size of the probation population.

2. Describe how the principles of public administration and the characteristics of the correctional process operate in Canada.

3. Identify the key features and elements of a well-performing correctional organization. What is a strategic management approach, and what effect would it have on the correctional service?

4. Explain the theory of administrative integration and give several examples of how it applies to corrections.

5. Describe the role of performance assurance in a correctional organization and how business lines can lead to key results.

6. Given that most offenders are managed in the community or are eventually returned to the community when they are released from prison, how can correctional organizations best contribute to public safety?

7. Suggest two statistical research initiatives, broad in scope, that would respond to current or anticipated priorities of the Correctional Service of Canada. How could the knowledge gained from these initiatives help the Service fulfill its mandate and meet its objectives?

WEBLINKS

Correctional Agencies

The following list of weblinks vary in their detail. Some sites provide only contact information while others provide more details on the administration and management of correctional services in the respective province.

Correctional Service Canada: **www.csc-scc.gc.ca**

British Columbia: **www.ag.gov.bc.ca/programs/index.htm#Corrections**

Alberta: **www.gov.ab.ca/just**

Saskatchewan: **www.saskjustice.gov.sk.ca**

Manitoba: **www.gov.mb.ca/chc/archives/J/j5.html**

Ontario: **www.sgcs.gov.on.ca**

Quebec: **www.msp.gouv.qc.ca/index.htm**

New Brunswick: **www.gov.nb.ca/solgen/index.htm**

Nova Scotia: **www.gov.ns.ca/just/services.htm#CS**

Prince Edward Island: **www.gov.pe.ca/caag/cacs-info/index.php3**

Newfoundland and Labrador: **www.gov.nf.ca/just**

Northwest Territories: **www.gov.nt.ca/Justice**

Yukon: **www.gov.yk.ca/govt.html**

Other Government

National Parole Board: **www.npb-cnlc.gc.ca**

Royal Canadian Mounted Police: **www.rcmp-grc.gc.ca**

Treasury Board: **www.tbs-sct.gc.ca**

Associations

Canadian Criminal Justice Association (CCJA): **home.istar.ca/~ccja/angl**

Network for Research in Crime and Justice (RCJ-Net): **www.qsilver.queensu.ca/rcjnet**

American Correctional Association (ACA): **www.corrections.com/aca/index.html**

American Probation and Parole Association (APPA): **www.appa-net.org**

American Society of Criminology (ASC): **www.asc41.com**

International Community Corrections Association (ICCA): **www.iccaweb.org**

International Corrections and Prisons Association (ICPA): **www.icpa.ca**

NOTES

1. The opinions expressed by L.L. Motiuk are solely his and not intended to represent the policies or practices of Correctional Service of Canada.

2. Adult correctional services is responsible for offenders over 18 years of age. Statistics Canada estimates that there were approximately 23,086,400 adults (18 years or older) in 1998.

3. The 1998/99 budget was spent on salaries ($649.5 million), capital expenditures ($153.5 million), and operating costs ($377.9 million).

4. The numbers include two new centres and growth within the institutions and offices in all sectors since 1997.

REFERENCES

Archambeault, W.G., and **B.J. Archambeault**. 1982. *Correctional Supervisory Management: Principles of Organization, Policy, and Law.* Englewood Cliffs, NJ: Prentice-Hall.

Boin, A. 1998. *Contrasts in Leadership: An Institutional Study of Two Prison Systems.* Delft, The Netherlands: Eburon.

Correctional Service of Canada. 1999a. *Basic Facts about Federal Corrections.* Ottawa: Public Works and Government Services Canada.

————. 1999b. *Performance Report for the Period Ending March 31, 1999.* Ottawa: Correctional Service of Canada.

Ekstedt, J. W., and **C.T. Griffiths**. 1984. *Corrections in Canada: Policy and Practice.* Toronto: Butterworths.

Hammer, M., and **J. Champy**. 1993. *Re-engineering the Corporation: A Manifesto for Business Revolution.* New York: Harper Business.

Ingstrup, O., and **P. Crookall**. 1998a. *The Three Pillars of Public Management.* Montreal and Kingston: McGill-Queen's University Press.

————. 1998b. The Three Pillars of Public Management. Corrections Management Quarterly 2, 1–9.

Mitchell, J.R., and **S.L. Sutherland**. 1999. Ministerial Responsibility: The Submission of Politics and Administration to the Electorate. In M.W. Westmacott and H.P. Mellon (Eds.), *Public Administration and Policy.* Scarborough: Prentice-Hall.

Motiuk, L.L. 1995. Refocusing the Role of Psychology in Risk Management: Assessment, Communication, Monitoring, and Intervention. In T. Leis, L. Motiuk, and J. Ogloff (Eds.), *Forensic Psychology: Policy and Practice in Corrections.* Ottawa: Correctional Service of Canada.

————. 1997. Factors Influencing the Correctional Population in Canada. In *Prison Population in Europe and North America: Problems and Solutions*. Helsinki: European Institute for Crime Prevention and Control, affiliated with the United Nations.

Office of the Auditor General. 1997. *Report of the Auditor General of Canada to the House of Commons*. Ottawa: Supply and Services Canada.

Statistics Canada. 1990. *Adult Correctional Services in Canada 1989/90*. Ottawa: Canadian Centre for Justice Statistics.

————. 1998. *Adult Correctional Services in Canada 1997/98*. Ottawa: Canadian Centre for Justice Statistics.

Westmacott, M.W., and **H.P. Mellon**. 1999. *Public Administration and Policy*. Scarborough: Prentice-Hall.

Wright, K. 1994. *Effective Prison Leadership*. New York: William Neil.

C h a p t e r

5

PROBATION

John Anderson
Criminology Department
Malaspina University-College
Nanaimo, British Columbia

LEARNING OBJECTIVES

After reading this chapter, you should be able to:

- Understand the concept of probation as a sentence of the court, with mandatory and optional conditions;
- Appreciate the original intention of probation and how it has changed over the last century;
- Identify the trends in the use of probation by the courts in Canada;
- Know the role of the probation officer, the types of supervision styles, and the significant issues they face;
- Understand the effects of external environment on the nature and volume of work done by probation officers; and
- Describe the features of successful supervision probation programs.

"If every country had an adequate system of probation, the immediate result would be an automatic reduction of the prison population and consequently of the number of prisons."

—Manuel López-Rey y Arrojo

This chapter provides an overview of standard probation and how it is used and looks at the significant issues that define this sentence. There is little Canadian information about some aspects of probation, but research conducted in the United States can be used to make generalizations that are relevant to the situation in Canada.

GENERAL FEATURES OF PROBATION

Probation is a sentence of the court where someone convicted of a criminal offence serves all or part of the sentence in society under the supervision of a designated authority. Probationers are directed by the court to abide by certain conditions, the violation of which may lead to a new criminal charge (i.e., breach of probation). Thus, probation contains four main elements: offenders must be *selected* as suitable for serving their sentence in the community; a *conditional suspension of punishment* is imposed (i.e., imprisonment); *personal supervision* is entailed; and this supervision involves *surveillance* or *treatment* (Harris 1995a, 4).

Probation is an act of **judicial clemency** that lays claim simultaneously to punishment and therapeutic values. Punishment is accomplished by legally enforceable obligations placed on offenders so they can serve their sentence in the community. Ideally, the therapeutic values come from a **probation officer** who facilitates change in the offender's behaviour, values, or the thinking processes that led to the crime in the first place.

Although rehabilitation was clearly the original intent behind probation, especially for young offenders, it is now changing from its original mandate. A brief overview of the history of probation will help to provide some context for its form and use today. First, let us start with a few comments about how probation is viewed by the public.

Public Perception of Probation

Despite its long history, probation has a poor public image and is widely seen as a sentence that avoids punishment and is "soft on crime" (Couglan 1988, 267, 329; Goff 1999, 133; see also Chapter 3). This negative perception is reinforced by rare and highly publicized crimes committed by probationers, such as the 1992 sexual assault and murder of a child by Jason Gamache in British Columbia. Despite the fact that there was no information available to the court or probation authorities to indicate that Gamache might hurt or kill someone during a sexual assault, events like these provoke strong public emotions and cast doubt on the ability of community-based sentences to protect the public (Fisher 1994).

The negative public views about probation cannot be divorced from wider perceptions that the entire criminal justice system is failing in its role to protect the public (Roberts 1987). Although police reports indicate that the crime rate has been dropping in Canada since the early 1990s, the fear of crime remains high, according to recent opinion polls. Even in this context, Canadians show support for non-custodial punishments that focus on effective control, supervision, and treatment (Solicitor General of Canada 1998). Probation offers many of the features in sentencing that Canadians apparently endorse.

Early Development of Probation

The word "probation" originates from the Latin word *probare* or "to prove." The use of the term probation, however, can be traced back to the medieval era when there was a common-law practice to release wrongdoers after they acknowledged an obligation to the monarch to behave and keep the peace. Later in history, after the Westminster court system had been established in Britain, a magistrate could order a person to serve a sentence outside the confines of prison as a test of the person's character.

The use of probation in Canada was strongly influenced by the reformers in the U.S. at the turn of the 19th century. Historical records show that earliest mention of probation in North America dates from the time of a relationship between **John Augustus** (1784–1859)—the father of modern probation—and a drunkard in Boston. Augustus provided bail for the man, who signed an oath to remain sober between his first and second court appearances. The judge was pleased by the man's turn of character and fined him one cent plus costs. According to Augustus, the man remained industrious and sober, and without doubt had been saved from a drunkards' grave (Augustus 1852). Pleased by this outcome, Augustus then provided probation for about 2,000 women and men who had been charged with petty crimes in Massachusetts (Enos et al. 1992, 30–31).

One cannot consider the acceptance and use of probation in Canada without also considering the causes of crime in the specific historical era in which it emerged. Until the 1930s, biological explanations about the causes of crime were prominent among many European scholars. Alternatively, the Chicago School focused on environmental factors associated with crime, leading reformers to direct attention to the influences of the home and neighbourhood as causes of delinquency. Concerned about the impact of industrialization, urbanization, and high levels of immigration from Europe, reformers believed that a person's immediate surroundings could encourage criminal behaviour, especially among the young.

Like the situation today, many solutions to youth crime one hundred years ago advocated a diversity of responses, based on varying ideas about human nature, the causes of crime, and their remedy. While some advocated a structured response such as hard labour or religious instruction in a reformatory or industrial school, others believed that the youth would be best served if they were separated from their parents and raised in caring, adoptive families. If children were to be left in their homes after being found delinquent, it was best done under the supervision of a responsible adult (that is, a probation officer) who could monitor their well-being and ensure social obligations were fulfilled. Historical records show that probation was originally conceived as a relationship of guidance and support between an errant child and a law-abiding authority. For the moral guidance that families of the day could not provide, the probation officer would substitute.

The *Report of Inquiry into the Prison Reformatories System* in 1891 was the earliest official document to advocate that probation be introduced for children in Ontario (Carrigan 1991, 413). The first legislated sign of probation was a law based upon the *British Probation of First Offenders Act* (1887), which was proclaimed in Canada in 1889. By 1908, the *Juvenile Delinquents Act* specifically provided for the supervision of children in the community under the guidance of a probation officer (Winterdyk 2000, 266). Juveniles were to remain in the community instead of being placed in reformatories or industrial schools. Federal provisions for probation supervision were enacted in 1921 and the law was later consolidated in the 1927 Canadian Criminal Code. Under this statute, first-time offenders convicted of offences that were punishable by less than two years' imprisonment were eligible for probation. The Royal Commission to Investigate the Penal System of Canada (the Archambault Commission) recommended a nation-wide probation service staffed by trained social workers in 1936. It took until 1951 before an effective probation system emerged in

Ontario and British Columbia, generally located in large municipalities where police, sheriffs, and other court officials could supervise probationers (Harris 1995b, 36).

After World War II, Canadian penal policy was dominated by notions of crime and its cure based upon the **medical model**, in which crime was seen as evidence of an underlying behavioural disorder requiring specialized intervention (Harris 1995a, 62). Probation was well suited to this perspective because it offered the potential for therapeutic involvement by trained professionals. It also appealed to the subsequent focus on community corrections recommended by the Ouimet Commission (1961), which directed legislators to seek penal interventions in the context where crime originates: the community. By 1967, the provinces and territories had enacted legislation to create probation services (Ekstedt and Griffiths, 1988). Today, probation is used frequently in Canadian courts for both juvenile and adult offenders.

WHEN AND HOW PROBATION IS USED

Probation is used for less serious offences, meaning that it is not available as part of a sentence for those serving more than two years' imprisonment. Probation is consistent with the 1996 sentencing reforms contained in section 718 of the Criminal Code. It specifies that offenders "should not be deprived of liberty, if less restrictive sanctions may be appropriate in the circumstances" (see Box 5.1). These principles provide judges with some direction in sentencing because they are intended to protect the public, assist victims, and promote accountability in offenders. Since World War II, several Canadian commissions of inquiry and government reports have recommended less use of imprisonment as a means of achieving sentencing goals. As discussed in Chapter 6, prisons are expensive and have a very limited ability to change undesirable behaviour (see Braithwaite 1989).

Probation is a sentence of the court and should not be confused with parole.[1] Section 731 in the Criminal Code requires that the judge take into account the "age and character of the offender, the nature of the offence, and the circumstances surrounding its commission" in order to determine if probation is appropriate. Probation can be ordered in addition to a fine *or* imprisonment of less than two years, but it cannot be used with *both* a fine and imprisonment.[2] Probation may actually shorten a jail term if the judge combines imprisonment with probation, rather than opting for a long prison sentence. The public would not be well served by having high-risk provincial offenders released without some means of facilitating their return to the community.

Today, probation is always accompanied by another punishment such as imprisonment, a conditional discharge, or an intermittent or suspended sentence. Judges take into consideration several things before deciding whether probation is an appropriate sentence for eligible offenders:

- The nature and seriousness of the offence committed;
- The degree of threat to the community that the offender may present if allowed to serve the sentence outside the confines of prison; and
- Any individual circumstances that may have caused the accused to commit the offence. If the crime arose because of a drug or alcohol abuse problem, a trial judge may order specific conditions such as abstinence from alcohol or drugs. If a weapon was used to commit crime, the trial judge will likely direct that the accused not be in possession of a firearms or other weapon.

BOX 5.1	**Purpose and Principles of Sentencing (from the Canadian Criminal Code, 1998)**

Section 718 The fundamental purpose of sentencing is to contribute, along with crime prevention initiatives, to respect for the law and maintenance of a just, peaceful, and safe society by imposing just sanctions that have one or more of the following objectives:

  i) Denounce unlawful conduct;

 ii) Deter the offender and other persons from committing offences;

iii) Separate offenders from society, where necessary;

 iv) Assist in rehabilitating offenders;

  v) Provide reparations for harm done to victims or to the community; and

 vi) Promote a sense of responsibility in offenders, and acknowledgement of the harm done to victims and to the community.

Section 718.1 A sentence must be proportionate to the gravity of the offence and the degree of responsibility of the offender.

Section 718.2. A court that imposes a sentence shall also take into consideration the following principles:

a) A sentence should be increased or reduced to account for any relevant aggravating or mitigating circumstances relating to the offence or the offender, and without limiting the generality of the foregoing:

  i) Evidence that the offence was motivated by bias, prejudice, or hate based on race, national or ethnic origin, language, colour, religion, sex, age, mental or physical disability, sexual orientation, or any other similar factor;

 ii) Evidence that the offender, in committing the offence, abused the offender's spouse or child; and

iii) Evidence that the offender, in committing the offence, abused a position of trust or authority in relation to the victim shall be deemed to be aggravating circumstances.

b) A sentence should be similar to sentences imposed on similar offenders for similar offences committed in similar circumstances;

c) Where consecutive sentences are imposed, the combined sentence should not be unduly long or harsh;

d) An offender should not be deprived of liberty, if less restrictive measures may be appropriate in the circumstances; and

e) All available sanctions other than imprisonment that are reasonable in the circumstances should be considered for all offenders, with particular attention to the circumstances of Aboriginal offenders.

Before making a probation order, the judge ensures that the terms of probation are understood by the accused and a copy of the order is given to him or her. The accused is also informed of the consequences of failure to comply with terms of probation order (MacIntosh 1995, 416–417). The probationer agrees to fulfill certain compulsory or **mandatory conditions**, such as to keep the peace and maintain good behaviour, to appear before the court when required to do so, and to notify the court or probation officer concerning any change in name, address, or employment.

A judge may also order **optional conditions**, such as the frequency of reporting to a probation officer, and whether the offender needs written permission before leaving the jurisdiction of the court. The judge can require a probationer to provide support and care for dependants, or to perform up to 240 hours of community service over a period not exceeding 18 months. The offender may be ordered to "actively participate in a treatment program," but only if the offender consents. It is important to note that the conditions of probation are meant to secure good conduct and not impose additional punishment.[3] The judge can order the offender to comply with any "other reasonable conditions," including that the probationer be strictly confined to his or her home and property except to attend work or other sanctioned activities.[4]

The probation order may be changed at the request of the offender, the parole officer or the Crown—but only with the court's consent. The requested changes can seek an alteration to the optional conditions, or a decrease the period of probation.[5] In this respect, probation is a dynamic sentence and can be modified to suit the special needs of the offender. Alternatively, if a greater degree of supervision is required by the probation officer, the conditions can also be made more restrictive.

Breach of Probation

There is a difference between failing to comply with a probation order and committing an offence while on probation. Both are criminal offences and carry different consequences. If a police officer discovers that an offender is on probation and has violated the terms of the probation order, the officer may write a report to the Crown counsel recommending a breach of probation. The Crown counsel then decides if the matter will go to court. Probationers who violate the terms of their probation order can be charged with failure to comply (a "hybrid" offence[6]) that carries a maximum sentence of two years' imprisonment.

A probationer who commits a crime during his or her term may have the probation order revoked and the court can issue "any sentence that could have been imposed if the passing of sentence had not been suspended." Alternatively, changes can be made to the optional conditions set out in the probation order, or the court can extend the probationary period for up to one year (see sections 732.5(d) and (e) in the Criminal Code).

For non-serious violations of probation orders, probation officers may be able to gain compliance from probationers by threatening to "breach" a client for non-compliance, or by raising the possibility of an unfavourable review before the court. However, probation officers must consider whether it is worth the time and effort to charge offenders with breaking the terms of their community sentence, especially if the anticipated consequence might only be an alteration of curfew hours. The breaching option requires careful deliberation. Compliance to the probation order might be achieved through other strategies besides revocation, particularly with young, first-time offenders.

Trends in the Use of Probation

The historical and recent patterns in the use of probation provide us with some insights as to how we punish law-breakers in Canada. Moreover, we can relate these trends to other developments in society that affect the work of probation officers.

Increase in the Use of Probation

One notable trend during this century is the increasing proportion of sentences handed down by the courts that include probation as the sentence. During the 1950s, probation counted for less than 3 percent of the total Canadian offender population. Prisons were used 16 times more frequently than probation, and 60 percent of probation orders came from three large counties in Ontario (Jaffary 1963). Today, probation is the most frequently used punishment, comprising over 40 percent of all sentences ordered by judges. That should not be surprising, given that most of the offences that come before the courts are relatively minor.[7]

Canadian sentencing practices rely on imprisonment to a lesser extent than those in the U.S. Since 1991, there has been a slight reduction in the use of imprisonment in Canada, relative to the number of adults charged by the police. Simultaneously, we are seeing a greater use of community dispositions such as probation (Boe and Muirhead 1998) and conditional sentences (Roberts 1999). Unlike in the U.S., where the numbers of adults on probation and parole are expanding with their prison populations, the use of sentencing alternatives such as probation appears more likely to be used as an alternative to incarceration in Canada (McMahon 1992). Overall, Canadian probation admissions increased 5 percent from 1995/96 to 1996/97 for a national average of 1,463 per 10,000 adults charged, but there is considerable regional variation in the use of probation. Probation varies from 627 (Quebec) to 3,544 (Prince Edward Island) per 10,000 adults charged with a crime (Reed and Roberts 2000, 8).

Trends and Patterns in Probation

Information compiled by the Canadian Centre for Justice Statistics (1998a), a division of Statistics Canada, allows us to make some generalizations about the use of probation as a sentence (see Reed and Roberts 2000):

- Probation was part of a sentence in 43 percent of adult convictions. The average probation sentence is 14 months and the most frequently imposed length in 1996/97 was 12 months, accounting for 27 percent of the total.

- The median age for probationers was 31, similar to the median age of those admitted to institutional corrections.

- Female offenders made up a greater percentage of probationers than prison admissions to provincial and territorial prisons (16 percent compared to 9 percent). Women tend to be convicted of less serious offences and are sentenced proportionately.

- Three quarters of the cases where probation was ordered had terms between 6 and 24 months. Offenders were usually given lengthier probation terms when they were convicted of more than one offence, at least for crimes against the person, drug-related offences, and other federal statutes (see Table 5.1). This information suggests that judges vary the length of probation orders based upon the severity of the offence, providing evidence for the principle of proportionality in sentencing (Roberts 2000, 91).

TABLE 5.1	Median Length of Probation Sentence in Days for Single/Multiple Charge Cases, 1997/98	

Offence Group	Probation/Type of Case	
	Single Charge	Multiple Charge
Crimes against the person	365	540
Crimes against property	365	450
Other Criminal Code offences	365	365
Traffic	180	360
Drug-related	365	540
Other federal statutes	365	365
Total offences	365	365

SOURCE: Canadian Centre for Justice Statistics 1998b.

- According to the Canadian Centre for Justice Statistics (1998a), probation is less likely to be used for property crimes than for other crimes, including those involving violence. Roberts (2000, 93–95) provides two reasons for this outcome. First, the majority of incidents scored as violent offences are Level 1, the least serious form of assault. Second, the criminal record of property offenders may be lengthy and likely included probation dispositions in the past, leaving judges to impose other sentences.

- Harassment charges and making indecent telephone calls were the offences with the highest percentage where probation was imposed as the most severe sentence. Two thirds of all offences related to uttering threats received a sentence of probation (Roberts 2000). Courts view probation as an appropriate disposition in cases where an external dimension of control is believed to act as a deterrent for offenders. Keeping one person apart from another to prevent conflict can be enforced through a probation order.

Provincial statistics reveal increased institutional and community populations. For example, in British Columbia from 1991/92 to 1996/97, the institutional counts increased 24 percent while the community caseload went up 58 percent. There was no increase in budget to manage these numbers. The B.C. Corrections Branch responded by double-bunking inmates and increasing caseloads in the community. More specifically, adult probation caseloads increased by 5500 offenders (or 60 percent) between 1991/92 and 1997/98. The increased use of probation has led to changes in the nature and volume of work for probation officers.

SUPERVISING PROBATIONERS

In industrialized countries, probation officers typically have college or university education, supplemented with specific occupational training.[8] These credentials are seen as necessary for a profession that conducts investigative and reporting work for the court, and whose practitioners are often required to make decisions that may have far-reaching consequences for the people they supervise. Many probation officers also administer risk assessment tools or make judgements about the likelihood of offenders to pose a risk to society in the future. They must prepare detailed reports in a short period of time, and need the tact and diplomacy to work around bureaucratic obstacles in pursuit of humanistic goals (Jacobs 1990).

Entry into these jobs requires competition in public service positions, where selection criteria may include pre-employment training, interviews, role-playing in simulated "what if" scenarios, background checks, and report-writing exercises. According to one Canadian province that responded to an international survey of probation jurisdictions, the most important quality for promotion within the probation bureaucracy is demonstrated common sense, despite the difficulties in measuring this trait. Apparently, common sense is more important than experience and education (Hamai and Villé 1995, 159). Perhaps the value of common sense is the reason why some countries use volunteers to take on some probationary duties.[9]

Probation officers often act like investigators, trying to build a body of information on their clientele through contact with employers, family, and friends. Because they have an obligation to the courts to monitor offender compliance to judicial orders, high-quality information about probated offenders is crucial to the job. They may have access to contact reports by police agencies that list the names, times, and places where people have been stopped for routine inquiries or in response to calls for service. These techniques would be used for monitoring high-risk probationers.

The role of probation officers—and the reality of their daily work—is affected by decisions made in government at the highest levels. Governments today are responding to contradictory pressures to reduce taxation, to increase public services, and to provide an economic climate favourable to foreign investors. These social and economic forces have an impact on probation officers and their clientele.

Government Fiscal Policies and Their Effects on Probation

The task of probation officers is shaped by the ideological and material context in which they do their work. If provincial governments reduce expenditures on public services, more supervision is done by fewer probation officers, affecting their workload and ability to provide meaningful counselling and supervision. The push to get more service for less money has led to a situation in Ontario where probation officers may have caseloads as high as 130 to 150 people, making their work excessive and unmanageable. These pressures, and the deinstitutionalization of at-risk populations in order to save money, may contribute to a loss of public confidence in the criminal justice system (Probation Officers Association of Ontario 1998). Probation, however, will not achieve rehabilitative goals when it tries to function in a resource-poor environment (Petersilia 1998).

One of the most difficult issues for probation agencies is negotiating the optimal sizes of their caseloads with governments. Caseload sizes of 35 to 50 have been proposed as an ideal by probation authorities, but supervision levels of up to 300 offenders have been noted in the U.S. (Enos et al. 1992; Petersilia and Turner 1997). Probation offices with high caseloads make it unlikely or impossible that their staff will have much opportunity to use the counselling skills acquired during training and experience. In these types of environments, probation agencies will make judgements about which offenders require the highest levels of supervision and allocate scarce resources for this group; leaving little left over for the rest of the offenders. Some probationers will require little more than token supervision, perhaps only required to report twice a week by telephone to confirm residency, program enrollment, or occupational status. High-risk offenders will receive more attention, but intense surveillance should not be automatically equated with greater public protection. High-risk probationers are more likely to have their probation revoked for violating the terms of their probation order, not necessarily for committing new offences (Klein 1997). The dilemma in this scenario is that some of today's low-risk probationers—who will receive little counselling—may go on to become tomorrow's high-risk offenders. Early focused interventions through probation services hold the promise of facilitating a departure from criminal pathways, at least for some proportion of delinquent youth.

In the context of reduced provincial expenditures in Canada, Ontario is responding with a "new model" of probation supervision. With an average daily count of about 61,000 probationers, the province has different modes of supervision to funnel probationers into one of four options after an intake assessment (Evans 1998). Those convicted of less serious offences will be required to complete a court-ordered task. Once completed, the offender will no longer have to report, or will have the probation order terminated. The second stream uses mass reporting so that groups of offenders will show up for education, orientation, or rehabilitative programming. The third and fourth options focus on the traditional model of individual or intensive supervision, the latter option reserved for those who present a public safety risk or are likely to harm themselves. Despite the reform-minded discourse behind recent developments in probation supervision, the real, material conditions of the modern state are the driving force behind these changes.

Recent developments in how probation is delivered in Ontario and the U.S. must be interpreted against the backdrop of contradictory pressures facing industrialized nations. The decline of corporate tax revenues since the early 1970s has led governments to seek reductions in the costs associated with providing social services to the public (Teeple 1995). At the same time, reported crime rose throughout part of this same period, leading voters to demand increased penalties for offenders on the belief that "getting tough" would address concerns about public safety. This trend is best exemplified in the U.S. where prison populations have tripled since 1980 (Gottfredson and Hirschi 1995), and doubled in the past 12 years, despite a decrease in officially recorded index crimes (United States Department of Justice 1999). Fiscally conscious governments find themselves caught between managing overcrowded prisons, the prospect of having to build new ones, and a citizenry demanding lower taxes. Probation and other community sentences are seen as cheaper alternatives, but must be legitimated in the language of crime prevention in order for the public to accept them. The discourse of deterrence is used as a means of responding to crime and disorder: if potential offenders are certain that severe punishments will be swiftly applied as a consequence of their criminal acts, they will be deterred and society will be safer, or so the story goes. Probation is marketed as a means of protecting society, saving money, and punishing wrongdoers without prison. This new ideology of deterrence strays from the original rationale for probation practice, where rehabilitation and reintegration were dominant correctional policies. Each provincial jurisdiction in Canada will vary to the extent that its probation services are directed by rehabilitation or deterrence ideals.

As the ideological basis for probation changes in most industrialized countries, probation officers are under pressure to employ a range of new disciplinary methods such as electronic monitoring and home confinement (Enos et al. 1992; also see Chapter 13). Probation shifts from being a helping profession to being one that embraces control technologies to satisfy retributive goals in sentencing (Harris 1995b; Bunzel 1995). Probation supervision may become more intensive (i.e., intensive supervision probation or ISP, discussed below) to control those for whom prison bed space is not available. Probation officers become more like police officers concerned with control and surveillance, abandoning the earlier role of helping offenders (Hamai et al. 1995).

Some jurisdictions have professional guidelines and codes of ethics to assist in defining their role, such as probation officers in Ontario (see Box 5.2). In Canada, there is no national professional association of probation officers, although the Probation Officers Association of

BOX 5.2   Code of Ethics for Probation Officers in Ontario

Code of Ethics

To assist Probation Officers in maintaining the integrity of their profession by upholding and advancing the purpose, knowledge, ethics, and values of the probation field at all times. This code of ethics will thereby provide a standard of practice to enable all probation officers to fulfill their goals and objectives to the Offender, the Courts, the Community, and the Criminal Justice System.

Responsibility to the Profession

Probation Officers shall:

- Encourage ethical conduct by all members of the profession.
- Have a responsibility to colleagues to develop a working relationship of mutual respect and cooperation.
- Promote the philosophy and ethics of the profession with new colleagues.
- Seek advice and utilize the expertise of colleagues and supervisors.
- Contribute their expertise in order to promote the integrity and competence of the profession to the public.
- Keep current with emerging knowledge relevant to the probation field and shall contribute to the knowledge base of the profession.

To Courts, Criminal Justice System, and Community

Probation Officers shall:

- Strive to provide the highest calibre of service to the Courts and Judiciary through the preparation of quality reports, testimony, and investigations. Probation Officers shall at all times conduct themselves in a manner that upholds the dignity of the Court.

- As an integral part of the total Criminal Justice System uphold and respect the tenants, rules and functions of that System.
- Promote awareness among other members of the Criminal Justice System, of the philosophies, functions, and roles of the Probation Officers.
- Be aware of their role in protecting the community from criminal activity and in the promotion of programs for the prevention of crime.

To The Offender

Probation Officers shall:

- Provide service to the offenders to the maximum of their professional skill, ability, and competence.
- Maintain a professional relationship at all times to avoid conflict of interest situations.
- Promote equality in every respect thereby preserving the dignity and rights of offenders.
- Create a positive atmosphere for change that will encourage offenders to realize their goals and potentials by taking advantage of training, treatment, and services provided.
- Inform the offender of legal rights and his or her responsibilities in the Criminal Justice System.
- Make the offender aware of the responsibilities and duties of the Probation Officer within the Criminal Justice System.
- Respect the privacy of the offender and the confidentiality of information subject to legal and policy parameters.

Reprinted with the permission of the Probation Officers Association of Ontario.

Ontario promotes the interests of its members, including writing position papers when the government is considering changes to the law that may affect their mandate. The U.S. has a similar national organization for community corrections—the American Probation and Parole Association. A national organization of probation officers in Canada could work to educate government officials, policy-makers, and the general public to promote rehabilitative ideals.

The Conflicting Roles of Probation Officers

As mentioned earlier, probation originally focused almost exclusively on the offender's needs as a prerequisite to rehabilitation. However, in the early 1970s, the rehabilitation ideal came under attack and was deemed by policy-makers to be unrealistic (Cullen and Gilbert 1982), largely because a single evaluation of studies announced that few rehabilitative interventions could change offenders (see Martinson 1974). As the rehabilitative ideal fell into disfavour among politicians and policy-makers, probation officers found their roles to be changing as well (Enos et al. 1992). Importantly, Canadian correctional policy has shown some resistance against the American experiment with getting tough on crime through mandatory minimum sentencing. Canadian researchers have dominated efforts to discover what rehabilitative strategies are most effective in reducing recidivism (Bonta and Cormier 1999).

The tension between rehabilitative and deterrence philosophies means that probation officers juggle two conflicting roles in the course of their jobs. Especially when working with youth, they are often expected to provide support for treatment through counselling or by acting as a referral agent to community resources. Alternatively, they play a law enforcement role in order to ensure that probationers are abiding by the court's mandatory and optional conditions. They can exercise discretion in ignoring a violation if a probationer fails to meet the requirements stipulated in the probation order, or they can choose to deal with it outside of the formal legal apparatus or invoke the state's resources to have the probationer arrested for breach of probation. This asymmetry in power between the two parties in this relationship affects how each party presents itself to the other, what they choose to say, and the perceived value of each encounter.

Depending upon the nature of the offence, caseload levels, and the organizational goals of the probation officers, officers will put more emphasis on surveillance than on promoting the rehabilitative needs of their clients. These tensions are obvious when an offender breaches a condition of probation and subsequently finds that his or her future hangs on the discretion of a probation officer. While there may be the legal grounds for charging an offender with a breach, doing so might jeopardize an otherwise productive relationship between the officer and probationer. Where probation serves the multiple functions of rehabilitation, punishment, and reparation, these conflicting purposes will be more pronounced (Hough 1995).

Abadinsky (1997) identifies three probation supervisory styles along a continuum of control and social service orientations. The **control model** focuses on monitoring the probationer's activities through random visits, urinalysis, and a close relationship with law enforcement agencies. The **social service model** is oriented towards meeting client needs through employment, housing, and counselling, often through private service providers (such as the John Howard or Elizabeth Fry Societies in Canada). Somewhere in between these two points lies the **combined model,** which provides social services while still endorsing the need to control probationers. The nature of the supervisory style for any jurisdiction can be revealed by such things as the formal qualifications of the probation officers, their legal mandate and access to treatment resources, and their relationship to the courts and law enforcement agencies.

Another emerging trend in probation identified by Harris (1995a) concerns the professionals in probation, who were once held in high esteem and believed to have expertise in rehabilitating offenders. These women and men in probation and other corrective agencies have been attacked by skeptics who dismiss their claims to therapeutic expertise. Probation officers in the United Kingdom—many with a background in the social sciences—have been accused by former prime minister Margaret Thatcher of giving "sociological alibis" to criminals. In this milieu, the requirement of a degree in social work has been eliminated in favour of in-service training modules for probation officers. Apparently, practitioners of retributive-style justice have no need for higher education (Rumgay and Brewster 1996).

Moving against the trend of having probation officers assume police-like roles is the emerging popularity in many Canadian jurisdiction for **restorative justice** (Umbreit 1994; Zehr 1990). Based on the concept of reintegrative shaming (Braithwaite 1989), this option generally avoids some part of formal processing in the criminal justice system. Instead, the offender and victim meet face to face with their respective support groups to work towards reconciliation. A trained facilitator mediates between the two parties until a mutual restorative agreement is reached, usually in the form of victim compensation or community service. Probation officers are uniquely situated to become agents of change in this process, either as program coordinators, facilitators, or mentors to help a probationer comply with the restorative agreement.

The Pre-Sentence Report

One of the fundamental roles of probation officers is to provide detailed information to the courts about the background and disposition of the accused. Earlier in history, when the rehabilitation model directed judges to fashion the most appropriate treatment, the informal reports by probation officers to judges gave way to standardized, written documents (Bunzel 1995). Rejecting the notion that the punishment should fit the crime, early probation advocates in the U.S. and Canada believed that treatment should fit the criminal. Today, these same purposes surface when the sentencing goal is to match the offender's needs with resources in the community to make available the necessary corrective interventions.

The **pre-sentence report** will contain information about the offender's age, maturity, character, previous convictions, behaviour, attitude, and, where applicable, willingness to make amends. This profile is intended to help the court match a sentence with the needs of the offender. Although many probation officers may make recommendations about the appropriateness of probation or imprisonment, one provincial appellate court has ruled that these reports are to have no other content than a social-biographical profile of the offender.[10] A copy must be made available to the accused or his or her lawyer. The information will also be used to help determine the appropriate level of supervision for the offender, once the judge has listed the conditions to be fulfilled.

Unfortunately, we have little information in Canada on the extent to which judges act on the recommendations of probation officers when it comes time for sentencing. According to Griffiths and Verdun-Jones (1994), some judges rely heavily on the recommendations of the probation officers, while others may give them less consideration. Research from the U.S. suggests that courts generally accept pre-sentence recommendations (United States Department of Justice 1997). Interestingly, research funded by the Rand Corporation "found in general no statistical difference in the recidivism rates of those persons probation officers recommended for probation from those they recommended for prison" (cited in Klein 1997, 29).

Field research into the work of probation officers suggests that the defendant's attitude or subjective orientation towards the crime has a strong effect on the type of recommendations made by the officers. Defendants who accept the probation officer's definition of the situation and have acceptable attitudes are likely to receive more positive evaluations before the court (Spencer 1989).

CURRENT ISSUES IN PROBATION

Some common themes in the literature on probation concern its effectiveness as a sentence of the court and whether more intensive forms of probation can meet the twin objectives of reducing prison populations and deterring offenders.

Intensive Supervision Probation

The control of crime has been politicized in the U.S. (and, to a lesser extent, in Canada) so that what works to rehabilitate offenders becomes less important than what sells to an anxious and largely misinformed public. One simplistic response to control crime has been to advocate tougher probation conditions and more intensive supervision.

Intensive supervision probation (ISP) is one form of intermediate sanctions that focuses on offender risk management in the community through a number of strategies. ISP resources are directed at offender control using tactics such as lower caseloads for probation officers, random curfew checks, frequent and irregular demands for drug testing through urinalysis, mandatory community service, and the requirement that probationers pay for some portion of their supervision costs. Offenders may be selected on the basis of a risk assessment instrument and may have a history of drug and alcohol abuse (Klein 1997). If they are willing to participate on an ISP and have been recommended for it in a pre-sentence report, they may be eligible for this program. ISP programs also have an ideological appeal when they are called a means of "punishing smarter," or, as Erwin (1986, 17) initially claimed, "we are in the business of increasing the heat on probationers . . . satisfying the public's demand for just punishment . . . criminals must be punished for their misdeeds"). The idea that offenders can remain in the community and be punished at the same time has an obvious appeal for governments wishing to save money by not having to build more prisons and yet still being seen as tough on crime.

In theory, the use of ISP frees up scarce prison space as intermediate-risk offenders live out their sentence in the community under stricter controls than regular probation might provide. Two general indicators can tell us whether ISP has been successful: its ability to reduce prison populations by diverting intermediate-risk offenders and its ability to prevent recidivism, meaning that offenders on ISP would be less likely to re-offend compared to similar clients on regular probation.

Early ISP programs in the southern U.S. were conducted under optimal conditions and showed favourable results in terms of their ability to divert offenders, reduce costs, and generate lower rates of recidivism. Later evaluations have been less encouraging (Fulton, Stone, and Gendreau 1994; Petersilia and Turner 1997). There are problems with ISPs in the U.S. that have been identified by a number of researchers, including the finding that some programs showed an *increase* in recidivism from 2 to 5 percent (Gendreau and Little 1993). Furthermore, ISP programs have shown poor results where inappropriate offenders were selected, the supervision caseloads were high, and treatment was poorly designed or non-existent. ISP can work effectively, however, but only under certain conditions with specific offender groups. Programs that show promise are accompanied by treatment participation, community service, and employment programs. The supervision of high-risk probationers must be structured and intensive, and must have accountability mechanisms for program participation and integrate the offender with pro-social social networks and activities.

In a review of evaluations on ISPs in the U.S., Abadinsky (1997) argued that most programs do not actually divert offenders. Many candidates placed on ISP would have received regular probation, but the availability of this sentencing option has promoted a tremendous growth in U.S. correctional populations since 1985. The data show that probation and prison counts are increasing steadily (United States Department of Justice 1999), undermining any claim that these innovations are "diversionary" (Petersilia and Turner 1997).

Some U.S. critics point out that intermediate punishments, such as intensive probation, are part of a wider array of instruments to control marginalized populations more effectively—clothed in the rhetoric of a "war on drugs" and "getting tough on crime" (Petersen and Palumbo 1997). Abadinsky (1997) questioned the assumption that "more is better" with respect to increased contacts between probation officer and offender. If probation officers have more time to supervise their clientele because of smaller caseloads, this discretionary time could be used to discover technical violations, resulting in a higher failure rate, which will inflate prison populations, especially where the client population consists of drug offenders (Turner, Petersilia, and Deschenes 1992). Goff (1999) notes the continued existence of ISP programs, despite their higher-than-expected recidivism rates, mainly because ISP offers higher levels of surveillance and punishment. This approach is consistent with the crime control model of justice. However, if poorly implemented, intensive supervision may produce unanticipated results. Notwithstanding these issues, effective probation interventions still hold promise.

The Effectiveness of Probation

Even though probation is the most common sentence used by the courts in Canada, there is surprisingly little information about its use and effectiveness[11] (Goff 1999). In the United States, where national figures are compiled, the Bureau of Justice Statistics reports that 65 percent of probationers completed their probation successfully, but almost one in three jail inmates were on probation during the time of their most recent arrest (United States Department of Justice 1999).

If probation is to reduce offender motivation effectively, the research tells us that high-risk offenders may benefit from what has been described as "the principles of effective intervention" (Gendreau 1996) delivered outside prison walls. These include intensive services that are behavioural in nature, such as concrete skill-building, problem-solving, and the use of positive reinforcement for pro-social styles of thinking, feeling, and acting. In programs like these, offenders are treated sensitively without using aggression or humiliation. Program involvement is firmly and fairly enforced to disrupt delinquent or criminal peer networks. Re-offending is prevented by teaching the probationer to monitor and anticipate situations that will lead to crime, and having the individual practice new, pro-social behaviours in increasingly challenging situations. Family and friends are trained to provide positive reinforcement for such behaviour and follow-up sessions may be necessary. The integrity and success of treatment interventions will vary, depending on program resources and the training provided to program staff (Fulton, Stone, and Gendreau 1994; Gendreau 1996). Community-based programs show more promise because they can deliver lower rates of recidivism—ranging from 25 percent to 60 percent—than their institutional counterparts (Gendreau 1996; also see Chapter 11).

Successful interventions are meant to correct thinking and perceptual errors, modify the offender's values and expectations that maintain antisocial behaviour, develop self-control, and facilitate problem-solving (Gendreau 1993). Although it sounds clinical, many of the treatment strategies described here are similar to what some self-help groups have been doing with people in need of treatment of some sort, such as Alcoholics Anonymous, Narcotics Anonymous, and the 12-Step Program (i.e., relapse prevention). Only a minority of all probationers will need this kind of focused intervention.

Studies that review the effectiveness of a wide range of correctional programs (called meta-analyses) also show which treatment interventions do not work. Offender recidivism is least likely to be affected by programs that claim to be "punishing smarter." These include those with a focus on punishments such as boot camps, random drug testing, electronic monitoring, restitution, and "shock incarceration" (Gendreau 1996). Non-punitive, treatment-oriented programs may be expensive to design and implement, but the savings to be gained from the reduced costs and victimization associated with repeat offenders makes them a worthwhile social investment (Petersilia and Turner 1997).

We have the knowledge to design and implement effective probation services for high-risk offenders, provided that these programs are based on cognitive-behavioural models, are adequately funded, and are staffed by suitable, trained individuals (Gendreau 1996; Andrews and Bonta 1990). Consistent with the Criminal Code sentencing guidelines, which state that "an offender should not be deprived of liberty, if less restrictive measures may be appropriate in the circumstances" (section 718.2; see Box 5.1), provincial governments have the potential to reduce their reliance on imprisonment by building consensus and strategies for non-custodial alternatives (Nuffield 1997).

SUMMARY

Probation is a flexible sentence that is typically used with offenders who do not present a risk to the public. The specific conditions of the order can be tailored to meet the needs of the offender and society. Compliance with probation orders is accomplished through monitoring the probationer, the potential for further criminal sanctions, and, in some cases, the treatment delivered or brokered by the probation officer.

The use of probation and other community-based sentences in Canada is expanding. There is some evidence that the growth of prison populations in Canada has stabilized because of 1996 Criminal Code amendments that direct judges to seek non-custodial sentencing options.

The difficult and sometimes conflicting role of the probation officer is affected by a lack of government funding for rehabilitative and treatment options that might assist high-risk probationers. The pre-sentence report is an important dimension of probation work because it provides sentencing authorities with guidance to match the offender's needs with available resources.

High-risk offenders may be suitable for more intensive forms of probation supervision and treatment, especially when the interventions focus on using cognitive-behavioural programs to address risk/need factors that may predispose an offender to future criminal behaviour. If implemented poorly, intensive supervision probation can have no effect, or can produce higher rates of recidivism than regular probation. Probation for higher risk offenders must be accompanied by meaningful, relevant, and timely rehabilitative programs.

KEY TERMS AND CONCEPTS

John Augustus	judicial clemency	probation
combined model of supervisory style	mandatory conditions of a probation order	probation officer restorative justice
control model of supervisory style	medical model	social service model of supervisory style
intensive supervision probation (ISP)	optional conditions of a probation order	
	pre-sentence report	

STUDY AND DISCUSSION QUESTIONS

1. If you were a probation officer, what supervisory approach would you take towards your probationers: a social worker orientation or one focused on surveillance and control? Why?

2. How has the role of the probation officer changed during the 20th century? What external forces have influenced these changes?

3. What features of probation make it a flexible sentence?

4. How is intensive supervision probation different from regular probation? After reading about the evaluations of ISP in the United States, do you think it would be a good idea for Canadians to adopt a similar program? Why or why not?

5. Is probation an appropriate sentence for high-risk offenders? If so, under what kinds of conditions?

WEBLINKS

American Probation and Parole Association: **www.appa-net.org**

New York Department of Probation: **www.ci.nyc.ny.us/html/prob/home.html**

Probation Officers Association of Ontario: **www.eagle.ca/~poao/index.html**

United States Department of Justice: **www.ojp.usdoj.gov/bjs**

NOTES

1. Parole is a form of sentence administration, or "conditional release" for offenders. It is not ordered by a judge. Parole eligibility is decided by the National Parole Board or by provincial decision-making bodies, and allows prisoners to be released and serve a portion of their sentence in the community under supervision. As with probation, parolees must abide by certain conditions or their parole may be revoked.

2. *R. v. St. James* (1981), 20 C.R. (3d) 389 (Que. C.A.).

3. *R. v. Ziatas* (1973), 13 C.C.C. (2d) 287 (Ont. C.A.).

4. See *R. v. M.* (D.E.S.) (1993), 21 C.R. (4th) 55, 80 C.C.C. (3rd) 372 (B.C. C.A.).

5. For example, a probationer convicted under the *Young Offenders Act* might request the court to change the conditions of the probation order if a situation emerged where the probationer had schooling, recreational, job-related, or other social obligations. Curfews or reporting obligations might need to be adjusted to facilitate the broader intentions of community supervision.

6. In the Criminal Code, offences are categorized as summary or indictable. The former are less serious offences carrying maximum sentences of 18 months or less, or a fine of $2,000, or both. Indictable offences are more serious and carry higher maximum penalties. At the discretion of the Crown, some crimes can be processed as either summary or indictable, and are so called hybrid offences (see Griffiths and Verdun-Jones 1994, 216–221).

7. According to the Canadian Centre for Justice Statistics (1998a), the top three most frequently occurring offences in 1997/98 were impaired driving (15 percent), common assault (12 percent), and theft (11 percent). These three crimes accounted for four in ten of all cases heard in nine Canadian jurisdictions. These are offences for which judges may view probation as an appropriate disposition because it meets the sentencing guidelines in section 718 of the Criminal Code (see Box 5.1). Based on the data for 1996/97, 65 percent of the adult correctional population (n = 151,850) was on probation.

8. The Justice Institute in New Westminster, British Columbia, offers a pre-employment program for adult probation officers. Successful applicants are required to pay for their training, and are expected to hold a university degree in a related discipline such as social work, criminology, sociology, psychology, law, counselling, or education. Applicants are also expected to have one year of full-time, recent, related work experience. The Employment Readiness Program consists of a comprehensive 12-week training program to provide applicants with the necessary skills and knowledge for work as an adult probation officer. The screening process involves a language proficiency test, a short panel interview, a role-playing exercise, and a written exercise, along with criminal record and reference checks.

9. Some countries, such as Japan, use an extensive network of volunteers to carry out the supervision of probation orders. Similarly in Sweden, there are few probation officers but many lay supervisors, who are paid only their expenses and a modest fee. These volunteers may lack professional qualifications but possess personal qualities and mature judgement (Harris 1995a, 11).

10. *R. v. Edwards* (1986), 60 Nfld. & P.E.I.R. 36 (P.E.I. C.A.).

11. Many studies on the effectiveness of probation have failed to meet the criteria for good-quality evaluations, such as being sure that it is the program that is causing the changes in offender behaviour, and not some other variable(s) (Fulton, Stone, and Gendreau 1994).

REFERENCES

Abadinsky, H. 1997. *Probation and Parole: Theory and Practice* (6th ed.). Upper Saddle River, NJ: Prentice-Hall.

Andrews, D.A., and **J. Bonta**. 1998. *The Psychology of Criminal Conduct*. Cincinnati: Andersen Publishing.

Augustus, J. 1852. *A Report of the Labors of John August, In Aid of the Unfortunate*. Boston: Wright and Hasty.

Boe, R., and **M. Muirhead**. 1998. Have Falling Crime Rates and Increased Use of Probation Reduced Incarceration? Some Trends and Comparisons. *Forum on Correctional Research* 10(2): 3–6.

Bonta, J., and **R.B. Cormier**. 1999. Corrections Research in Canada: Impressive Progress and Promising Prospects. *Canadian Journal of Criminology* 41(2): 235–247.

Braithwaite, J. 1989. *Crime, Shame, and Reintegration*. Cambridge: Cambridge University Press.

Bunzel, S.M. 1995. The Probation Officer and the Federal Sentencing Guidelines: Strange Philosophical Bedfellows. *Yale Law Journal* 104(4): 933–968.

Canadian Centre for Justice Statistics (Statistics Canada, *Juristat*, Catalogue No. 85-002). 1998a. Adult Correctional Services in Canada, 1996–97. *Juristat* 18(3).

———. 1998b. Adult Criminal Court Statistics, 1997/98. *Juristat* 18(14).

Carrigan, O.D. 1991. *Crime and Punishment in Canada: A History*. Toronto: McClelland and Stewart.

Couglan, D.W.F. 1988. The History and Function of Probation. In R.C. McLeod, *Lawful Authority: Readings on the History of Criminal Justice in Canada*. Toronto: Copp, Clark, and Pittman.

Cullen, F., and **K.E. Gilbert**. 1982. *Reaffirming Rehabilitation*. Cincinnati: Anderson Publishing.

Ekstedt, J., and **C.T. Griffiths**. 1988. *Corrections in Canada: Policy and Practice* (2nd ed.). Toronto: Butterworths.

Enos, R., **C.M. Black**, **J.F. Quinn**, and **J.E. Holman**. 1992. *Alternative Sentencing: Electronically Monitored Correctional Supervision*. Bristol, IN: Wyndham Hall Press.

Erwin, B.J. 1986. Turning Up the Heat on Probationers in Georgia. *Federal Probation* 50: 17–24.

Evans, D.C. 1998. Ontario's New Probation Supervision Model. *Corrections Today* August, 128–129.

Fisher, B. 1994. *Report on the Process and Procedure in Supervising Jason Karl Gamache*. Victoria: Ministry of the Attorney General.

Fulton, B.A., **S.B. Stone**, and **P. Gendreau**. 1994. *Restructuring Intensive Supervision Programs: Applying "What Works."* Lexington, KY: American Probation and Parole Association.

Gendreau, P. 1993. The Principles of Effective Intervention with Offenders. Unpublished paper for the International Association of Residential and Community Alternatives, Philadelphia, November 3.

———. 1996. Offender Rehabilitation: What We Know and What Needs to Be Done. *Criminal Justice and Behavior* 23(1): 144–162.

Gendreau, P., and **T. Little**. 1993. A Meta-Analysis of the Effectiveness of Sanctions on Offender Recidivism. Unpublished manuscript.

Goff, C. 1999. *Corrections in Canada*. Cincinnati: Anderson Publishing.

Gottfredson, M.R., and **T. Hirschi**. 1995. National Crime Control Policies. *Society* 32(2): 30–37.

Griffiths, C.T., and **S. Verdun-Jones**. 1994. *Canadian Criminal Justice* (2nd ed.). Toronto: Harcourt Brace.

Hamai, K., and **R. Villé**. 1995. Probation as a Profession. In K. Hamai, R. Villé, R. Harris, M. Hough, and U. Zvekic (Eds.), *Probation Round the World*. New York: Routledge.

Hamai, K., R. Villé, R. Harris, M. Hough, and **U. Zvekic** (Eds.). 1995. *Probation Round the World*. New York: Routledge.

Harris, R. 1995a. Studying Probation: A Comparative Approach. In K. Hamai, R. Villé, R. Harris, M. Hough, and U. Zvekic (Eds.), *Probation Round the World*. New York: Routledge.

———. 1995b. Origins and Developments. In K. Hamai, R. Villé, R. Harris, M. Hough, and U. Zvekic (Eds.), *Probation Round the World*. New York: Routledge.

Hough, M. 1995. Variations in Probation Function. In K. Hamai., R. Villé, R. Harris, M. Hough and U. Zvekic (Eds.), *Probation Round the World*, New York: Routledge.

Jacobs, M.D. 1990. *Screwing the System and Making It Work: Juvenile Justice in the No-Fault Society*. Chicago: University of Chicago Press.

Jaffary, S.K. 1963. *Sentencing of Adults in Canada*. Toronto: University of Toronto Press.

Klein, A.R. 1997. *Alternative Sentencing, Intermediate Sanctions, and Probation* (2nd ed.). Cincinnati: Anderson Publishing.

MacIntosh, D.A. 1995. *Fundamentals of the Criminal Justice System* (2nd ed.). Toronto: Carswell.

Martinson R. 1974. What Works? Questions and Answers about Prison Reform. *National Public Interest* 35: 22–54.

McMahon, M.W. 1992. *The Persistent Prison? Rethinking Decarceration and Penal Reform*. Toronto: University of Toronto Press.

Nuffield, J. 1997. *Diversion Programs for Adults*. Ottawa: Solicitor General Canada.

Petersilia, J. 1998. A Decade of Experimenting with Intermediate Sanctions: What Have We Learned? *Federal Probation* 62(2): 3–10.

Petersen, R.D., and **D.J. Palumbo**. 1997. The Social Construction of Intermediate Punishments. *Prison Journal* 77(1): 77–93.

Petersilia, J., and **S. Turner**. 1997. Intensive Probation and Parole. In M. Tonry (Ed.), *Crime and Justice: An Annual Review of Research*. Chicago: University of Chicago Press.

Probation Officers Association of Ontario. 1998. Submission to the Crime Control Commission, January 21, 1998. www.eagle.ca/~poao/papers/crime.htm (April 2000).

Reed, M., and **J. Roberts**. 2000. Correctional Trends. In J. Roberts (Ed.), *Criminal Justice in Canada*. Toronto: Harcourt Brace.

Roberts, J. 1987. *Empirical Research on Sentencing*. Ottawa: Department of Justice, Research and Development Directorate.

———. 1999. Sentencing Research in Canada. *Canadian Journal of Criminology* 41(2): 225–234.

———. 2000. *Criminal Justice in Canada*. Toronto: Harcourt Brace.

Rumgay, J., and **M. Brewster**. 1996. Restructuring Probation in England and Wales: Lessons from an American Experience. *Prison Journal* 76(3): 331–348.

Solicitor General of Canada. 1998. *Corrections Population Growth, Second Progress Report*. Ottawa: Solicitor General of Canada.

Spencer, J. 1989. Accounts, Attitudes, and Solutions: Probation Officer-Defendant Negotiations of Subjective Orientations. In D.H. Kelly (Ed.), *Deviant Behavior: A Text Reader in the Sociology of Deviance* (3rd ed.). New York: St. Martin's Press.

Teeple, G. 1995. *Globalization and the Decline of Social Reform*. Toronto: Garamond Press.

Turner, S., J. Petersilia, and E.P. Deschenes. 1992. Evaluating Intensive Supervision Probation/Parole (ISP) for Drug Offenders. *Crime and Delinquency* 38(4): 539–557.

Umbreit, M. 1994. *Victim Meets Offender: The Impact of Restorative Justice and Mediation*. Monsey, NY: Criminal Justice Press.

United States Department of Justice, Bureau of Justice Statistics. 1997. *Characteristics of Adults on Probation, 1995*. Washington, DC.

———. 1999. *Correctional Populations in the United States, 1996: Executive Summary*. Washington, DC.

Winterdyk, J. 2000. *Young Offenders in Canada: Issues and Perspectives* (2nd ed.). Toronto: Harcourt Brace.

Zehr, H. 1990. *Changing Lenses: A New Focus for Crime and Justice*. Scottsdale, PA: Herald Press.

INCARCERATION IN CANADA: PAST AND PRESENT

Michael G. Young[1]
Camosun College
Victoria, British Columbia

LEARNING OBJECTIVES

After reading this chapter, you should be able to:

- Describe methods of punishment in early Canada;
- Identify the factors that contributed to the emergence of incarceration as a dominant method of correction;
- Trace and understand the shifts in correctional paradigms over the past two centuries;
- Identify possible social factors associated with the shifts in correctional paradigms and models of correctional practice;
- Identify and understand the influence of competing objectives on institutional corrections;
- Provide a profile of incarcerated offenders;
- Understand two of the contemporary issues facing institutional corrections: the construction of new facilities and privatization; and
- Assess the overall effectiveness of incarceration.

Kindness is shown to all convicts, and if punishment is meted out occasionally it is because the cases are such that it cannot be avoided.

—John Creighton (fourth warden of Kingston Penitentiary, 1876)

Correctional institutions, like most social institutions, are reflexive. That is, they respond to pressures in their operational and policy environments. To be sure, prisons did not emerge in a vacuum but were the product of sociohistorical and economic forces and changing conceptions about the nature of humanity in western history. As a response to crime, however, the use of incarceration is a relatively recent phenomenon. Prior to the 18th century, the methods to punish or correct social deviants were often arbitrary, brutal, and inhumane (see Chapter 1). In addition to being an alternative means of punishment, prison brought with it the promise of humane treatment and the possibility of the reform of offenders.

This chapter examines the evolution of incarceration in Canada, starting with the identification of early punishments and the emergence of prisons during the colonial period. The development and organization of institutions at both the federal and provincial levels of government over the past two centuries are discussed and statistical data are used to identify basic trends and characteristics in offender populations. Particular attention is paid to changes in correctional paradigms and philosophical models of punishment (see Table 6.1), and to the impact of these changes on incarcerated offender populations. An undercurrent running through this chapter is that incarceration has succeeded in punishing offenders but failed in reforming them. The discussion concludes with an analysis of current issues facing institutional corrections.

PRE-INSTITUTION PUNISHMENT IN EARLY CANADA

The philosophy of punishing in early Canada was influenced by the English and French. Both New France and English Canada adapted the law of their mother countries to the "new world" context. Prior to the 18th century in Europe, prisons were primarily used as holding tanks and rarely held offenders for any length of time. Generally, punishment was intended to serve two purposes, deterrence and revenge. Unlike deterrence as formulated by the philosophers of the Enlightenment, in this context **deterrence** meant that the punishment or execution of offenders in public would serve as a lesson to others. **Revenge** referred to *lex talionis*, or an eye for an eye, and originates from the Code of Hammurabi, circa 18th century BC in Babylon (Bowker 1982).

TABLE 6.1	Corrections Paradigms		
Paradigm	**Time Period**	**Cause of Crime**	**Purpose of Corrections**
Pre-institution	1700–1830	Endemic to society	Punish and deter
Punishment and Penitence	1830–1867	Offender's social environment	Punish and reform
Punishment and Penitence	1867–1938	Offender's social environment	Punish
Rehabilitation	1938–1970	Individual pathology	Treat and reform
Reintegration and Opportunity	1970–1978	Individual choice	Treatment and reintegration
Reparation, Risk Assessment, and Reintegration	1978–present	Individual choice influenced by social risk factors	Punish, risk assessment, treatment, and reintegration

SOURCE: Adapted from Ekstedt and Griffiths 1988; Ekstedt and Jackson 1997.

In addition, punishment reflected the influence of Christianity in western thought. Criminal acts were considered crimes against the king's peace and his majesty. The doctrine of divine rule held that acts against the king were acts against God and therefore merited punitive attention in the most sensational way. Punishment allowed the condemned criminal to make an *amende honorable* to God and king through the admission of guilt and display of remorse during a ritual of tortuous punishment and public repentance or execution (Foucault 1977).

By the 15th century, the most popular method of execution in England was hanging, which meant death by slow strangulation, until 1783 when it was replaced by the "snapping drop" method. It is estimated that under the 38-year reign of Henry VIII there were more than 78,000 hangings (Blanchfield 1985).

In Europe and North America, executions were considered public theatre and intended to act as a deterrent; for justice to be done, it had to be seen to be done. Families would pack a lunch and go to an execution, and it was not uncommon for entire villages to attend (Carrigan 1991). The methods used for execution in Europe were applied with similar vigour in New France. Sixty-seven Europeans were executed during the French regime in Canada: 54 were hanged, six were broken on the wheel, one had his head crushed, three were shot, and three were decapitated (Blanchfield 1985). Those fortunate enough to be spared execution were banished or enslaved on the galleys, large fighting ships powered by sail and as many as 500 men on oars (Carrigan 1991). Slaves were poorly clothed or fed and frequently whipped to increase their performance output. If the ship was boarded during battle, the slaves were slaughtered and, if sunk, they went down with the ship.

By the late 17th century in England, galleys were replaced by more advanced sailing vessels; French galleys were decommissioned in 1748 (Blanchfield 1985). However, the 18th century also witnessed a population explosion and a surge in crime rates. Members of the upper classes, frightened by masses of unemployed people in the cities, called for "law and order" and sought to achieve it by the use of savage and exemplary punishment. In England, Sir William Blackstone identified 160 offences punishable by death in 1760, which grew to over 200 by the late 18th century (Bowker 1982). Commonly referred to as the **Bloody Code**, people were executed for the most minor crimes, such as stealing bread (Carrigan 1991). The code was adopted by Lower Canada in 1763 and Upper Canada in 1793 and applied to everyone: children as young as seven were put to death for petty crimes.

Not all convicts condemned to death were executed. Given the severity of punishment, plaintiffs were sometimes unwilling to prosecute and judges and juries often refused to convict. Blanchfield (1985) observes that by 1810 fewer than 10 percent of those sentenced to death in the colonies were actually hanged. The court also had the option of commuting a convict's sentence to Transportation—the removal of an offender to another country. English convicts were sent to the American colonies, where they essentially worked as slave labourers for the duration of their sentence (Spierenburg 1995). By 1775, England was transporting 2,000 convicts a year to the colonies. However, after the War of Independence, other options were urgently sought by the English government. Australia became the next dumping ground for transported prisoners. The first shipload of prisoners arrived at what is now Sydney Harbour in 1787. Although the use of Transportation declined dramatically in the 19th century, Transportation from Canadian colonies to Tasmania and New South Wales did not end until 1853 (James 1990).

Obviously, not all convicts with a commuted sentence could be transported, and those sentenced to death were not always executed immediately. Consequently, there was severe overcrowding in local prisons and lockups. In England, the solution to this problem was the use of decommissioned warships as prisons. Frequently referred to as floating hells, hulks were initially modified for "temporary" use as prisons after the American colonies achieved independence in 1775. They remained in service for over 80 years, far beyond the time originally intended. The conditions on these vessels were disgusting. In addition, they were full of people who did not belong there: the mentally ill, the sick, the poor, vagrants, the infirm, women, and even illegitimate children as young as two years old were incarcerated in hulks. Not surprisingly, one out of every four convicts died (Blanchfield 1985).

Given the emphasis on physical punishment throughout this period, the use of imprisonment as punishment was rare. Those who were incarcerated were held in the dungeons of old castles constructed during the Middle Ages, the archetype being Newgate in London, which was originally constructed as a city "gatehouse" in the 12th century. The dungeons were dark, damp, filthy, crawling with vermin, and ridden with disease. There was no attempt to segregate or classify prisoners by sex, age, or gravity of crime; women, children, civil debtors, first-time offenders, repeat offenders, and hardened criminals all shared the same cell (James 1990).

During the 16th century, cities in England became crowded with peasants who had been thrown off their land without any other means to support themselves. While some were treated and punished as criminals, others were sent to early correctional institutions— **bridewells** and workhouses (see Chapter 1). Bridewells quickly gained popularity and, within a short period of time, were located in every county (James 1990). Workhouses were established with similar goals but they were for the urban poor. However, for prisoners in these institutions work was hard to come by. Within a few decades, a seemingly humanitarian attempt to deal with convicts degenerated to the point where the conditions of bridewells and workhouses resembled those found in common jails and debtors prisons (James 1990).

The deplorable conditions of bridewells and workhouses in England did not prevent their adoption in Canada. The first bridewell opened in Halifax in 1758. In 1936, Williams (cited in Carrigan 1991, 306) observed that the bridewell was to house "all disorderly and idle persons, such as drunkards, persons of lewd behaviour, vagabonds, runaways, stubborn servants and children, and persons who failed to support their families." The conditions of the bridewell at Halifax quickly resembled those in England (see Box 6.1).

BOX 6.1 **The Bridewell at Halifax**

The Bridewell was constructed of wood and was thirty feet wide by forty feet long. The motley array of inhabitants, combined with the lack of sanitation and proper ventilation, quickly made the jail unfit for human habitation. A nauseating stench from vomit and human waste permeated the building. It was too hot in summer and too cold in winter. Though punishment enough, jail conditions were not the only misery criminals had to endure. Thieves were usually given thirty-nine stripes before being incarcerated for up to one year. Prostitutes and drunks did a stint in stocks before being sent to jail, usually for three months. In addition, each inmate received ten lashes on admission to jail. In keeping with this general attitude toward criminals, little concern was given to their health during incarceration. Their diet was sparse, consisting usually of bread and molasses tea. Sleeping on vermin-infested straw mattresses laid on damp floors, prisoners sometimes became ill. Seldom did they get the benefit of medical attention.

SOURCE: Carrigan 1991, 306. Reprinted with the permission of Oxford University Press.

Convicts in the colonies were also housed in county jails and city lockups. Like in bridewells, conditions in these jails were disgusting and cruel. Although the application of the law and the treatment of inmates varied across the colonies, the brutality of justice remained a dominant theme. As well, convicts were expected to pay for their meals and were required to pay the jailer for his services upon release. Inmates without means remained imprisoned until someone, such as a family member, paid their way out or they were given permission to leave the jail in order to beg for money. Generally, debtors received superior treatment than convicts. They were allowed outdoors for exercise, could receive packages of food and clothing, and were not subjected to physical abuse (Carrigan 1991). Apparently, the distinction between the punishment of what are now considered white-collar offenders and street criminals was established very early in Canada.

For the most part, 18th-century Canadian jails were holding tanks for offenders waiting to be tried, punished, or executed. The worst features of prisons on the east coast were adopted in Upper and Lower Canada, thus the conditions of jails and lockups were no better in the other colonies than in Nova Scotia. The prison at Montreal was noted for its small cells, 12 square feet (1.12 square metre), inadequate heating and bedding, and an abusive jailer (Carrigan 1991).

The notion that offenders could be reformed through industry, education, and religious instruction was promoted in bridewells and workhouses; however, it was unable to compete with that of punitive deterrence, which remained popular well into the late 18th century. Corporal punishment, the most popular being public flogging, was inflicted even for the most minor offences. For example, a Charlottetown man received 39 lashings in three different locations for theft. Similarly, capital punishment was applied unsparingly to a broad spectrum of offenders. In Montreal, at least 44 men were hanged for a variety of offences including sacrilege and petty theft (Carrigan 1991). When combined with an uneducated and untrained judiciary, the dispensing of justice in the colonies was arbitrary, capricious, and brutal.

THE INFLUENCE OF THE ENLIGHTENMENT ON CRIME AND PUNISHMENT

By the late 18th century in England and France, the ability of corporal or capital punishment to deter was questioned by governments and reformers alike. That thieves and pickpockets were known to practice their trades during public executions severely challenged the "deterrence through punishment" approach to crime. Moreover, by then public support for corporal and capital punishment had declined substantially (Foucault 1977).

As punishment became less focused on the body, the social response to crime became influenced by Enlightenment philosophers. At the core of this philosophy are the classical school principles of free will, hedonism, and the **social contract**. As noted in Chapter 1, these ideas were expressed in Cesare Beccaria's 1764 treatise *On Crimes and Punishments*. Beccaria argued that punishment was justified only to protect the social contract and to deter future transgressions in behaviour. As such, punishment was to be proportional to the crime (Beccaria [1764] 1963).

Not surprisingly, the decline of corporal and capital punishment in England led to overcrowding and deplorable prison conditions. This promoted John Howard (1726–1790) to call for major penal reforms (see Chapter 1). Many of his ideas were presented in his 1777 treatise *The State of Prisons in England and Wales with Preliminary Observations and an Account of Some Foreign Prisons*. Howard's recommendations resulted in several major reforms to the use of prisons, not the least of which included separate cells for sleeping, the segregation of men from women and children, the abolition of the fee system, and the provision of sanitation systems (Blanchfield 1985).

Many of Howard's recommendations for reform were adopted by British Parliament and enshrined in the *Penitentiary Act* of 1779. Subsequently, Howard's initiatives were embodied in the first penitentiary. In addition, Howard's recommendations were embraced by the English philosopher Jeremy Bentham, who developed the **panopticon** prison in 1787. The panopticon, Greek for "all-seeing," was designed to give offenders the chance to reflect on their criminal behaviour so that they might become model citizens in the future. The original design was a four-storey structure, with a central observation tower encircled by all of the cells. The intent was to provide constant surveillance of prisoners without the prisoner ever being aware of being observed. The structure was to be built out of brick and cast iron, which made it fireproof. It included separate cells with individual sanitation, a glass roof, and ventilation and heating ducts (Bowker 1982).

The Emergence of the Penitentiary

Although a pure version of the panopticon was never built, long-term penitentiaries based on the concept appeared in the U.S. shortly after the War of Independence in 1776. Millbank, Britain's first **penitentiary**, opened several decades later in 1816 (McGowen 1995). The physical design of the penitentiary served to enhance what James (1990, 10) identifies as a "trio of penal regimes . . . solitude, separation and silence." Influenced by the dominant religious practices of the day, these regimes formed the ideological base for the control and punishment of inmates based on two different models of American penitentiary. The **Pennsylvania model** called for the total isolation of prisoners day and night. Prisoners had no contact with the outside world whatsoever and even work duties were completed in isolation. Through religious instruction, the trio of penal regimes intended to provide the prisoner the opportunity to reflect on past actions, seek forgiveness from God, and return to society a changed and reformed person.

Based on the State Penitentiary at Auburn, New York, the **Auburn model** also called for the isolation of prisoners at night, but by day prisoners laboured and ate together. Here, too, silence was enforced at all times for fear that more hardened criminals would contaminate less serious criminals (Taylor 1988). Another feature of the Auburn model was the belief that it could be self-sufficient, which may explain why the first penitentiary that opened at Kingston in 1835 emphasized this model (Baehre 1977). However, the moral education element of the Philadelphia system also figured into the reform of offenders at Kingston and the other Canadian penitentiaries to follow.

Although the conditions that led to the construction of Kingston Penitentiary are the subject of much debate, it is clear that there was a hardening of public attitudes towards crime between the late 1700s and the 1830s. Bellomo (1972) points out that a common sentence for assault in the early 1800s was a small fine. However, by 1840 a similar offence could result in two years' imprisonment as apprehension towards the dangerous classes grew. In addition, the decline of corporal and capital punishment may have necessitated the construction of the penitentiary as local jails were overcrowded and otherwise ill equipped to deal with the growing number of offenders. This was exacerbated by a dramatic increase in prisoner populations. Living conditions in prisons were deplorable and prisoners were often indiscriminately housed together. Finally, there was a growing belief in society that the moral architecture of the penitentiary (Taylor 1988) would lead to the reform of offenders (also see Chapter 2 for further discussion). Rothman (1971, 82–83) observes:

> The penitentiary, free of corruptions and dedicated to the proper training of the inmate, would inculcate the discipline that negligent parents, evil companions, taverns, houses of prostitution, theaters, and gambling halls had destroyed. Just as the criminal's environment had led him into crime, the institutional environment would lead him out of it.

PUNISHMENT AND PENITENCE: 1830–1867

In theory, the penitentiary was to bring about the reform of offenders through punishment and discipline. At the time, criminals were thought to be lazy and idle, and thus required regular work schedules and the inculcation of good work habits. Beattie (1977, 4) observes that "men fell into crime because they had not learned the personal and social discipline that religion imparted and had not learned to curb their baser instincts."[2] Thus, each prisoner was to be isolated and his spirit broken through rigid discipline and punishment. Only then could his passions be tamed and his reform achieved (Beattie 1977). Discipline was accomplished through enforcement of rules and regulations. A quasi-military approach was applied to daily activities, which were controlled by the ringing of bells. When needed, punishment included a variety of corporal measures, which were swift, brutal, and frequent. In 1845, the slightly fewer than 500 convicts in Kingston received 2,102 official punishments. This figure increased to 6,063 by 1847 (Shoom 1966). Many of these punishments were administered to the few women and children also housed in Kingston (see Table 2.1 in Chapter 2 for examples of the corporal punishment in use in 1843).

Despite the frequent and often brutal punishment of prisoners, the ability of the penitentiary to discipline and reform remained questionable. It had failed to impose discipline or to break the spirits of the prisoners. The severe and incessant punishment appeared to have defeated the purpose of the penitentiary as indicated in high rates of recidivism, 25 percent by 1841 (Baehre 1977), and an increase in the population of the penitentiary from 55 in 1835 to 454 in 1848. This growth outstripped increases in the general population over the same time (Beattie 1977).

Following the recommendations of the Brown Commission in 1848 (see Chapter 2), the application of corporal punishment was curtailed but remained on the books until its abolishment in 1972 (Correctional Service of Canada 1998). As well, there was an attempt to segregate young and first-time offenders from the general population and the rules surrounding isolation and silence were relaxed. The Commission also supported the notion of convict labour to offset institutional expenses, despite protests from trade groups in the community that prison labour interfered with the market system (Palmer 1980). Despite the apparent failure of the penitentiary to discipline and reform, its underlying philosophy was never challenged. In fact, the penitentiary was to serve as a model for society by encouraging temperance and clean living habits and by providing moral and religious instruction (Rothman 1971).

PUNISHMENT IN WESTERN CANADA

Although detailed information is lacking, the need for prisons and penitentiaries in Rupert's Land emerged in the early 19th century. At Red River, Manitoba, the pressing need for a jail was noted in 1812 (James 1978/79). Under the administration of the Hudson's Bay Company, a single-floor, two-room prison finally opened in 1835 at Upper Fort Garry, which was replaced by a more permanent limestone structure eight years later (Anderson 1960). Two jails were constructed in neighbouring Saskatchewan in 1886, one in Regina and the other in Prince Albert (Ekstedt and Griffiths 1988). Further west, in 1852 the Hudson's Bay Company opened a small barracks for prisoners at Fort Victoria on the Colony of Vancouver Island (Doherty and Ekstedt 1991). Similar structures soon appeared throughout the west as European settlers established cities and towns. Estimates place the number of provincial institutions at 104 in 1887 (Department of Justice 1883–1897). This number had increased to 140 by 1897 but like in the colonial jails that preceded them, conditions were harsh and none held more than a couple of dozen prisoners at a time (Zubrycki 1980). By the late 19th century, workhouses in Nova Scotia had deteriorated to the point where they were unfit for human beings.

Punishment and Penitence: 1867–1938

Despite proof of effectiveness, faith in the penitentiary led to the construction of four new institutions shortly after Confederation: St. Vincent de Paul, Quebec, 1877; Stoney Mountain, Manitoba, 1877; British Columbia Penitentiary, 1878; and Dorchester, New Brunswick, 1880 (Curtis et al. 1985; also see Box 2.3 in Chapter 2). The practice of housing offenders sentenced to more than two years' imprisonment in penitentiaries started in 1841 in Upper Canada and was codified with the enactment of the *British North America Act* in 1867, now the *Constitution Act* in 1982. At this time, the provinces were given legislative jurisdiction over offenders sentenced to less than two years. Although the reasons for this split in corrections have been the subject of much debate, to date 11 governmental reviews have failed to introduce any significant changes to this arrangement (Solicitor General Canada 1996).

Although comprehensive data and more consistent methods of collecting corrections statistics were not available until later in the 19th century, estimates place the number of offenders in federal penitentiaries at approximately 1,400 per year from the early 1880s to late 1890s (Department of Justice 1883–1897). By this time, faith in the penitentiary to reform the morals of offenders had started to decline. Instead, attention shifted to the social causes of crime—lack of self-discipline, poor parenting, and intemperance—and the conditions within penitentiaries that mitigated against the reform of offenders. Corrections had adopted a **social hygiene model** of reform. Accordingly, accommodations for the small population of women in Kingston Penitentiary was established in 1853 but truly separate facilities within Kingston did not open until 1913. As well, an asylum for the criminally insane was opened in the 1880s; however, there were major concerns about the haphazard mixing of offenders due to lack of proper classification procedures.

Although, at 15 to 20 percent, recidivism rates were low by today's standards, the idea that prisons were "high universities" in crime led to repeated requests for the congregate or **Crofton system** (Department of Justice 1883–1897). Comparable to the Auburn system, the Crofton system emphasized the separation of offenders, but it elaborated on the concept of discipline by providing rewards as well as punishments. Zubrycki (1980) points out that the eventual adoption of the Crofton system in the late 19th century was based on the notion of producing compliant and obedient workers during their incarceration and after their release. Hailed as one of the first "scientific" developments in penology, the Crofton system influenced the development of earned remission (parole) and the eventual enactment of the *Ticket of Leave Act* in 1899.

Throughout much of the early 20th century, the populations of both federal penitentiaries and provincial institutions remained fairly stable. As indicated in Appendix A,
increases in federal populations can be attributed to increases in the general population and
the associated construction of new penitentiaries in Saskatchewan earlier in the century and
Collins Bay in 1931. Similar growth patterns were experienced in provincial corrections; however detailed information is lacking. Topping (1929) notes that in 1927 the provinces controlled 149 of the 158 correctional institutions in operation.

The stable population trend changed in the late 1920s, a time marked by a severe economic downturn with the onset of the Great Depression in 1929. Along with an increase
in crime, the apparent failure of penal reform measures as indicated by an increase in
recidivism rates prompted the Superintendent of Penitentiaries to recommend the total
isolation of habitual offenders from younger and "redeemable" offenders (Department of
Justice 1927). It had long been recognized that many offenders were destitute on arrival at
the penitentiary gates. In 1927, over 25 percent of new arrivals to penitentiaries required
medical attention and were unfit to perform ordinary work tasks. In addition, inmate illit-
eracy was estimated at upwards of 30 percent and those who could read and write had
limited capability. The delivery of physical and mental services were improved and the
focus of offender reform shifted to include instruction in personal hygiene, clean living
habits, and basic education. So strong was the belief that the cause of crime was rooted in
the offender's social environment that it was attributed to the downfall of 85 percent of
arrivals at Canadian penitentiaries.

Much to the surprise of penitentiary officials, however, attempts to segregate younger
offenders did not have any appreciable impact on the type of offender admitted, nor did the
remuneration for work carried out in the institution (Department of Justice 1936). Conditions
in federal penitentiaries deteriorated rapidly in the 1930s to the point where several riots
forced officials to re-examine the social hygiene approach to reform. These problems led to
the formation of the Royal Commission to Investigate the Penal System in Canada headed
by Justice J. Archambault. One of the recommendations made by the committee was that
incarceration should contribute to the reform of offenders, and not just the short-term protection of society through punishment (Archambault 1938). Ironically, this approach would
set corrections at odds with itself as it simultaneously attempted to punish and treat offenders. The resulting "control care dialectic" remains at the core of much controversy surrounding corrections today (Goff 1999).

Rehabilitation: 1938–1970

The transformation from punishment and penitence to rehabilitation coincided with the
expansion of the **medical model.** In contrast to preceding eras, attention shifted from social
and environmental causes to theories based on individual pathology. Offenders were considered to be suffering from physical, mental, or social illnesses and the institution became a
hospital for those suffering from the disease of crime (Griffiths and Cunningham 1999). In this
context, the importance of proper classification techniques became paramount and extensive evaluation procedures were developed in an effort to place offenders in appropriate
"treatment" programs. Treatment covered a broad range of corrections intervention. At the
social level, programs involving academic, physical, and vocational training were developed. Emphasis was placed on treating offenders for their poor upbringing in order to make

them law-abiding citizens. Individual level treatment included psychotherapy, group counselling, aversion therapy, behaviour modification, and, in some cases, electroconvulsive or shock therapy and plastic surgery for those with facial deformities. Andersen (1993) notes that more than 600 plastic surgery operations were conducted on inmates in Okalla Prison in British Columbia in the hope that it would improve self-esteem and thus reduce recidivism.

Given the medical emphasis of rehabilitation, the importance of the institution as a place of treatment grew well into the 1960s, at which time the number of penitentiaries had grown to 12. Several more federal institutions were constructed later that decade, bringing the total by 1969 to 19 (Posner 1991). Similarly, although the two-year rule meant that sentences in provincial institutions were shorter, many provinces added or upgraded the capacity of existing institutions. Interestingly, the growth in institution construction occurred during this period despite the observation by the Commissioner of Penitentiaries that incarceration was not conducive to reform (Department of Justice 1953). The total number of incarcerated offenders remained roughly proportionate with the general population (see Appendix A), which suggests that incarceration was having little effect on behaviour.

As in the previous era, rehabilitation was fraught with problems. High recidivism rates (40–50 percent) continued to plague institutional corrections. By 1952, there were approximately 14,000 offenders incarcerated in provincial and federal institutions with admissions totalling over 85,000 annually (Department of Justice 1952). The number of inmates in provincial institutions and federal penitentiaries remained fairly constant but admission rates to provincial institutions increased dramatically in the late 1940s (see Appendix A). These trends were evidence of the apparent failure of the medical model. Responding to concerns about the abusive aspects of treatment and high recidivism rates, the Ouimet Committee on corrections recommended that the institution was not the best place for reform (Ouimet 1969). Later, an infamous study on rehabilitation efforts in the U.S. by Martinson (1974) led to the conclusion that "nothing works." Martinson's findings confirmed what was already suspected and corrections was again forced to re-evaluate what it was doing. Rehabilitation was not totally abandoned; rather, following the direction of the Ouimet Committee, it was conjoined with community-based corrections and the notion of reintegration (see Chapter 13).

Reintegration and Opportunity

Following the lead of the Ouimet Committee, the 1970s marked a time of correctional reform including a renewed interest in community-based corrections. Combined with growing dissatisfaction with the rehabilitation model, witnessed by recidivism rates upwards of 80 percent, this shift was also the result of a crisis in Canadian correctional institutions, particularly penitentiaries. Between 1975 and 1976, there were 69 major incidents in federal penitentiaries, four more than for the entire period of 1932 to 1974. They included several "smash-ups" of institutions and 92 hostage-taking incidents, which culminated in the murder of a correctional officer and also one of the hostages. An investigation into these and many other incidents conducted by the Sub-Committee on the Penitentiary System in Canada revealed that the incidents

> were born of anger, frustration and oppression within the tight and unnatural confines of prison over unresolved grievances, transfers, harassment and provocation by both sides (staff and inmates in adversary attitudes) as "mind" games (MacGuigan 1977, 5).

Dissatisfaction with imprisonment was based on the grounds that it had failed to reform or correct offenders and had consequently failed to protect society. In fact, MacGuigan (1977) expressed concern about the potential of incarceration to make non-violent offenders violent and dangerous offenders more dangerous. When combined with the high cost of building and operating prisons, the use of imprisonment for rehabilitation was rejected and the "personal reformation" approach advanced. Under this model, community-based alternatives to incarceration and the provision of aftercare programs for offenders released from institutions were expanded. In essence, offenders were expected to avail themselves of the opportunity to participate in the programs deemed necessary for their rehabilitation. At the heart of this approach was the assumption that offenders needed basic social and living skills in order to lead law-abiding lives and these skills were best provided in the community (Ekstedt and Griffiths 1988). In addition to programs established by the state such as probation and parole, many of the programs were delivered from non-governmental organizations such as the John Howard Society, the Elizabeth Fry Society, and the St. Leonard's Society.

Incarceration was justified for the protection of society and the denunciation of criminal behaviour. Interestingly, the number of adults charged with Criminal Code offences increased a whopping 65 percent, from 197,557 in 1970 to 326,132 in 1978 (Boe and Myara 1993).

As noted previously, however, prison populations remained relatively constant in contrast to the growth in the use of non-custodial sanctions (see Appendix A). In effect, the net of social control had expanded bringing more offenders under control of corrections.

Reparation, Risk Assessment, and Reintegration

As a correctional philosophy, reintegration has enjoyed mixed success. Like other western nations, Canada experienced a gradual shift towards punishment starting in the late 1970s. As a product of a law-and-order philosophy, or "creeping conservatism," this approach emphasizes:

> 1) support for more extensive law enforcement practices; 2) the introduction of increasingly harsher, and more punitive measures; 3) the manipulation of public fear of crime; and 4) an ideological emphasis on individual responsibility, traditional values, morality, and the sanctity of the family (Hatt, Caputo, and Perry 1992, 248).

The return to punishment philosophy was also influenced by several high-profile crimes, including murders committed by offenders released on parole. Members of the public, press, and law enforcement agencies demanded harsher sentences and stricter guidelines for the release of offenders. In 1992, Bill C-36, the *Corrections and Conditional Release Act* (CCRA) introduced changes to the sentencing and **conditional release** of offenders. Under the Act, accelerated review provides for the release of less serious offenders at one third of their sentence. However, for more serious offenders, day parole eligibility has been changed from one sixth of the sentence to six months prior to full parole eligibility date. As well, sentencing judges can now stipulate that more serious offenders serve up to half of their sentence before being eligible for parole. Boe (1992) predicted that the net effect of these changes would be an increase in the number offenders incarcerated in federal institutions. He was correct. Crime rates have gone down but the number of inmates admitted to and incarcerated in correctional institutions increased dramatically during the 1980s and 1990s. For the period of 1989/90 to 1994/95, federal penitentiary populations grew by 22 percent, while the growth of provincial populations was more modest at 12 percent (Boe, Motiuk, and Muirhead 1998). At the provincial level, growth was attributed to increased admissions as sentencing judges handed down more custodial sentences and for longer periods of time. At the federal level, the number of conditional releases granted has decreased. In addition, the number of "lifers," offenders serving life or long sentences for violent crimes, in federal institutions has increased, which reduces the space available for new admissions (Boe, Motiuk, and Muirhead 1998). Although other countries have experienced increases, Canada remains high in comparison to most (see Box 6.2).

A significant issue emerges from conservative criminal justice policies that stress punishment and curtail conditional release: **overcrowding**. By the early 1990s, approximately 40 percent of federal institutions had experienced overcrowding (Posner 1991), as did many institutions at the provincial/territorial level. According to the Solicitor General of Canada (1997), British Columbia, Alberta, Saskatchewan, Manitoba, Ontario, New Brunswick, Newfoundland, and Labrador have reported significant increases in correctional institution populations. Prison populations peaked in 1995 and have declined slightly since then. For 1997/98, the number of offenders sentenced to federal and provincial/territorial institutions declined by 3.4 percent and 6.2 percent respectively. Ironically, this trend is associated with lower crime rates and not the result of release policies contained in the CCRA (O'Neill 1999). Unfortunately, at the federal level, incarceration rates for Aboriginal people have actually increased slightly during this same period. As noted below, Aboriginal people continue to be over-represented in the criminal justice system.

Whether the decline in prison populations will have any impact on overcrowding is unclear; however, the Solicitor General of Canada (1997) suggests that growth in prison populations and overcrowding will continue to plague many correctional institutions in the future. One response to this issue is to construct new prisons. However, Canada has been reluctant to follow the U.S. example of expansive prison construction for two reasons. First, correctional institutions are expensive to build and maintain and, as indicated thus far, are not always conducive to reform. For 1994/95, corrections expenditures accounted for $1.98 billion of the $9.94 billion total allotted to justice spending. Slightly over 50 percent ($97 million) of this amount went to the provinces and territories (Canadian Centre for Justice Statistics 1997). In 1995/96, the annual average cost for housing an offender in a federal institution was $50,375, ranging from a low of $32,811 for community corrections centres to $74,965 for women's institutions (Solicitor General of Canada 1997). Annual costs for provincial offenders also vary. For example, the per diem cost for offenders in Ontario institutions averages $125 or $45,625 annually (Attorney General of Ontario 1998), while the per diem cost in Saskatchewan is $95 or $23,725 annually (Watson 1999).

BOX 6.2	International Incarceration Rates per 100,000 for Selected Countries, 1998–1999		
Russian Federation	685	Switzerland	90
United States	645	Austria	85
England and Wales	125	Italy	85
Scotland	120	Denmark	65
Canada	115	Finland	55
France	90	Norway	55
Germany	90	SOURCE: Walmsley 1999.	

Currently, the Correctional Service of Canada operates 64 institutions in five regions: 10 maximum security institutions, 20 medium security institutions, 12 minimum security institutions, 7 women's institutions, and 15 community correctional centres, also minimum security. Exchange of service agreements between the various provinces and the federal government provide shared responsibility for women's institutions (Solicitor General of Canada 1997). At the provincial/territorial level, there are 151 adult correctional institutions ranging from minimum security work camps to maximum security prisons (see Table 6.2) (Canadian Centre for Justice Statistics 1998).

The second factor limiting the construction of new facilities is the continuing trend toward reintegration. Public demand for punishment has been offset by the growth of community-based sentencing options, which started in the 1970s (see Table 6.3). However, the placement of offenders in community-based programs is based on more sophisticated assessment techniques. The Correctional Service has developed risk assessment techniques to identify the criminogenic factors associated with an offender's criminal behaviour. Offenders can then access the specific "core" programs necessary to deal with those factors. These programs target domains tied to conventional behaviour, but are not limited to the value of employment, supportive marital and family relations, positive peer associates, living without substance abuse, community functioning or living skills, being in control of one's life (personal and emotional), and law-abiding attitudes (Motiuk 1998).

TABLE 6.2	Provincial Institutions[a]		
Newfoundland	6	Manitoba	8
Nova Scotia	9	Saskatchewan	15
New Brunswick	10	Alberta	10
Prince Edward Island	2	British Columbia	19
Quebec	19	Yukon Territories	2
Ontario	47	Northwest Territories	4

[a] Does not include municipal jails, city lockups, or community training residences.

SOURCE: Canadian Centre for Justice Statistics 1999, adapted from *Juristat*, Catalogue No. 85-002.

TABLE 6.3	Total Admissions to Canadian Corrections, 1990–1991 and 1995–1996			
Types of Admissions	**Year**	**Provincial**	**Federal**	**Total**
Custodial	1990/91	207,946	4,296	212,242
	1995/96	230,330	4,402	234,732
Non-custodial	1990/91	70,428	5,423	75,851
	1995/96	82,252	7,724	89,976
Total	1990/91	278,374	9,719	288,093
	1995/96	312,582	12,126	324,708
Percentage Change	Custodial	10.8	2.5	10.6
1990/91 to 1995/96	Non-custodial	16.8	42.4	18.6
	Total	12.3	24.8	12.7

SOURCE: Solicitor General of Canada 1997. Reproduced with the permission of the Minister of Public Works and Government Services Canada, 2000.

Community-based sentences are more commonly intended for less serious types of offences. However, due to the increasing costs associated with incarceration, they are chosen over a wider range of offences. The provinces and territories are following the lead of the Correctional Service and developing similar core programs that deal with cognitive skills, anger management, family violence, substance abuse, education, and sex offending. Limited resources are reserved for high-risk offenders who are also exposed to core programs such as British Columbia's Breaking Barriers. This motivation program emphasizes that change is not only possible but necessary for law-abiding behaviour in the community (Johnson 1998).

A PROFILE OF INMATES IN CANADIAN CORRECTIONAL FACILITIES

Recent census research in 1996 on incarcerated offenders in both federal and provincial/territorial facilities reveals that inmates are more likely to be young, male, and Aboriginal. In addition, inmates are less likely to be married, more likely to have fewer years of schooling, and less likely to be employed at the time of their admission to correctional facilities. In 1996, the median age in the general population was 41. In federal institutions, in contrast, the median age was 34 and in provincial/territorial prisons it was 31. While Aboriginal people constituted only 2 percent of the general population, they represented 18 percent of the population in provincial/territorial prisons and 14 percent of the population in federal facilities. The over-representation of Aboriginal people in correctional facilities was most pronounced in the western provinces. For example, Aboriginal people comprise more than 50 percent of the population in Manitoba prisons (Solicitor General of Canada 1998). Where information on education was available, 36 percent of inmates had not achieved more than a grade 9 education. More than half (52 percent) of inmates were unemployed at time of admission and fewer than one third were married. Almost half (49 percent) of all inmates were incarcerated for committing crimes against the person; significantly, 73 percent of federal inmates and 33 percent of provincial/territorial inmates had committed a crime against the person. Not surprisingly, the majority (83 percent) of provincial/territorial inmates had at least one previous criminal conviction. Finally, where information was available, nearly one half (49 percent) of inmates in provincial/territorial prisons were "at risk" of re-offending. Risk was determined by combining needs factors, including employment stability and substance abuse, with criminal history factors such as prior failure on release and previous convictions. (See Appendix B for selected characteristics of inmates.)

New Facilities and the Privatization of Corrections

The correctional philosophies of retribution and reintegration work at cross purposes. Corrections must constantly negotiate the boundaries of punishment and reform, which are influenced by its operational and policy environment. In many cases, community-based sanctions are favoured over incarceration; however, there remain certain groups of offenders who will require incarceration, whether for the protection of the public or for the denunciation of abhorrent criminal behaviour. Given public and political pressures and the growing population, there is a real need for new correctional facilities in both federal and provincial/territorial jurisdictions. However, several issues must be considered with regard to the design of new facilities or the renovation of existing institutions, and their placement in the community.

At the federal level, in the 1950s the Correctional Service of Canada started to move away from the penitentiary model or "big house" towards the "campus" model (Posner 1991).

The most recent development is the reconstruction of William Head Institution (WHI) at Victoria, B.C. In contrast to the prison, jail, or campus model, the design of WHI reflects a residential environment that emphasizes positive dynamic interactions between residents and staff. The anticipated result is the instillation of pro-social values in offenders through the normalization of the institutional environment. **Normalization** is achieved through a community design, which is composed of several neighbourhoods made up of residential units. Each unit contains five or six residents, each with a separate room. Although research on the effectiveness of WHI is yet to be conducted, former manager R. Scott has observed that recidivism rates appear lower than other medium security institutions in the region (Scott 1998).

A less formal design has also been used in the construction of new facilities for women. Traditionally, women offenders have been under-represented in both provincial and federal corrections. They have lacked relevant programs and when sentenced to federal institutions have had to relocate to the Prison for Women (P4W) at Kingston. In 1864, there were approximately 60 women in P4W. In 1996, there were approximately 360 women in federal institutions and 1,658 in provincial facilities. Taken together, women still comprise roughly less than 10 percent of incarcerated offenders (Canadian Centre for Justice Statistics 1998). A few years earlier, although 64 percent of women in federal institutions were serving time for crimes against the person (Canadian Centre for Justice Statistics 1998), the majority of women—88 percent—in provincial/territorial facilities were charged and convicted of non-violent offenses (Canadian Centre for Justice Statistics 1995).

Starting in 1973, exchange of service agreements between the federal and provincial governments provided that some federally sentenced women offenders be housed in provincial facilities. By the 1980s, a similar type of agreement resulted in the construction of regional facilities and the proposed closure of P4W. Construction of the new facilities began in the early 1990s in all regions except the Pacific, where the Burnaby Correctional Centre for Women was already established. The new sites are in Truro, Nova Scotia; Kitchener, Ontario; Joliette, Quebec; Edmonton, Alberta; and the Maple Creek healing lodge for Aboriginal women at Nakaneet, Saskatchewan. The rationale behind the construction of these facilities was to reduce the distance between women offenders and their families and to improve the quality of and access to programming designed to meet the specific needs of women offenders (Leblanc 1994). Ultimately, this approach would also aid in reintegration because women would be less isolated from their support networks in their home community.

Regardless of the type of inmate, the location of new institutions is often the subject of heated controversy (Young 1998; 1999). Although the current public demand for punishment is tempered with reintegration, new institutions are currently under construction in several jurisdictions. Community acceptance or resistance of construction, however, is difficult to predict. Recently, several Ontario communities competed for the construction of a prison in their neighbourhood because the prison ostensibly provides economic benefits in terms of jobs and services. The Ontario government is building new high-volume prisons and retrofitting older institutions. The new "ultra efficient" institutions will hold more inmates than conventional prisons (up to 5,000) with fewer staff. It is believed that this approach will free up resources for rehabilitation programs (Attorney General of Ontario 1998). Alternatively, in British Columbia, the **NIMBY** (not in my back yard) **syndrome** led to the termination of the construction of two new prisons in 1996. The host communities voiced concern that prisons increased citizens' risk of criminal victimization and had a negative impact on property values. Community resistance was eventually overcome after the provincial government presented research documenting the positive attitudes and experiences of citizens living in close proximity to prisons in British Columbia (Young 1998; 1999).

The high costs of constructing and operating prisons have led some jurisdictions to consider the option of **privatization**. In addition to financial savings, the supposed benefits from private prisons include insulation from political pressure and the infusion of new people and ideas into the institutional context. Drawbacks include concerns that the profit motive will be an incentive to build more prisons and that the quality of services may decline if a profit is not realized from operation. Moreover, there is a risk that a company or group of companies may monopolize services, resulting in decreased government control. Schlosser (1998) points out that private prisons in the U.S. are managing increasing numbers and volumes of inmates. He says the rise of the "prison-industrial complex" represents a cash cow and not a concerted effort to prevent crime or rehabilitate offenders.

In Canada, non-profit and volunteer agencies, such as the John Howard Society and the Elizabeth Fry Society, deliver programs in correctional facilities and the community; many private agencies also supply goods and services within institutions such as health care (John Howard Society of Alberta 1992). Unlike in the U.S. and England, however, the construction and operation of private prisons have not occurred in Canada, with the exception of Nova Scotia, which entered into a partnership with a private consortium in 1996 with the aim of improving its adult jail system. This is not the first attempt by the province to privatize a corrections institution; the youth correctional facility at Halifax is fully operated by a non-profit organization (Honsberger 1998).

Whether prisons are private or public, ultimately the state is accountable to the public for safety and responsible for the well-being of inmates. Generally, most Canadians find something inherently wrong with the idea of punishment for profit but this may change if public demand for punishment continues in the face of decreased government revenues. However, there is a lesson to be learned from the U.S. experience; the prison-industrial complex is now a multibillion dollar industry with its own political, bureaucratic, and economic interests, which encourage growth regardless of demand. Currently, the state of California has several institutions that hold more than 6,000 inmates. Plans are underway for the construction of new "mega-prisons" with an estimated capacity of 20,000 inmates. If, as Schlosser (1998) argues, private prisons are factories for crime, the privatization of prisons without government control will add to human suffering, not alleviate it.

Privatization of Prisons

Private sector involvement in corrections can be traced to the early days of the penitentiary. Along with the goals of penitence and prevention of idleness, hard labour was expected to offset the costs of incarceration. Originally, inmates engaged in manual labour such as construction and farming to maintain the prison. Within a short time, however, inmates were contracted or leased to private employers. Social reformers criticized this as slave labour and labour unions felt it was unfair to ordinary workers. Eventually, inmate labour was confined to institution maintenance and government contracts with the enactment of the *Penitentiary Act* of 1906 (Gandy and Hurl 1987).

Interest in prison industries re-emerged in Canada during the 1950s, when it was assumed that work facilitated rehabilitation, reduced recidivism, and encouraged institutional stability. By the 1970s, prison industries in many western nations began to return to institutions, although private sector involvement in Canadian institutions was limited (Gandy and Hurl 1987). In the 1980s, with an economic recession, increasing crime rates, and a hardening of public attitudes towards the punishment of offenders, there was an unprecedented drive to reduce government spending and decentralize government. Along with many other government functions, corrections became the target of private sector interests. The privatization of government-controlled industries, agencies, and services, including prisons, received enthusiastic political endorsement in the U.S. and the U.K. under the Reagan and Thatcher governments (Ryan and Ward 1989). According to Easton (1998), in 1996 there were 17 management firms housing more than 85,000 offenders in 119 private prisons in Australia (6), Canada (1), the U.K. (6) and the U.S. (106). Not surprisingly, this number has increased significantly, with the U.S. alone now accounting for more than 90,000 inmates in some 27 states nation-wide (Schlosser 1998).

In the United States, the origin of privatized prisons can be traced to contracts awarded by the Immigration and Naturalization Service and the Marshals Service to small private firms during the early 1980s. The first significant federal contract occurred in 1985 when the Corrections Corporation of America was contracted by the Immigration and Naturalization Service to manage the Houston Processing Center. In the same year, the first state-level contract was established between Kentucky and the United States Corrections Corporation (Thomas 1998). The U.K. was slower to develop the option of privatized prisons and its first privately managed remand institution opened in 1992 at Wolds. By the mid 1990s, the U.K. had five correctional institutions that were either privately constructed or managed. Ultimately, the government intends to have at least 10 percent of prisons (13) managed by the private sector (Wilson 1998).

Arguments For and Against Privatization of Prisons

Arguments favouring privatization generally turn on economic, operational, and administrative efficiency. The general advantages of privatization include:

1. On average, they are 10 percent less costly than government-run institutions;
2. Reduced bureaucracy allows flexibility and the capacity to implement new ideas faster;
3. Public consultation is not required prior to construction;
4. The government can stipulate what is required of the contractor;
5. Overcrowding of other (public) institutions can be reduced; and
6. The company assumes the risk for unoccupied space during times of reduced inmate populations (John Howard Society of Alberta 1992).

Despite the perceived advantages, privatized prisons present a myriad of difficult issues. The provision of punishment for profit is controversial and the profit motive has actually proved to be an incentive to build more prisons. The Corrections Corporation of America, the largest private corrections corporation in the U.S., is in the process of building three prisons in California without a contract to fill them (Schlosser 1998). Corporation officials are confident that once constructed, these prisons will be filled.

Comparisons between the effectiveness of private and public institutions are difficult to make. A recent study on cost-effectiveness and quality of services between private and public prisons in Tennessee found that private prisons were slightly less expensive and provided higher quality service. However, private prisons outperformed public prisons by only a slight margin and both kinds of institutions scored higher in comparison to prisons elsewhere in the U.S. (Thomas 1998). Other research on the performance of private prisons in New Mexico indicated similar positive results. Logan (1992) found that the privatized prison for women provided higher quality services than the public prison it replaced. As indicated in Box 6.3, however, research indicating the efficiency of private prisons may be the exception, not the rule.

Determining the efficiency and effectiveness of private prisons is complicated by several factors. According to Thomas (1998), standards vary from state to state and this is further complicated by the three levels of prisons operating in the U.S. (county, state, and federal). Initially, private institutions in the U.S. operated without legislative guidelines but a series of problems including guard-to-inmate brutality and prisoner escapes forced state governments to enact legislation on private prisons (Schlosser 1998). For example, in Texas, two escapees from a facility run by the Corrections Corporation of America in Houston could not be charged with escape because it was not unlawful to escape from a private prison. In another setting, an investigation into the conditions of Dickens County Prison in Texas operated by the Bobby Ross Group found that inmates were going for days without food or medical attention. As a result of these and other problems, many states have introduced separate statutes governing the establishment and operation of private prisons.

The issues extend beyond assessing cost-effectiveness and efficiency. While it is not the norm for privatized prisons, the Texas example illustrates the potential for abuse of prisoners' basic human rights, a concern taken seriously by the American Civil Liberties Union (ACLU). In addition to state legislation, Schlosser (1998) points out that the ACLU has established safeguards for prisoners, including guidelines for inmate labour. These are not legally binding, but they should nonetheless bring attention to the issues surrounding private prisons. For example, an investigation into United States Corrections Corporation's misuse of inmate labour in Kentucky revealed that the company benefited from unpaid inmate labour (Schlosser 1998).

| **BOX 6.3** | **Fresh Doubts Cast on U.S. Private Prisons** |

Claims made for the benefits of private prisons in the U.S. have been seriously undermined by the findings of a new report. The General Accounting Office (GAO) of the U.S. federal government has analyzed five recent studies comparing the operational costs and quality of service in public and private prisons. The GAO's report, published on August 16, 1996, found:

• No conclusions about cost savings or quality of service could be drawn as four studies assessing operational costs indicated little difference or mixed results;

• Two studies that addressed quality of life reported equivocal findings or no differences between private and public facilities;

• The studies provided little information that could be applied to different correctional settings, since states may differ widely in terms of correctional philosophy, economic factors, and inmate population characteristics.

SOURCE: Fresh Doubts Cast on U.S. Private Prisons 1996.

Currently, in most states legislation governing the operation of private prisons provides clear guidelines for both state and private company liability. However, in the event that market conditions force private corporations into bankruptcy, the state will, by default, be held responsible for the care and control of offenders (John Howard Society of Alberta 1992). This is unlikely to occur in the near future, given the current rate of incarceration and the associated growth in privatized corrections. Moreover, private prisons employ "bed brokers" who search for inmates to fill spaces in private prisons lacking "clients" (Schlosser 1998). This practice is analogous to the Transportation of offenders from England to penal colonies in the 18th century.

To date, private sector involvement in Canadian corrections has been limited to contracting of services (e.g., community attendance centres, community residential centres, food services). On the one hand, contracting is considered cost effective and administratively efficient. Competition among contractors results in value for money, and private sector companies can respond quickly to demands for changes in the delivery of services. On the other hand, private sector companies lack the same level of accountability as the public sector; competition may lead to cost cutting and a decline in service quality. In addition, there is no protection for companies during times of "market instability" (e.g., during government cutbacks), leaving them vulnerable to economic forces, which, in turn, threaten service delivery (John Howard Society of Alberta 1992). Moreover, although limited, the Canadian experience with private prisons has produced mixed results. As a privatized pilot project, the Miramichi Youth Facility in New Brunswick seems a limited success, but cost overruns and hidden expenses belie the anticipated savings (New Brunswick, New Conflict 1997). As suggested in Box 6.4, other efforts have met with less success.

American experience shows that the privatization of prisons brings new problems. In addition to the issues already raised, privatized prisons threaten the job security of public

---

BOX 6.4	**Boot Camp Debacle**

The official opening by the Solicitor General on 28 August of Ontario's first private prison, the Project Turnaround boot camp, was to have been a triumph for the government's get tough on young offenders' strategy. But it turned into an embarrassment when two teenagers escaped the day before—thanks to a bolt of lightening that exposed flaws in the facility's security. Early in the evening of 27 August, two prisoners had been arrested and removed for allegedly assaulting a guard. Later, during a storm, the prison's power supply was shut down and, as there was no backup, all the doors remained unlocked. In the chaos, two prisoners escaped but they were recaptured the next day. The Solicitor General has promised an internal review.

The boot camp is run by Encourage-Youth Corporation Inc. But since the breakout, eight state-employed corrections officers have been drafted in to guard the facility. Opposition politicians have renamed the facility "Camp Getaway." Ontario's Child Advocate has complained about the inappropriate transfer of young offenders away from their schooling and programming at their regular facilities and being brought to the boot camp in order to try and fill the 32 beds.

SOURCE: Boot Camp Debacle 1997.

employees because private prisons typically pay staff less, offer fewer benefits, and are less open to union activity. At same time, privatization expands the net of corrections control. The decision of the Corrections Corporation of America to build prisons in California entirely on speculation is evidence of the confidence held by private companies about the tendency of the criminal justice system to fully utilize available facilities. There are no guarantees that privatized prisons will be any more cost efficient or effective at protecting the public. Given that tax payers are ultimately responsible for the costs involved in housing offenders, the decision to privatize requires a critical assessment of the potential outcomes beyond financial considerations.

SUMMARY

Clearly, the development of prisons and the establishment of the penitentiary were influenced by the humanitarian element of Enlightenment thought. However, the transformation from seemingly barbaric punishments to a calculated formula of punishments under Enlightenment philosophy was also influenced by changes in the political and economic structures of society. On the economies of scale, incarceration was more effective in controlling the growing number of unruly populations suffering from unemployment. Fear of the dangerous classes resulted in pressure on corrections as dominant middle and mid-Victorian class interests demanded harsher penalties for offenders.

Arguably, the humanitarian element associated with early incarceration weaves through the correctional paradigms that have followed punishment and penitence. At the base of any change in corrections philosophy is the anticipated reform of offenders, a humanitarian ideal in corrections. The subtle shift in thinking associated with the post-Confederation period of punishment and penitence transferred the cause of crime, and its cure, from a religious to social base. A religious deficit was replaced by shortcomings in socialization. Not inadvertently, this transformation aligned with a broader social movement to instill social values in the broader population. The influence of the moral architecture of the penitentiary was reaffirmed with the construction of penitentiaries across the country. Ironically, the focus of concern remained on the individual despite the recognition that offenders were products of their environment. Although reduced in status, religion remained a part of this movement because it supported the general drive to sanitize society.

Advances in scientific knowledge, coupled with the dismal success of incarceration to instill pro-social values in offenders, set the stage for the transformation from punishment to rehabilitation in the 1930s. However, the impact of the Great Depression on corrections cannot be overlooked as a contributing factor to the emergence and popularity of the medical model. The progressive individualization of the criminal corresponded well with the focus on individual pathology. Despite the fact that prisons and penitentiaries were increasingly filled with the poor and indignant, an observation that is as true now as it was then, poor economic conditions and high unemployment rates were considered secondary factors to criminal behaviour.

The demise of the medical model is often explained by the failure of corrections, including incarceration, to rehabilitate offenders. However, the shift to reintegration and community-based corrections was also motivated by factors external to corrections itself, such as increases in the crime rate between the 1960s through to the early 1990s. Like other components of the criminal justice system, corrections was forced to respond to public and media criticism that it was not living up to its mandate to protect society. Another shift involved the growth of institutional populations, which forced corrections to explore and develop sentencing options that would allow offenders to remain in their communities while at the same time provide protection to society. Undoubtedly, this approach was influenced by developments in corrections theory and research that underscored the potential damaging effects of incarceration and those aspects of community-based sanctions that facilitate successful reintegration.

The reintegration/opportunity approach to corrections was short lived, but it was pivotal in the transformation to reparation, risk assessment, and reintegration. Reparation enjoys wide support but public attitudes towards reintegration remain cynical. This cynicism manifests itself in the call for harsher penalties, usually in terms of increased use of incarceration for longer periods of time. In addition, public knowledge of risk assessment techniques is generally limited, thus public opinion on conditional release policies is often critical and support is limited.

Since the emergence of the first jails in the colonies, corrections, particularly incarceration, has been the subject of criticism and controversy. Corrections finds itself in the unenviable position of having little or no control of its clientele but having complete responsibility for it. In addition, corrections is subject to governmental authority and external influences over which it may or may not have control. When added to the struggle over control versus care, where corrections is expected to simultaneously punish and reform offenders, corrections operates under competing agendas. The melding of retribution and reintegration that currently guides corrections is clear example of this competition.

Ironically, the number of individuals charged with criminal offences is increasing in the face of falling crime rates. Equally ironic is the fact that at least one half of offenders incarcerated have been convicted of a non-violent offence. Like their 19th-century predecessors, many offenders lack the basic skills to lead law-abiding lives and to function adequately in society. As is evident by the number of offenders sentenced to custodial settings and the high rates of recidivism, retribution does not seem to be an effective or safe correctional option.

There is a potential crisis with regard to institutional corrections. Whether we develop alternative means of punishment or adopt the American "prison binge" approach remains to be seen. Regardless of the paradigm, experience indicates that the latter is neither an effective nor a safe option. However, knowledge of the shortcomings of incarceration tends to be limited to those involved with corrections itself. Educating the public about the realities of incarceration may represent the first step in solving the problem of what to do with criminals.

KEY TERMS AND CONCEPTS

amende honorable	*lex talionis*	penitentiary
Auburn model	medical model	Pennsylvania model
Bloody Code	NIMBYsyndrome	privatization
bridewell	normalization	revenge
conditional release	overcrowding	social contract
Crofton system	panopticon model	social hygiene model
deterrence		

STUDY AND DISCUSSION QUESTIONS

1. How did the punishment of offenders in Europe influence pre-institution corrections in early Canada?
2. What factors led to the emergence of the penitentiary?
3. Identify the two early models of the penitentiary in the U.S. What model did Canada eventually adopt?
4. What are the key features of the various paradigms in Canadian corrections history? Besides punishment, can you identify any of these features in contemporary corrections?
5. What are the positive and negative aspects of privatization in corrections? Should Canadian corrections move towards privatization?
6. Would you approve or disapprove of the construction of a new prison in your community? Why?
7. Using the data in this chapter, speculate on the future of institutional corrections in Canada.
8. Discuss the effectiveness of incarceration. Given the profile of the typical offender, what alternatives to incarceration might be a more effective method of correction?

WEBLINKS

American Correctional Association: **www.corrections.com/aca**

Solicitor General of Canada: **www.gsc-scc.gc.ca**

Statistics Canada: **www.StatCan.CA/english/Pgdb/State/justic.htm**

NOTES

1. The author would like to thank Russel Ogden and Margaret Jackson for their comments on an earlier draft of this paper.
2. It is interesting to note that in early times little to no reference was made of female offenders. This is an issue and area that has only recently, since the 1970s, received notable attention in criminology and criminal justice studies.

REFERENCES

Andersen, E. 1993. *Hard Place to Do Time: The Story of Okalla Prison 1912–1991.* New Westminster: Hillpoint Publishing.

Anderson, F.W. 1960. Prisons and Prison Reforms in the Old Canadian West. *Canadian Journal of Corrections* 2: 209–215.

Archambault, J. (Chairman). 1938. *Report of the Royal Commission to Investigate the Penal System of Canada.* Ottawa: King's Printer.

Attorney General of Ontario. 1998. *Preparing to Prevent.* www.sgcs.gov.on.ca:80/english/fmprevent.htm (May 1999).

Baehre, R. 1977. Origins of the Penitentiary System in Upper Canada. *Ontario History* 69: 185–207.

Beattie, J.M. 1977. *Attitudes Towards Crime and Punishment in Upper Canada, 1830–1850: A Documentary Study.* Toronto: Toronto Centre of Criminology, University of Toronto.

Beccaria, C. [1764] 1963. *On Crimes and Punishment.* Indianapolis: Bobbs-Merrill.

Bellomo, J.J. 1972. Upper Canadian Attitudes Towards Crime and Punishment (1832–1851). *Ontario History* 69: 9–26.

Blanchfield, C. 1985. Crime and Punishment: A Pictorial History. *Let's Talk* 10(7): 1–6.

Boe, R.E. 1992. *CSC Offender Population Forecast for 1993 to 2002.* Ottawa: Correctional Service of Canada.

Boe, R.E., and **A. Myara**. 1993. *Canadian and International Crime and Incarceration Trends, 1962 to 1991: A Compendium of Source Statistics.* Ottawa: Correctional Service of Canada.

Boe, R., **L. Motiuk**, and **M. Muirhead**. 1998. *Recent Trends and Patterns Shaping the Corrections Population in Canada: 1983/84 to 1996/97.* Ottawa: Correctional Service of Canada.

Boot Camp Debacle. 1997. *Prison Reform Trust* 13. www.penlex.org.uk/pages/prtpre13.html (April 2000).

Bowker, L.H. 1982. *Corrections: The Science and the Art.* New York: Macmillan.

Canadian Centre for Justice Statistics. 1995. Canadian Crime Statistics, 1994. *Juristat* 15: 2.

———. 1997. Canadian Statistics: Justice Spending. *Juristat* 17: 3.

———. 1998. A One-Day Snapshot of Inmates in Canada's Adult Correctional Facilities. *Juristat* 18: 8.

———. 1999. *The Juristat Reader: A Statistical Overview of the Canadian Justice System.* Toronto: Thompson Educational Publishing Inc.

Carrigan, D.O. 1991. *Crime and Punishment in Canada: A History.* Toronto: Oxford University Press.

Correctional Service of Canada. 1998. *50 Years of Human Rights Legislation in Federal Corrections.* Ottawa: Human Rights Division, Correctional Service of Canada.

Curtis, D., A. Graham, L. Kelly, and **A. Patterson**. 1985. *Kingston Penitentiary: The First Hundred and Fifty Years 1835–1985.* Ottawa: Minister of Supply and Services.

Department of Justice. 1883–1897. *Report of the Minister of Justice as to the Penitentiaries in Canada.* Ottawa: Queen's Printer.

———. 1927. *Annual Report of the Superintendent of Penitentiaries.* Ottawa: F.A. Acland, King's Printer.

———. 1936. *Annual Report of the Superintendent of Penitentiaries.* Ottawa: F.A. Acland, King's Printer.

———. 1952. *Annual Report of the Superintendent of Penitentiaries.* Ottawa: Edmond Cloutier, Queen's Printer.

———. 1953. *Annual Report of the Superintendent of Penitentiaries.* Ottawa: Edmond Cloutier, Queen's Printer.

Doherty, D., and **J.W. Ekstedt**. 1991. *Conflict Care and Control: The History of the Corrections Branch in British Columbia.* Burnaby: Simon Fraser University Publications.

Easton, S.T. 1998. *Privatizing Correctional Services.* Vancouver: The Fraser Institute.

Ekstedt. J.W., and **C.T. Griffiths**. 1988. *Corrections in Canada: Policy and Practice* (2nd ed.). Vancouver: Butterworths.

Ekstedt, J.W., and **M.A. Jackson**. 1997. *The Keepers and the Kept: Introduction to Corrections in Canada.* Toronto: ITP Nelson.

Foucault, M. 1977. *Discipline and Punish: The Birth of the Prison.* New York: Vintage Books.

Fresh Doubts Cast on U.S. Private Prisons. 1996. *Prison Reform Trust* 4. www.penlex.org.uk/pages/prtprep4.html (April 2000).

Goff, C. 1999. *Corrections in Canada.* Cincinnati: Anderson Publishing.

Gandy, J., and **L. Hurl**. 1987. Private Sector Development in Prison Industries: Options and Issues. *Canadian Journal of Criminology* 29,185–204.

Griffiths, C.T., and **A. Cunningham**. 1999. *Canadian Corrections.* Toronto: ITP Nelson.

Hatt, K., **T. Caputo**, and **B. Perry**. 1992. Criminal Justice Policy under Mulroney, 1984–1990: Neo-Conservatism, Eh? *Canadian Public Policy* 18: 254–260.

Honsberger, F. 1998. Nova Scotia Configuration Project. In S.T. Easton (Ed.), *Privatizing Correctional Services.* Vancouver: The Fraser Institute.

James, J.T.L. 1978/79. Gaols and Their Goals in Manitoba 1870–1970. *Canadian Journal of Criminology* 20/21: 34–42.

———. 1990. *A Living Tradition: Penitentiary Chaplaincy.* Ottawa: Minister of Supply and Services.

John Howard Society of Alberta. 1992. *A Review of the Literature on the Privatization of Corrections.* Alberta: John Howard Society of Alberta.

Johnson, D. 1998. Core Programs and Community Corrections. *Corrections Techniques Quarterly* 20: 7, 12.

Leblanc, T. 1994. Redesigning Corrections for Federally Sentenced Women in Canada. *Forum on Corrections Research* 6(1): 11–12.

Logan, C.H. 1992. Well Kept: Comparing Quality of Confinement in a Public and a Private Prison. *Journal of Criminal Law and Criminology* 83: 577–613.

MacGuigan, M. (Chairman). 1977. *Sub-Committee on the Penitentiary System in Canada.* Ottawa: Minister of Supply and Services.

McGowen, R. 1995. The Well-Ordered Prison. In N. Morris and D.J. Rothman (Eds.), *The Oxford History of the Prison.* New York: Oxford University Press.

Martinson, R. 1974. What Works: Questions and Answers about Prison Reform. *The Public Interest* 35: 22–54.

Motiuk, L. 1998. Using Dynamic Factors to Better Predict Post-Release Outcome. *Forum on Corrections Research* 10(3): 12–15.

New Brunswick, New Conflict. 1997. *Prison Reform Trust* 7. www.penlex.org.uk/pages/prtprep7.html (April 2000).

O'Neill, J. 1999. Lower Crime Rates Cited for Sharp Drop in Imprisonments. *Ottawa Citizen*, 7 April, B10.

Ouimet, R. (Chairman). 1969. *Report of the Canadian Committee on Corrections—Toward Unity: Criminal Justice and Corrections.* Ottawa: Information Canada.

Palmer, B.D. 1980. Kingston Mechanics and the rise of the Penitentiary, 1833–1836. *Social History* 8: 7–32.

Posner, C. 1991. An Historical Overview of the Construction of Canadian Federal Prisons. *Forum on Corrections Research* 3(2): 3–5.

Rothman, D.J. 1971. *The Discovery of the Asylum.* Boston: Little, Brown and Company.

Ryan, M., and **T. Ward.** 1989. *Privatization and the Penal System.* Milton Keynes: Oxford University Press.

Schlosser, E. 1998. The Prison-Industrial Complex. *Atlantic Monthly* December, 51–77.

Scott, R. 1998. Personal communication with author, 23 October.

Shoom, S. 1966. Kingston Penitentiary: The Early Decades. *Canadian Journal of Corrections* 8: 215–220.

Solicitor General of Canada. 1996. *Corrections Population Growth: Report for Federal/Provincial/ Territorial Ministers Responsible for Justice.* Ottawa: Solicitor General of Canada.

———. 1997. *Basic Facts about Corrections in Canada.* Ottawa: Solicitor General of Canada.

———. 1998. *Corrections Population Growth Second Report on Progress.* Regina: Solicitor General of Canada.

Spierenburg, P. 1995. The Body and the State: Early Modern Europe. In N. Morris and D.J. Rothman (Eds.), *The Oxford History of the Prison.* New York: Oxford University Press.

Taylor, C.J. 1988. The Kingston, Ontario Penitentiary, and Moral Architecture. In R.C. Macleod (Ed.), *Lawful Authority.* Toronto: Copp Clark Pitman.

Thomas, C.W. 1998. Issues and Evidence from the United States. In S.T. Easton (Ed.), *Privatizing Correctional Services.* Vancouver: The Fraser Institute.

Topping, C.W. 1929. *Canadian Penal Institutions.* Canada: Ryerson Press.

Walmsley, R. 1999. World Prison Populations: An Attempt at a Complete List. In D. van Zyl Smit and F. Dünkel (Eds.), *Imprisonment Today and Tomorrow* (2nd ed.). Deventer: Kluwer.

Watson, K. 1999. Personal correspondence with author.

Wilson, T. 1998. Contractual Management of Custodial Services in the United Kingdom. In S.T. Easton (Ed.), *Privatizing Correctional Services.* Vancouver: Fraser Institute.

Young, M.G. 1998. Rethinking Community Resistance to Prison Siting: Results from a Community Impact Assessment. *Canadian Journal of Criminology* 40: 323–327.

———. 1999. Win, Lose or Draw: The Battle over Site Selection in British Columbia. *Corrections Compendium* 24(3): 3–5, 25–30.

Zubrycki, R.M. 1980. *The Establishment of Canada's Penitentiary System: Federal Correctional Policy 1867–1900.* Toronto: University of Toronto, Faculty of Social Work.

APPENDIX A

Incarceration in Canada, Selected Census Years[a]

Year	Population	Federal Actual-in	Federal Admissions	Inmates per 100,000 Pop.	Provincial Actual-in	Provincial Admissions	Inmates per 100,000 Pop.	Total Inmates per 100,000
1901[b]	5,371,315	1,382	–	25.3	–	–	–	–
1906[b]	6,170,649	1,439	1,971	23.3	–	–	–	–
1911[b]	7,206,643	1,865	2,697	37.4	–	–	–	–
1916[b]	8,035,584	2,118	3,004	26.3	1,977	–	24.6	50.9
1921[b]	8,787,949	2,150	1,038	24.4	2,748	38,171	31.2	55.6
1926[b]	9,389,300	2,473	1,132	26.3	2,439	40,416	26.0	52.3
1931[b]	10,374,196	3,714	1,189	35.8	4,467	59,358	43.1	78.9
1936[b]	11,028,000	3,097	1,558	28.1	–	–	–	–
1941[b]	11,506,655	3,688	1,625	32.1	3,816	56,358	33.2	65.3
1946[b]	12,307,000	3,362	1,794	27.3	–	–	–	–
1951[b]	14,009,429	4,817	2,334	34.4	5,422	88,555	38.7	73.1
1956[b]	16,080,791	5,508	3,112	34.3	5,901	106,563	37.0	71.3
1961[b]	18,238,247	6,738	4,973	36.9	7,629	–	41.8	78.7
1966[b]	20,014,880	7,437	5,991	37.2	8,415	–	42.0	79.2
1971[b]	21,568,311	7,486	–	34.7	10,165	–	47.4	81.5
1976[b]	22,992,604	8,971	4,421	39.0	12,736	137,149	55.4	94.4
1981[c]	24,343,200	8,651	4,794	35.5	13,835	168,548	56.8	92.3
1986[c]	25,354,064	11,214	6,083	44.2	16,178	183,021	63.8	108.0
1991[d]	27,300,000	12,008	6,331	43.9	17,994	207,817	65.9	109.8
1996[d]	29,819,900	14,143	4,569	47.4	20,023	225,462	67.1	114.5

[a] Does not include adult or youth reformatories.

[b] Statistics Canada. 1906–1979. Canada Yearbook, 11-202. Ottawa: Statistics Canada.

[c] Statistics Canada. 1980–1986. Canada Yearbook, 11-402. Ottawa: Statistics Canada.

[d] Solicitor General of Canada. 1998. *Corrections Population Growth: Second Report on Progress*. Regina: Solicitor General of Canada.

Reproduced with the permission of the Minister of Public Works and Government Services Canada, 2000.

APPENDIX B

Selected Characteristics of Inmates[a]

	Adult[b] Population in Canada	Provincial/ Territorial Inmates	
Median age (years)	41	31	
	%	Total Sample	% of Sample
Male[c]	49	23,678	93
Aboriginal[d]	2	23,494	18
Grade 9 or less[e]	19	19,903	34
Unemployed[f]	7	9,239	54
Married[g]	63	18,682	24
	Federal Inmates		**Total Inmates**
Median Age (Years)	34		32
	Total Sample	% of Sample	Total Sample
Male[c]	13,862	98	37,540
Aboriginal[d]	13,862	14	37,356
Grade 9 or less[e]	5002	46	24,905
Unemployed[f]	2620	43	11,859
Married[g]	13693	41	32,375
	Total Inmates		
Median age (years)	32		
% of Sample			
Male[c]	95		
Aboriginal[d]	17		
Grade 9 or less[e]	36		
Unemployed[f]	52		
Married[g]	31		

[a] Statistics Canada. 1998. Adapted from One-Day Snapshot of Inmates in Canada's Adult Correctional Facilities (*Juristat* 18(8), Catalogue No. 85-002). Ottawa: Canadian Centre for Justice Statistics.

[b] 1996 Census data.

[c] Missing data for one provincial/territorial inmate.

[d] Missing data for 185 provincial/territorial inmates.

[e] Missing data for 3,776 provincial/territorial inmates and 8,960 federal inmates.

[f] Missing data for 14,440 provincial/territorial inmates and 11,242 federal inmates.

[g] Refers to those inmates married at time of admission. Missing data for 4,997 provincial/inmates and 169 federal inmates.

PRISON LIFE AND DAILY EXPERIENCES

Shivu Ishwaran
Toronto, Ontario
Robynne Neugebauer
Department of Sociology
York University
Toronto, Ontario

LEARNING OBJECTIVES

After reading this chapter, you should be able to:

- Understand the process of socialization that occurs behind prison walls;
- Describe inmate subculture and codes of conduct;
- Describe and assess the extent of prison crowding;
- Describe the impact of prison violence on corrections; and
- Understand and describe how corrections deals with dangerous inmates in Special Handling Units.

There are prisons, into which whoever looks will, at first sight of the people confined, be convinced, that there is some great error in the management of them . . . I think it will show plainly, that much is yet to be done for the regulation of prisons; and I am not without hope, that the legislature will finish what was so laudably begun.

—John Howard

129

The prison is easily one of the most controversial and popular areas within corrections. Popular culture, news media, and academic discourse have paid considerable attention to the prison (see Chapter 3). Since their inception in North America in the mid 1900s, prisons have been a concern of reformers, community workers, and politicians (see Chapters 2 and 6). This chapter provides an examination of prison life—the world of inmates, correctional officers, and the prison environment. This exploration includes a discussion of the process of socialization behind prison walls, inmate subculture and social systems, the experiences of inmates in sometimes crowded cells and often violent prisons, and the management of dangerous inmates in Special Handling Units.

PRISONS AS TOTAL INSTITUTIONS

Numerous critical studies have been conducted on the maximum security prison. Early research by Clemmer (1958), Cloward et al. (1960), Cressey (1961), Sykes (1958), Sykes and Messinger (1970), Caron (1978), and Mann (1967) represent some important work in this field. Much has been written about inmate culture and behaviour within prisons and the influence of the structure of prisons in these social processes. A central theme in the analysis of prisons is the "total institution." In his groundbreaking work on prisons, hospitals, concentration camps, and psychiatric institutions, Erving Goffman developed the concept of the "total institution" to capture the impact of the controlling structure and social organization of the institution on the individual. As described in his book *Asylum*, Goffman (1961, 6) defines a **total institution** as "a place of residence and work where a large number of like-situated individuals, cut off from the wider society for an appreciable period of time, together lead an enclosed, formally administered round of life." All activities take place within the physical environment of the prison. All activities are closely monitored and sanctioned by prison authorities. Moreover, there is a lack of privacy as all aspects of daily life occur in close quarters and in full view of other inmates. The behaviour of individual prisoners is scrutinized by fellow inmates as well as by authorities.

As well, prisons are not all alike. Some prisons exert more control over their population than others do. For instance, maximum security institutions exercise greater control both in terms of correctional staff behaviour and structure of the institution.

Goffman further argues that life in total institutions is conducted according to the following parameters:

- All aspects of life take place within the confines of the institution and under the same authority;
- All aspects of life are conducted in the immediate company of a large group of strangers who are expected to do things together;
- All phases of daily life are rigidly routinized and monitored by authority structures and prison staff and maintained by a system of formal rules; and
- All aspects of daily life in these institutions is designed to fulfill the needs and requirements of the governing body.

ENTERING THE INSTITUTION: THE INITIATION PROCESS

The initiation process for entering a total institution involves a radical shift in the social self. This adjustment to prison involves a psychological process, which Goffman (1961) refers to as the **mortifications of the self**. This process of adjusting to the institution requires the loss of a civilian identity and the incorporation of a new institutional identity. The new inmate is stripped of her or his civilian identity. Personal possessions such as clothing, money, and personal effects are removed. Various demoralizing and identity-altering practices, such as hair cutting, disinfecting, and finger printing, are also performed on the individual. Clemmer (1958) maintains that forcing inmates to wear identical prison uniforms further demeans the individual. Consequently, the individual is denied individuality. Goffman (1961, 16) describes this process as follows: "Admission procedures might better be called 'trimming' or 'programming' because in thus being squared away the new arrival allows himself to be shaped and coded into an object that can be fed into the administrative establishment, to be worked on smoothly by routine operations."

The initiation rituals reinforce the inmates' isolation from the wider society—a forced separation from the outside world of activities and intimate relationships. Garfinkel (1956) refers to the process of stripping the individual of his or her identity as status degradation ceremonies. Feelings of isolation and loneliness are also felt strongly by inmates. Under the harsh circumstances of imprisonment, the inmate is inclined to seek out the "comfort" of the prison subculture. According to Clemmer, the prisoner's loss of autonomy promotes an identification with a hierarchical system similar to that of the outside world. Grasping this familiar status enables the individual to gain prestige and self-worth.

The individual must maintain one's status in the wider society and simultaneously within the prison hierarchy in order to obtain goods and services that otherwise would be unattainable. Another factor motivating newcomers to associate with the prison subculture is the maintenance of safety and protection. It is also important for inmates to adhere to the rules of the prison in order to placate prison staff and other relevant authorities and to reduce their sentence and avoid further punishment. In *The Prison Community* (1958), based on research in a maximum security prison, Donald Clemmer introduced the concept of **prisonization** to describe the process of socialization into the inmate culture of the prison. This socialization process involves learning the inmate subculture, including values, beliefs, and behaviour that challenge and run counter to those expected by prison staff. Hence, although the stated goals of imprisonment are to correct and rehabilitate offenders (see Chapter 4), the prison experience may in fact reinforce deviant behaviour. In *Society Behind Bars*, W.E. Mann (1967) argues that the degree of prisonization is determined by several factors, including the age of the prisoner, the length of sentence, the number of prison terms that individual has served, and any attachments to the world outside the prison walls. Mann's research demonstrates that recidivists are more likely to have internalized the values and belief system of the prison subculture.

THE INMATE SUBCULTURE

The term subculture refers to the distinctive values, beliefs, norms, symbols, language, and ideologies embraced by a particular group or community set apart from the larger society. Thus, the **inmate subculture** is the totality of norms, beliefs, values, language and ideologies shared by inmates within correctional institutions.

There are two approaches to explaining the inmate subculture: the deprivation model and the importation model. Both theories are valid. Nevertheless, both pre-prison socialization and socialization within the prison environment can be seen to have an impact on behaviour inside the prison. The relative weight of each influence is yet to be determined.

The Deprivation Model

According to the **deprivation model**, prisoners experience considerable suffering and frustration attendant with the deprivation of the following basic needs (Sykes 1958; Sykes and Messinger 1970):

- Liberty;
- Privacy;
- Free access to goods and services;
- Heterosexual relationships;
- Autonomy; and
- Security.

This model thus argues that the prison subculture represents a coping mechanism for dealing with the **pains of imprisonment**. In other words, the pains of imprisonment produce the inmate subculture. Although prisons purport to punish and rehabilitate offenders, they reinforce criminal behaviour instead. Nonetheless, inmates are known to vary in terms of their coping strategies with institutional life. A Canadian study examined coping strategies employed by inmates in federal prisons (Zamble and Porporino 1988). Findings from this research suggest that rehabilitation programs were relatively unsuccessful in diverting inmates away from inappropriate strategies for coping with the pains of imprisonment. This study noted that inmates were primarily preoccupied with surviving and developing a comfortable routine while in prison. In addition, these concerns distracted inmates' attention from productive problem-solving and positive forecasting about their future (see Chapters 9 and 11).

Purport : to act in the publics best interest (convey)

The Importation Model

The second approach to explaining prison subculture is the **importation model**, which attributes the development of the prison subculture to the values, roles, beliefs, and inclinations that prisoners bring with them into the prison (Clemmer 1958; Irwin and Cressey 1961). In other words, according to this approach, the prison is a microcosm of the outside society, a reflection of the world outside the prison walls and not due to the "pains of imprisonment." Clemmer argues that the prison subculture is influenced by the social structure of the prison and identifies a number of elements that characterize prison society. These involve the following:

- The prisoner-staff binary dynamic;
- The three types of inmates;
- The various racial groups within the prison population;
- The type of offence committed;
- The record of recidivism (re-offending);
- Personality differences as a reflection of socialization prior to imprisonment;
- The power of "politicians" (those at the top of the inmate social hierarchy);
- Work gangs and groups; and
- Sexual "deviation."

THE INMATE SOCIAL SYSTEM

Although there are institutions for both male and female offenders, most of the research into prison life has focused on male offenders. Accordingly, almost all prisons have developed an inmate social system. The inmate social system comprises a code of behaviour, an economic system for the distribution of illicit goods and services, a power hierarchy, and, lastly, "argot" roles.

Inmate Code

According to Sykes (1958) and Sykes and Messinger (1970), the five elements of the **inmate code** are the following:

- *Don't interfere with the interests of other inmates.* Never "rat on a con." The most crucial norm in this category is concerned with preventing the betrayal of fellow inmates to guards.

- *Don't lose your head.* Emphasis is placed on avoiding emotional friction between inmates and the pains of daily life. The main idea behind this maxim is "playing it cool" and "doing your own time."

- *Don't exploit inmates.* A central theme is that the exploitation and manipulation of fellow prisoners should be outlawed. This element suggests that inmates share scarce resources. Other maxims in this category include "Don't steal," "Don't break your word," and "Be right."

- *Don't weaken.* Emphasis is on maintaining autonomy, dignity, and the ability to be strong in the face of frustration or threatening situations without breaking down or resorting to subservience. The inmate should try to maintain integrity in spite of deprivation.

- *Don't be a sucker.* Guards are to be treated with suspicion and distrust. Inmates should not allow themselves to become committed to the values of hard work or to the submission to authority. Thus, it is essential that inmates "don't trust the guards or staff."

Sykes (1958) argues that conformity to the inmate code decreases the pains of imprisonment. Theoretically, a cohesive inmate society provides the individual with a group identity, solidarity, and defence against guards. Additionally, inmate solidarity in the form of mutual tolerance would alleviate the problem of personal security and in the form of sharing gifts and favours. Yet, despite the fact that inmates give strong verbal support to a code that emphasizes group cohesion, the actual behaviour of the community of prisoners varies between two extremes: complete conformity and complete deviation to the code. Moreover, even if all inmates fully adhere to the code, the pains of imprisonment would only be partially alleviated given that the deprivations of prison life are too severe for human beings to cope with (Sykes and Messinger 1970).

Prison Argot Roles

Argot is a set of terms invented by inmates to refer to the various roles displayed in the prison. A variety of roles are expressed in the prison argot. Sykes (1958, 90–98) reveals the following:

- *Fish.* This term implies the vulnerability of the new inmate who must learn to adjust to the prison environment, in other words to sink or swim.

- *Rat.* This role refers to the prisoner who has violated the code by providing damaging information about a fellow prisoner's behaviour to prison guards. This behaviour represents the most serious form of betrayal of the inmate code. Rats, also referred to as squealers, are informants who trade information with guards in exchange for contraband goods, personal benefits, or preferential treatment.

- *Gorilla.* These individuals are physically strong inmates who prey on those who are weak and vulnerable. Gorillas use force or the threat of force against other inmates in order to gain cigarettes, food, or clothing.

- *Centre-Men.* Centre-men are also very unpopular with the other inmates. These men are inmates who attempt to ingratiate themselves with prison authorities. They go to great lengths to please prison staff. They are overly helpful and cooperative.

- *Merchant/Peddler.* The merchant or peddler is an inmate who sells when he is in the position to give. According to the inmate subculture, giving, as opposed to selling for profit, is seen as an expression of group solidarity and strengthens the bonds between inmates. The inmate population regards the merchant as someone who exploits his companions.

- *Ball Buster.* This inmate is blatantly disobedient, sometimes verbally and physically abusive towards staff, and constantly creates a disturbance.

- *Tough.* The tough is violent and verbally abusive towards fellow prisoners. The tough exhibits an aggressive stance at all times. He is prone to frequent outbursts of anger.

- *Real Man.* The real man "does his own time." He is an inmate who endures his imprisonment with dignity. He represents an attempt to maintain integrity in the face of severe deprivation—he tries to maintain some autonomy by denying the guards the power over his self.

- *Wolf.* Wolves are inmates who take on the male role in the sexual encounter. These individuals are very aggressive.

- *Fag.* Fags are inmates whose sexual orientation was gay prior to entering the prison. While in prison, they maintain their gay identity and behaviour. Fags thus take on the "female role" in sexual interaction.

- *Punk.* Punks are inmates who are forced into the female role. They are forced into submission by wolves.

The presence of identifiable homosexual roles demonstrates the extent of homosexual behaviour within the men's prison subculture. With the absence of females within the same prison walls, homosexual behaviour is common. The inmates in Sykes' (1958) research recognized and labelled a variety of sexual acts. The inmates also distinguished between those who had genuine homosexual orientation and those who engaged in such behaviours in response to the deprivation of heterosexual contact and affection. Homosexuals were divided between those who play an active role and those who play a more passive role in the encounter. Fags professed a genuine homosexual orientation and engaged in homosexual behaviour prior to entering prison; wolves and punks engaged in same-sex relations only while in prison, as a result of the prison environment.

Other Argot Roles

- *Politician.* The politician is at the top of the inmate social hierarchy. The politician is chosen on the basis of age, criminality, length of sentence, and outside contacts. The politician is usually an older man, with vast experience in prison life. He has done his time; he has seniority, so to speak, within the prison. Moreover, politicians typically have an impressive criminal record, which earns them the respect of the prison population (Kalinich and Stojkovic 1985). Politicians have a respected position within the hierarchy of prison subculture and have important ties with prison staff, other inmates, and medical practitioners.

- *Square John.* This term describes the inmate who does not adequately embrace the prison subculture. The square john has turned away from his criminal past; conversely, these inmates are interested in treatment programs and participate stridently in their own rehabilitation and reform.

- *Right Guy.* The prisoner who is intent on making crime a career is referred to as a right guy. As such, this type of prisoner strongly avoids developing relationships with prison staff and avoids rehabilitation programs.

Roger Caron's personal account of life in prison as described in his book *Go-Boy* (1978) identified other types of prisoners, which include the following:

- *The Legalist.* This prisoner is someone who gains knowledge of the legal system while in prison. The legalist uses his legal expertise for his own case and provides legal expertise to fellow inmates.

- *The Colonist.* The colonist views prison as home and feels more comfortable in prison than on the outside. Once released from prison, this type of inmate often commits further crimes in an effort to be confined to prison again.

- *The Radical.* The radical views society as hierarchical system of inequality and defines the justice system as an extension of this system. Radicals promote ideas about justice for prisoners, reform, and revolution. Thus, they identify themselves as political prisoners.

Inmate Social Systems in Women's Prisons

Information about inmate social systems in women's prisons is limited by the paucity of available research in the area (see Chapter 10 for more details). However, research by Dobash, Dobash, and Gutteridge (1986) suggest that social systems in women's prisons differ from those in male prisons. When compared to men's correctional institutions, notable differences in staff training and attitudes, organizational rules and staff expectations of inmates have been found in women's prisons (Wilson 1986). Gender roles and gender socialization outside the institution also influence the development of roles and inmate interactions within prison. According to Wilson, female inmates deal with pains of imprisonment differently from their male counterparts. For example, female prisoners cope with the loss of emotional relationships by developing and maintaining significant relationships or "pseudo families" with other prisoners. There is a lower level of violence in prisons for women. While sexual behaviour among male inmates is characterized by dominance, in contrast, female prisoners develop family and lesbian relationships with other inmates on a voluntary basis to strictly fulfill emotional needs.

As well as differences between men and female inmates, the growth in Aboriginal and other ethnic, racial, and cultural groups also have an impact on prisons today. The over-representation of Aboriginal people in federal prisons is considerable. In 1997/98, they represented about 2 percent of the adult population in Canada, and approximately 15 percent of admissions to provincial/territorial facilities and 17 percent of federal inmates (Finn et al. 1999). The authors also found that Aboriginal inmates have more defined needs than non-Aboriginal inmates in terms of substance abuse, employment, and personal and family needs. These and other differences between ethnic, racial, and cultural groups can foster an "us against them" mentality. Given that Canadian institutions house an increasingly heterogeneous group of inmates, perhaps no one inmate code exists. Rather, the contemporary inmate social world can be characterized as being pluralistic. The formation of various subcultures, groups, and gangs as well as individual differences are a constant source of conflict, competition, and tension in prison.

OVERCROWDING

In addition to the initiation process for entering the total institution and the establishment of inmates subcultures and social systems, inmates in prison must cope with living in a harsh physical environment. Correctional researchers are well aware that Canada has a high rate of incarceration compared to other nations. As described in Chapters 1 and 6, although Canada's incarceration rate is about a one fifth (114 of every 100,000 adults) of the United States (547), it is higher than other Western European and industrialized countries.

The Canadian criminal justice system is under constant fiscal pressure. At the same time, people are concerned about crime, particularly violent crime, and demands for harsher sentences are increasing. Prison overcrowding and insufficient funds for programming and counselling are some of the symptoms of this paradox.

There are various ways to measure overcrowding in prisons. **Prison crowding** has been described as an instance of **double-bunking**: housing two inmates in a cell originally designed for one. Double-bunking was introduced in Canada in 1984 as a temporary measure. However, between 1986 and 1993 the inmate population grew from 10,500 to 13,200, while penitentiary cell capacity increased only from 11,656 to 12,061. Based on the projections of the Correctional Service, inmates will continue to be double-bunked, even though this goes against the Standard Minimum Rules for the Treatment of Prisoners that Canada has endorsed (Marron 1996) (see Box 7.1).

Recently, the Correctional Service of Canada (1996a) conducted a **National Inmate Survey** (NIS) of 4,425 inmates in federal prisons to help gain insight into prisoners' experiences and opinions about the conditions of their confinement. The NIS also features comparative data from the United States and prison services in Britain and Scotland (see Table 7.1).

Among Canadian inmates, in 1995 26.4 percent reported that they were currently sharing a cell. Among these inmates, 37 percent were sharing for less than 4 months while 17 percent shared a cell for 12 or more months.

Comparatively, inmates in Canada experience double-bunking less often than inmates in the British and Scottish jurisdictions, and about half as often as inmates in the United States.

BOX 7.1	Standard Minimum Rules for the Treatment of Prisoners

- Men and women in detention are to be held in separate facilities; likewise, untried and convicted prisoners, those imprisoned for civil offences and criminal offenders, and youths and adults shall be housed separately.

- Cells for individuals should not be used to accommodate two or more persons overnight; dormitory facilities are to be supervised at night.

- Prisoners shall be provided with adequate water and toilet articles, and required to keep themselves clean.

- Prisoners not allowed to wear their own clothing are to be provided with an adequate and suitable outfit, with provisions for laundry and changes of clothes.

- Prisoners outside an institution for an authorized purpose are to be allowed to wear their own clothing.

- Every prisoner shall be provided with a separate bed and clean, separate, and sufficient bedding.

- Wholesome, well-prepared food is to be provided to prisoners at usual hours.

- Drinking water shall be available whenever needed.

- If not employed in outdoor work, every prisoner shall have at least one hour of exercise in the open air, weather permitting.

- Young prisoners and others of suitable age and physique are to receive physical and recreational training.

- A medical officer with some knowledge of psychiatry is to be available to every institution.

- Prisoners requiring specialized treatment are to be transferred to a civil hospital or appropriate facility.

- A qualified dental officer shall be available to every prisoner.

- Prenatal and postnatal care and treatment are to be provided by women's institutions; where nursing infants are allowed to remain with their mothers, a nursery staffed by qualified persons is needed.

- Every prisoner shall be examined by the medical officer shortly after admission; prisoners suspected of contagious diseases are to be segregated.

- The medical officer shall see all sick prisoners daily, along with those who complain of illness or are referred to the medical officer's attention.

- The medical officer is to report to the director on prisoners whose health is jeopardized by continued imprisonment and on the quality of the food, hygiene, bedding, clothing, and physical regimen of the prisoners.

- Every institution shall maintain a library with recreational and instructional books for the use of prisoners.

- Transport is to be at the expense of the prison administration, and equal conditions shall obtain for all prisoners.

- The administration shall carefully select every grade of personnel and maintain in their minds and the public's the important social service they provide.

- To these ends, pay, conditions, and benefits shall be suitable to professional and exacting service.

- Personnel are to be sufficiently educated and to receive ongoing courses and training.
- As far as possible, personnel should include psychiatric, social work, and education professionals.
- The director shall be a qualified administrator, retained on a full-time basis and residing on the premises or in the immediate vicinity.
- Staff personnel are to be able to speak the language of the greatest number

of prisoners, and to retain the services of an interpreter when necessary.

- In large institutions, at least one medical officer should reside on the premises or in the immediate vicinity.
- In others, a medical officer shall visit daily and reside near enough to be available for emergencies.
- Prison officers are to receive physical training in the use of force.

SOURCE: United Nations 1957.

TABLE 7.1   Cross-jurisdictional Comparison of Rates of Double-Bunking in Cells

Jurisdiction	% Double-Bunked
Correctional Service of Canada	26.4
British Prison Service	35.0
Federal Bureau of Prisons (U.S.)	50.0
Scottish Prison Service	32.0

SOURCE: Correctional Service of Canada 1996a.

Prison crowding can also be defined in psychological terms. For instance 61 percent of the NIS respondents reported "feeling" overcrowded (Correctional Service of Canada 1996a). Such a feeling is a subjective experience that is a function of many factors including spatial density (i.e., the actual amount of space available per inmate in a cell) and social density (i.e., the number of inmates per square metre in a given cell). Beyond the physical environment, feeling crowded is also influenced by personality factors such as sociability and the ability to cope with stress and adverse conditions.

Prison crowding can also be measured as an instance when the number of prisoners exceeds the capacity of a prison (i.e., the number of permanent beds in the facility) on a given day.

Although this seems like a simple method, the number of inmates in correctional facilities varies from day to day. There is a constant movement of inmates into and out of facilities. Some are admitted and released, others are on temporary absence to serve an intermittent sentence in the community or are away for medical reasons, court appearances, and so on. In order to obtain an accurate measure of the prison population, correctional researchers conducted the first "one-day snapshot" census of inmates in all adult federal and provincial/territorial correctional facilities (Correctional Service of Canada 1996a; also see Table 7.2). The census contains data based on two counts of inmates: those who are "on register" (i.e., the number of inmates on record who have been sentenced to a facility) and "actual in"

TABLE 7.2 Distribution of Correctional Facilities and Inmate Populations on October 5, 1996a

Jurisdiction	# of Facilities	Total Capacity[b]	On-Register Count	On-Register Capacity (%)	Actual-In Count[c]	Actual-In Capacity (%)
Newfoundland	6	351	346	99	299	85
Prince Edward Island	2	107	66	62	66	62
Nova Scotia	9	512	490	96	432	84
New Brunswick	10	388	496	128	396	102
Quebec	19	3,483	5,766	166	3,424	98
Ontario	47	7,914	8,416	106	..	..
Manitoba	8	976	1,062	109	942	97
Saskatchewan[d]	15	1,228	1,153	94	1,117	91
Alberta	10	2,412	2,889	120	2,176	90
British Columbia	19	2,259	2,603	115	2,324	103
Yukon	2	131	79	60	76	58
Northwest Territories	244	313	128	273	112	4
Provincial/Territorial Total	151	20,005	23,679	118	...	...
Provincial/Territorial Total (excluding Ontario)	...	12,091	...	...	11,525	95
Federal	48	12,721	13,862	109	13,610	107
TOTAL	199	32,726	37,541	115	...	...
TOTAL (excluding Ontario)	...	24,812	...	...	25,135	101

.. Figures not available.

... Figures not appropriate or applicable.

[a] Includes all facilities that were operational on Snapshot Day.

[b] Defined as the number of permanent beds in the facility.

[c] "Actual-in" counts were not available for Ontario.

[d] Includes two facilities that were operational but that had no inmates.

SOURCE: Robinson, et al. 1998.

population or the total number of prisoners who are physically present at the facility on census day. In terms of crowding, the actual-in count is a conservative estimate as it excludes inmates who are absent from the prison.

Calculations of crowding based on the registered data show that the Correctional Service of Canada (responsible for federal level institutions) and seven provincial/territorial jurisdictions were operating over capacity. Based on the conservative actual-in data, the Correctional Service was operating at 7 percent beyond its capacity and the provincial/territorial jurisdictions (excluding Ontario) were operating at only 5 percent below their maximum capacity. Crowding was as high as 12 percent over capacity in the Northwest Territories and as low as 38 percent below capacity in the Yukon.

Explanations of Overcrowding

Crime Rate

There are several explanations for prison crowding. One explanation is that it is a function of the crime rate—an increase in the number of offences results in more charges, convictions, and, hence, an increase in admissions to custody. However, prison populations are also influenced by fluctuations in the number of offenders held on remand (i.e., non-convicted), convicted prisoner admissions, length of sentence, and the availability and use of alternatives to imprisonment and early-release mechanisms (Kuhn 1996). Therefore, fluctuations in crime do not always result in fluctuations in the prison population. For instance, in the United States the national crime rate declined steadily between 1980 and 1984, the prison rates continued to rise during that same period. Joutsen (1997) points out that in many Central and Eastern European countries crime rates have been stable or even decreasing for several years, while prison populations in many of those nations have continued to increase. In Canada, the inmate population has grown faster in the past several years than either crime or the overall population, despite an increase in the use of probation and other sanctions (Boe and Muirhead 1998).

Demography

One of the basic facts known to criminologists is that males between the ages of about 18 to 25, a group whose numbers has increased since 1960, commit the majority of crimes. Accordingly, some argue that overcrowding is rooted in social changes such as the baby boom, typically defined as the increase in the birth rate that occurred between the late 1940s and 1960s. In the year 2000, baby boomers are between 30 and 50 years of age. Thus, demographers predict that the crime rate and correctional populations will continue to decline as they have in recent years. On the other hand, given that the prison populations in Canada and the United States grew faster than the crime rates or the overall populations did, demographics alone cannot totally account for the rising inmate populations (Boe and Muirhead 1998).

The Media, Public Opinion, and Legislation

As discussed in Chapter 3, some experts argue that the media can play a role in determining prison populations. Media accounts of crime are often misleading, giving an image of crime that is increasing and typically more violent than is the case. A recent study from Argentina compared official statistics with media accounts. By tracking the number of crime-related articles found in major newspaper publications, Argentina's Ministry of Justice recorded about a 90 percent increase in crime over a two-year period (1991–1993), while crime increased only about 2 percent, according to official counts (Chavez 1997). Recent crime statistics in Canada indicate that violent crimes have dropped, although 45 percent of Canadians believe that it is on the rise (Edwards and Hughes 1997). Fear of crime, heightened by sensationalized media accounts, can result in punitive attitudes. Public opinion and concern demand a tough response to crime (i.e., restrictive early-release policies and longer sentences for repeat and violent offenders). Under public pressure, politicians begin to argue in favour of punitiveness. Recent legislation in the United States is an example of how the "three strikes and you're out" principle can add to the rising inmate population, and illustrates how overcrowding is partially rooted in social change such as the creation of new legislation. Moreover, the three-strikes rule demonstrates how some strategies are triggered by social, economic, or political movements, which are not always supported in research literature (see Box 7.2).

In Canada, harsher measures for serious crimes may also contribute to the inmate population. As described by the Correctional Service of Canada (1996b, 7), these policies include following:

- New firearms legislation includes a mandatory four-year minimum sentence for serious personal injury offences involving use of a firearm, as well as new offences under the gun registration system.

- Recent changes to the *Young Offenders' Act* makes it easier to charge 16- and 17-year-olds with murder and other serious offences tried in adult court, and also lengthens their periods of parole ineligibility if they are convicted.

BOX 7.2   Three Strikes

Although many people believe that harsher penalties and longer prison sentences offers the public a sense of safety, the expansion of the prison system and use of incarceration have not proved to be effective deterrents or cures for crime. Yet, under the recent "three strikes and you're out" legislation in the United States, an offender convicted of a third felony automatically receives a mandatory long-term sentence, usually life in prison. Turner, Sundt, and Applegate (1995) suggest that the recent interest in tougher sentences is in part due to public disillusionment with the effectiveness of the criminal justice system.

Because this three-strikes rule has not been in place long, its effectiveness is still undetermined and heavily debated. Overall, initial reports suggest that it is having little effect on reducing crime (Stolzenberg and D'Alessio 1997). It is also noted that it might have more negative than positive effects. For instance, Turner, Sundt, and Applegate suggest that the policy might result in population growth throughout the system, as well

as in fiscal burdens and constitutional issues. Population increases will be driven by more "lifers" going to prison—and more offenders going to prison for longer periods of time can potentially result in prison crowding. As well, it will contribute to the surmounting need for geriatric care. Increases in the system will also be related to the amount of cases going to trial. Because of the severity of mandatory sentences, defending lawyers will demand jury trials in far more cases, and far less often enter a plea of guilty. Thus, Turner and his colleagues argue that the three-strikes rule can have the effect of increasing fiscal pressure by raising the prisoner populations and increasing costly litigation. Moreover, the courts will see an increase in constitutional challenges, such as claims that the legislation violates the eighth amendment, which protects against cruel and unusual punishment, or that interpreting the law as totally precluding judicial discretion "in the furtherance of justice" is unconstitutional.

SOURCE: *People v. Superior Court* 1996.

- The amendments to the *Corrections and Conditional Release Act*, among other things, make it easier to detain sex offenders who commit crimes against children until the expiry of their sentence, and require offenders whose conditional release is revoked to serve a longer period in prison before becoming once again eligible for release.
- The new provisions for collection of forensic DNA evidence from criminal suspects may soon be complemented by a DNA data-banking scheme covering offenders convicted of personal injury offences.
- Forthcoming legislation will deal with high-risk violent offenders. This could have far-reaching consequences for the Correctional Service, since it would allow the courts to designate an individual as a "long-term offender" and require that person to remain under supervision in the community for up to 10 years following completion of his or her sentence.

Nevertheless, many offenders are being sentenced to prison for relatively minor crimes. Fine defaulters, for instance, account for 22 percent of provincial/territorial admissions to custody in 1997/98 (Reed and Roberts 1999). Under increasing public concern with prison crowding, the Correctional Service has embarked on a plan to provide flexible alternatives to incarceration such as community-based programs for low-risk offenders. The Conditional Sentence of Imprisonment (section 742.1 of the Criminal Code) is an example of legislation that attempts to reduce crowding by allowing judges to order an offender to serve the sentence in the community instead of in prison.

Adult Correctional Expenditures

A realistic long-term solution to reducing prison crowding does not lie in spending additional tax dollars to build more prisons, the effectiveness of which is continually being called into question. As noted in Chapter 4, in 1998/99 Canada spent $1.3 billion on correctional operating expenditures. Alternatively, the Correctional Service of Canada has been promoting community corrections as a less expensive solution to the prison. The Service's 1999 *Basic Facts* booklet estimates that the average annual cost of incarcerating an inmate in a federal institution during 1998/99 was approximately $61,000 per inmate, compared to 13,000 to supervise an offender on parole or statutory release.

Effects of Overcrowding

Crowding, in conjunction with other adverse prison conditions, can lead to a range of psychological and physical illnesses, an increased likelihood of recidivism (Farrington and Nuttal 1980), suicide, violence, and disciplinary infractions. One inmate explains the affect of double occupancy cells (Marron 1996, 22): "You've got two guys living in a toilet. It could be your best friend. After a while you want to kill him. Everybody's entitled to some dignity, some privacy. You need time for quiet on your own. When you're double-bunked, there is no such thing as time out. The pressure keeps building."

Overcrowding also has strains prison resources and programs and presents challenges to correctional staff and administrators. Because space is limited, overcrowding results in offenders being classified on the basis of space rather than by the official procedures. Thus, inmates classified as medium security can be found in maximum security institutions, and vice versa (Botterell 1984). Misclassification can impede rehabilitation and the progress of inmates through the correctional system (Clements 1982).

Prison crowding also stretches the resources available for rehabilitative programs such as opportunities for work, academic advancement, employment, vocational training, and access to recreational material. Without appropriate rehabilitative and constructive time-consuming activities, inmates tend to spend more time in crowded cells. This can lead to inmate idleness, frustration, discontent, and disruptive behaviour (Cox, Paulus, and McCain 1984). Moreover, competition and conflict over resources that are available can bring about aggression and violence (Johnston 1991).

Reducing Overcrowding

Criminal justice systems across the globe have initiated a number of strategies to reduce prison crowding. According to Skovron, Scott, and Cullen (1988), these efforts can be classified into three general strategies: front-end strategies to reduce the number of admissions to prison and shorten the length of sentences, back-end strategies to increase the number of offenders released from prison, and capacity expansion to expand the prison system by the design and construction of new institutions.

Front-End Strategies

The introduction of the conditional terms of imprisonment allows judges, after imposing a term of imprisonment of less than two years in provincial/territorial facilities, to order the offender to serve the sentence in the community, under supervision. This legislation was designed to reduce the large number of admissions of low-risk offenders.

Back-End Strategies

Conditional terms of release constitute an example of a back-end policy that can help to alleviate crowding There are three types of conditional release by which federal offenders can be released into the community, all intended to help inmates reintegrate into the community: day parole, full parole, and statutory release. Offenders on day parole reside in halfway houses or correctional institutions located in the community. Offenders on full parole serve part of their sentence in the community. Most federal inmates are eligible to apply for full parole after having served one third of their sentences. Statutory release requires that federal inmates serve the final one third of their prison sentence in the community under supervision.

Capacity Expansion and Design

The William Head Institution in British Columbia represents the first major correctional facility that was planned to incorporate much of what has been learned about the effects of crowding in prisons and the impact of physical environments. The building's layout is designed to provide inmates with more personal space and control over their environment by easing restrictions on inmate movement and activity. Cells are equipped with individual climate controls and inmates are allowed to decorate their cells. Different colours, light, textures, and fixtures enhance inmates' feelings of identity or belonging to a certain cell block. This fosters interaction among inmates, yet affords a certain amount of privacy. Other measures include retrofitting existing institutions, building temporary units, transferring offenders between regions, and using bed space in provincial facilities.

PRISON VIOLENCE

In addition to the stress caused by living in a overcrowded environment, inmates and staff face a constant threat of being victimized or being exposed to major and minor security incidents (see Table 7.3).

Types of Prison Violence

Prison violence can be broken down into types of personal violence or self-injury (i.e., suicide, self-mutilation, etc.), inmate-on-inmate violence, inmate-staff incidents, and the use of force by staff on inmates.

Suicide

Suicide, the ultimate personal injury, continues to be the most frequent cause of death in custodial institutions, accounting of 35 percent (32) of all deaths (92) in federal and provincial institutions in 1997/98. This is more than twice as high as in the general population (Reed and Roberts 1999). A profile of 16 inmate suicides conducted by the Correctional Service of Canada (1992) found that in one quarter of the suicides, inmates had served less than one year of their term, while another quarter had served 10 years or more. Eight inmates would have reached their mandatory supervision release dates within two years at the time of committing suicide. The study suggests that "the prospect of serving a very long sentence was perhaps too much to handle, while for others, the difficult issue may have been the prospect of being out on the street again" (5).

Assaults by Inmates

The 1995 National Inmate Survey breaks down prison violence into reports of assault by inmates on inmates and staff and reports of assault by staff on inmates. Findings indicate that

TABLE 7.3   Prison Violence in Federal Facilities, 1995/96–1998/99

	1995/96	1996/97	1997/98
Murders – Staff	0	0	0
Murders – Inmates	2	5	2
Major assaults – Staff	4	1	5
Major assaults – Inmates	54	45	45
Hostage taking	3	1	4
Major inmate fights	4	4	5
Major disturbances	1	10	12
Inmate suicides	17	10	9

SOURCE: Adapted from Correctional Service of Canada 1998.

about one in five inmates (21 percent) reported being physically assaulted by other inmate. Comparable information from the British and Scottish Prison Services indicate that physical assaults are experienced less often (9 percent and 13 percent, respectively) than by Canadian inmates.

Assaults by Staff

In terms of assaults by staff on inmates, about 8 percent of inmates surveyed reported being assaulted by staff in the past six months. Most assaults occurred in maximum security facilities (16 percent), followed by 6 percent in medium and 2 percent in minimum security. Given the lower level of reported violence in minimum security institutions, it is not surprising to find that minimum security inmates report having a better relationship with staff than inmates in higher security facilities.

Assaults on Staff

The potential for conflict between inmates and correctional officers is always present in the prison setting. For instance, about 22 percent of the inmates surveyed agreed with the statement that "male staff members were likely to be assaulted" and 12 percent agreed that female staff members were likely victims. Again, the threat of violence is believed to be greater in higher security facilities than in minimum ones (high security: 19 percent; medium security: 13 percent; minimum security: 7 percent).

Official reports and surveys of correctional officers show that they are exposed to violence, the threat of victimization, and critical events. Table 7.4 shows a list of traumatic events that a sample of 122 officers were exposed to during their careers (Rosine 1992). On average, the correctional officers were exposed to 27.9 incidents of "critical events." Only two officers in the sample did not experience at least one critical incident.

TABLE 7.4   Percentages of Officers Exposed to Traumatic Events

Event	Frequency of Event				
	0	1	2	3	>3
Suicide attempt	56	16	6	5	17
Completed suicide	42	21	15	10	12
Murder	55	14	10	4	17
Hostage taking	66	17	9	5	3
Been taken hostage	91	7	2	0	0
Potential to shoot another	60	16	12	7	5
Been physically assaulted	54	18	9	4	15
Seen the physical assault of another	16	16	10	8	50
Riot	35	25	13	7	20
Slashing	64	6	1	3	26
Other	59	29	6	6	0

SOURCE: Rosine 1992.

Official figures illustrated in Table 7.3 show that major assaults on staff decreased from six incidents in 1994/95 to one recorded incident in 1996/97.

Special Handling Units

In 1977, the Correctional Service of Canada introduced **Special Handling Units** (SHUs), the highest level of security, to house dangerous inmates who could not be managed in current maximum security facilities because of the high risk of danger they posed to staff and other inmates (see Table 7.4). Inmates were considered dangerous if they caused serious harm, caused death, jeopardized the safety of others, escaped or attempted to escape, or took hostages. Originally, SHUs were used reactively, that is, in response to dangerous behaviour. A minimum two-year program consisted of 23 hours of solitary confinement in a heavily guarded, top-security prison. Inmates were allowed to exercise for 30 minutes per day (Culhane 1985).

The SHU environment is also a challenge for correctional staff. One officer describes SHU inmates as "a collection of very volatile men, who are potentially explosive at any moment and could not be held anywhere else . . . [t]hey tend to demonstrate that they do not have an appropriate attitude to authority" (Marron 1996, 63).

More recently, SHUs have been used proactively by admitting inmates who are deemed to present a threat (Lowman and MacLean 1991). For instance, an inmate may be considered for transfer to a SHU if he or she has caused or committed an act of violence, or is suspected of having done so; similarly any inmate who makes serious threats or otherwise shows a propensity for serious violence may be considered for transfer. In addition, in line with the new philosophy and objectives of the Correctional Service of Canada, the policies governing SHUs were reviewed and revised in 1992 (see Box 7.4). The overall objective of the SHU is to create an environment in which dangerous inmates are motivated and assisted to behave responsibly so as to facilitate their integration in a maximum security institution.

As a result, the environment in SHUs encourages staff-inmate interactions; physical separations are minimized and controls are less restrictive, but there are enough to ensure a necessary level of safety for staff and inmates. Restraint equipment is used only in exceptional circumstances, and restrictions are gradually reduced as the inmate demonstrates more responsible behaviour. Psychiatric intervention, employment opportunities, and personal development opportunities are provided to SHU inmates, and the National Review Committee provides for an objective process when considering SHU inmates.

BOX 7.3   Special Handling Units

An inmate describes the Special Handling Unit environment in a letter sent to Culhane (1985):

The meals here are unliveable. The bare minimum is one tea, one milk, two slices of bread . . . and the main course. Not enough to feed a cockroach . . . served in small amounts, just enough to keep us alive and forever hungry. Every day we have to *stand* for the count, otherwise get charged. They command us to stand by yelling at us and using foul language to intimidate us. We only get twenty to thirty minutes' exercise outside, instead of one hour.

BOX 7.4	Correctional Service of Canada's Policy Governing Special Handling Units

- Introduction of a 90-day assessment period for inmates under consideration for admission to a Special Handling Unit (SHU).

- Integration of essential components in programming, including psychiatric intervention, employment opportunities, and personal development opportunities.

- Promotion of staff-inmate interaction and fewer physical controls so that the correctional environment will be conducive to inmates changing their behaviour.

- Establishment of a National Review Committee, which provides for a more objective decision-making process when considering inmates' admission to and transfer from the SHUs.

- Annual reviews of the SHUs, resulting in a report on the progress of the SHUs with recommendations for improvement.

SOURCE: O'Brien 1992.

Assessment of Dangerous Inmates

Inmates transferred to a Special Handling Unit undergo various assessments including psychological and psychiatric evaluations. Based on this assessment the National Review Committee reviews the case history of the inmate and determines whether correctional programming in the SHU is necessary. During 1991/92, 103 inmates were transferred to SHUs for assessment. The majority were transferred as a result of their involvement in a major assault on another inmate, hostage takings, or potential hostage takings. At the national level, just over half of the inmates (51.5 percent) who were transferred to the SHU for assessment were actually admitted by the National Review Committee. Of those admitted, almost one quarter (22.6 percent) had previously been admitted to a SHU, and in 7.5 percent of these cases, it had been between 2 and 10 years since the inmate was last in the SHU (O'Brien 1992).

DOING TIME: FILLING THE VOID

While programs are available to SHU inmates and the general prison population, many inmates often say that they are only interested in "doing their time," and participating in rehabilitative exercise is only a means of reducing their sentence. In order to fill the void of prison life, many inmates rely on drugs, contraband, and illegal activities. For instance, the national inmate survey conducted by Robinson and Mirabelli (1996) found that 38 percent of inmates incarcerated in federal institutions said they had used illegal drugs at least once in their current institution. The most frequently used drugs were cannabis (59 percent), heroin (19 percent), and cocaine or crack (17 percent). Moreover, 25 percent of the survey respondents believed that inmates are pressured to smuggle drugs into their facility. Drugs are part of an underground economy that exists in prisons. Drugs, contraband, and cigarettes are traded, sold, and bought in this informal system. Cigarette smoking is a significant time killer among inmates, and has become a contentious issue for correctional management.

The national inmate survey found, for example, that 72 percent of inmates smoke (49 percent of whom smoke at least 20 cigarettes a day). Meanwhile, correctional institutions are moving to become smoke-free environments. In 1999, a smoking ban at the Whitby jail in Ontario was met with strong inmates resistance including hunger strikes and a six-hour riot that caused thousands of dollars in damage.

SUMMARY

This chapter detailed prison life, inmate subculture, and the reality of life behind bars. The prison can be viewed as a microcosm of the wider society, with the values, beliefs, and roles of society at large imported and reproduced. Simultaneously, the structure of the prison—the environment of the institution—also affects the prison populations by influencing the development of specific subcultures. The chapter also describes the daily life of prisoners in crowded and violent prisons, and discusses the handling of dangerous inmates.

The prison has been a source of considerable attention and continues to challenge criminal justice officials in Canada and abroad. The shape of prisons in the future will undoubtedly depend on whether the media, public opinion, and legislators will advocate for punitive or rehabilitative sanctions.

KEY TERMS AND CONCEPTS

deprivation model	mortifications of the self	prisonization
double-bunking	National Inmate Survey	Special Handling Units
importation model	pains of imprisonment	(SHUs)
inmate code	prison crowding	total institution
inmate subculture		

STUDY AND DISCUSSION QUESTIONS

1. What is prisonization?
2. What are the pains of imprisonment?
3. Discuss the importation model and deprivation model as explanations for the development of prison subculture. What are the strengths and weaknesses of each model?
4. What shape will prisons take in the future?
5. How can prison crowding and violence be reduced?
6. Can dangerous inmates be successfully reintegrated back into mainstream prison life? If so, describe how.

WEBLINKS

Summary report of the National Inmate Survey:
   www.csc-scc.gc.ca/text/rsrch/briefs/b14/toce.shtml

United Nations Crime and Justice Information Network (UNCJIN): **www.uncjin.org**

Basic Facts about Federal Corrections (Correctional Service of Canada):
www.csc-scc.gc.ca/text/faits/facts07_e.shtml

Forum on Correctional Research: **www.csc-scc.gc.ca/text/pblct/forum/index_e.shtml**

REFERENCES

Boe, R., and **M. Muirhead**. 1998. Have Falling Crime Rates and Increased Use of Probation Reduced Incarceration? Some Trends and Comparisons. *Forum on Corrections Research* 10(2): 1–5.

Botterell, E. (Chairman). 1984. *Report of the Study Team: Seven Suicides in the Atlantic Region.* Ottawa: Correctional Service Canada.

Caron, R. 1978. *Go-Boy: Memories of a Life Behind Bars.* Toronto: McGraw-Hill Ryerson.

Chavez, J. 1997. *Media Reporting of Crime in Argentina.* Albany, NY: School of Criminal Justice, University of Albany.

Clements, C. 1982. The Relationship of Offender Classification to the Problems of Prison Overcrowding. *Crime and Delinquency* 28: 71–85.

Clemmer, D. 1958. *The Prison Community.* New York: Holt, Rinehart, and Winston.

Cloward, R.A., **D.R. Cressey**, **G.H. Brosser**, **R. McCleery**, **L.E. Ohlin**, **G.M. Sykes**, and **S.L. Messinger**. 1960. *Theoretical Studies in Social Organization of the Prison.* New York: Social Science Research Council.

Correctional Service of Canada. 1992. Violence and Suicide in Canadian Institutions: Some Recent Statistics. *Forum on Crime Research.* 4(3): 1–5. www.csc-scc.gc.ca/text/pblct/forum/e043/e043b.shtml (April 2000).

———. 1996a. *1995 National Inmate Survey: Final Report.* Ottawa: Correctional Service of Canada.

———. 1996b. *Outlook 1996/97 to 1998/99.* Ottawa: Correctional Service of Canada.

———. 1998. *Performance Report for the Period Ending March 31, 1998.* www.csc-scc.gc.ca/text/pblct/perform/repe-03.shtml (April 2000).

———. 1999. *Basic Facts about Federal Corrections.* Ottawa: Public Works and Government Services Canada.

Cox, V., **P. Paulus**, and **G. McCain**. 1984. Prison Crowding Research: The Relevance of Prison Housing Standards and a General Approach Regarding Crowding Phenomena. *American Psychologist* 39: 1,148–1,160.

Cressey, D.R. (Ed.). 1961. *The Prison: Studies in Institutional Organization and Change.* New York: Holt, Rinehart, and Winston.

Culhane, C. 1985. *Still Barred from Prison: Social Injustice in Canada.* Montreal: Black Rose Books.

Dobash, R.P., **R.E. Dobash**, and **S. Gutteridge**. 1986. *The Imprisonment of Women.* New York: Basil Blackwell Publishing.

Edwards, G., and **J. Hughes**. 1997. 45% Believe Violent Crime Is on the Rise. *Gallup Poll* 57(44): 1–3.

Farrington, D., and **C. Nuttal**. 1980. Prison Size, Overcrowding, Prison Violence, and Recidivism. *Journal of Criminal Justice* 8: 221–231.

Finn, A., **S. Trevethan**, **G. Carrière**, and **M. Kowalski**. 1999. Female Inmates, Aboriginal Inmates, and Inmates Serving Life Sentences: A One-Day Snapshot. *Juristat* 19(5): 1–15.

Garfinkel, H. 1965. Conditions of Successful Status Degradation Ceremonies. *American Journal of Sociology* 61: 420–424.

Goffman, E. 1961. *Asylums*. New York: Doubleday.

Irwin, J., and **D.R. Cressey**. 1961. Thieves, Convicts, and the Inmate Code. *Social Problems* 10(1): 142–155.

Johnston, J.C. (1991). A Psychological Perspective on the New Design Concepts for William Head Institution (British Columbia). *Forum on Corrections Research* 3: 14-21.

Joutsen, M. 1997. *Prison Rates in Eastern Europe*. Helsinki: European Institute for Crime Prevention and Control, affiliated with the United Nations.

Kalinich, D.B., and **S. Stojkovic**. 1985. Contraband: The Basis for Legitimate Power in a Prison Social System. *Criminal Justice and Behaviour* 12(4): 435–451.

Kuhn, A. 1996. Incarceration Rates Europe vs. U.S.A. *European Journal on Criminal Policy and Research* 45: 46–73.

Lowman, J., and **B. MacLean**. 1991. Prisons and Protest in Canada. *Social Justice* 18(3): 130–154.

Mann, W.E. 1967. *Society Behind Bars*. Toronto: Social Science Publications.

Marron, K. 1996. *The Slammer: The Crisis in Canada's Prison System*. Toronto: Doubleday Canada.

O'Brien, R. 1992. Special Handling Units. *Forum on Correctional Research* 4(3): 1–5.

People v. Superior Court, 917 P.2d 628 (Cal. Sup. 1996), modified and rehearing denied, 1996 Cal. LEXIS 4699 (Cal. 1996).

Reed, M., and **J. Roberts**. 1999. Adult Correctional Services in Canada, 1997/98. *Juristat* 19(4): 1–14.

Robinson, D., and **L. Mirabelli**. 1996, March. *Summary of Findings of the 1995 CSC National Inmate Survey*. Ottawa: Research Division, Correctional Service of Canada.

Robinson, D., **F.J. Porporino**, **W.A. Millson**, **S. Trevethan**, and **B. MacKillop**. 1998. A One-Day Snapshot of Inmates in Canada's Adult Correctional Facilities. *Juristat* 18(8): 1–15.

Rosine, L. 1992. Exposure to Critical Incidents: What Are the Effects on Canadian Correctional Officers? *Forum on Correctional Research* 4(1): 1–11.

Skovron, S.E., **J.E. Scott**, and **F. Cullen**. 1988. Prison Crowding: Public Attitudes Toward Strategies of Population Control. *Journal of Research in Crime and Delinquency* 25: 150–169.

Stolzenberg, L., and **S.J. D'Alessio**. 1997. Three Strikes and You're Out: The Impact of California's New Mandatory Sentencing Law on Serious Crime Rates. *Crime and Delinquency* 43: 457–469.

Sykes, G.M. 1958. *The Society of Captives: A Study of Maximum Security Prison*. New Jersey: Princeton University Press.

Sykes, G.M., and **S.L. Messinger**. 1970. The Inmate Social Code. In N. Johnston (Ed.), *Sociology of Punishment and Corrections*. New York: John Wiley and Sons.

Turner, M.G., **J.L. Sundt**, and **B.K. Applegate**. 1995. "Three Strikes and You're Out" Legislation: A National Assessment. *Federal Probation* 59: 16–35.

United Nations. 1957. *The Standard Minimum Rules for the Treatment of Prisoners*. Resolution 663 C1 (XXIV). 31 July.

Wilson, T.W. 1986. Gender Differences in the Inmate Code. *Canadian Journal of Criminology* 28: 397–405.

Zamble, E., and **F. Porporino**. 1988. *Coping Behaviour and Adaptation in Prison Inmates*. New York: Springer-Verlag.

LIMITING THE STATE'S RIGHT TO PUNISH

Kelly Hannah-Moffat
Department of Sociology
Erindale College, University of Toronto
Toronto, Ontario

LEARNING OBJECTIVES

After reading this chapter, you should be able to:

- Understand the evolution of prisoners' rights in Canada;
- Understand the significance of these rights;
- Understand some of the basic methods of ensuring and protecting prisoners' rights; and
- Consider the gap between legal norms and correctional practice.

One must resist the temptation to trivialize the infringement of prisoners' rights as an insignificant infringement of the rights of people who do not deserve any better. When a right has been granted by law, it is no less important that such rights be respected because the person entitled to it is a prisoner; indeed, it is always more important that the vigorous enforcement of rights be effected in the cases where the right is the most meaningful.

—Justice Louise Arbour

What are the limits on the state's right to punish an offender? What constitutes too much punishment? When is punishment excessive? Why should prisoners have rights—after all, they are coddled and they have more rights than the law-abiding citizen. Prisoners' rights are, without doubt, highly controversial. To answer such questions we need to reflect on the meaning, context, purpose, and history of imprisonment and on the significance of human rights in limiting the power of the state. The debate about prisoners' rights is filled with misconceptions and often inappropriately juxtaposed with concerns about victims' rights (or lack of rights). We do not deny the insufficiency and importance of victims' rights; however, pitting victims' rights against prisoner's rights fails to capture the significance and complexity of the issue. The breadth of the debate is expansive. The debate about prisoners' rights is not simply about colour televisions, varied meals, and new recreation facilities, but more fundamentally speaks to our views on human rights and the civility of our society. As Melnitzer (2000, 186) notes, "the civil rights of prisoners are the lowest common denominator of democracy." The power of the state is ominous, and those subject to that power—particularly those confined out of public view, like prisoners—need some assurances of accountability and protection from the arbitrary uses and abuses of power by correctional officials, who control virtually every aspect of a prisoner's life. Rights allow prisoners to have some autonomy and control over their living conditions.

The debate about rights, which legally and morally ensure conformity with a particular norm, is not to be confused with privileges, which are often equated with an advantage or source of pleasure granted to a person. This discussion of rights speaks to the protection of basic legal, democratic, and human rights, such as access to lawyers, privacy, limits on the use of solitary confinement, limits on the use of force, the right to be informed about decisions, the right not to be subject to cruel and unusual punishments, and the right to basic amenities such as showers, sanitary products, clothing, medical treatment, and exercise.

The recognition and acknowledgement of such rights, along with the development of laws and administrative processes to secure those rights, are a relatively new phenomenon. The objectives of this chapter are to provide a brief history of prisoners' rights legislation, to outline some of the official avenues of redress available to prisoners, and to discuss some of the gaps between the legal norms that protect prisoners and reinforce the rule of law and correctional practice.

THE SIGNIFICANCE OF PRISONERS' RIGHTS

The administration of a prison sentence is linked to the administration of justice and as such is governed by the rule of law, which implies that everyone from the most ordinary citizen to the head of state is subject to the law. The rule of law in this context means that the authority to punish comes from the law. In a society governed by the rule of law, the state (for the purposes of our discussion, this means the Correctional Service of Canada and its employees) must respect the fundamental rights of citizens. The premise is that either human rights belong to everyone or they are guaranteed to no one. The coercive authority of the state to punish individuals by confining them and depriving them of their liberty (a precious and taken-for-granted freedom) is justified in law. The guarantee and enforcement of the rule of law ensures that punishment is fair and not arbitrary, and that the experience of punishment is not inconsistent with the expectation of that punishment. For example, if a judge exercises legal authority to sentence a person to a period of incarceration, that judge expects that the offender will be removed from society and denied liberty for a defined period of time. The judge may also expect the offender to have access to programs and services that facilitate his or her reintegration into society while at the same time maintaining the safety of the community. Judges who impose sanctions expect that their sentence will be administered in accordance with the law (Arbour 1996, 183). When the experience of incarceration is unduly harsh or unjust, it deviates from legal expectations and, thus, the integrity of the sentence is compromised.

The central point here is that prisoners are sentenced to a period of incarceration *as* punishment, not *for* punishment. The 1975 United Nations Minimum Standards for the Treatment of Prisoners, to which Canada subscribes, clearly indicates that:

- A prisoner's sense of dignity and worth as a human being must be respected and maintained through the entire course of imprisonment;
- The suffering that results from the loss of liberty and freedom by the fact of incarceration is punishment enough; and
- Prisons should not be punishing places; rather, they should help prisoners rehabilitate themselves (Correctional Service of Canada 1998a, 15).

Subsequently, the Correctional Service has a duty and an obligation to ensure that incarcerated offenders who are denied their liberty and freedom as a consequence of their sentence are treated humanely and fairly. Prisoners retain all the same rights as law-abiding citizens, except those that are necessarily removed because of their imprisonment (i.e., mobility and freedom of association). Today, both domestic and international human rights laws affirm that people deprived of their liberty have a right to be treated fairly and not subject to cruel, inhumane, or degrading treatment or punishment. Article 6 of the United Nations Universal Declaration of Human Rights states that all people, including those imprisoned, have the right to full and equal recognition and protection before the law. This means that prisoners have, or should have, certain inalienable and fundamental rights and freedoms, such as the right to life, liberty, and security of person.

These rights are of utmost importance to individuals who find themselves in situations wherein they need protection. In her examination of the Correctional Service of Canada's flagrant violations of federal women prisoners rights, Justice Louise Arbour (1996, 182) argues that "one must resist the temptation to trivialize the infringement of prisoners' rights as either an insignificant infringement of rights, or as an infringement of rights of people who do not deserve any better." She says that

> For example, the right not to be subjected to body cavity searches is not particularly valuable to those who are unlikely ever to be subjected to such an intrusive procedure. It is only valuable, and therefore should be enforced with the greatest vigour, in cases where such searches are likely to be undertaken (Arbour 1996, 82–183).

In summary, Arbour argues that even though law-abiding citizens may not identify with the position of prisoners, respecting and protecting prisoners' rights are critical because of the potential for abuse. Failing to protect the rights of prisoners jeopardizes the rights of all citizens.

THE EVOLUTION OF PRISONERS' RIGHTS

The premise that the correctional system should be bound by the rule of law and to the same due process standards as other parts of the criminal justice system is a relatively new concept. Traditionally, the judiciary adopted a hands-off approach to prisoners' rights, particularly in terms of inmate discipline and institutional management (Campbell 1997; Landau 1984; Jackson 1983; Jacobs 1980). The relative importance of prisoners' rights has changed over time. Historically, prisoners were afforded few rights and subjected to hard labour and physical punishment. Punishments were harsh, severe, and, by today's standards, inhumane (see Chapters 1 and 2). Corporal punishments, such as hosing inmates with a powerful stream of cold water (used until 1913), dunking prisoners in troughs of ice (used until 1930), whipping and strapping (used until 1972), long periods of solitary confinement on bread and water diets (used until 1976), and the death penalty (also used until 1976), were commonplace (MacGuigan 1977). This approach to corrections was influenced by a prevailing belief in the deterrent effect of imprisonment in austere conditions. Correctional officials believed that the harsher and more unpleasant the punishment, the greater the likelihood of conformity to the penal regime and the greater the chances of reform upon release from prison. While this belief still prevails today, academic research does not support the premise that harsh penalties or sparse and unpleasant conditions of confinement either deter offenders, prevent crime, or elicit conformity.

Until the mid 1930s, there was little public or political interest in exposing these harsh conditions to external scrutiny. There were few substantive rights and procedural protections for prisoners (Campbell 1997). According to Landau (1984), the prison was an autonomous and secret system, with its own norms over which there was no form of external scrutiny. Prisoners were proverbially "out of sight, out of mind" and matters of prison discipline were left to penitentiary wardens. Prisoners' only method of focusing public attention on their living conditions was through the occasional riot. When riots did occur, they were often the result of the absence of meaningful programs and ineffective or non-existent complaint processes. In 1938, the Archambault Commission raised some concerns about prison conditions and prison discipline; however, government attention to prisoners' rights and significant developments in prisoners' rights litigation did not occur until the mid 1960s.

The overall correctional philosophy shifted in the postwar period from an ethos of deterrence and hard labour to one of rehabilitation. The intent of the rehabilitation model or medical punishment was to turn the prison into a hospital to "treat" the "disease" of criminality. While the rehabilitative approach yielded many positive developments, including the introduction of programs such as individual counselling, it also led to further indiscretions and abuses of prisoners' rights. A wide variety of interventions and "treatments" were imposed on often-involuntary patients (see Box 8.1). For example, some of the new treatment techniques employed in the British Columbia's Oakalla Prison included plastic surgery, which was first used in 1953 to correct "any disability which might have contributed towards delinquency, such as scars, squints, unsightly or obscene tattoos" (Richmond 1975). Under the benevolent guise of treatment and rehabilitation, prisoners were subjected to cruel and dehumanizing treatments such as shock therapy, experimental drugs, forcible injections of mind-altering drugs, experimental surgeries, forced sterilization, prolonged segregation and sensory deprivation, indefinite periods of incarceration, and, in some instances, physical abuse (Ekstedt and Griffiths 1988). Some of these abuses continue today and few prisoners are compensated by the state for these indiscretions. The introduction of a rehabilitative ethos raised several concerns about the professional ethics, consent, and the right to be informed of and refuse treatment. At present, it is acknowledged that prisoners retain the right to self-determination and that incarceration does not remove an individual's basic right to refuse medical and psychological treatment. The individual's right to autonomy and control over his or her body is one of the most fundamental rights of today's legal system. This right is extended to prisoners and "it can only be limited in very narrow circumstances when mental incompetence prevents an individual from giving informed consent to treat-

BOX 8.1	Dorothy Proctor's Case

The 1998 statement of claim (pending law suit) filed by Dorothy Proctor verifies the existence of a experimentation program at the Prison for Women in the early 1960s that consisted of administering mind-altering drugs, primarily lysergic acid diethylamide (LSD-25) in conjunction with other potent drugs, and with the administration of electrical currents to the brain ("electroshock"). One of the purposes of this experimentation was an attempt to modify the behaviour of prisoners and in particular to "alter the criminal disposition of offenders" and reduce recidivism. Approximately 30 female inmates were involved in these experiments. Ms. Proctor, 17 at the time, was serving a three-year sentence at the Prison for Women when she was identified as a participant in this experiment. According to court records, during the first year of her incarceration Ms. Proctor was placed in solitary confinement for lengthy periods of time, as punishment for breaches of various prison rules. While incarcerated she was compelled to undergo experiments under the direction of a contract psychiatrist. These experiments continued throughout the second and third years of her incarceration at the Prison for Women and while she stayed at the Institute of Psychotherapy. This series of experimentation shows an extreme exercise of disciplinary power and a flagrant abuse of individual rights, which existed, at the Prison for Women.

After several denials of any wrongdoing in this case, in March of 1997, the Commission of the Correctional Service of Canada ordered a Board of Investigation under section 20 of the *Correctional and Conditional Release Act* to investigate and report on Ms. Proctor's allegations. Even though this board of investigation was not able to obtain several relevant Correctional Service of Canada records, it did produce a final report, which found, among other things, that Ms. Proctor was administered, without her informed consent, LSD-25 while in solitary confinement and that she had sustained long-term negative effects as a result (including brain damage). There is some issue here as to whether or not an incarcerated prisoner can ever provide informed consent. In this particular case, the defendant, Ms. Proctor was not informed of the potential long-term consequences of this drug, and as a minor and prisoner she did not feel that she was in a position to decline treatment. There are outstanding allegations of assault and battery, a breach of fiduciary duty, intentional infliction of mental suffering, negligence, and a resulting claim for punitive and exemplary damages. The board recommended compensation and an apology for Ms. Proctor and the other unnamed inmates involved in the experiments, the lawsuit is still pending (as of July 1999).

SOURCE: Ontario Court General Division 1998.

ment or when the person has a communicable disease covered by provincial legislation" (McKinnon 1995, 47).

By the mid 1970s, conditions in prison had worsened to the point that they could no longer be hidden. Society's tolerance for these prison violence and the indiscretions of prison authorities was lessening. The growing disillusionment with rehabilitative approaches and concerns about prisoner's rights led to another shift in correctional philosophy to more community-based interventions. This period of penalty saw a "humanizing of punishment" with the abolition of corporal punishment in 1972 and of the death penalty in 1976. Throughout the 1960s and 1970s, there were several prison riots and the penitentiary system was increasingly subject to the scrutiny of public and parliamentary committees (Gosselin 1982). The infamous riot at Kingston Penitentiary marked a turning point in corrections. The 1971 Swackhamer inquiry, which criticized Kingston Penitentiary for the curtailment of programs and activities in the years before the riot, argues that:

> Such things as access to hobby craft and sports, freedom to decorate cells and to dress in non-prison clothing on certain occasions, were not trivial privileges that could be limited or withdrawn without negative impact—but rather that these were significant factors in reducing the dehumanizing effects of incarceration (Campbell 1997, 297).

This commentary, along with similar indictments of the prison system's overall failure to rehabilitate or protect such as the MacGuigan Committee's 1977 report (which characterized Canadian corrections as "a system in crisis"), supported a shift away from punitive conditions of confinement towards the normalization of the prison experience. Campbell (1997) argues that a recognition of these deplorable circumstances contributed to additional government inquiries, the establishment of new legal frameworks and support systems that allowed for external scrutiny and accountability through systematic monitoring and prisoners' rights litigation (see Box 8.2).

BOX 8.2	Selected Government Inquiries and Related Developments

1959 The Parole Act and the National Parole Board—This act allowed for the creation of the National Parole Board. For the first time in Canadian correctional history, parole decisions were determined and administered by an independent, national decision-making body.

1960 The Canadian Bill of Rights—This bill affirms the dignity and worth of the human person and recognizes and declares fundamental freedoms. Although replaced to some extent by the Charter of Rights and Freedoms in 1982, the Bill of Rights continues to apply to acts of federal government.

1965 Ouimet Committee—This rehabilitation-orientated committee argued that punishment for the sake of retribution was expensive and fruitless.

It favoured community correctional options and in-person parole hearings, and it was critical of corporal punishment, which was still used in some institutions.

1971 Swackhamer Inquiry—This inquiry recommended the development of a "visitors' committee" to oversee the operation of penitentiaries. This recommendation led to the creation of the Office of the Correctional Investigator in 1973.

1972 Hugessen Task Force—This report made a series of recommendations to improve fairness and accountability in release decision-making, including access to information, right to reasons, and the right to have assistance at parole hearings. It recommended the creation of five regional parole boards at the federal level.

3

1973 Office of the Correctional Investigator—This office was established as a result of the Swackhamer Inquiry. The function of the Correctional Investigator is to conduct investigations in to the problems of offenders. The powers of the correctional investigator were redefined in the 1992 *Corrections and Conditional Release Act*.

1972 Abolition of Corporal Punishment—The use of corporal punishments such as whipping and strapping, which were previously imposed as a sanction from the court or as a penalty for institutional offences, was abolished.

1973 Queen's University Correctional Law Project—This project, which began as a research study, was instrumental in litigating many of the major correctional law cases. It provides mechanisms that allow prisoners to challenge the conditions of their confinement and correctional decisions in court (Campbell 1997, 302).

1974 Goldenberg Committee—This report echoed the concerns of the Hugessen.

1975 Millhaven Inquiry—This report is noted for its articulation of the vulnerability of prisoners in a climate where there is a absence of rights, the rule of law, and due process.

1975 The United Nations Standard Minimum Rules for the Treatment of Prisoners—This comprehensive international document recognizes and outlines the rights of legally incarcerated persons. Many countries including Canada have integrated these principles into their legal and policy frameworks.

1976 The Abolition of the Death Penalty—Although the death penalty was officially abolished on July 26, 1976, the last execution in Canada occurred in December 1962. All death sentences between 1962 and 1976 were commuted to life imprisonment in 1977.

1977 The Métis and Non-status Indian Crime and Justice Commission Reports—This commission reported on the over-representation of Native offenders in federal and provincial prisons and recommended increased involvement of Natives in the development of correctional policy.

1977 Canadian Human Rights Act—This act provides all citizens including prisoners with access to information about them held by the government. This meant that for the first time offenders were able to access significant portions of their institutional files and evaluate the information contained in the file used to inform correctional and release decisions. This act also established the Canadian Human Rights Commission, which was mandated to monitor and report on human rights concerns. This Commission has made a number of influential rulings on the conditions of confinement at the Prison for Women, on privacy issues, and on the employment of female guards in men's prisons.

1977 National Advisory Committee on the Female Offender (Clark Report)—This report outlined some of the longstanding inadequacies in the treatment of federally sentenced women. Like many previous reports, it called for the closure of the Prison for Women and for substantial improvements in programs and services for incarcerated women, including francophone and Aboriginal prisoners. This report was one of a series of reports over the next 20 years calling for substantial reforms and for the acknowledgement of women prisoners' rights to equality.

1980 Martineau v. Matsqui Institutional Disciplinary Board and the Duty to Act Fairly—In this case the Supreme Court of Canada, for the first time, acknowledged and reaffirmed that prison officials have a duty to act fairly when making decisions about offenders involving their rights. The duty to act fairly includes the duty to inform prisoners about reasons for all administrative decisions that affect an offender's liberty.

1982 Canadian Charter of Rights and Freedoms—Inspired by international human rights documents, the Charter protects the rights and freedoms of all citizens.

1982 Access to Information Act—This act allowed citizens broad access to internal Correctional Service reports, inquiries, and studies.

1990 Report of the Task Force on Federally Sentenced Women—The primary recommendations of this task force were the closure of the Prison for Women and the construction of five new regional facilities to be dispersed across the country, including an Aboriginal healing lodge. This report marks a significant change in women's corrections. For the first time, the government acknowledged and accepted the specific and unique needs and experiences of women.

1992 Corrections and Conditional Release Act (CCRA)—This act completely replaces the *Penitentiary and Parole Acts* that previously governed the operations of the Correctional Service of Canada. The CCRA incorporates important legal developments in administrative law, and reflects the rights expressed in the Canadian Charter of Rights and Freedoms. The CCRA covers three areas: matters pertaining to the custodial portion of the sentence, conditional release under the jurisdiction of the National Parole Board, and the Office of the Correctional Investigator.

1996 Arbour Commission—This commission was mandated by the Solicitor General of Canada to investigate and report on an incident that occurred at the Prison for Women in April of 1994. The report argued that respect for rule of law and a culture of rights were not evident in correctional practice, in spite of a plethora of laws and policies aimed to the contrary.

1997 Task Force on Administrative Segregation—This task force was established in response to a recommendation of the Arbour Commission. It provided a complete review of the use of administrative segregation by the Correctional Service. The task force was to ensure that all correctional staff and managers were knowledgeable of the legal and policy requirements and procedural compliance with the law. It found that Correctional Service staff did not fully appreciate their obligation to comply with legislative and policy provisions in the management of administrative segregation.

Inquiries recommended improvements in general living conditions and the development of a formalized grievance process. These recommendations contributed to the eventual creation of the Office of the Correctional Investigator and the development of a formal institutionally based system for handling complaints and grievances in 1973. (These devices are discussed in greater detail below). In addition to these procedural developments, there was a series of legislative changes and influential legal decisions. Some of the most notable legislative changes included the enactment of the *Canadian Human Rights Act* (1977), the

Canadian Charter of Rights and Freedoms (1982), and the *Corrections and Conditional Release Act and Regulations* (1992). The *Canadian Human Rights Act* allowed citizens, for the first time, to access information about them held by the government; most significantly, it established the Canadian Human Rights Commission. Prior to the enactment of the Charter of Rights and Freedoms, this tribunal provided prisoners and their advocates a legal avenue of redress. The Commission investigated and reported on several matters relating to prisoners. Two of the most notable cases involved balancing the rights of female guards to work in men's penitentiaries against a prisoner's right to privacy, and the conditions at the Prison for Women. After a comprehensive year-long investigation of the controversy surrounding the Prison for Women, the Human Rights Commission upheld the complaint by Women for Justice and declared that "federal female offenders were discriminated against on the basis of sex, and that in virtually all programs and facility areas, the treatment of federal women inmates was inferior to that of men" (Cooper 1987, 139). The Canadian Human Rights Commission said that the state had a legal and moral obligation to provide women with programs and facilities "substantively equivalent" to those provided to male inmates. The investigation also noted that there were few women involved in the development of policies and in senior management of the prison, and it was suggested that increased involvement of women in this area could facilitate improvements (Hannah-Moffat 2000).

Legal decisions played a critical role in reshaping the correctional landscape by further defining and refining laws, policies, and their interpretations as they pertained to the rights and privileges of offenders. For example, in *Martineau v. Matsqui Institutional Disciplinary Board* (1978), the Supreme Court of Canada reversed its "hands-off approach" and for the first time in correctional law, it declared that correctional authorities had a **duty to act fairly** when making decisions concerning the rights of prisoners (Correctional Service of Canada 1998a, 21). Subsequent litigation clarifies that the duty to act fairly exists "whenever the rights, privileges and interests of the offender are at stake" and this includes:

> The right to be given notice to the allegations, an account of the information being considered by the decision-maker, sufficient time and opportunity to respond to allegations, the right to be heard, the right to a hearing free of bias, and the right to be given reasons for a final decision. Depending on the nature of rights and privileges and interests at issue, the duty of fairness may also include the right to legal assistance and the right to a full hearing (Correctional Service of Canada 1998a, 22).

Prior to this case judicial authorities were reluctant to interfere with the internal administration of penitentiaries.

In addition to this case, the enactment of the Charter of Rights and Freedoms in 1982 led to increases in litigation on prisoners' substantive rights and on procedural fairness. Although the Charter has brought forth an unprecedented number of challenges to corrections and conditional release matters, and although it has allowed for real recourse to remedies through the courts, prisoners have not had a high degree of success in their claims (Campbell 1997, 310). In general, the courts tend to be conservative in their rulings on prison issues. Section 7 of the Charter, which refers to protections for life, liberty, and security of person, is one of the most heavily litigated sections of the Charter. Issues raised under this section include concerns about correctional and conditional release decision-making processes, disciplinary hearings, transfers, urinalysis, double-bunking (which incidentally also violates the UN Minimum Standards for the Treatment of Prisoners), unescorted temporary absences, revocation of parole, parole conditions, and detention decisions (Campbell 1997, 313). The

Charter was also used to litigate concerns about the right to legal counsel, the use of segregation as arbitrary form of detention, searches (in particular by officers of the opposite sex), the imposition of cruel and unusual punishments (including challenges to the constitutionality of indefinite confinement permitted through dangerous offender legislation, doublebunking, and segregation—none of which was ruled in violation of section 12), equality (as it pertains mainly to accommodations, programs, and services for federal female prisoners).

The Charter and related litigation, as well as the findings of earlier inquires, played a critical role in shaping the ***Corrections and Conditional Release Act*** (CCRA), the legislation that currently governs the federal corrections. This act ensures that prisoners retain the same rights and privileges of all members of society, except those necessarily removed as a consequence of incarceration. The CCRA replaced the *Penitentiary and Parole Acts* that previously governed corrections and conditional release. This act affirms the **rule of law** and it reflects many of the principles, values, and corporate objectives outlined in mission statement of the Correctional Service of Canada, which was adopted in 1989 (Correctional Service of Canada 1998a). The CCRA has three components: part one relates to matters involving the custodial portion of the prisoner's sentence, part two deals with matters related to the National Parole Board and conditional release, and part three governs the Office of the Correctional Investigator.

AVENUES OF REDRESS

Unlike the past, today prisoners have several official and legal avenues of redress available to them. In addition to independent litigation, prisoners in theory have unfettered access to the institutional grievance and complaint process, and to the Office of the Correctional Investigator.

The Offender Grievance System

Federal offenders have had access to a formal grievance procedure since 1973. This process was formalized and refined in the 1992 CCRA. Sections 90 and 91 require that:

- There be fair and expeditious procedures for resolving offender's complaints on matters within the jurisdiction of the Commissioner; and

- Offenders have complete access to these procedures without negative consequences.

The intention of this legislation is to provide prisoners with access to a fair, timely, and effective method of redress when needed. The grievance system is a three-stage process, wherein the complaint or grievance is first filed at the institutional level, where the warden has authority. Each institution has a grievance coordinator, who manages the institutional grievance process. Some wardens have the grievance coordinator investigate issues directly, while others have complaints and grievances refer to the correctional manager in charge of the area or of the individual being grieved (Mainwaring 1998). If the outcome is not satisfactory the complaint can be escalated to the second level, which is regional headquarters, and then to the third level, national headquarters, for resolution. At the regional and national levels, there are teams of analysts who investigate grievances and prepare responses for the Deputy Commissioner's signature in the region and for the signature of the Assistant Commission, Corporate Development, at the third and final level.

The Correctional Service of Canada receives in excess of 23,000 formal written complaints and grievances each year that require investigation and response. Grievance data appear to suggest that a relatively small portion of the correctional population is responsible for the vast majority of complaints and grievances submitted. For example, 5 percent of the prisoner population accounted for 16,191 or 69 percent of complaints and grievances during the 1996 calendar year (Correctional Service of Canada 1998b, 9). However, given that the Correctional Service is bound by law to ensure that all offenders have complete access to the grievance process, it is required to treat these complaints with the same rigour as any complaint filed by prisoners who rarely invoke this process.

According to the Correctional Service, an offender receives a response to a grievance in on average between 11.6 and 17 working days. Only 5.8 percent are submitted to the final level of the grievance procedure for investigation—most grievances and complaints are dealt with at the lowest level between the offender and the correctional workers. Subsequently, the Correctional Service (1998b) states that it is providing offenders with a timely and efficient responses to their complaints and grievances. Given that 19 percent of the complaints filed by prisoners in 1996 were upheld in whole or in part, the Correctional Service reports that it considers "grievances in a serious light and utilizes the system to contribute to the fair treatment of offenders." Interestingly, it states that grievances are increasingly being resolved in favour of offenders at lowest level of the grievance procedure.

From the prisoner's perspective, however, there remains some skepticism about the effectiveness of this process, which until recently was severely backlogged. The Correctional Service (1998b) notes that while some offenders actively engage the grievance process, that process may not be accessible to others. For example, Aboriginal offenders comprise 15 percent of the federal offender population but only submitted 7.5 percent of the total complaints and grievances in 1995/1996. The Correctional Service has expressed some concern about the cultural appropriateness of this complaint process, which may preclude offenders, for various reasons (including language barriers) from using this method.

Julius Melnitzer (2000), an incarcerated former criminal lawyer, suggests that prisoners are often subject to arbitrary decision-making and violations of their rights and that often prisoners do not engage formal complaint processes when, or if, they realize that their rights have been compromised. This failure to access formal process can be attributed to ignorance of their legal protections, concerns about pending administrative decisions such as transfers, passes, and parole, fear, or a lack of faith in "the system." Prisoners' right advocates such as Kim Pate (1998) note that the impact of rights is often curtailed by the fact that few prisoners are actually fully aware of the extent to the rights. Melnitzer (2000, 186) argues that various systemic factors and the status of being a prisoner often inhibit seeking redress. Some tasks—such as calling a lawyer, which is a simple and straightforward right guaranteed to everyone under the Charter of Rights and Freedoms, including prisoners—are difficult to exercise if a person is denied access to a telephone. He raises some important systemic issues about prisoners' access to this internal complaint process as well as its perceived fairness. He also argues that the powerless status that accompanies being a prisoner inhibits an offender's ability to exercise his or her rights. When institutional staff hear complaints about the conduct of other institutional staff, the legitimacy of the complaint process is compromised. Because of their incarcerated status, prisoners often rely on the cooperation of institutional staff when they request access to their lawyer or others, such as the Correctional Investigator.

Similarly, Mann (1998) argues that while the grievance and complaint procedure appears to be bureaucratically noble in appearance, in practice the effectiveness, confidentiality, and objectivity of the process are viewed by many prisoners with widespread cynicism. Prisoners often "fear that simply lodging a complaint can be detrimental and that the only constructive way to achieve conflict resolution is by circumventing the complex grievance system and directly involving the Federal Court of Canada by way of litigation." Many prisoners believe that the Correctional Service's commitment to human rights represents a form of "bureaucratic window dressing" that frequently fails in practice.

The Office of the Correctional Investigator

The Office of the Correctional Investigator plays a central role in protecting the rights of prisoners and ensuring Correctional Service of Canada's compliance with the law. The **Correctional Investigator** is an independent and neutral body. It is neither an agent of the Correctional Service nor an advocate for the prisoner. The mandate of the Correctional Investigator is

> To conduct investigations into problems of offenders related to decisions, recommendations, acts, or omissions of the Commissioner (of Corrections) or any person under the control or management of, or performing services for or on behalf of, the Commissioner, that affect offenders either individually or as a group (Correctional Investigator 1997, 5).

The Correctional Investigator conducts investigations and makes recommendations on the problems of prisoners as they relate to the operations and activities of the Correctional Service. The office is afforded a substantial amount of discretion and investigative authority; it can require the production of all relevant information pertaining to a complaint, and, when required, it can conduct a formal hearing involving an examination under oath. In addition to investigating complaints, the Correctional Investigator makes a series of unscheduled visits to penitentiaries and regularly meets with inmate committees. The Correctional Investigator's recommendations, however, are not legally binding on the Correctional Service of Canada. The Correctional Investigator provides an annual report each year documenting its activities to the Solicitor General, who in turn is required by law to present each report to Parliament.

In the 1996/97 reporting year, the Correctional Investigator received 6,366 complaints and 5,463 complaints in 1997/98. A detailed list of the complaints received in 1997/98 is presented in Table 8.1.

The 1996/97 annual report of the Correctional Investigator indicates that the majority of complaints received are resolved at an institutional level through discussion and negotiation. When a case is not resolved at this level, the matter is referred to regional or national headquarters. If in the opinion of the Correctional Investigator, the matter is not sufficiently addressed in a reasonable and timely way at this level, the matter can be referred to the Solicitor General.

According to the Correctional Investigator, there are many recurring areas of complaint, which reflect broader systemic problems. These include the operation and management of Special Handling Units, inmate pay, grievance procedures, case preparation and programming, double-bunking, temporary absence programming, transfers, the management of the aftermath of a hostage-taking incident at Saskatchewan Penitentiary in 1991, the handling of mentally incompetent prisoners, disciplinary court decisions, the investigation of use of

TABLE 8.1	Complaints Received by the Correctional Investigator, by Category in 1996/97

Administrative segregation		Health care	
a) Placement	182	a) Access	76
b) Conditions	41	b) Correction	232
Case preparation		Mental health	
a) Parole	222	a) Access	22
b) Temporary absence	112	b) Programs	8
c) Transfer	272	Other	63
Cell effects	287	Pen placement	45
Cell placement	86	Private family visiting	168
Claims		Programs	257
a) Decisions	66	Request for information	294
b) Processing	50	Security classification	103
Correspondence	53	Sentence administration	66
Diet		Staff	263
a) Food services	22	Temporary absence decision	102
b) Medical	22	Telephone	89
c) Religious	19	Transfer	
Discipline		a) Decision	301
a) Independent chairperson's decisions	31	b) Involuntary	276
b) Minor court decisions	20	Use of force	60
c) Procedures	106	Visits	220
Discrimination	35		
Employment	89	**Outside Terms of Reference**	
Financial matters		National Parole Board decisions	184
a) Access to funds	71	Outside court	21
b) Pay	184	Provincial matters	14
Grievance procedure	157	Total	5,463

SOURCE: Correctional Investigator 1998. Reproduced with the permission of the Minister of Public Works and Government Services Canada, 2000.

force and follow-up on these investigations, and the investigation of inmate injuries (Correctional Investigator 1993; 1994; 1995; 1997; 1998).

According to the 1996/97 annual report, the common areas of complaint continue to focus on "longstanding issues" that are repeatedly raised in successive reports. In addition to the systemic concerns mentioned above, an overriding theme in the Correctional Investigator's annual reports, as well as in other independent inquiries and investigations such as the Arbour Commission (1996) and the Task Force on Administrative Segregation (1997), is a concern with objectivity and fairness in decision-making. Another common theme is the Correctional Service of Canada's investigations into the complaints and concerns of inmates, advocacy groups, and independent investigators and the Service's responses to those issues. For example, the Correctional Investigator has repeatedly denounced the practice of double bunking. It argues that:

> The housing of two individuals in a secure cell, designed for one individual, for up to twenty-three hours a day, for months on end, is inhumane. This practice, which continues unmonitored at either the regional or national level, defies not only any reasonable standard of decency but also the standards of international convention (Correctional Investigator 1997, 30).

Repeatedly, the response of the Correctional Service on this particular issue is that it is researching the problem; in the meantime, the practice continues. In a similar vein, the Correctional Investigator (1997) notes that it has repeatedly raised concerns about Correctional Service of Canada's ongoing failure to consistently conduct investigations on the use of force and to follow up on those investigations in accordance to its policy. Similar concerns are raised about the Service's internal investigation process in relation to other matters, such as the investigation of prisoner's injuries. On this issue, the Correctional Investigator (1997, 37) notes that "our areas of concerns have and continue to focus on the objectivity, thoroughness, and timeliness of investigations and the management of the process itself." With respect to the institutional grievance process, the Correctional Investigator (1997, 26) reports that "the difficulties inherent in the operation of this process have been related to *an absence of commitment and acceptance of responsibility on the part of those mandated to make the process work*" [emphasis added].

Nonetheless, the Correctional Investigator's 1997/98 annual report points out that it has been invited to participate in several task forces, focus groups, and meetings in the areas of administrative segregation, Special Handling Unit reviews, inmate grievance policy, federally sentenced women, healthcare redress, Aboriginal issues, and the review of the CCRA (Correctional Investigator 1998). The Correctional Investigator reports that some significant progress was made over the past year in improving Canada's handling of prisoners' concerns.

Concerns about the Correctional Service of Canada's unresponsiveness and indifference to infringements on prisoners' rights are raised in many contemporary forums. Of particular concern is the Service's lack of accountability to the rule of law and the inability of the Correctional Investigator and of administrative processes, such as the grievance and complaints process, to make meaningful substantive and systemic changes. Justice Louise Arbour also stated these concerns, in the course of her investigations into incidents that occurred at the Prison for Women in 1994. In the report of the **Arbour Commission**, she argued that the role of the Correctional Investigator, while extremely valuable, is severely limited by its inability to compel compliance by the Correctional Service to its recommendations for changes and improvements in correctional operations (Arbour 1996). This lack of compliance is further complicated by what she called the Correctional Service's "disturbing lack of commitment to the ideals of justice" (198). For these reasons, Justice Arbour recommended increased judicial scrutiny and supervision of correctional practices. She also recommended that when there are serious violations of prisoners' rights legal remedies such as the reduction of the prisoner's sentence might be an appropriate way of ensuring accountability. She argues:

> If illegalities, gross mismanagement of unfairness in the administration of a sentence renders the sentence harsher than that imposed by the court, a reduction of the period of imprisonment may be granted, such as to reflect the fact that the punishment administered was more punitive than the one intended (Arbour 1996, 183).

This legal remedy is akin to the exclusionary rule contained in the Charter, which allows for the exclusion of evidence illegally obtained by the police. Arbour (1996, 183–184) argues that this exclusionary rule has been the single most effective means ever in Canadian law to ensure compliance by state agents with the fundamental rights of individuals in the area of search and seizures, arrest and detention, right to counsel, and the giving of statements to persons in authority. She further argues that such an exclusionary provision would not actually benefit the prisoner in the same way, because the exclusionary rule appears to benefit the accused. Rather, she notes that "a reduction in the term of imprisonment to reflect the illegality of unjustly imposed harsher conditions of imprisonment *merely restores the original sentence to its full intended effect. There is truly no windfall for the inmate"* [emphasis added] (184). While the practicalities of such a mechanism of redress are difficult to comprehend, Justice Arbour's proposal has certainly drawn attention to this issue.

The recommendations of the Arbour Commission were far reaching and had implications far beyond women's corrections, because Justice Arbour highlighted a variety of systemic violations that seriously compromised prisoners' rights. Her numerous recommendations are still being reviewed in various correctional forums. The 1997 **Task Force on Administrative Segregation** was one such forum; it was established in response to a recommendation of the Arbour Commission. It provided a complete review of the use of administrative segregation by Correctional Service of Canada. The Task Force was to ensure that all correctional staff and managers were knowledgeable of the legal and policy requirements and procedural compliance with the law. It ultimately confirmed the findings of Justice Arbour through its findings that Correctional Service staff did not fully appreciate their obligation to comply with legislative and policy provisions in the management of administrative segregation (Task Force on Administrative Segregation 1997, 12) and, furthermore, that "overall CSC staff members and managers demonstrated a casual attitude towards the rigorous requirements of law and their sense of being bound by it" (Task Force on Administrative Segregation 1997, 12).

At the crux of Justice Arbour's findings and recommendations is an awareness of the systemic nature of this problem of prisoners' rights. The violations of a prisoner's rights are sometimes the result of the malicious abuse of power of a particular guard or group of guards. More often, however, it is a consequence of a systemic failure to endorse and respect the rule of law. The system as a whole is unresponsive to outside criticisms. Arbour, like many observers, attributes the Correctional Service of Canada's defensiveness and lack of accountability for and protection of rights to a "corporate culture which fails to appreciate the need to obey both the spirit and the letter of the law" (Arbour 1996, 181) (see Box 8.3).While the Correctional Service of Canada maintains that "humanizing the incarceration experiences through a rights-oriented correctional model promotes responsible behaviour that favours the safe and timely reintegration of offenders back into society" (Scott 1998), recent evidence seems to suggest that Canada is still struggling with the concept of prisoners' rights. The legal framework of corrections includes several laws, directives, and policies designed to protect prisoners from abuses and arbitrary decisions, but these rules are often ignored and compromised in practice. While it is clear that the Correctional Service of Canada operates as a legal entity, the degree to which corrections functions consistently within the rule of law is less obvious (Ekstedt and Griffiths 1988, 6).

Recent evidence suggests that the introduction of the rule of law with procedural and administrative guidelines has not eliminated abuses of power and violations of prisoners'

BOX 8.3   Image Mattered Most, Prison Probe Reveals

When six of the Kingston Prison for Women's toughest inmates broke the law by picking a fight with guards in April, 1994, they were punished by being locked in isolation cells and eventually had months added to their sentences.

But when prison officials broke the law by having inmates stripped by a male riot squad, not letting them call lawyers, taking away exercise and basic amenities and leaving them for months in segregation, no one was punished.

Instead, the Correctional Service of Canada issued a misleading report defending staff actions and ignoring any hints of impropriety.

What has emerged as the inquiry moved from prisoners to guards to prison management and eventually all the way to the CSC commissioner himself is a portrait of a complacent bureaucracy that valued image over substance, accepted without question anything that fit its concepts of reality, disregarded anything that didn't and appeared incapable of critical self-examination.

Even though, two years later, no one has been disciplined or even reprimanded, the inquiry headed by Madam Justice Louise Arbour of the Ontario Court of Appeal did elicit a grudging acknowledgment from CSC Commissioner John Edwards that he may have erred by failing to ensure that people who work for him paid sufficient attention to the rules.

The Correctional Investigator, a federal prisoners' ombudsman who also reports to the Solicitor General, had issued his own report on events at the Prison for Women and it was scathing. He denounced the CSC's report as "incomplete, inconclusive and self-serving," and suggested that prisoners deserved to be compensated for the way they had been treated.

Most important, news media finally had succeeded in obtaining a copy of a videotape made by the riot squad, which not only contained graphic images of nearly naked women being manhandled by men who looked like Darth Vader but proved that the CSC had not revealed everything about the strip-search.

Although the inquiry started by delving into the incidents that triggered the whole affair, what emerged during the hearings was a pattern of astonishing ignorance of, or indifference to, rules by prison staff and CSC officials.

For example, the CSC gave a four-member board of investigation only days to probe events at the prison but spent months editing the board's report—in the process removing references in men being involved in strip-searching women and to the existence of a videotape.

That allowed the CSC to maintain for almost a year—until the videotape surfaced—the official fiction that men had not been involved in the strip-search.

If nothing else, however, the commission's hearings provided one clear lesson: The search for justice inside a Canadian penitentiary can be a long, arduous process, with the balance heavily weighted on the side of authority. And without the videotape, it is unlikely there would have been a Prison for Women inquiry.

SOURCE: Adapted from Hess 1996. Reprinted with permission from *The Globe and Mail.*

rights. Prisoners' rights activists, such as the late Claire Culhane, have spent many tireless hours fighting for the implementation of legal and administrative protections of prisoners' rights. Now that many of these mechanisms exist, critical observers are questioning and challenging the efficacy of these laws and policies. After all, what good is legal protection if prisoners are unaware of it or unwilling to use it, if correctional officials misinterpret or reinterpret the law because it is administratively convenient, or because the state that concedes the right fails to make the necessary structural alterations for its exercise?

However, there is reason to be hopeful, since the Solicitor General of Canada has acknowledged this problem. Nevertheless, the solution to this problem is complex—there are no easy answers to finding a balance between the rights of the prisoner and the state's power to punish. While ultimately the accountability for violations of prisoners' rights rests with individual administrators and guards, society at large is also responsible for and feeds this "corporate culture" through its willingness to turn a blind eye.

SUMMARY

What are the limits on the state's rights to punish? This chapter examined the importance of human rights as they relate to Canadian prisoners. It outlined the social, legal, and political significance of prisoners' rights by examining international and national laws. It also provided a brief discussion of the rule of law, a history of prisoners' rights in Canada. Common methods of redress for rights violations including the grievance system, the Office of the Correctional Investigator, and individual litigation were outlined. The findings of the Arbour Commission and the Task Force on Administrative Segregation were discussed, and the views of the Correctional Investigator and prisoners were also presented to raise questions about the capacity of these systems to enforce the rule of law and to protect the right of prisoners.

KEY TERMS AND CONCEPTS

Arbour Commission	Corrections and	rule of law
Correctional Investigator	Conditional Release Act	Task Force on Administrative
	duty to act fairly	Segregation

STUDY AND DISCUSSION QUESTIONS

1. How does the rule of law influence the operation and organization of the Correctional Service of Canada? Is it enforced in correctional practice?

2. How should the state respond when a prisoner's rights are violated?

3. List and discuss the significance of five legislative or administrative developments in prisoners' rights.

4. What is the role of the Office of the Correctional Investigator? How is the effectiveness of that office limited?

5. Identify three gaps between legal norms and correctional practice. Show how they reflect a systemic problem rather than an individual problem.

6. Discuss Justice Louise Arbour's proposition to reduce a prisoner's term of imprisonment to reflect the illegality of unjustly imposed harsher conditions of imprisonment than defined by law.

WEBLINKS

Journal of Prisoners on Prisons: **www.jpp.org**

Canadian Association of Elizabeth Fry Societies: **www.elizabethfry.ca**

John Howard Society of Canada: **www. johnhoward.ca**

Amnesty International: **www.amnesty.ca**

Prison Activist Resource Center: **www.prisonactivist.org**

REFERENCES

Arbour, L. (Chair). 1996. *Report of the Commission of Inquiry into Certain Events at the Prison for Women in Kingston.* Ottawa: Public Works and Government Services Canada.

Campbell, M. 1997. Revolution and Counter Revolution in Canadian Prisoners' Rights. *Canadian Criminal Law Review* 2: 285–329.

Cooper, S. 1987. The Evolution of the Federal Women's Prison. In E. Adelberg and C. Currie (Eds.), *Too Few to Count.* Vancouver: Press Gang.

Correctional Investigator. 1993. *Annual Report of the Correctional Investigator, 1992-1993.* Ottawa: Minister of Public Works and Government Services.

———. 1994. *Annual Report of the Correctional Investigator, 1993-1994.* Ottawa: Minister of Public Works and Government Services.

———. 1995. *Annual Report of the Correctional Investigator, 1994-1995.* Ottawa: Minister of Supply and Services Canada.

———. 1997. *Annual Report of the Correctional Investigator, 1996-1997.* Ottawa: Minister of Public Works and Government Services.

———. 1998. *Annual Report of the Correctional Investigator, 1997-1998.* Ottawa: Minister of Public Works and Government Services.

Correctional Service of Canada. 1998a. *Commemorating the 50th Anniversary of the United Nations Universal Declaration of Human Rights.* Ottawa: Human Rights Division, Correctional Service of Canada.

———. 1998b. *CCRA Five-Year Review: The Offender Grievance System.* Ottawa: Solicitor General of Canada.

Ekstedt, J., and **C.T. Griffiths**. 1988. *Corrections in Canada: Policy and Practice.* Toronto: Butterworths.

Gosselin, L. 1982. *Prisons in Canada.* Montreal: Black Rose Books.

Hannah-Moffat, K. 2000. *Punishment in Disguise: Canadian Federal Women's Penal Reform.* Toronto: University of Toronto Press.

Hess, H. 1996. Imagine Mattered Most, Prison Probe Reveals. *The Globe and Mail* 9 January.

Jacobs, J.B. 1980. The Prisoner's Rights Movement and Its Impacts, 1960–1980. *Crime and Justice: An Annual Review* 2: 429–448.

Jackson, M. 1983. *Prisoners of Isolation: Solitary Confinement in Canada.* Toronto: University of Toronto Press.

Landau, T. 1984. Due Process, Legalism, and Inmates' Rights: A Cautionary Note. *Canadian Criminology Forum* 2: 151–163.

MacGuigan, M. 1977. *Report to Parliament by the Sub-Committee on the Penitentiary System in Canada.* Ottawa: Supply and Services.

Mainwaring, B. 1998. Offender Affairs. *Let's Talk* 23(4): 22–23.

Mann, T. 1998. Human Rights within CSC: One Prisoner's Perspective. *Let's Talk* 23(4): 14–15.

Martineau v. Matsqui Institution [1978]. 1 S.C.R.118, 33 C.C.C. (2d) 366.

McKinnon, C. 1995. The Legal Right of Offenders to Refuse Treatment. *Forum on Corrections Research* 7(3): 45–47.

Melnitzer, J. 2000. Prisoners' Rights: Inhuman Rights. In J. Roberts (Ed.), *Criminal Justice in Canada: A Reader.* Toronto: Harcourt Brace.

Ontario Court General Division. 1998. Statement of Claim. Dorothy Mills Proctor and Her Majesty the Queen in Right of Canada. Court File 98cv-6618.

Pate, K. 1998. Correcting Corrections for Federally Sentenced Women. *Let's Talk* 23(4): 16–17.

Richmond, D.J. 1975. *Prison Doctor.* Surrey, British Columbia: Nunaga Publishing Company. Quoted in J. Ekstedt and C.T. Griffiths, *Corrections in Canada: Policy and Practice,* Toronto: Butterworths, 1988, 75.

Scott, A. 1998. Human Rights and Corrections. *Let's Talk* 23(4): 2–3.

Task Force on Administrative Segregation. 1997. *Commitment to Legal Compliance, Fair Decisions, and Effective Results: Reviewing Administrative Segregation.* Ottawa: Correctional Service of Canada.

SPECIAL POPULATIONS WITHIN CORRECTIONS

D.A. Andrews, Craig Dowden,
and L. Jill Rettinger
Department of Psychology
Carleton University
Ottawa, Ontario

CHAPTER OBJECTIVES

After reading this chapter, you should be able to:

- Identify and describe the characteristics of the five major special prison populations;
- Describe the dynamic risk/need factors for each population discussed;
- Describe the range of issues that relate to responsivity; and
- Describe the different intervention issues for the special populations addressed in this chapter.

We are all related.

—Aboriginal belief

This chapter examines five special populations in the prison system: young offenders, female offenders, Aboriginal offenders, mentally disordered offenders, and sex offenders. The "specials" may be compared with "others" in a number of ways. Of course, we are interested in differential rates and types of offending and re-offending. We are also interested in common and/or differential risk and protective factors for criminal behaviour. **Risk factors** refer to characteristics of individuals and their circumstances that are associated with an increased chance of offending or re-offending. Some of these risk factors are fixed or stable factors, such as having been arrested or growing up in particular socioeconomic circumstances. Other risk factors are dynamic in that individuals and/their circumstances may change (such as changes in social skills or attitudes).

Dynamic risk factors are called **criminogenic needs** in order to differentiate them from other dynamic variables that may be considered problematic but are unrelated to criminal behaviour (that is, non-criminogenic needs). In this chapter, we will also discuss individuals' differential **responsivity** to different types of naturally occurring events (for example, sexual victimization) and to deliberate and controlled interventions (such as arrest or access to treatment services). Additionally, we will look at how and whether subgroups are responded to in ethical, legal, humane, decent, and cost-efficient ways and, in particular, in a manner consistent with human rights provisions. The latter includes exploration of possible bias in the judicial and correctional processing of special populations.

This discussion also recognizes that special populations may present special strengths or needs, and corrections may be expected to respond to their uniqueness even when those strengths or needs may be irrelevant to the analysis of criminal behaviour.

We begin with an interdisciplinary theoretical perspective on criminal conduct and corrections that is so general in its applicability that it may assist in understanding any special population. Note that this perspective applies directly to a host of factors that can influence our understanding of any special population. Therefore, its applications are best guided by the pursuit of ethical, legal, decent, just, efficient, and humane applications. You will see as well that this general perspective receives research support. In addition, unfortunately, you will see that we know very little about some very complex processes.

The level of research support in part reflects our knowledge of the magnitude of the correlation between various variables and offending behaviour. Throughout this chapter we will refer to correlation coefficients wherein a correlation coefficient of .00 demonstrates no association between a variable and criminal behaviour and a value of 1.00 demonstrates a perfect linear association. Rosenthal (1991) made a valuable contribution to the field by showing that the interpretation of these coefficients is very direct and very easy to understand. Assuming that 50 percent of any group are criminal and that 50 percent are judged to be at risk for criminal behaviour, the strength of the association between risk and recidivism is the direct difference between the offending rates of those judged high risk and the group judged low risk. Thus, if 60 percent of the high-risk group offended and 40 percent of the low-risk group offended, the difference is 20 percentage points (60 – 40) and the correlation coefficient is .20. This approach will also be employed in the interpretation of the effects on re-offending of deliberate and controlled interventions.

A GENERAL PSYCHOLOGY OF CRIMINAL CONDUCT

We draw upon a general **psychology of criminal conduct (PCC)** because it is relatively advanced in terms of the four criteria crucial for understanding human behaviour. These criteria are the ability, or potential, to:

- Predict criminal behaviour through the identification and assessment of major risk factors;

2 • Produce shifts in the chances of criminal behaviour through the selection of criminogenic needs as targets of intervention and the use of powerful styles, modes, and strategies of change;

3 • Apply knowledge of the interrelationships among risk factors, including how they influence each other and how those relationships with each other and with criminal behaviour may shift over the life course; and

4 • Use the research findings implied by each of the above criteria should represent applied deductions from a coherent, parsimonious, and logical theoretical perspective.

In the field of corrections, we start from a perspective of general personality and social learning that we call the **personal, interpersonal, and community-reinforcement theory (PIC-R)** (Andrews 1982; Andrews and Bonta 1994, 1998).[1] There are four major criteria for understanding human behaviour. Briefly, PIC-R identifies the predictors of criminal behaviour and differentiates between major and minor risk factors (see Table 9.1). It distinguishes between fixed historical/static risk factors and dynamic risk factors and also between criminogenic and non-criminogenic needs (see Table 9.2 for promising and less promising targets for change). It is very specific about the causal processes for behavioural change.

TABLE 9.1   Major and Minor Risk/Need Factors

Major Risk Factors: The Big Eight

1. Antisocial cognition: Antisocial/pro-criminal attitudes, values, beliefs, and rationalizations, and cognitive emotional states such as anger and resentment.

2. Antisocial associates/interpersonal support for crime: Association with criminal others and isolation from anti-criminal others.

3. Antisocial personality pattern: Restlessly aggressive energy, adventurous pleasure seeking, egocentric, weak problem-solving/self-regulation skills, impulsive/non-reflective, taste for risk, weak socialization, psychopathic personality, conduct disorder plus attention deficit disorder, hyperactivity.

4. History of antisocial behaviour: Evident from an early age, in a variety of settings and involving a number and variety of antisocial acts (e.g., lying, stealing, aggression, and substance abuse).

5. Problematic circumstances at home: Poor scores on the parenting variables of nurturance/caring/affection and supervision/appropriate discipline; parental and/or sibling criminal history.

6. Problematic circumstances at school/work: Weak attachment to school, discipline problems at school; among adults, unstable employment history.

7. Leisure/recreation: Low levels of involvement in organized anti-criminal activities.

8. Substance abuse: Alcohol and/or drug abuse.

Minor Risk Factors

9. Low class origins: Poverty in family of origin, low-class neighbourhood (magnitude of risk increases slightly with long-term reliance on welfare and intergenerational states of disadvantage).

10. Personal distress: low self-esteem, anxiety, worrying, depression, internalizing disorder; psychopathology.

11. Low verbal intelligence.

12. Biological indicators: A host of biological/neuropsychological indicators that have yet to be integrated convincingly in theory or in practice through systematic risk/need assessment.

NOTE: The predictive contributions of class, being young, and being a minority group member are greatly reduced once the above-noted major risk factors are introduced.

TABLE 9.2	More Promising and Less Promising Targets for Change

A. Promising Targets for Change (targeting criminogenic needs)

- Changing antisocial attitudes.
- Changing/managing antisocial feelings (anger, resentment, defiance).
- Reducing antisocial peer associations.
- Promoting familial affection/communication.
- Promoting familial monitoring and supervision.
- Promoting child/family protection (preventing neglect/abuse).
- Promoting identification/association with anti-criminal role models.
- Increasing self-control, self-management and problem-solving skills.
- Replacing the skills of lying, stealing, and aggression with more pro-social alternatives.
- Reducing chemical dependencies and substance abuse.
- Shifting the density of the personal, interpersonal, and other rewards and costs for criminal and non-criminal activities in familial, academic, vocational, recreational and other behavioural settings, so that the non-criminal alternatives are favoured.
- Providing the chronically psychiatrically troubled with low pressure, sheltered living arrangements and/or effective medication (risk is greatest during periods of active psychosis).
- Insuring that the client is able to recognize risky situations, and has a concrete and well-rehearsed plan for dealing with those situations (an intermediate goal of relapse prevention).
- Confronting the personal and circumstantial barriers to service (client motivation; background stressors with which clients may be preoccupied).
- Reduce individualized need factors (if reasonably linked with crime).

B. Less Promising Targets (targeting non-criminogenic needs)

- Increasing self-esteem (without simultaneous reductions in antisocial thinking, feeling, and peer associations).
- Focusing on vague emotional/personal complaints not linked to criminal conduct (anxiety, depression, worrying, etc.).
- Increasing the cohesiveness of antisocial peer groups.
- Improving neighbourhood-wide living conditions, without touching the criminogenic needs of high-risk individuals and families.
- Showing respect for antisocial thinking on the grounds that the values of one culture are as equally valid as the values of another culture.
- Increasing conventional ambition in the areas of school and work without concrete assistance in realizing these ambitions.
- Attempting to turn the client into a "better person," when the standards for being a "better person" do not link with recidivism.
- Focusing on deterrence, increased fear of official punishment.

SOURCE: Based on Andrews and Bonta 1994, 1998.

In brief, the modelling of criminal and non-criminal behaviour, the rewards and costs for criminal and non-criminal alternative behaviour, and the signalled rewards and costs are in part personally mediated. Antisocial cognition contributes to the standards of conduct that influence whether personally mediated control favours the criminal over the non-criminal.

Antisocial cognition also contributes to the set of exonerating and justification self-statements that may be employed to release one from the moral code (i.e., "the victim deserves it").

Antisocial associates influence the immediate situations in which one finds oneself or that one creates for oneself. They also indicate whether the actions and reactions of others will be favourable or unfavourable to criminal activity. A history of antisocial behaviour indicates that the immediate rewards of crime have been tasted and that one has learned that the costs are uncertain, delayed, and often not apparent at all. The major personality and temperamental factors reflect the fact that many criminal acts are exciting, tension-reducing, and fun, and their inhibition requires the skills of restraint and reflection. For adventurous pleasure-seekers, for the restlessly aggressive, and for low-restraint folk, many types of acts that are subject to the label "antisocial" or "criminal" are high on their behavioural repertoire across a wide range of situations.

These immediate situational, personal, and interpersonal risk factors are themselves to be understood in the context of interpersonal relationships and the patterns of modelling and reinforcement in the major social settings within which human behaviour occurs. These settings include those of home, school, and work, as well as recreation and leisure. Thus, additional major risk factors are problematic relationships and circumstances in the domains of home (see #5 in Table 9.1), school/work (#6), and leisure/recreation (#7). The behaviour modelled and the rewards and costs for criminal and non-criminal behaviour in those contexts are influential in producing, maintaining, and altering the more immediate contingencies established at the personal and interpersonal level. Substance abuse (#8) is often associated with problematic circumstances in these behaviour settings and often limits the rewards and satisfactions from non–drug-oriented behaviour.

Minor risk factors include lower socioeconomic origins and personal distress. The theories that emphasize such factors have proven to be very weak relative to the general PCC that affords those variables only minimal causal significance. Note, however, that low class origins is differentiated from the antisocial traits and educational/employment functioning, which are in the major set (see #6 in Table 9.1). Personal distress factors such as low self-esteem, worrying, anxiety, and even major psychiatric disorders such as schizophrenia are very weak risk factors relative to, for example, antisocial attitudes and feelings or to psychopathic personality (#1 and #3). Biological and neuropsychological factors are also listed as minor at this time because the many established biological correlates have yet to be integrated either theoretically or into an empirically validated and powerful prediction system. We expect that genetics and neuropsychology link with the major personality domain through, for example, the cognitive skills underlying self-management. In time, biological factors will almost certainly enter the major set (see Winterdyk 2000a: Chapter 5).

All these considerations yield several strongly validated principles for achieving reduced offending through primary prevention or reduced re-offending in the case of corrections (see Table 9.3). As noted, the general PCC, in particular PIC-R, is explicit not only about the major risk factors but also about how behaviour is influenced. Specifically, variations in behaviour are to be understood through the fundamental principles of behavioural psychology, social learning, and cognitive behavioural processes. This yields the general responsivity principle of effective treatment: Match the mode, style, and treatment strategies to the learning style and abilities of cases—hence, and most generally, employ behavioural, social learning, and cognitive behavioural strategies.

Although much more detail could be offered, in this chapter issues regarding special populations in corrections will reflect the more general correctional context. In Canada, this

TABLE 9.3	Some Indicators of Effective Programs for Dealing with Offenders

An effective program:

- Is an empirically validated theory underlying the intervention (in particular a general personality and social learning perspective);
- Does not rely on variations of themes of official punishment;
- Introduces human service or correctional treatment programs;
- Applies more intensive treatment to high-risk cases;
- Targets criminogenic needs; does not emphasize non-criminogenic needs;
- Targets multiple criminogenic needs;
- Uses concrete social learning/cognitive behavioural style, mode, and strategy of service;
- Amplifies service by high level of core correctional practice (CCP):
  - Workers are enthusiastic, engaged, and can establish high-quality relationships in combination with structuring skills and the establishment of appropriate contingencies;
  - Workers are able to handle their authority, without domination/abuse, but with respectful guidance towards compliance with the rules;
  - Workers are able to recognize antisocial thinking, feeling, and acting, and are able to demonstrate and reinforce concrete alternatives with high levels of modelling, approval, and disapproval;
  - Workers are able to offer concrete problem-solving and to engage in structured skill-building (describe the skill, model the skill, role play, and rehearsal with corrective feedback);
  - Workers engage in advocacy/brokerage actively involving relevant others in the offenders social network (home, extended family, school, work, leisure, peers, and official agencies such as the police, court, corrections, child welfare, social assistance, mental health, etc.);
- Involves specific responsivity: matches service to the personality, aptitude, ability, and motivation of cases; enhances fit with gender, age, race/ethnicity;
- Prefers a community-based setting over a custodial one;
- Uses structured follow-up/booster sessions/relapse-prevention strategies;
- Engages pro-social others in the broader social network including family, peers, school, work, leisure, and neighbourhood, and/or shifts them in the pro-social direction;
- Maintains integrity of implementation and program delivery:
  - Adequate dosage;
  - Service deliverers trained and supervised in relevant practices;
  - Printed training/program manual;
  - Small units;
- Uses professional discretion: having considered risk, need, general responsivity, and other concerns, makes decisions that appear appropriate for this case.

Community: Practice/Apply — Promotion/Rehabilitation

context entails the ethical, legal, decent, humane, fair, and efficient administration and management of the sanction or disposition imposed by the courts. Of course, what is fair and decent may be the subject of considerable debate, and patterns of abuse have been documented. The overarching and justice-specific purposes of sentencing are reasonably well established in criminal law. Three of these purposes have to do with controlling re-offending.

As discussed in greater detail in Chapter 1, **deterrence** focuses on reducing the chance that the sanctioned offender will re-offend. Readers will see in this chapter, and again in

Chapter 11, that increases in the severity of the penalty, are associated with, at best, mild increases in recidivism.

Incapacitation refers to sentences that limit the possibility of re-offending through controls such as a custodial placement or very high levels of supervision in the community. We will see that the post-sanction effects on reduced recidivism of both custodial and community sanctions depends on the delivery of quality treatment services within those contexts. At the same time, we have few experimentally controlled estimates of the magnitude of the effects of incapacitation on both in-program and post-program re-offending.

Rehabilitation refers to the delivery of human service to offenders in the context of the disposition. Ideally, however, the service should be consistent with the principles of risk, need, and general responsivity. Of course, as will be seen with special populations in this chapter, and again in Chapter 11, treatment services that are inconsistent with the principles of effective treatment have either no effect or negative effects on recidivism.

Some of the purposes of sentencing in their intent have nothing at all to do with influencing re-offending. For example, retribution has to do with doing harm, taking revenge, on those who violate the law. Just desert places some limits on retribution by suggesting that the harm imposed should be proportionate to the seriousness of the offence and the culpability of the offender. There is a tendency to confuse the raw nature of the harm and injury underlying retribution and just desert by referring not to retribution but instead to holding offenders "responsible" or "accountable."

Restorative justice is very attractive to many who feel uneasy about retribution. This is due to the fact that the restorative approach is not about doing harm to offenders but about restoring balance through the healing of victims and the broader community. However, despite the fact that it is not clear that reduced re-offending on the part of the offender is a major concern, the approach favours community-based, voluntary, and non-professional programming if rehabilitation is a concern (see Chapter 13). A balanced approach, we think, would combine the goal of reduced future offending with restorative approaches to current and past victims.

Among the standard punishing purposes of sanctioning, one of the most relevant to corrections is the incapacitation element of incarceration. The prevention of escapes is a major security concern. In Canada, the punishment is said to reside in the fact of incarceration or in the fact of supervision, and hence it is not expected that corrections administer punishment (or hold offenders accountable) beyond managing the disposition. The ideal of rehabilitation, in Canada, largely rests with corrections because Canadian judges, under existing legislation, are primarily concerned with retribution, deterrence, incapacitation, and just desert. Thus, correctional discretion in regard to treatment services is the primary route to maximizing reduced recidivism through human service in the justice context.

YOUNG OFFENDERS

Young offenders constitute a particularly interesting subpopulation. Young people have been viewed as being so different from adults that separate justice systems have been established for young offenders and adult offenders. What is always recognized is that the young have special needs reflecting their level of physical, emotional, moral, and cognitive development and reflecting limitations on their ability to function independent of parents or other caregivers.

We begin with a brief overview of crime rates and youth processing, turn to legislation, and proceed through risk/need factors and the effects on re-offending of judicial interventions. The analyses of risk/needs and intervention effects will be presented in some detail so that the most basic and most widely applicable findings need not be repeated in the subsequent discussions of female offenders, Aboriginal offenders, sex offenders, and mentally disordered offenders.

In any given year, nearly 10 percent of Canadians aged 12 to 17 years are arrested by the police for a violation of the Criminal Code or other federal statutes (Hung and Lipinski 1995). In 1992, 211,700 youth were arrested, 140,000 were charged, and 71,000 were dealt with informally. On any given day in 1992, 4,700 Canadian youth were residing in open custody, secure custody, or pre-trial detention facilities. Another 34,000 were on probation. Sixty percent of the youths were charged with property offences and only 14 percent with a violent offence.

Of course, officially processed youth represent a small proportion of the youth engaged in criminal activity. Self-report surveys of young people reveal that the vast majority admit to acts that would be judged "criminal" if detected and processed. For example, 88 percent of more than 500 high school students surveyed in a medium-sized central Canadian city and its surrounding rural areas admitted to at least one offence in the last year (Watkins 1999a, 1999b; see Table 9.4). The corresponding figures were 91 percent for young men and 85 percent for young women. Of course, the vast majority of these offences were minor. The top 10 antisocial activities among young Canadians, according to their reports on their own behaviour, are under-age drinking (49 percent), reckless driving/speeding (36 percent), trespassing (34 percent), stealing things worth less than $200 (33 percent), threatening harm or injury (31 percent), possession of stolen goods (31 percent), creating a disturbance (31 percent), obtaining money by false pretence (31 percent), driving a car without a license (30 percent), and possession of marijuana and/or hashish (28 percent). Incidentally, if cheating on exams were criminalized, the pool of identified young offenders could be increased because 41 percent of the students reported school-based cheating.

Young Offender Legislation in Canada

For decades, the judicial processing of Canadians aged seven through sixteen years was governed by the *Juvenile Delinquents Act* of 1908. Guided by *parens patriae* (the law of the state to act on behalf of those unable to act for themselves), judges and childcare officials were asked to respond to a youth's crime with particular attention to the child's best interests. Judges had great discretionary powers, were not required to attend to seriousness of the offence, and were able to impose dispositions ranging from no consequences or supervision at all through to the young person being made a ward of the state until the age of 21 (see Fetherston 2000).

The Act came to be seen as unjust and in 1984 the ***Young Offenders Act*** **(YOA)** was introduced in Canada in an attempt to address the justice issues through combined attention to criminal law and civil libertarian orientations (see Winterdyk 2000a: Chapter 14). Clearly a product of social science leanings in the 1960s and 1970s, it contained distinct pro-punishment and anti-rehabilitation themes and displayed a lack of trust in authority. The YOA was clearly a legislation focusing on criminal law and not on child welfare, although the special needs of young people were to be considered (Winterdyk 2000b). First,

TABLE 9.4	Rates[a] of Self-Reported Delinquency[b] by Gender, Age, and Type of Behaviour					
Item[c]	**Females**		**Males**		**Combined**	
	14–15	**16–19**	**14–15**	**16–19**	**14–15**	**16–19**
1. Bribe/attempt bribe of officials	0.94	1.52	7.29	6.32	3.96	4.01
2. Used force to get money/valuables	5.66	1.02	11.46	12.07	8.42	6.43
3. Bought beer/wine/liquor while minor	26.42	52.02	32.63	68.97	29.35	59.89
4. Sold illegal drugs (not marijuana or hashish)	2.83	5.05	5.21	13.79	3.96	9.36
5. Carried razor, switchblade, or gun	3.77	5.56	20.00	14.94	11.44	10.16
6. Attacked someone/intent to injure	7.55	5.56	13.54	18.39	10.40	11.76
7. Taken part in gang fight	3.77	0.51	5.21	10.92	4.46	5.61
8. Stolen things worth more than $200	0.95	3.05	3.13	9.77	1.99	6.43
9. Break and entering	2.86	2.03	12.63	11.70	7.50	6.49
10. Possession of marijuana or hashish	13.21	25.25	25.00	43.35	18.81	33.78
11. Joyriding	6.60	14.14	12.50	30.81	9.41	21.77
12. Sex or attempted sex by force	1.89	0.51	2.11	5.78	1.99	2.96
13. Started a fist fight unprovoked	11.43	10.10	22.92	21.97	16.92	15.82
14. Purposefully damaged property	16.98	10.66	23.96	33.91	20.30	21.72
15. Driven car without license	31.13	22.73	44.79	31.03	37.62	26.47
16. Gave false information	6.60	11.62	16.67	23.12	11.39	17.16
17. Sold marijuana or hashish	5.66	6.06	6.25	23.56	5.94	14.44
18. Set fire to a building	0.00	0.00	5.32	5.85	2.50	2.70
19. Participated in illegal gambling	7.55	10.10	27.08	36.78	16.83	22.73
20. Stolen things (worth $5 to $200)	25.47	33.50	29.17	39.88	27.23	36.56
21. False alarms (fire, ambulance, etc.)	11.32	11.74	19.79	20.12	15.35	15.86
22. Reckless driving/speeding	5.66	41.84	14.58	59.54	9.90	50.13
23. Trespassing	34.91	18.18	53.68	39.88	43.78	28.42
24. Threatened harm or injury	26.42	19.70	37.50	42.53	31.68	30.48
25. Stolen things (less than $5)	25.47	22.56	31.25	32.18	28.22	26.95
26. Possession of stolen goods	21.70	23.35	31.58	45.98	26.37	34.05
27. Cheated on exams/assignments	36.79	41.41	35.42	47.70	36.14	44.39
28. Impaired driving	3.77	17.68	3.16	35.63	3.48	26.20
29. Created a disturbance in public	26.41	25.25	36.84	38.51	31.34	31.55
30. Drug possession (marijuana and/or hashish)	4.76	11.62	7.37	26.44	6.00	18.72

TABLE 9.4	Rates[a] of Self-Reported Delinquency[b] by Gender, Age, and Type of Behaviour (continued)

Item[c]	Females		Males		Combined	
	14–15	16–19	14–15	16–19	14–15	16–19
31. Sold beer, wine, liquor to minors	4.72	12.18	9.47	30.46	6.97	20.91
32. Automobile theft (not joyriding)	0.00	1.01	1.05	2.30	0.50	1.60
33. Obtained money, etc., via false pretence	29.25	25.89	36.84	34.48	32.84	30.03
Number of respondents	106	198	96	174	202	372

[a] Rates for a particular item are expressed as a percentage of number of respondents.

[b] Delinquent acts committed one or more times within the last year.

[c] Statements below are shortened versions/examples of actual questionnaire items.

NOTE: Watkins 1999a, 1999b.

the judge was required to specify not only the type but also the duration of supervision. Second, the upper limit of supervision was set at no more than two years (the principle of limited sanctioning). Third, the selection of disposition was expected to reflect the seriousness of the offence (the principle of just desert rather than the child's best interests). Fourth, the extraordinary power of the state relative to the young person was recognized by enhancing the youth's access to representation by a lawyer (and thereby the opportunity for enhanced compliance with due process and concern for rules of evidence and such).

Fifth, access to treatment services from the child welfare and mental health systems was limited to those contacts to which the youth gave his or her consent. This limitation on access to human services, we think, reflected certain anti-rehabilitation themes within a just-desert philosophy. Briefly, this philosophy refers to the "dignity of punishment," where consent is not required—as opposed to the "tyranny of treatment," where consent is required.

Sixth, the YOA opened up the possibility of a whole range of alternative diversionary community-based non-judicial responses to crime. The alternatives occurred outside the justice system but did hold offenders accountable while allowing negotiation of conditions that the offender, the victim, and representatives of the broader community found "just." Consider, for example, the potential positives of seeking an alternative mode of processing that might avoid the negative effects of official judicial processing. The community might avoid, for example, paying the high costs of court and custodial placements. The victims may feel that they are part of the process. The offender may escape the negative effects of experiencing official punishments that do not deal with the causes of antisocial behaviour.

Seventh, the YOA raised the minimum age and lowered the maximum age for juvenile justice processing. The YOA applies to persons aged 12 to 17. Once again, recognizing the potential negative aspects of judicial processing, children under 12 years of age were to be spared involvement even in the juvenile justice system. Dealing with the antisocial behaviour of people under 12 is left to parents, schools, child welfare agencies, mental health agencies, and any other community resource that may step in. It is often the police, however, who initiate and support intervention by non-judicial agencies. Reflecting the belief that exposure to adult justice is harmful to young people, offenders under 18 years of age were to be spared exposure to the adult system.

Ironically, for all of the distrust of judicial and correctional discretion, among the best documented consequences of the YOA was an actual increase in the punishment of Canadian youth through custodial sanctions accompanied by a dramatic drop in the delivery of treatment services through child welfare and mental health agencies. The increased use of custody was somewhat mitigated by a reduction in the average length of custodial placement but the latter finding was really an underestimate of the drop in services to young offenders. Systematic research is required on this point but anecdotal reports suggest that child welfare agents sometimes stopped working with a youth once the individual became involved with youth court.

Interestingly, the themes of due process, just desert, and anti-treatment in pro-YOA legal and criminological scholarship became intertwined with the "nothing works" perspective on rehabilitation. Leschied, Andrew, and Hoge (1995) have documented how personal and bitter the debate became when scholars brought forth evidence suggesting that judicial sanctions without human service were criminogenic and that the decline in rehabilitative programming was criminogenic (see Box 9.1).

BOX 9.1   Interview with Dr. Alan Leschied

Dr. Alan Leschied and his colleagues at the London Family Court Clinic in London, Ontario, led the evidence-based crusade for pro-rehabilitative changes in the YOA. Dr. Leschied is now a professor at the University of Western Ontario.

How did you become so involved in the debate over the Young Offenders Act?

I graduated in clinical psychology from the University of Western Ontario in 1980. During the last three years of my graduate work, I worked part-time at the Family Court Clinic providing assessments for the youth court in southwestern Ontario. The Clinic was developed in 1975 as a children's mental health centre dedicated to providing assessments to youth court judges under the *Juvenile Delinquents Act*. The JDA was committed to the needs of kids and the Clinic's work depended on the ability of judges to do two things. The first was to make referrals for assessment, and the second was to act on the recommendations that, in the main, were geared to linking community services to the rehabilitative needs of kids and their families.

The Clinic has always been committed to looking at the empirical base of whatever it was that we were involved in. Whether that meant looking at assessment needs, making recommendations consistent with the available literature supporting certain interventions over others, or examining the impact of legislation on the ability of service providers to allocate resources consistent with the needs of youth. The YOA, which was enacted in 1984, was obviously going to mean a major shift in how kids would be dealt with in the forum of court.

How would you summarize your research findings?

We published results in three areas during the early years of the YOA. Those were on the section for the consent to treatment, which required youths between the ages of 12 to 17 to decide upon their own treatment needs; on the frequency at which judges would use the assessment section of the Act; and on the utilization rates of custody by youth court judges. Underlying the principles section of the Act was a tension among crime control, the justice model, and rehabilitation. Clearly, the way in which the Act was written and how judges would interpret it would make some of those principles incompatible with one another. Our guess, based upon literature primarily from the U.S., was that whenever crime control provisions were written into legislation, competing principles would be overridden. Hence we predicted that custody rates would escalate, the consent section would be overly restrictive in eliminating some kids' chances from experiencing treatment programs, and the needs for assessment would decrease in the drive towards standardizing sentencing outcomes under the justice provisions. In all of these areas, our predictions were correct. While I know that there has been some criticism of the methodology that we employed in comparing certain data, defining terms, etc., our findings were replicated and reported on by many other observers involved in Canadian juvenile justice.

Were you heavily criticized for your stance?

Yes! We advocated for changing the consent to treatment provision, suggesting that kids who had adopted an antisocial life style, and who had also experienced many of the major predictors of risk—including substance abuse, a history of personal violence, etc.—may not be in the best position to judge on the basis of their own treatment needs. There were some who thought we were advocating for some kind of extreme authoritarianism in youth and juvenile justice policy. Providing youth with the most appropriate intervention in influencing future outcomes (pro-social versus antisocial) over the youth's right to choose upset quite a few, particularly those who prided themselves in being ardent civil libertarians. The rhetoric was out of control. But it was an early lesson for us in just how volatile the debate in the area of youth justice was becoming for the public.

Compared to the *Juvenile Delinquents Act,* the YOA was judged a success by most observers on several counts. That is, due process was enhanced for young people through greater access to lawyers during the investigation, court, and correctional periods of processing. Enhanced access to lawyers also introduced increases in court processing time through lawyer-driven delays. In addition, children under 12 years of age were removed from the juvenile justice system, and 16- and 17-year olds were removed from the adult system.

The YOA was under attack from several directions from its inception. Critics who placed a high value upon deterrence and incapacitation were offended by the raising of the minimum age, by the limits upon duration of sanction implementation, by the availability of alternative processing, and by the emphasis on due process. In fact, prior to the proposal for a completely new act in 1999 (most likely to be called the *Youth Criminal Justice Act*), a series of YOA reforms reflected an ever-increasing emphasis on "getting tough." Consider, for example, that the longest duration of disposition was raised from two to five and then to ten years for very serious offences. Moreover, conditions favourable to transfers to adult court were facilitated in these reforms.

Critics with an interest in human service questioned the apparent overemphasis upon due process, just desert, and deterrence relative to the provision of human service and rehabilitative services. Many critics were upset by the failure of some provinces to encourage the development of the alternative sanctioning aspects of the YOA (Quebec is typically celebrated in this regard while Ontario is viewed as slow to respond to the opportunity). A few critics were concerned that the YOA was fundamentally a reflection of human rights and justice perspectives that were seriously out of contact with a theoretically serious empirically based human and social science of antisocial behaviour. The positive effects of human service were becoming widely recognized by the mid 1980s (Andrews 1980; Gendreau and Ross 1979; Palmer 1975) and yet under the YOA there was increased use of custody and dramatic reductions in human service/treatment delivery through child welfare and mental health agencies. Grand steps were taken in 1994 for the introduction of a strong statement that protection of the public would be enhanced through the introduction of rehabilitative programming (Kirven 1995). This type of statement was missing in the original YOA.

The proposed new act is said to rest on the following three pillars:

- Recognizing that responsibility for crime control must extend beyond the justice system, the proposed act will facilitate community-based crime prevention efforts and promote the use of non-justice alternative responses for those low-risk cases admitting to non-violent and less serious offences[2];

- Young offenders will be held accountable through meaningful sanctions. This is the retributive response although the supportive rhetoric appeals to notions of responsibility and accountability rather than that of the state-imposed punishment of children. There is some chance that principles of restorative justice may become more prominent but retribution appears to be the emphasis; and

- The rehabilitation of serious and violent offenders will be emphasized.

While the rhetoric surrounding the proposed reforms certainly suggests that community-based sanctions are preferred over custodial placements, it appears clear that custody is a major part of the plan for dealing with serious and violent offenders. The proposal contains a number of other indicators of "getting tough." Among those indicators are the following: 1) Even though there is little evidence that the YOA increased crime, the government seems to want to be seen to be "getting tougher" with serious offenders; 2) even though the YOA actually did "get tough" with young offenders compared to the JDA, apparently that was not a sufficient level of "toughness"; 3) transfers of young offenders to adult court will even easier to accomplish; 4) judicial processing will occur in the regular courts rather than family courts; and 5) periods of custody will be followed by periods of supervision in the community. There is the promise for enhanced service under the proposed legislation but there are also strong elements of enhanced criminal justice and non–service-oriented processing.

Young Offender Profiles

Who are these young people caught up with the justice system? They are predominately male (80 percent); 48 percent are aged 16 to 17 years, 22 percent are 15 years old, 15 percent aged 14 years, and 11 percent are 12 or 13 years of age. Note that this pattern of increasing involvement through older adolescence is a well-established age-based finding, and rates of crime involvement begin to fall off after the age range between 18 and 21 years. As already noted, only 14 percent were charged with a violent offence, but overwhelmingly the majority of the offences are non-serious (although certainly irritating if you happen to be a victim). A recent sample of young people aged 12 to 15 years on the caseloads of Toronto probation officers were studied in some detail by Leschied, Andrews, and Hoge (1995). The findings revealed that less than 10 percent of the cases were involved in major damage offences or in offences involving serious personal injury. Looking at their prior offences, less than 3 percent of the young people presented with a history of serious offences and only 5 percent had three or more prior offences.

Less than 10 percent of the cases would not admit responsibility for their offence or showed no concern for victims. Only 2 percent of the families were involved heavily with criminal justice agencies and only 1 percent of the families were caught up in the psychiatric system. However, generalized and chronic emotional distress characterized 14 percent of the families. Many of the families were involved in crises related to marriage and parenting but only 14 percent were in socioeconomic or financial crisis. The areas of need most evident were as follows:

- Peer relationships (some need evident in 77 percent of the cases);
- Family discipline/problem-solving deficits (76 to 73 percent depending upon specific indicator);
- Leisure/recreation (75 percent);
- School-related (63 to 67 percent);
- Emotional distress (58 percent);
- Alcohol/drugs (43 percent);
- Employment issues (38 percent);
- Health concerns (20 percent); and
- Sexuality/sexual behaviour (14 percent).

The latter two need areas were confined largely to the young women and were nearly non-existent among the young men. Even within the most frequently represented need areas, the percent of cases identified as high need at most was in the area of only 20. We will see below how these need areas on their own and in combination relate to re-offending, but note that 45 percent of these officially identified urban young Canadian offenders were clearly "low risk" in that they scored below average on all of the major risk and need factors (Simourd et al. 1994).

The Major Risk/Need Factors

The major risk factors for the antisocial behaviour of young people are very similar to the risk factors for the antisocial behaviour of adults. It would be surprising indeed if this were was not the case because, according to a general personality and social learning perspective, the major variables responsible for variation in human behaviour are personal, interpersonal, and immediate situational. At present, the best validated of the risk factors are antisocial cognition, antisocial associates, antisocial personality, a history of antisocial behaviour, and problematic circumstances in the domains of school and/or work, home, and leisure/recreation, and substance abuse. Among the weak risk factors are low class origins, personal distress, and biological factors. These domains were expanded upon in Table 9.1 and a meta-analytic examination of some of these predictors of youth crime is summarized in Table 9.5.

TABLE 9.5	Meta-Analytic Tests of Risk/Need Factors and the Criminal Behaviour of Young People: Mean Adjusted Correlation Coefficients by Gender (number of tests)		
	Total	Male	Female
Antisocial attitudes/Associates	.41 (106)	.40 (53)	.39 (53)
Personality/Behavioural history	.38 (90)	.36 (45)	.35 (45)
Parenting factors	.20 (82)	.22 (41)	.20 (41)
Education/Employment	.26 (68)	.23 (34)	.24 (34)
Family structure/Parent problems	.07 (28)	.09 (14)	.07 (14)
Personal distress/Mental disorder	.07 (34)	.09 (17)	.10 (17)
Low class origins	.05 (38)	.06 (19)	.07 (19)

NOTE: The r statistic may take a value between 0 (no predictive accuracy) to 1.0 (perfect predictive accuracy). The mean values tabled and noted above give an idea of what may be expected reasonably on the basis of prior research. The Binomial Effect Size Display (Rosenthal 1991) provides a neat way of interpreting r values: Assuming that the overall base rate of recidivism is 50 percent and that equal numbers of cases have been assigned to the low- and high-risk groups, the r value reflects directly the percentage point difference in the recidivism rates of the low- and high-risk groups. For example, if r = 0.00, recidivism rates of the low- and high-risk groups were the same (that is, each 50 percent). If r = 1.00, the recidivism rate in the high-risk group is 100 percent and 0 percent in the low-risk group. If r = .40, the recidivism rate in the low-risk group is 50 percent minus 40/2 or 30 percent, and the recidivism rate in the high-risk group is 50 percent plus 40/2 or 70 percent. Thus, the r of .40 reflects a 40 percentage point difference (70 − 30 = 40).

SOURCE: Simourd and Andrews 1994.

The information in Table 9.5 is important because it reveals that there is a distinct pattern based on the findings of many studies. There is a body of knowledge that replicates these sums and is widely applicable (see also Lipsey and Derzon, 1998). For example, Table 9.4 shows us that the major and minor risk factors for youthful offending are very similar for males and females. As will be seen in the section on female offenders, there are gender-specific risk and need factors, but the general PCC applies well to young men and young women (and, indeed, to adult men and adult women). Similarly, we explore applicability in the analysis of Aboriginal offenders, mentally disordered offenders, and sex offenders later in the chapter.

Just as the predictive validity of the major risk factors is reasonably well understood, so is it understood that it is possible to build valid risk/need composite scales by surveying a number and variety of major risk factors.[3] There are many examples of composite risk/need scales for young people in conflict with the law (see Hoge and Andrews 1996). The Level of Service Inventory (LSI) (Andrews and Bonta 1995) is perhaps the most researched and best validated of the instruments, albeit in various forms (Hoge and Andrews 1996; Mattson, Williams, and Guerra 1998; Shields and Simourd 1991). The latest versions of the LSI for young offenders provide a sum of scores on the "big eight" of attitudes, associates, behavioural history, antisocial personality pattern, substance abuse, and problematic circumstances in the behavioural domains of home, school/work, and leisure/recreation. A study by Andrews (1997) reveals that increases in LSI risk levels of young offenders aged 16 through 17 years were accompanied by orderly increases in the proportion of offenders who reoffended over a several year follow-up period (see Table 9.6, wherein for young offenders the probability of recidivism varied from .09 for very low-risk cases through 1.00 for very high-risk cases). Being younger was itself a risk factor but the strength of that association was reduced substantially with the introduction of LSI risk/need scores.

TABLE 9.6	Re-offending Rates by Intake Risk/Need Level of Subgroups of Probationers Based on Age, Gender, and Reliance on Social Assistance (N = 561; number of cases in parentheses)

	Intake Risk Level				
Subgroup	Very Low	Low	Medium	High	Very High
Being young (r = 15 with recidivism, r = .11 when risk controlled)					
Young (16–17)	.09 (32)	.31 (39)	.59 (51)	.88 (16)	1.00 (2)
Adult	.09 (119)	.17 (130)	.44 (145)	.63 (27)	— (0)
Being male (r = .09 with recidivism, r = .06 ns when risk controlled)					
Women	.05 (37)	.11 (27)	.38 (24)	.78 (9)	— (0)
Men	.11 (114)	.22 (142)	.49 (172)	.71 (34)	1.00 (2)
Young women	.00 (8)	.14 (7)	.29 (7)	.80 (5)	— (0)
Young men	.13 (24)	.34 (32)	.64 (44)	.91 (11)	1.00 (2)
Adult women	.07 (29)	.01 (20)	.41 (17)	.75 (4)	— (0)
Adult men	.10 (90)	.18 (110)	.45 (128)	.61 (23)	— (0)
Poverty: Relies on social assistance (r = .16 with recidivism, r = 02 ns when risk controlled)					
Yes	.09 (11)	.25 (24)	.47 (78)	.77 (22)	— (0)
No	.09 (140)	.19 (145)	.48 (124)	.67 (21)	1.00 (2)
Young male offenders relying on social assistance	.00 (1)	— (0)	.73 (11)	1.00 (3)	— (0)
Young female offenders relying on social assistance	.00 (1)	.00 (1)	.33 (3)	1.00 (2)	— (0)
Adult male offenders relying on social assistance	.17 (6)	.38 (13)	.46 (48)	.67 (15)	— (0)
Adult female offenders relying on social assistance	.00 (3)	.10 (10)	.30 (10)	1.00 (2)	— (0)
Young male offenders, not depending on social assistance	.13 (23)	.34 (32)	.61 (33)	.88 (8)	1.00 (2)
Adult male offenders, not depending on social assistance	.09 (84)	.15 (97)	.44 (80)	.50 (8)	— (0)
Young female offenders, not depending on social assistance	.00 (7)	.17 (6)	.25 (4)	.67 (3)	— (0)
Adult female offenders, not depending on social assistance	.08 (26)	.10 (10)	.57 (7)	.50 (2)	— (0)

NOTE: The correlation of the five-level LSI Risk Score with recidivism was .44, and was .40 when age, gender, and poverty were statistically controlled. The contributions of gender and poverty were reduced to non-significant (ns) levels once risk was entered. Being young continued to make a contribution, albeit minor, once risk was considered (r = .11). The correlation coefficients for Risk-Recidivism were .37, .49, .51, and .64 for adult men, adult women, young men, and young women respectively. Data based on the original LSI sample, reanalyzed according to LSI-OR guidelines (Andrews 1997).

In addition, inspection of Table 9.6 reveals that assessment of the major risk and need factors was associated with the re-offending of young men and young women as well as adult men and adult women. The data further revealed that general risk/need scores predicted the criminal behaviour of the young and old, male and females, the more and the less financially disadvantaged and did so for all six combinations of age, gender, and social class. This pattern of results challenges the social location perspectives that suggest that youthful offending is primarily a reflection of being young, being poor, and being male. The contributions of age, poverty, and gender were all reduced substantially by considering the major personality and social learning variables.

Studies of risk/need factors have reached a new level of sophistication with the emergence of **developmental criminology** (Farrington 1999; Stouthamer-Loeber et al. 1993). Early onset delinquency, with aggression evident as early as preschool, and with hyperactivity and impulsivity, is associated with chronic and serious criminal behaviour in adulthood, with estimates that 70 to 80 percent of adult violent offenders were aggressive as children. Other young people display antisocial behaviour in adolescence but do not go on to become adult offenders. One of the interests of this subdiscipline is gaining an understanding of patterns of criminal behaviour over the course of a life.

Developmental criminologists also raise the issue of a differentiation between risk factors and protection, or between strength factors and resiliency processes. The notion of strength factors has tremendous appeal for a number of reasons. First, the human service and human science practitioners do not appear to focus exclusively on negatives when strength is addressed. Second, building on existing strengths may enhance the positive effects of treatment. Third, a consideration of strengths may help explain why not all high-risk cases actually offend. The problem is that the field has yet to settle on what is actually meant by a **strength factor**, by "protection" or "resilience," or both (see Stouthamer-Loeber et al. 1993).

Currently we know that risk factors, as discussed herein, are the best established predictors of offending. That is, the vast majority of suggested strength and protective factors represent the other end of well-established risk factors. However, the idea of strength provides additional predictive value if, for example, young people with "above average intelligence" have lower re-offending rates than both those of "average intelligence," who in turn have lower re-offending rates than those with "below average intelligence." Under these hypothetical conditions, "above average intelligence" is a strength factor, "below average intelligence" is a risk factor, and "average intelligence" is neutral. At this time, the evidence favourable to considering strength for predictive purposes is limited primarily to children under 12 years of age. This is an issue for ongoing research with both the under-age and those subject to justice processing.

Another definition of strength, protection, and resilience entails evidence of a "statistical interaction" or a finding that "it depends." For example, consider the following hypothetical example: Poverty is associated with the antisocial behaviour of young people who scored below average on intelligence but is unrelated to the antisocial behaviour of other young people. Under these conditions, "average or above average intelligence" would be described as a resilience factor, a factor that protected children from the criminogenic nature of poverty. To date, no protective factors as described in this hypothetical illustration have been established to any convincing degree. As described below, however, a number of risk/need factors have been shown to interact with treatment.

The Effects on Re-offending of Official Punishment and Treatment in the Youth Justice Context and the Effects of Primary Prevention

The general principles of clinically relevant and psychologically informed treatment (as outlined in Table 9.3) appear to apply very well in studies of young offenders. A close look at Table 9.7 reveals that the average difference in the recidivism rates between experimental and comparison groups was enhanced with adherence to the human service principle. The effect of increases in the severity of the disposition was a mild increase in recidivism of two percentage points on average in 47 separate tests. In dramatic contrast, the average effect of introducing human service into the youth justice context was a reduction of re-offending by 13 percentage points (in 146 tests). In brief, and in the context of justice, deliver human service and do not rely on punishment without service. Inspection of Table 9.7 further reveals that the positive effect of human service was enhanced by delivery of more intensive service to high-risk rather than low-risk cases, by a focus on a greater number of criminogenic needs targeted than non-criminogenic needs, and by the use of social learning/cognitive behavioural strategies.

Moreover, and consistent with the principle of community-based treatment (see Chapter 13), the mean difference in recidivism rates of treatment and control groups reached 37 percentage points in the 21 tests of clinically appropriate treatment delivered in non-residential community settings. The difference of 37 percentage points corresponds to a mean recidivism rate of 68.5 percent in the control groups, compared to a mean recidivism rate of 31.5 percent in the groups receiving clinically appropriate human service.

TABLE 9.7 **Mean Effect Size by Adherence to Principles of Effective Correctional Treatment in 193 Tests with Young Offenders and Correlation of Adherence with Effect Size (k = number of tests of treatment)**

Adherence to Principle

Principle	No	Yes	Correlation with Effect Size
Human service	−.02 (47)	.13 (146)	.31
Risk: Services delivered to high-risk cases	.02 (50)	.11 (143)	.20
Criminogenic needs: Number of criminogenic needs targeted exceed number of non-criminogenic	−.01 (102)	.20 (56)	.52
General responsivity: Social learning/Cognitive behavioural strategies	.03 (137)	.23 (56)	.43
Full adherence: Clinically appropriate treatment (adheres to all of the above)	.04 (152)	.27 (41)	.46
Community-based full adherence: Clinically appropriate treatment	.05 (123)	.37 (21)	.55
Residential-based full adherence: Clinically appropriate treatment	.03 (29)	.17 (20)	.41

It is interesting to observe that community-based youth justice programs that failed to adhere to any of the four clinical principles averaged only a five percentage point difference between treatment and comparison groups. Indeed, community-based youth justice programs that did not introduce any human service component yielded a very mild increase in re-offending rates. Adding eight additional studies that introduced human service inconsistent with each of risk, need, and general responsivity yielded an even less impressive result. These findings are devastating for the application of specific deterrence theory in youth court.

On the other hand, community-based justice programs that introduced human service consistent with risk, need, and general responsivity, or any combination of the three, yielded a more promising effect. Based on these findings, which have also been replicated with adult offenders, proposed new youth justice legislation is well advised to emphasize community-based rehabilitation if reduced re-offending is valued. It appears that rehabilitation agents would do well to attend to the clinically relevant and psychologically informed principles of human service in a justice context. Meanwhile, residential-based sanctioning without human service and residential-based clinically inappropriate human service are even less promising for purposes of reduced re-offending. Therefore, if re-offending is sought and custodial sanctions are unavoidable for reasons of justice, the criminogenic potential of custody can be reduced by the introduction of clinically appropriate human service. The average effects of residential-based human service consistent with risk, need, and responsivity, or any combination of them, were positive for both youth and adult samples.

Even though the effects of residential-based treatment are smaller than community-based effects, the consequence of not treating in custody may well be an increase in re-offending rates. Our interpretation is that high-risk cases in custody should receive clinically appropriate human service, and continued access to human service should be arranged upon return to the community.

The specific criminogenic needs and non-criminogenic needs targeted in the tests of treatment are summarized in Table 9.8 (criminogenic needs; recall Table 9.2, part A) and Table 9.9 (non-criminogenic needs; recall Table 9.2, part B). The young offender findings are consistent with the general model. Indeed, the mean effect of treatment increased directly with the number of criminogenic needs targeted. More generally, these findings provide strong support for yet an additional principle of effective treatment in youth justice contexts: **multimodal service**. Multimodel service is supported, at least when it refers to the targeting of multiple criminogenic needs.

In direct contrast, the mean effect of young offender treatment systematically decreased with increases in the number of non-criminogenic needs targeted. As noted earlier, when criminogenic needs targeted exceeded number of non-criminogenic needs targeted, reduced re-offending was enhanced. In other words, when reduced re-offending is desired, clinically relevant and psychologically informed human service is best introduced in the context of youth justice. Note, however, that in only 21 of 193 tests (a mere 11 percent of the tests) were rehabilitative services delivered in the community to high-risk cases with criminogenic needs targeted and social learning strategies employed. In other words, the vast majority of tests of juvenile justice interventions (that is, 89 percent of them) were conducted under conditions not favourable to positive effects. Looked at in this way, no wonder many people decided that rehabilitation does not work! Nonetheless, there is little doubt about what the research evidence shows: Rehabilitative service does not work when non-structured non-behavioural services are delivered to low-risk cases with a focus on non-criminogenic

TABLE 9.8 **Criminogenic Needs Rank Ordered by Magnitude of Correlation with Effect Size: Percentage of 193 Tests with Criminogenic Need Targeted, Mean Effect Size When and When Not Targeted, and Correlation of Need Area Targeted with Effect Size**

Need Area Targeted		Mean Phi (k)		
	Percentage	Not a Target	Targeted	Correlation with Effect Size
Personal criminogenic targets: Antisocial cognition and skill deficits	33	.04 (130)	.20 (63)	.39
Antisocial cognition	25	.05 (145)	.21 (48)	.33
Self-control deficits	19	.06 (156)	.21 (37)	.28
Interpersonal criminogenic targets: Family and peers	23	.05 (149)	.22 (44)	.33
Family process	13	.06 (167)	.28 (26)	.37
Antisocial associates	14	.07 (166)	.22 (27)	.26
Individualized matching with need (specific needs not identified)	19	.06 (156)	.22 (37)	.30
School/work	26	.06 (143)	.15 (50)	.23

NOTES:

a) Some targets occurred in less than 5 percent of the studies: Relapse prevention (f = 5, r = .03 ns), Barriers to treatment (f = 8, r = .27), Substance abuse (f = 6, r = .02 ns), Medication for mentally disordered offenders (f = 0).

b) Components of antisocial cognition: Antisocial attitudes (f = 16, r = .12), Anger (f = 39, r = .31).

c) Components of family process: Affection (f = 21, r = .31), Supervision (f = 15, r = .31).

d) Components of antisocial associates: Increase contact with pro-social (f = 19, r = .22), Decrease contact with antisocial (f = 8, r = .13).

e) Components of school/work: School (f = 46, r = .20), Vocational skills (f = 15, r = .12), Vocational skills plus obtaining work (f = 8, r = .26).

f) Components of substance abuse treatment (f = 1, r = −.01 ns), Information (f = 5, r = .03 ns).

g) Sum criminogenic needs targeted and effect size: r = 58.

needs. Otherwise, rehabilitation works to a socially significant degree. Although our focus is on corrections, the literature is building in support of risk-targeted primary prevention programs—in the words of the developmental criminologists, it appears that prevention programming is never too early and never too late (Farrington 1999).

Core Correctional Practice

Adherence to general responsivity scores positively when the influence strategies incorporated modelling, reinforcement, graduated practice, and role-playing. These are the major elements of social learning strategies; however, such textbook descriptions are best amplified by descriptions that are called the core elements of effective correctional practice, or **core correctional practice (CCP)** (Andrews and Carvell 1998). Modelling and reinforcement effects are greatly enhanced under conditions of open, warm, and enthusiastic communication,

TABLE 9.9   Percentage of 193 Tests with Non-criminogenic Need Targeted, Mean Effect Size When and When Not Targeted, and Correlation with Effect Size

Need Area Targeted		Mean Phi (k)		
	Percentage	Not a Target	Targeted	Correlation with Effect Size
Personal non-criminogenic targets	45	.13 (107)	.05 (86)	−.20
Fear of official punishment	7	.10 (180)	−.05 (13)	−.19
Personal distress	29	.11 (137)	+.03 (56)	−.18
Physical activity	18	.10 (159)	+.07 (34)	−.05 ns
Conventional ambition	6	.09 (182)	+.11 (11)	+.02 ns
Interpersonal non-criminogenic targets	17	.11 (161)	+.00 (32)	−.20
Family: Other	9	.10 (175)	+.06 (18)	−.13

NOTES:

a) Low frequency targets: Targeting of respect for criminal thinking: f = 6, r = −.04 ns; Cohesive peers: f = 15, r = −.00 ns.

b) Components of personal distress: Self-esteem (f = 12, r = −.13), Other distress (f = 46, r = −.11 ns).

c) Sum of non-criminogenic needs targeted and effect size: r = −.22.

and thus a major dimension of effective practice is the interpersonal relationship one. Another is the structuring or contingency dimension reflecting the interpersonal influence skills of modelling and differential reinforcement. The structuring elements include a specification of effective anti-criminal modelling, anti-criminal reinforcement, and anti-criminal expressions of disapproval.

Structured learning procedures, as outlined by Goldstein and Glick (1987) for purposes of skill-building and problem-solving, are also highlighted. As many parents and most coaches and teachers know, to build a new skill, certain steps are important: Describe the skill, model the skill, use role-playing to practice the skill, use reinforcement and corrective feedback, practice some more. High levels of advocacy and brokerage are also indicated. Treatment effects are enhanced when the service agent stands up for the young person's legitimate efforts in his or her interactions with the court, corrections, welfare, and other agencies such as school. Effective use of authority is "firm but fair," definitely not "shaming," and not simply monitoring and then initiating negative sanctioning upon discovery of non-compliance. Effective use of authority entails respectful guidance towards compliance.

The information in Table 9.10 reveals that each element of CCP enhanced effect sizes over and above the contributions of risk, need, and general responsivity. The one exception was use of authority. Of the CCP elements, relationship skills and structured learning skills made incremental contributions once all CCP elements were allowed to enter after appropriate treatment had been introduced. The lack of attention to CCP is another noteworthy finding. Only 3 percent of the tests (5 out of 193) attended to staff relationship skills and less than 5 percent of the tests revealed any attention to high-quality reinforcement or effective disapproval. Once again, the state of the existing research literature suggests that there are great opportunities to improve the quality of treatment services offered young offenders. What can correctional managers, policy-makers, and legislators do?

TABLE 9.10   Mean Effect Size by Elements of Core Correctional Practice with Young Offenders

Element of CCP	Element Present No	Yes	Correlation with Effect Size	Partial	Partial b
Relationship skills	.08 (188)	.48 (5)	.31	.15	.17
Structuring skills	.06 (169)	.27 (24)	.34	.15	ns
Effective reinforcement	.08 (185)	.31 (8)	.22	.15	ns
Effective modelling	.06 (170)	.28 (23)	.35	.20	ns
Effective disapproval	.08 (187)	.30 (6)	.19	.14	ns
Structured skill-learning	.06 (172)	.31 (21)	.37	.23	.14
Problem-solving	.07 (170)	.25 (23)	.29	.18	ns
Advocacy/brokerage	.07 (156)	.16 (37)	.16	.16	ns
Effective authority	.09 (189)	.27 (4)	.13	.03 ns	ns

NOTES:

a) The correlation of the simple sum of the nine elements with effect size was .44.

b) All tabled correlation coefficients with effect size are statistically significant at least at the .05 level (one-tailed) except where noted non-significant (ns).

c) "Partial" refers to the correlation with effect size after general responsivity: behavioural is entered.

d) "Partial b" refers to the correlation after appropriate treatment is entered.

e) The r moves to .63 with the introduction of CCP from .57 with appropriate treatment on its own.

Integrity in Program Implementation and Service Delivery

Managers of rehabilitation programs, and indeed funders of programs, must be knowledgeable beyond the legislative and policy base for programming and beyond the requirements for ethical, legal, decent, humane, and cost-efficient programming. Knowledge of "what works" (as we have just reviewed) plus skills in program development and implementation are crucial aspects of successful programming for young offenders. "Integrity" refers to implementation according to the standards and procedures established by the program designer (Hollin 1995). Major indicators of integrity include staff factors such as the selection of staff on program-relevant characteristics, the pre-service and in-service training of staff, and the clinical supervision of staff by trained and skilled supervisors. Table 9.11 indicates that a number of indicators of integrity linked with effect size. In this context, "dosage" refers to a sufficient level, duration, and intensity of treatment. Once again, it is notable that the majority of tests of treatment directed for Table 9.11 were not conducted under high integrity conditions.

Specific Responsivity Classification Systems

A number of personality-based classification systems have been proposed for differentiating among young offenders. None has proved as empirically or theoretically powerful as the risk, need, and general responsivity approaches for purposes of prediction and treatment

TABLE 9.11   Mean Effect Size by Indicators of Integrity of Implementation and Service Delivery (K = 193)

Indicator	Indicator Present		Correlation with Effect Size
	No	Yes	
Staff selected for relationship skills	.08 (188)	.48 (5)	.31
Staff trained	.02 (88)	.15 (105)	.32
Clinical supervision of staff	.07 (152)	.18 (41)	.22
Number of hours of service	metric non-binary variable	.41 (k = 53)	
Rated appropriate dosage	.07 (115)	.12 (78)	.11 ns
Printed/taped manuals	.05 (147)	.21 (46)	.32
Monitor process and/ or intermediate change on targets	.07 (100)	.11 (93)	.07 ns
Specific model	.02 (80)	.14 (113)	.27
New/fresh program	.06 (115)	.14 (78)	.19
Small program/sample	.05 (107)	.14 (86)	.19
Involved evaluator	.04 (142)	.24 (51)	.42

but all are useful as guides for specific responsivity. Unfortunately, a comprehensive meta-analysis of specific responsivity has not been conducted as yet and we are unable to report on how useful they may be.

Perhaps the most widely represented approach—although not always acknowledged—is a theoretically derived classification system based on the Freudian model of personality and psychosexual development. Although this theme is developed more fully in Andrews and Bonta (1998) than we can present it here, these subtypes emerge over and over again in various classification systems, including explicitly non-Freudian empirically derived ones. The subtypes are those of "weak superego," "weak ego," "normal antisocial offender," "neurotic offender," "situational offenders," and a host of exceptional types such as the "psychotic," "retarded," and "substance abusers."

The weak superego offender is "without conscience" and "without ego-ideal." The former refers to the lack of an internalized value system representing socially proscribed behaviour and the latter to the lack of an internalized value system representing socially prescribed behaviour. This behaviour is subject only to the individual's need for immediate gratification and the demands of the immediate situation. Thus, without superego, antisocial and self-serving behaviour is to be expected. If the superego is not formed by the age of six or seven, one can expect generalized disregard for conventional rules and procedures, antisocial thinking, freedom from guilt, conflict with authority figures, a lack of a life plan, weak conventional ambition in the domains of school and work, and even displays of bravado, flirtatiousness, and exhibitionism. These characteristics are all deducible from the Freudian notion of what happens when very young people are not provided an early opportunity to deal with early family circumstances through identification with a morally mature, nurturing, and supervising caregiver (Glueck and Glueck 1950). Readers may recognize the description, if not the theoretical interpretation, as a description closely related to the Cleckley (1982) and Hare (1990) notions of psychopathy (we return to that construct in the section on mentally disordered offenders in this chapter).

A number of psychological classification systems have been developed over the years, some based on research and others based on theory (for detailed examples, see Hewitt and Jenkins 1946; Van Voorhis 1994). The empirically based systems reflected factor analytic and related correlation strategies aimed at identifying the minimum number of dimensions required to describe the personality of delinquents. Quay (1984) provided a useful summary of these approaches. Based on behaviour problem checklists, the coding of life history information and responses to paper-and-pencil questionnaires, the systems identify some combination of the following five types: inadequate immature offenders, unsocialized aggressive offenders, socialized-subcultural offenders, disturbed-emotional offenders, and situational offenders. These correspond roughly to the weak ego, weak superego, mature antisocial, neurotic, and situational respectively.

The Interpersonal Maturity system (I-Level) is based on a developmental theory that emphasizes stages of emotional and social maturity. At the low level of maturity (I-2) were the Unsocialized Aggressive and the Unsocialized Passive. At a high level (I-3) were the Immature Conformist (going along with the leader), the Cultural Conformist (association with delinquent others), and the Manipulator. At I-4, were the Situational Reactors, Neurotic Acting-out, Neurotic Anxious, and the Cultural Identifier who has internalized criminal values.[4]

As noted, specific responsivity according to case characteristics requires more original studies and a meta-analytic investigation to make statements as strong as the conclusions that can be made in regard to risk, need, and general responsivity. We expect that the recognition of certain fundamental dimensions of personality will guide specific responsivity more so than the typologies do. For example:

- Those who work with young people who score high on measures of anxiety, worrying, and interpersonal shyness should avoid heavy confrontational and "hot seat" strategies.
- Those who work with individuals who score below average on measures of verbal intelligence should employ structured intervention techniques and not rely on highly verbal, insight-oriented, or evocative approaches.
- Those who work with the extremely egocentric and antisocial should employ very structured intervention efforts and set up open communication among all involved workers.
- Those who with weakly motivated individuals should reduce all situational barriers to participation, be sure to establish high-quality relationships with them, deliver on matters of personal interest early on, and start where the "case is at."

This is only a sample of specific responsivity considerations. Age, race/ethnicity, language, and gender are other specific responsivity considerations.

Conclusion

The priorities for dealing with young offenders are relatively clear. In Canada, the first set of priorities must be enacting federal legislation that will govern the official processing of young offenders. Will the move towards blending together youth and adult justice be enhanced or weakened? Will we be able to achieve a balance among retribution, restoration, just desert, rehabilitation, prevention, and due process? How? Will true respect for protection of the public be displayed through the enhancement of both primary prevention and rehabilitative programs? The second set has to do with risk, need, responsivity, program integrity, and professional discretion. Will these factors be applied, and will research be conducted and attended to in order to enhance effectiveness?

FEMALE OFFENDERS

No set of research findings is better established than that the research into gender differences in patterns of antisocial behaviour. Women, young and old, are less likely than men, young and old, to engage in criminal acts, and women engage in fewer and less serious and violent criminal acts than do men. Re-examination of the data in Table 9.4 reveals that this pattern exists even when the self-confessed and officially undetected antisocial activity of high school students is examined. Thus substantially fewer young women and adult women are involved in the young offender and adult correctional systems than are men of similar ages.

The dramatic gender differences in criminal behaviour constitute a phenomenon of tremendous theoretical, empirical, and practical interest. Moreover, over the last 20 years, there have been serious challenges to a) the validity of theory and research on female criminality and b) the fairness and validity of the processing of female offenders (Chesney-Lind and Bloom 1997).

Perhaps the changes have been more visible in federal corrections than in provincial corrections, that is, in the Correctional Service of Canada. The provincial-federal distinction is important because the offences of adults subject to federal processing (those with custodial sentences of two years or more) may differ considerably from adults processed by the provinces and territories (Trevethan 1999). For example, women in federal facilities were typically incarcerated for violent offences (64 percent) while women in provincial-territorial facilities were in for non-violent offences (72 percent). Of course, proportionally more male inmates in both types of facilities presented with violent offences. In both settings, women were serving shorter sentences than were men.

Who are these incarcerated adult women? As presented in Chapter 10, on average they are young, uneducated, unemployed, and unattached, with an over-representation of Aboriginal women. This pattern is very similar to the findings for male adult incarcerates although fewer men were unemployed at time of admission. The majority of the women were classified as low risk and proportionally more of the men were high risk. The issue is whether the major risk/need factors apply regardless of age, gender, education, employment status, and ethnicity. Recall, from Table 9.6, that assessments of the best established of the major risk factors are very robust across categories of age and gender. In addition, the assessments were predictive for younger and older women trapped in poverty and for younger and older women not trapped in poverty. This pattern of results is also found with male offenders.

Table 9.12 indicates that level of risk/need once again is associated with the recidivism of younger and older women, but additionally with the re-offending of more and less well-educated women, employed and unemployed women, married and unmarried women,

Aboriginal women and non-Aboriginal women, abused women and non-abused women, and Black women and non-Black women. We have yet to find any subgroup of women for whom the survey of the big eight risk/need factors is not valid.

Rettinger's (1999) research further reveals that the "big four" of attitudes, associates, behavioural history, and personality could account for the vast majority of the explained variation in adult female re-offending in samples from both community and institutional corrections. In addition, financial problems and personal/emotional problems were also weak risk factors. There is a suggestion that accommodation problems are important for women and that the construct of home-based strength and risk factors might be expanded to include the quality and physical location of the home.

This is an extraordinarily important sample of provincially sentenced women because these women participated in Margaret Shaw's (1994) woman-centred interview study that allowed over 400 adult female offenders to report their concerns in their own voice. Shaw's interviews revealed high rates of victimization both as children and as adults. Fifty-four percent of the women reported experiencing some form of physical, sexual, or emotional abuse as a child; 72 percent reported some form of abuse an adult[5]; 82 percent reported some form of abuse as either a child or an adult. Every indicator of abuse except emotional abuse as an adult was significantly associated with increased recidivism. The strongest link between

TABLE 9.12 **Recidivism Rates of Provincially Sentenced Adult Women by Risk/Need Level as Assessed by a Composite of the Major Risk Factors and by Indicators of Socioeconomic Disadvantage and Abuse**

| | Intake Risk Level | | | | |
Sample	Very Low	Low	Medium	High	Very High
Total sample	.04 (51)	.15 (93)	.44 (146)	.80 (129)	1.00 (22)
Less than Grade 10	.00 (3)	.12 (67)	.34 (47)	.77 (61)	1.00 (15)
Relies on welfare	.08 (13)	.12 (52)	.44 (105)	.88 (88)	1.00 (14)
Often unemployed	— (0)	.25 (12)	.47 (59)	.85 (91)	1.00 (21)
Unmarried	.03 (33)	.14 (66)	.47 (103)	.80 (93)	1.00 (13)
Dissatisfied with marital circumstances	.11 (9)	.19 (31)	.44 (71)	.76 (55)	1.00 (9)
Black	.00 (8)	.00 (10)	.54 (13)	.91 (11)	1.00 (2)
White	.02 (37)	.20 (71)	.43 (109)	.80 (97)	1.00 (13)
Severe history of abuse: Abused as a child and as an adult including at least two of physical, sexual, and emotional abuse	.17 (6)	.16 (19)	.45 (58)	.80 (59)	.1.00 (14)

NOTE: In regression analyses, the only variable to contribute over and above risk/need was frequent unemployment (from an r of .41 to a still significant .10). Others contributed only via risk/need.

SOURCE: Adapted from Rettinger 1998, 1999.

abuse and recidivism was the measure that summed all three forms of abuse across both childhood and adulthood (although the magnitude of that link was itself much smaller than the association between the big four of the major risk factors and recidivism).

Many other areas of concern were found within the sample of female adult offenders. These areas ranged from having children (71 percent), being unmarried/unattached (70 percent), experiencing feelings of personal distress (69 percent), physical health problems (56 percent), dissatisfaction with marital circumstances (41 percent), and histories of suicide attempts (34 percent). With the exception of a history of suicide attempts, none of the above or any of many other women-specific risk factors linked with recidivism. As in the case of age, ethnicity, gender, and socioeconomic status, none of the measures of abuse or the other measures described as women-specific contributed to the prediction of recidivism (Rettinger 1999). They may well function as gender-specific responsivity factors in treatment services but that has yet to be tested (Dowden and Andrews 1999).

It is not clear that systematic controlled tests of women-centred programming will be forthcoming soon. Powerful advocates of the interests of women are arguing for the disregard of risk, criminogenic need, and general responsivity, and are arguing that systematic, controlled, and quantitative approaches to evaluation should not be used (see Covington and Bloom 1999). Nonetheless, we remain optimistic because what these advocates seem to want is not at all incompatible with clinically relevant and psychologically informed service. For example, the principles of risk, need, and responsivity are not incompatible with certain key features of the Covington-Bloom suggestions, including all of the following:

- Emphasize prevention (specifically, principles of effective prevention);
- Do no harm (avoid a reliance on specific deterrence and avoid inappropriate treatment);
- Create gender responsive services (attend to specific responsivity issues);
- Build community support (enhance community programming and consider associates and the settings of home, school/work, and leisure); and
- Emphasize the importance of interpersonal relationships (encourage quality interpersonal relationship in combination with structuring skills).

In a set of 374 controlled tests of correctional treatment, only 45 tests were conducted with samples composed primarily of female offenders (Andrews, Dowden, and Gendreau 1999) and thus controlled tests of correctional treatment with female offenders ought to be a high priority. While much fewer in number, the percentage of tests with female offenders that adhered to the principles of risk, need, and general responsivity was almost identical to the percentages found in the total sample of tests. Moreover, adherence with the principles of risk, need, and general responsivity was associated with reduced offending within the female tests of treatment as strongly as within the male tests of treatment.

As noted, the need for additional studies is obvious, but at this time the principles of human service, risk, need, and general responsivity—that is, of clinically relevant and psychologically informed human service—appear to apply very well with female offenders. In addition, reduced re-offending of female offenders was found in those treatments where staff possessed interpersonal relationship skills and structuring skills. The structuring skills of treatment staff included high levels of reinforcement, modelling, problem-solving, and skill-building. Similarly, effect sizes increased with a number of indicators of integrity in female offender program implementation and service delivery.

The Special Case of Federally Sentenced Offenders

Federally sentenced female offenders are special in the over-representation of violent offences and in the extraordinary attention paid to gender-specific needs. Unlike young persons, women have not been afforded a separate justice system but the possibility of their differential processing has been seriously investigated. According to Stableforth (1999)—the Deputy Commissioner for Women in Correctional Service of Canada—the first federal institution for women, the infamous Prison for Women in Kingston, was criticized from its opening in 1934 for emphasizing security more than was necessary. Other criticisms have focused on the lack of women-centred programming (see Chapter 10).

The federal response is summarized in the Correctional Service's fact sheet presented in Box 9.2. The major changes—the closing of the Prison for Women and the opening of new facilities across the country—constitute a textbook example of the possibilities when government and voluntary sector agencies interact.

To date, the best of the available research evidence supports, without qualification, the position that men are involved in more forms of criminal activity than are women. Additionally, the major risk and criminogenic need factors are very similar for men and women. Similarly, the human service principles of risk, need, general responsivity, core correctional practice, and program integrity appear to apply to women. And yet female offenders present with

---

BOX 9.2 Fact Sheet on Female Offenders

There are very few women inmates under federal sentence in Canada. They currently number just over 850, or about 4% of the total federal offender population. Of this number, about 40% are incarcerated in a penitentiary and the remainder are on conditional release under supervision in the community.

Because there are so few federally sentenced women, they were historically incarcerated away from their families and home communities at the sole federal facility for women, the Prison for Women in Kingston, Ontario, and the range of programming available to them was limited.

In 1989, the federal government set up a Task Force to review the overall situation of federally sentenced women and to chart a new direction. The Task Force Report on Federally Sentenced Women, *Creating Choices,* released in

April 1990, made one main long-term recommendation:

- to close down the Prison for Women and replace it with four regional facilities and a unique Aboriginal Healing Lodge. This would allow women offenders to move closer to their families and home communities.

These regional facilities and the Healing Lodge accommodate minimum and medium-security women offenders and are now all operational:

Name	Location
Nova Institution for Women	Truro, Nova Scotia
Établissement Joliette	Joliette, Québec
Grand Valley Institution for Women	Kitchener, Ontario

Name	Location
Edmonton Institution for Women	Edmonton, Alberta
Okimaw Ohci Healing Lodge	Maple Creek, Saskatchewan

In Ontario Region, Isabel McNeil House, a minimum-security facility for women offenders in Kingston, provides 13 beds.

Maximum-security women inmates are not housed in the regional facilities, but rather in Maximum-Security Women's Units in other existing institutions, where security and programming are consistent with their needs.

The Maximum-Security Women's Units are located as follows:

Springhill Institution	Springhill, Nova Scotia
Regional Reception Centre	Ste-Anne-des-Plaines, Que.
Prison for Women	Kingston, Ontario
Saskatchewan Penitentiary	Prince Albert, Saskatchewan

In British Columbia, the provincially run Burnaby Correctional Centre for Women accommodates women offenders of all security classifications under a joint federal/provincial agreement.

SOURCE: Correctional Service of Canada 1999b.

histories of higher rates of other-induced and self-induced abuse, with higher rates of internalization disorders and personal distress, and with more concerns in the domains of sexuality, family, and parenting. Gender-specific programming remains almost totally unexplored in the context of controlled experimental tests of specific responsivity considerations.

ABORIGINAL OFFENDERS

Aboriginal people and Aboriginal communities are over-represented among convicted offenders and as victims of crime in Canada. Box 9.3 contains the Correctional Service of Canada's fact sheet on Aboriginal offenders, and describes the Service's attempts to provide culturally sensitive settings and programs.

Wood and Griffiths (2000) have provided an interesting look at the patterns of Aboriginal crime, drawing on their own work, the work of their colleagues, and the work of LaPrairie (1992) and Trevethan (1993). Drawing heavily on LaPrairie, Woods and Griffiths compare non-Aboriginal and Aboriginal homicide, suspect, and victim rates per 100,000 population for selected cities in the 1980s. At one extreme for cities west of Toronto, consider the city of Regina where the rate for non-Aboriginal suspects was 0.9, compared to 76.6 for Aboriginal suspects, and the rate for non-Aboriginal victims was 1.2 compared with 45.3 for Aboriginal victims. At the other extreme was the city of Thunder Bay, where the rate for non-Aboriginal suspects was 1.3 compared to 17.4 for Aboriginal suspects, and the rate for non-Aboriginal victims was 1.5 compared to 15.3 for Aboriginal victims. The over-representation of Aboriginal people involved in crime is particularly evident in the case of violent crime. In the case of property crime, some Aboriginal communities have rates lower than the overall national rate and some have rates higher than the national rate. Notably, however, there is tremendous variability in crime rates among Aboriginal communities and within geographic regions.

BOX 9.3   Aboriginal Offenders

Aboriginal people come into contact with Canada's correctional systems in numbers hugely disproportionate to their representation in the general population. While representing three per cent of Canada's population, self-identified Aboriginal people represent approximately 16 per cent of all admissions to federal institutions.

Another way to look at this problem is to compare incarceration rates. At 129 per 100,000, Canada has one of the highest incarceration rates among developed countries. But adult Aboriginal people are incarcerated more than 6 times the national rate. In Saskatchewan, the adult Aboriginal incarceration rate is over 1,600 per 100,000, compared to 48 per 100,000 for adult non-Aboriginals. And to compound the problem, the current Aboriginal "baby-boom" will cause the number of Aboriginal offenders to rise dramatically over the next decade.

Today, there are about 2,400 Aboriginal people in federal institutions, provincial institutions under the federal-provincial Exchange of Services Agreement, or on conditional release in the community. An estimated 70 per cent of all Aboriginal people sentenced to penitentiaries are either residents of urban (non-reserve) communities, or committed their offenses while off-reserve.

Problems posed by the relatively high numbers of Aboriginal offenders are complicated by the fact that Aboriginal peoples do not form a homogeneous group, culturally, geographically or by way of status. The Aboriginal population in federal institutions is made up of 71 per cent self-identified Indians, 25 per cent Métis and four per cent Inuit.

In addition to being over-represented, a Ministry of the Solicitor General study entitled *Aboriginal Peoples in Federal Corrections* showed that Aboriginal inmates waive their rights to a parole hearing more frequently than do other inmates. Parole is also denied at a higher rate than for non-Aboriginal offenders, and when parole is granted, it is usually later in the inmate's sentence. In addition, the revocation rate for Aboriginal offenders on conditional release is higher than for the general offender population.

The Ministry of the Solicitor General has undertaken several initiatives to provide Aboriginal people with more effective, fair, and culturally sensitive treatment in the federal corrections system.

The Department of the Solicitor General works with the Aboriginal community to develop and support innovative projects to examine offender treatment and services within the context of restorative justice and healing. Examples include the Hollow Water Community Holistic Healing Circle in Manitoba and the Maison Waskeskun House in Montreal.

The Correctional Service of Canada (CSC) supports initiatives in federal penitentiaries and those designed to assist Aboriginal people with their successful release into the community. CSC has developed culturally appropriate substance abuse programs; Native liaison services; traditional cultural and spiritual programs within prisons; Elders' services; mandatory cross-cultural training for corrections staff; and post-release programs and services.

As part of its plan to close the Prison for Women, CSC has constructed a unique facility for federally-sentenced Aboriginal women. The Okimaw Ohci Healing Lodge in Maple Creek, Saskatchewan, is the first institution of its kind, developed with and for the First Nations community. Sixty per cent of the staff are of Aboriginal descent. The lodge operates on Aboriginal teachings and philosophy, and there is a strong emphasis placed on Aboriginal culture and spirituality.

In addition, the National Parole Board has implemented a program of Elder-assisted hearings, to ensure that its conditional release program is sensitive to and respectful of the languages and cultures of Aboriginal people.

SOURCE: Correctional Service of Canada 1999a.

There is a strong tendency in the social sciences to link high rates of Aboriginal crime to Aboriginal culture having suffered from colonization and Aboriginal people thereby being socioeconomically and otherwise disadvantaged. Substitute "patriarchy" for "colonization" and much of the social science of Aboriginal crime sounds almost indistinguishable from the victim theories of female crime (see Covington and Bloom 1999), except, however, that the rates and patterns of Aboriginal crime and female crime are dramatically different. Consistent with this chapter, Woods and Griffiths (2000) conclude their paper by suggesting that any understanding Aboriginal criminal behaviour may benefit from the consideration of theories that view criminal behaviour across all racial and ethnic groups.

Notably, in New Zealand an interest in Aboriginal crime is leading the systematic search for Maori-specific links to the more generally well-established risk and need factors such as antisocial attitudes, antisocial associates, and other members of the big eight risk factors (Maynard 1999). For example, Maxwell (1999) and colleagues are finding lower rates of re-offending among persons reporting cultural pride and cultural knowledge. Similarly, New Zealand researchers and policy scientists are searching for Maori-specific styles of learning, motivation, or interaction that might be attended to in treatment according the principle of specific responsivity (Maynard 1999). As Box 9.3 indicates, the Correction Service of Canada is exploring specific responsivity issues with Aboriginal offenders (male and female). Case studies reveal some promise for approaches reflecting Aboriginal spirituality (Waldrom 1994), particularly within the contexts of risk, need, general responsivity, and professional discretion. More broadly, Aboriginal perspectives on justice are having major impact on the implementation and development of restorative justice programs in Australia, Canada, and New Zealand.

Unlike the analysis of youthful and female crime, within Aboriginal studies we are unable to present relevant meta-analyses of the risk/need and treatment literatures because too few primary studies have been compiled of Aboriginal people and offenders. This identifies an extraordinary research need. At the present time, standardized risk/need scales appear to function equally well in Aboriginal and non-Aboriginal samples of both male (Bonta, LaPrairie, and Wallace-Capretta 1997) and female offenders (Rettinger 1999). Table 9.13 reveals that a systematic survey of the big eight risk factors functioned well overall in an Aboriginal female sample, and did so for follow-ups of probation and incarcerate samples, for the younger and older and for the less and more socially disadvantaged.

In regard to the treatment of Aboriginal offenders, the number of controlled outcome studies is once again so small that a meta-analytic summary is not possible. On the other hand, it is possible to examine that subset of our 374 tests of treatment that involved treatment of ethnic/racial minorities (106 tests in total conducted with Aboriginal, Black, and Hispanic offenders). All of the analyses that were conducted with young offenders and

TABLE 9.13 **Recidivism Rates of Provincially Sentenced Adult Aboriginal Women by Risk/Need Level as Assessed by a Composite of the Major Risk Factors and by Indicators of Socioeconomic Disadvantage and Abuse**

Sample	Intake Risk Level		
	Low	Medium	High
Total Aboriginal	.14 (7)	.38 (21)	.79 (24)
Setting			
Community	.14 (7)	.40 (15)	.60 (5)
Institutional	— (0)	.33 (6)	.84 (19)
Less than Grade 10			
No	.33 (3)	.33 (9)	1.00 (7)
Yes	.00 (4)	.42 (12)	.71 (17)
Poverty: Relies on social assistance			
No	.00 (3)	.33 (3)	1.00 (5)
Yes	.25 (4)	.39 (18)	.79 (19)
Frequently unemployed			
No	.14 (7)	.29 (14)	.50 (8)
Yes	— (0)	.57 (7)	.94 (16)
Severe history of abuse as a child and an adult			
No	.00 (5)	.38 (16)	.64 (11)
Yes	.50 (2)	.40 (5)	.92 (13)

NOTE: Only the main effect of risk/need was statistically significant in the tests of risk/need and each of setting, education, unemployment, poverty, and abuse history, and in tests of their interactions with risk/need.

SOURCE: Adapted from Rettinger 1998, 1999.

female offenders were repeated with minority samples. Perhaps not surprisingly, reduced re-offending was found in the treatment of minority samples when there was adherence to the principles of human service, risk, need, and general responsivity, and when the targeting of criminogenic needs was an emphasis, the targeting of non-criminogenic needs was minimized. High staff functioning on elements of core correctional practice but that of authority was associated with reduced re-offending, as were several indicators of integrity including staff selection, training, and clinical supervision.

This whole research area is a terrific one for students who wish to contribute to the greater good through understanding how Aboriginal people—sometimes marginalized and disrespected and other times not—get into crime or not, and, if they do, how they get out of crime or continue with crime.

MENTALLY DISORDERED OFFENDERS

Extraordinarily high proportions of officially identified offenders are, have been, or could be subject to a diagnosis of being mentally disordered according to applications of the criteria of the *Diagnostic and Statistical Manual of the American Psychiatric Association* (DSM-IV) (American Psychiatric Association 1994). Based on six large-scale surveys of mental disorder in North American pre-trial and prison samples, the rates of "any disorder" varied from a low of 75 percent to a high of 100 percent (Andrews and Bonta 1998: Table 11.1). At the same time, the prevalence of serious disorders such as schizophrenia and manic depressive disorder was very low in that the rates varied from lows of less than 2 percent to a high of 17 percent. Perhaps not surprisingly, in view of the general personality and social learning of criminal behaviour, the specific disorders of highest prevalence were "antisocial personality disorder" and "substance abuse." In the six studies, the prevalence rates of antisocial personality disorder or substance abuse or both varied within the range of 9 percent to 65 percent. Not surprisingly, rates of mental disorder are higher in pre-trial and pre-sentence samples where mental illness is suspected and fitness to stand trial is an issue. Similarly, **not guilty by reason of insanity (NGRI)** samples include large proportions of mentally disordered offenders.

Mental Disorder as a Risk Factor for Criminal Behaviour

Is being mentally disordered a risk factor for criminal behaviour? Overall, yes, but it is a minor one. Moreover, that psychiatric patients have higher arrest rates than non-patients can be attributed to those patients with symptoms involving antisocial cognition such as the belief that the world is a hostile place that one must sometimes attack in order to prevent attack by others. Indeed, that type of cognition also predicts the antisocial behaviour of non-patients.

Predictability of Criminal Behaviour of Persons with a Mental Disorder

Psychologists and other professionals can predict the criminal behaviour of persons with a mental disorder, as long as their assessment includes the major risk/need factors for criminal behaviour (as identified in Table 9.1 and in the risk/need findings reported in this chapter for young offenders, female offenders, and Aboriginal offenders (Bonta, Law, and Hanson 1998). Just as in the case of general offenders, the predictive value of measures of anxiety, depression, schizophrenia, low class origins, and low intelligence were weak risk factors. Table 9.14 reveals how a systematic risk/needs assessments linked with the general and violent recidivism of several samples of mentally disordered offenders. In brief, the field of forensic criminology made progress only when it turned away from traditional clinical and sociological models, and embraced the variables highlighted by a general personality and social psychology of crime.

However, it is important to note that the effectiveness of clinical prediction in relation to risk/need assessments is so poor that the average correlation between clinical judgement and the recidivism of mentally disordered offenders was .03 (Bonta, Law, and Hanson 1998), compared with an average of .39 for systematic assessments of risk/need factors. The former value of .03 compares with the average predictive validity of assessments of socioeconomic circumstances (.00 in samples of mentally disordered offenders and .05 in general offender samples).

The Special Case of Personality and Substance Abuse Disorders

Substance abuse is one of the well-known risk/need factors, as is an antisocial personality pattern (recall Tables 9.1 and 9.5). Thus formal clinical diagnoses reflecting these factors

TABLE 9.14 **General and Violent Recidivism Rates of Provincially Sentenced Mentally Disordered Offenders and of Sex Offenders by the Standardized Level of Risk/Need in Ontario (n)**

| | Intake Risk Level | | | | |
Sample	Very Low	Low	Medium	High	Very High
Mentally disordered offenders					
One: General R	.17 (18)	.33 (27)	.49 (55)	.70 (20)	1.00 (2)
One: Violent R	.00	.07	.09	.30	.50
Two: General R	.00 (7)	.13 (24)	.39 (51)	.56 (64)	.79 (42)
Two: Violent R	.00	.13	.20	.25	.33
Three: General R	.00 (17)	.16 (43)	.40 (52)	.75 (53)	1.00 (5)
Three: Violent R	.00	.00	.08	.23	1.00
Sex Offenders					
Two: General R	.00 (5)	.29 (7)	.33 (12)	.80 (15)	.67 (12)
Two: Violent R	.00	.14	.08	.27	.33

NOTE: Sample One (male and female): The original LSI sample (Andrews 1982), re-analyzed for the LSI-OR report (Andrews 1997). Sample Two (male): Girard 1999. Sample Three (female): Rettinger 1998, 1999.

do function as risk factors. Perhaps the best established of the personality disorders is antisocial personality disorder, and perhaps the best validated measure of antisocial personality is Hare's (1990) Psychopathy Checklist—Revised (PCL-R). The PCL-R is scored from interviews and reviews of official records. The item content reflects the description of a psychopath provided by Cleckley (1982), which includes being egocentric, being callous, being guilt-free, feeling a need for stimulation, impulsivity, and an early and persistent history of antisocial behaviour. The construct is compelling because images of the "morally insane," the "weak superego," and the "charming evil presence" among us are often evoked in the arts, in science, and in clinical practice.

Whether a special type of human being exists—the "psychopath"—is still debated. What is not debated, however, is the obvious predictive validity of the PCL-R. The average correlation between PCL scores and general offending is in the area of .17 to .29, and its average correlation with violent offending is between .13 and .30 (Gendreau and Goggin 1999). It would be remarkable if the PCL did not predict recidivism because its content reflects two of the big eight risk factors, that is, a history of antisocial behaviour and antisocial personality pattern, and it is strongly correlated with more general assessments of risk and need. Finally, we would be surprised if predictive accuracy could not be improved by assessing more than history and personality. Harris, Rice, and Quinsey (1993) in fact report that consideration of problems in school, alcohol abuse, and family/marital circumstances enhance prediction of the violent recidivism of mentally disordered persons.

Treatment of Mentally Disordered Offenders

Clinical treatment of the mental illness and personal distress of mentally disordered offenders generally follows the same treatments for people who are mentally troubled but are not criminal offenders. Offenders serving sentences of more two years or more have access to the Regional Psychiatric Facilities found in the regions of the Correctional Service of Canada. The great challenge is delivering correctional treatment services that will reduce re-offending. Experts in the field are pointing to the general literature on effective correctional treatment (Tables 9.2 and 9.3; see also Harris and Rice 1997). Psychopaths are a group that some people feel are incapable of responding to treatment, and yet few studies have been conducted that target the many criminogenic needs of the highest risk cases and employ powerful social learning and cognitive behavioural strategies of influence (Andrews and Bonta 1998: Chapter 11). Certainly, offering peer-oriented, self-directed encounter groups in marathon sessions involving nudity and LSD did not work with psychopaths (Harris, Rice, and Cormier 1994). The "treatability" of very high risk egocentric offenders is a major issue for theoretical and practical research.

SEX OFFENDERS

Sex offenders are an extraordinary subpopulation because of the level of fear and disgust that they elicit in the public and because of the often traumatic nature of their impact on victims. Their victims tend to be women and children. Sex offenders are also an ordinary population in that any and all of the prior noted subpopulations are represented within the sex offender set. That is, some sex offenders are young and some are old, most are male but some are female, some are Aboriginal persons and some are non-Aboriginal, some are mentally disordered and some are not, and some score high on measures of psychopathic personality and many do not. What sex offenders share in common is that they have been found to have engaged in sexual activities that are judged illegal. The range of these activities, however, is so diverse that the search for some commonality seems almost doomed from the start. Consider even the following partial list: uninvited exposure of genitalia, uninvited watching of others in more or less intimate circumstances, brushing against another person in a way defined as sexual, touching the private parts of others, engaging in any one of a host of less or more intrusive acts defined as sexual with a minor or without the consent of the other. The nature of the crime may be further differentiated according to the offender's relationship to the victim (for example, incest versus sexual molestation of an unrelated child).

In view of such diversity, is it reasonable to apply the general personality and social learning approach to sex offenders? Let's see.

The Major Risk/Need Factors

Hanson and Bussière (1998) conducted a major meta-analytic review of risk factors within sex offender samples. Among the major predictors were assessments of antisocial personality pattern, a history of criminal behaviour, antisocial cognition, and problematic family circumstances. These findings fit very nicely with the general psychological of criminal conduct. Additionally, low class origins and personal distress were very weak predictors of recidivism as the general PCC leads one to expect. At the same time, there were some deviations from expectations. For example, substance abuse and low levels of educational/ vocational achievement were weak predictors, while below-average intelligence yielded a higher mean correlation with recidivism than one might expect. Most notably, there were no tests of the effects of antisocial associates because, apparently, the psychopathological model that drove the research on sex offenders did not include it as a potential risk factor. In fact, the research reveals that the re-offending behaviour of sex offenders increased directly with their risk/need level as assessed with the composite LSI measures of the big eight risk factors. Let us consider, however, some of the major risk factors in more detail.

General criminal history was a predictor of the re-offending behaviour of sex offenders. However, an even stronger predictor was a history of sex offences in particular. In brief, the general PCC suggests that assessments of behavioural history (and attitudes and associates) are best made specific to the particular behaviour being predicted. Scott (1995) demonstrated that a general measure of personal tolerance for law violation was correlated with sex offending but a sexually specific attitude measure was still more strongly correlated with sex offending. She reported a similar pattern of findings with assessments of antisocial associates wherein there was correlation between having criminal friends and sex offending but a much stronger one between knowing other sex offenders and sex offending. Hanson and Scott (1996) went even further and found that child molesters knew other child molesters and rapists knew other rapists. Sexually specific assessment of cognition and associates is a major area for future research. Assessments of attitudes and cognition represent an important supplement to assessment of the imagining of sex offenders. Many of us may have considerable experience with masturbation and could likely speak to the role of fantasy in sexual arousal and sexual performance, and would not have difficulty believing that sex offenders too have fantasies that support some of their favourite pursuits.

Deviant sexual arousal in males, as assessed through phallometric techniques, was actually the single strongest risk factor in the Hanson-Bussière meta-analysis ($r = .32$). These devices measure penile tumescence while the subject is exposed to a variety of stimuli that include some sexually specific material and some neutral scenes. The stimuli may be presented by audio, by tapes, or visually with slides or videotapes or both. Assessments for pedophilia would incorporate images of nude children and nude adults, while assessments for rape propensity would include images of sex incorporating violence and power differentials as well as images of sexual activity without violence and with consent and equality. The index of "deviant" arousal would reflect level of arousal to inappropriate stimuli relative to appropriate or neutral stimuli or both.

Treatment of Sex Offenders

While the issue of the effectiveness of treatment programs for sex offenders is more controversial than the effectiveness of correctional treatment generally, a meta-analysis of recent treatment programs found that cognitive behavioural strategies were more effective than simple behavioural approaches (Hall 1995). Hormonal treatments also yielded larger effect sizes. The former is consistent with the general responsivity principle of effective treatment and the latter is consistent with the dominant predictive validity of assessments of deviant sexual arousal.

"Chemical castration" through drugs such as Androcur (CPA) and Provera (MPA) reduce testosterone levels, sexual fantasies, and masturbation frequency (Bradford and Pawlak 1993). Presumably these types of effects mediate reduced recidivism. Many observers remain to be convinced.

The range of therapeutic techniques in the behavioural and cognitive behavioural set includes aversive conditioning (to reduce deviant arousal) and masturbation combined with non-deviant images (to enhance non-deviant arousal). Specific social skill deficits may be targeted through structured learning of personal, interpersonal, and social skills. The most promising element of treatment today is relapse prevention. Offenders learn those aspects of their offence history that are highly patterned along with the particular situations are risky for them. They also learn ways of avoiding risky situations and practice new low-risk ways of thinking and acting in those situations. It is not at all unusual that involved others are part of the relapse prevention plan, including probation/parole officers, spouses, and peers. The relapse prevention approach was introduced in the treatment of substance abuse but is spreading into corrections generally.

Perhaps the major "intervention" issues in regard to sex offenders do not have to with human service or medical approaches to controlling recidivism. Rather, public fear and abhorrence seem to fuel approaches involving more and more punishment and more and more control. These approaches include low parole rates, sex offender registration lists organized by area of residence, and notification of the public of the presence of a sex offender in their midst. Advances in assessment and treatment will be made in this context of fear, and perhaps even in spite of it.

CONCLUSION

Special populations are readily identified within corrections. Some are identified by virtue of the type of offence that they present. In this chapter, sex offenders were the example, although many other subtypes include violent offenders, shoplifters, drug dealers, impaired drivers, etc. Such subtypes present special concerns but in this chapter we suggest that there is value in applying a general model of the personality and social psychology of crime and corrections as well as in a focus on uniqueness.

Mentally disordered offenders are identified not by the nature of their offence but by a diagnosis or label applied by mental health professionals or through assessment tools developed by mental health researchers and practitioners. Such offenders inspire both some level of fear and some level of compassion. In regard to the latter, for years being emotionally disordered was viewed incorrectly a major risk factor. Equally disturbing is the frequently reported observation that the mentally disturbed are sometimes managed through the justice system as a means of gaining access to mental health services. These positions aside, the major risk/need factors within samples of mentally disordered offenders are the generally well-known risk factors.

Young offenders, female offenders, and Aboriginal offenders are identified by their biological, psychological, and social location indicators of age, gender, and ethnicity and race. Perhaps not surprisingly, much of the research and theory on these types of offenders has been greatly influenced by the social science and human rights themes of ageism, sexism, and racism. Certainly, any applied efforts must represent ethical, legal, decent, just, humane, and cost-efficient efforts. In this chapter, we have emphasized just applications of the general personality and social learning approach. Here we saw that the major risk/need factors and the principles of effective treatment apply widely across categories of age, gender, and race and ethnicity. The major issues in research, service, and theory now reside in the identification of subgroup specific risk and need, careful distinctions between subgroup specific criminogenic and non-criminogenic needs, and specific responsivity considerations tied to subgroup membership.

KEY TERMS AND CONCEPTS

core correctional practice (CCP)

criminogenic needs

deterrence

developmental criminology

incapacitation

multimodal service

not guilty by reason of insanity (NGRI)

personal, interpersonal, and community-reinforcement theory (PIC-R)

psychology of criminal conduct (PCC)

rehabilitation

responsivity

restorative justice

risk factor

strength factor

Young Offenders Act (YOA)

STUDY AND DISCUSSION QUESTIONS

1. How do specific populations differ from "other" populations? Are these distinctions warranted? Explain.

2. How is the perspective used in this chapter interdisciplinary in nature? What are the advantages and disadvantages of such a perspective for corrections?

3. Identify the major risk/need factors for young people. How are they similar to the risk factors for the antisocial behaviour of adults?

4. Discuss how developmental criminology has affected corrections practices for special populations.

5. Describe the core elements of correctional practice. What are their strengths and weaknesses in regard to the various special populations discussed?

6. How have the theoretical challenges of female criminality influenced correctional responses over the years?

7. What advantages are there for correctional practices in attempting to understand Aboriginal criminal behaviour across other racial and ethnic groups?

8. How can focusing on general personality and social psychological factors enhance the treatment of mentally disordered offenders?

WEBLINKS

Forum on Corrections Research is a publication of the Correctional Service of Canada and has had several "special issues" on specific offender populations. These sites with the corresponding offender population are listed below:

Aboriginal Corrections (Canadian focus): **www.sgc.gc.ca/Epub/EAbocorrlist.htm**

Solicitor General of Canada, Aboriginal offenders: **www.csc-scc.gc.ca/text/pblct/forum/v12n1/indexe.shtml**

Solicitor General of Canada, Sexual offenders: **www.csc-scc.gc.ca/text/pblct/forum/e082/e082ind.shtml** and **www.csc-scc.gc.ca/text/pblct/forum/e034/e034ind.shtml**

Solicitor General of Canada, Women offenders: **www.csc-scc.gc.ca/text/pblct/forum/v11n3/indexe.shtml**

Solicitor General of Canada, Young offenders:
www.csc-scc.gc.ca/text/pblct/forum/v11n2/indexe.shtml

U.S. Federal Bureau of Prisons: **www.bop.gov**

U.S. National Institute of Justice: **www.ojp.usdoj.gov.nij**

U.S. Office of Juvenile Justice and Delinquency: **www.ojjdp.ncjrs.org/index.html**

NOTES

1. See also Elliott, Huizinga, and Ageton 1985, Henggeler et al. 1998, Jessor and Jessor 1977, Burgess and Akers 1966, Akers 1973, and Agnew (1992, in terms of social learning theory rather than strain theory).
2. Critics already doubt that adequate funding will accompany this provision.
3. First, be certain that you survey the major risk factors and do not concentrate on the minor ones. Similarly, limiting assessment to ideologically and/or professionally acceptable variables is not a good idea unless solid theory and research support those variables. Second, use multiple sources of information in scoring risk/need and in scoring re-offending. Third, keep the scoring procedures very simple and provide training and supervision to users so that computational and other errors do not interfere with accuracy. Fourth, if you are interested in reducing risk as well as assessing it, it is important to assess dynamic items because—according the criminogenic need principle—it is by focusing appropriately on dynamic risk factors that the chances of re-offending will be reduced. Fifth, if you wish to maximize predictive accuracy, include reassessments on dynamic risk factors because doing so promises significant gains in accuracy. The point is simple: the attitudes, interpersonal relationships, and circumstances of people change, and assessment of that change enhances predictive accuracy. Sixth, there is a set of technical issues that are not reviewed here but elsewhere (see Andrews and Bonta 1998).
4. Van Voorhis (1994), working with adult inmate samples, convincingly showed that five diverse classification systems converged on four types of offenders: committed criminal (subcultural, normal antisocial, cultural conformist), character disorder (unsocialized aggressive, manipulative), neurotic anxious, and situational.
5. According to the women interviewed, the experience of physical abuse (72 percent) was more frequent than emotional abuse (69 percent) or sexual abuse (49 percent).

REFERENCES

Agnew, R. 1992. Foundation for a General Strain Theory of Crime and Delinquency. *Criminology* 30: 47–87.

Akers, R.L. 1973. *Deviant Behavior: A Social Learning Approach*. Belmont, CA: Wadsworth.

American Psychiatric Association. 1994. *Diagnostic and Statistical Manual of Mental Disorders* (DSM-IV). Washington, DC: American Psychiatric Association.

Andrews, D.A. 1980. Some Experimental Investigations of the Principles of Differential Association through Deliberate Manipulations of the Structure of Service Systems. *American Sociological Review* 45: 448–462.

————. 1982. *A Personal, Interpersonal and Community-Reinforcement Perspective on Deviant Behaviour (PIC-R)*. Toronto: Ministry of Correctional Services.

————. 1997. *Reports and Analyses on the LSI-OR Project*. A report prepared for the Ministry of Correctional Services, Ontario.

Andrews, D.A., and J. Bonta. 1994. *The Psychology of Criminal Conduct*. Cincinnati: Anderson.

————. 1995. *The Level of Service Inventory—Revised*. Toronto: Multi-Health Services.

————. 1998. *The Psychology of Criminal Conduct* (2nd ed.) Cincinnati: Anderson.

Andrews, D.A., and C. Carvell. 1998. *Core Correctional Treatment: Core Correctional Supervision and Counseling: Theory, Research, Assessment, and Practice*. Ottawa: Carleton University.

Andrews, D.A., C., Dowden, and P. Gendreau. 1999. *Clinically Relevant and Psychologically Informed Approaches to Reduced Re-offending: A Meta-Analytic Study of Human Service, Risk, Need, Responsivity, and Other Concerns in Justice Contexts*. Manuscript submitted for publication.

Bonta, J., C. LaPrairie, and S. Wallace-Capretta. 1997. Risk Prediction and Re-offending: Aboriginal and non-Aboriginal Offenders. *Canadian Journal of Criminology* 39: 127–144.

Bonta, J., M. Law, and R.K. Hanson. 1998. The Prediction of Criminal and Violent Recidivism among Mentally Disordered Offenders: A Meta-Analysis. *Psychological Bulletin* 123: 123–142.

Bradford, J.M.W., and M.A. Pawlak. 1993. Double-Blind Placebo Crossover Study of Cyprotone Acetate in the Treatment of the Paraphilias. *Archives of Sexual Behavior* 22: 383–402.

Burgess, R.L., and R.L. Akers. 1966. A Differential Association-Reinforcement Theory of Criminal Behavior. *Social Problems* 14: 128–147.

Chesney-Lind, M., and B. Bloom. 1997. Feminist Criminology: Thinking about Women and Crime. In B. MacLean and D. Milovanovic (Eds.), *Thinking Critically About Crime*. Vancouver: Collective Press.

Cleckley, H. 1982. *The Mask of Sanity* (4th ed.). St Louis: Mosby.

Correctional Service of Canada. 1999a. *Aboriginal Offenders*. www.csc-scc.gc.ca/text/pubed/feuilles/off-fem_e.shtml (April 2000).

————. 1999b. *Female Offenders*. www.csc-scc.gc.ca/text/pubed/feuilles/off-fem_e.shtml (April 2000).

Covington, S., and B. Bloom. 1999. *Gender-Responsive Programming and Evaluation for Females in the Criminal Justice System: A Shift from What Works to What Is the Work?* A paper presented at the meetings of the American Society of Criminology, Toronto, Canada.

Dowden, C., and D.A. Andrews. 1999. What Works for Female Offenders: A Meta-Analytic Review. *Crime and Delinquency* 45: 438–452.

Elliott, D.S., D. Huizinga, and S.S. Ageton. 1985. *Explaining Delinquency and Drug Use*. Beverly Hills: Sage.

Farrington, D.P. 1999 *Presidential Plenary: Developmental Criminology*. A session presented at the meetings of the American Society of Criminology, Toronto, November.

Fetherston, D.W. 2000. The Law and Young Offenders. In J.A. Winterdyk (Ed.), *Issues and Perspectives on Young Offenders in Canada* (2nd ed.). Toronto: Harcourt Brace.

Gendreau, P., and C. Goggin. 1999 *Comparing the LSI and PCL: A Meta-Analysis*. A paper presented at the meetings of the Canadian Psychological Association, Halifax, October.

Gendreau, P., and **R.R. Ross**. 1979. Effectiveness of Correctional Treatment: Bibliography for Cynics. *Crime and Delinquency* 25: 463–489.

Girard, L. 1999. *Validation of the LSI-OR.* Unpublished doctoral dissertation. University of Ottawa, Ontario.

Glueck, S., and **E.T. Glueck**. 1950. *Unraveling Juvenile Delinquency.* Cambridge, MA: Harvard University Press.

Goldstein, A.P., and **B. Glick** 1987. *Aggression Replacement Training: A Comprehensive Intervention for Aggressive Youth.* Champaign, IL: Research Press.

Hall, G.C. 1995. Sexual Offender Recidivism Revisited: A Meta-Analysis of Recent Treatment Studies. *Journal of Consulting and Clinical Psychology* 63: 802–809.

Hanson, R.K., and **M.T. Bussière**. 1998. Predicting Relapse: A Meta-Analysis of Sexual Offender Recidivism. *Journal of Consulting and Clinical Psychology* 66: 348–362.

Hanson, R.K., and **H. Scott**. 1996. Social Networks of Sexual Offenders. *Psychology, Crime and Law* 2: 249–258.

Hare, R.D. 1990. *The Hare Psychopathy Checklist—Revised.* Toronto: Multi-Health Systems.

Harris, G.T., and **M.E. Rice**. 1997. Mentally Disordered Offenders: What Research Says about Effective Service. In C.D. Webster and M.A. Jackson (Eds.), *Impulsivity Theory: Assessment and Treatment.* New York: The Guilford Press.

Harris, G.T., **M.E. Rice**, and **C.A. Cormier**. 1994. Psychopaths: Is a Therapeutic Community Therapeutic? *Therapeutic Communities* 15: 283–299.

Harris, G.T., **M.E. Rice**, and **V.L. Quinsey**. 1993. Violent Recidivism of Mentally Disordered Offenders: The Development of a Statistical Prediction Instrument. *Criminal Justice and Behavior* 20: 315–335.

Henggeler, S.W., **S.K. Schoenwald**, **C.M. Borduin**, **M.D. Rowland**, and **P.B. Cunningham**. 1998. *Multisystemic Treatment of Antisocial Behavior in Children and Adolescents.* New York: The Guilford Press.

Hewitt, L.E., and **R.L. Jenkins**. 1946. *Fundamental Patterns of Maladjustment: The Dynamics of Their Origin.* Springfield: John Wiley.

Hoge, R.D., and **D.A. Andrews**. 1996. *Assessing the Youthful Offender: Issues and Techniques.* New York: Plenum.

Hollin, C.R. 1995. The Meaning and Implications of "Programme Integrity." In J. McGuire (Ed.), *What Works: Reducing Reoffending.* Chichester, UK: John Wiley and Sons.

Hung, K., and **S. Lipinski**. 1995. Questions and Answers on Youth and Justice. *Forum on Corrections Research* 7(1): 6–9.

Jessor, R., and **S.L. Jessor**. 1977. *Problem Behavior and Psychosocial Development: A Longitudinal Study of Youth.* New York: Academic Press.

Kirven, M.A. 1995. Canada's Youth Justice System—Under Review. *Forum on Corrections Research* 7(1): 41–42.

LaPrairie, C. 1992. *Dimensions of Aboriginal Over-representation in Correctional Institutions and Implications for Crime Prevention.* Ottawa: Ministry of Solicitor General.

Leschied, A., D. A. Andrews, and **R.D. Hoge**. 1995. *A Report on the Toronto Case Management System*. A report to Ontario Ministry of Community and Social Services.

Lipsey, M.W., and **J.H. Derzon**. 1998. Predictors of Violent or Serious Delinquency in Adolescence and Early Adulthood. In R. Loeber and D.P. Farrington (Eds.), *Serious and Violent Juvenile Offenders*. Thousand Oaks, CA: Sage.

Mattson, B.A., K.R. Williams, and **N. Guerra**. 1998. *Reliability and Validity of the CYO-LSI*. A Report to Colorado Judicial Department's Office of Probation Services.

Maynard, N.K. 1999. *An Analysis of the Cultural and Gender Appropriateness of the Risk/Needs Assessment Tool Used by Community Probation Service*. A discussion document within New Zealand Department of Corrections.

Maxwell, G. 1999. Personal correspondence with authors.

Palmer, T. 1975. Martinson Revisited. *Journal of Research in Crime and Delinquency* 12: 133–152.

Quay, H.C. 1984. *Managing Adult Inmates: Classification for Housing and Program Assignments*. College Park, MD: American Correctional Association.

Rettinger, L.J. 1998. *Risk/Need Assessment with Provincially Sentenced Adult Women*. Unpublished doctoral dissertation, Department of Psychology, Carleton University, Ottawa.

———. 1999. *A Recidivism Follow-up Study Investigating Risk and Need within a Sample of Provincially Sentenced Women*. Unpublished doctoral dissertation. Carlton University, Ottawa.

Rosenthal, R. 1991 *Meta-Analytic Procedures for Social Research* (rev. ed.). Newbury Park, CA: Sage.

Scott, H.A. 1995. *The Determinants of Rape: An Examination of Risk Factors in Self-Reported and Convicted Rapists*. Unpublished doctoral dissertation, Department of Psychology, Carleton University, Ottawa.

Shaw, M. 1994. *Ontario Women in Conflict with the Law: A Survey of Women in Institutions and under Community Supervision in Ontario*. North Bay: Ontario Ministry of the Solicitor General and Correctional Services.

Shields, I.W., and **D.J. Simourd**. 1991. Predicting Predatory Behavior in a Population of Incarcerated Young Offenders. *Criminal Justice and Behavior* 18: 180–194.

Simourd, D.J., and **D.A. Andrews**. 1994. Correlates of Delinquency: A Look at Gender Differences. *Forum on Corrections Research* 6(1): 26–31.

Simourd, D.J., R.D. Hoge, D.A. Andrews, and **A.W. Leschied**. 1994. An Empirically Based Typology of Male Young Offenders. *Canadian Journal of Criminology* 4: 447–461.

Stableforth, N.L. 1999. Effective Corrections for Women Offenders. *Forum on Corrections Research* 11(3): 3–5.

Stouthamer-Loeber, M., R. Loeber, D.P. Farrington, Q. Zhang, W. van Kammen, and **E. Maguin**. 1993. The Double Edge of Protective and Risk Factors for Delinquency: Interrelations and Developmental Patterns. *Development and Psychopathology* 5: 683–701.

Trevethan, S. 1993. *Police-Reported Aboriginal Crime in Calgary, Regina, and Saskatoon*. Ottawa: Canadian Centre for Justice Statistics.

———. 1999. Women in Federal and Provincial-Territorial Correctional Facilities. *Forum on Corrections Research* 11(3): 9–12.

Van Voorhis, P. 1994. *Psychological Classification of the Adult Male Prison Inmate*. Albany: State University of New York.

Waldram, J.B. 1994. Aboriginal Spirituality in Corrections: A Canadian Case Study in Religion and Therapy. *American Indian Quarterly* 18: 197–213.

Watkins, R.E. 1999a. *A Social Psychological Examination of the Relationship between Athletic Participation and Delinquent Behaviour*. Unpublished doctoral dissertation, Carleton University, Ottawa.

———. 1999b. Personal communication with author.

Winterdyk, J. 2000a. *Canadian Criminology*. Don Mills: Pearson.

———. (Ed.). 2000b. *Issues and Perspectives on Young Offenders in Canada* (2nd ed.). Toronto: Harcourt Brace.

Wood, D. S., and **C.T. Griffiths**. 2000. Patterns of Aboriginal Crime. In R.A. Silverman, J.J. Teevan, and V.F. Sacco (Eds.), *Crime in Canadian Society* (6th ed.). Toronto: Harcourt Brace.

Chapter

10

WOMEN IN PRISON

Helen Boritch
Department of Sociology
University of Alberta
Edmonton, Alberta

LEARNING OBJECTIVES

After reading this chapter, you should be able to:

- Understand the role that different historical perspectives have played in the handling of women in prisons;
- Describe and understand the significance of the various commissions and reports that were instrumental in effecting changes for women in prison;
- Describe the social and demographic characteristics of female prisons;
- Critically assess some of the major issues confronting the incarceration of women prisoners;
- Describe the similarities and differences between federal and provincial facilities for women prisoners;
- Understand the need for correctional reform to address the problems facing women prisoners.

I am never quite as incompetent as I think I am or as competent as I would like to be.

—Ann Wilson Schaff

The traditional treatment of women prisoners in Canada has been described as a curious and contradictory "mixture of neglect, outright barbarism, and well-meaning paternalism" (Cooper 1993, 33). Historically, women prisoners have been disadvantaged in relation to men because of their relatively small numbers, and because traditional gender stereotypes have defined policies and practices in women's prisons. As a result, compared with men, women prisoners are more likely to be geographically separated from family and friends; women are more likely to be incarcerated in higher security environments than they require; women have access to fewer educational and vocational programs, and lack the same physical and mental health services; and women may serve a greater portion of their sentences because there are fewer services and facilities for female offenders reentering the community than their male counterparts (Law Society of British Columbia 1992; Moffat 1991).

Although the many inequities existing in women's prisons have been documented in numerous government reports over the last century and a half, it has only been since the late 1970s that serious attention has been devoted to reforming correctional policies and programs for female offenders. Many factors have converged to help reverse the long history of bureaucratic neglect of women prisoners, including the increasing strength of the feminist movement, the increase in women's involvement in correctional administration and criminology, the enactment of the Canadian Charter of Rights and Freedoms, and increased awareness of the special problems of Aboriginal women offenders (Adelberg and Currie 1993; Shaw 1993).

THE HISTORY OF WOMEN'S PRISONS IN CANADA

Kingston Penitentiary for Women

The history of women imprisonment is one in which "small numbers of women have been housed in often unsuitable accommodations, under regimes stressing the domestic role of women in society and providing little access to program or training" (Shaw 1994, 13). To a large extent, the current realities of women's prisons are the historical legacy of practices and policies that emerged with the establishment of penitentiaries in the early part of the 19th century and separate women's prisons in the latter part of the 19th century (see Chapter 6). Prior to these developments, there was little difference in the treatment of male and female offenders. This policy of uniformity meant that women were incarcerated in the same jails as men and subject to the same severe physical punishments, including whipping, branding, being put in irons, and hanging (Carrigan 1991; Phillips 1994).

As discussed in Chapter 6, during the early decades of the 19th century, correctional philosophy and practice shifted when the use of corporal punishment was reduced in favour of imprisonment as the primary method of punishing criminals (see Chapter 1). In 1835, Kingston Penitentiary became the first institution to house women sentenced to long terms. Although the original plans for the penitentiary called for a separate prison for women on the same general site, no special accommodations for women were actually built (Carrigan 1991).

Ostensibly, the penitentiary was the central component of a more enlightened penal philosophy but, in practice, physical deprivations, torture, and brutality were pervasive features of prison life in the 19th century (Beattie 1977). However, in a system designed, operated by, and housing primarily men, the plight of women prisoners was especially bleak. In the absence of any special accommodations for women prisoners, the first female inmates were kept in a small attic space above the men's dining hall (Cooper 1993, 35). From the beginning, prison officials viewed women as nuisance to be warehoused, managed, and moved around in whatever ways were least disruptive to the management of the larger male population. In 1836, a prison inspector noted that the "sentencing of females to the Penitentiary causes some inconvenience" and a female matron was hired to supervise the women (Faith 1993, 129).

By the end of the 1850s, a total of 68 women were confined to the penitentiary. With no permanent facility to house them, and denied access to the workshop or recreational facilities available to male inmates, the women spent their time making and mending prison bedding and clothing for male inmates. Over the next 50 years, women were shifted to at least two more temporary locations within the penitentiary; in each case, the move was precipitated because the existing location was required for male inmates (Cooper 1993).

The conditions under which women prisoners at Kingston were forced to live were considerably worse than those of male inmates, and their suffering was commensurately greater. While the small number of women prisoners was one determinant of their inferior treatment, equally important was the attitude of correctional officials who saw female offenders as "fallen women." In this respect, prison officials reflected prevailing 19th-century gender stereotypes in general, and stereotypes of women offenders in particular. Nineteenth-century ideology held women to a higher moral standard than men, so that women who committed crimes not only violated the law but also breached their prescribed social and moral roles to a much larger extent than men. Women offenders frequently were depicted as mentally subnormal, emotionally disturbed, sexually deviant, and more unruly and difficult to manage than male inmates. Moreover, since they were seen as more morally depraved than male criminals, they were also considered less capable of being redeemed (Feinman 1983; Rafter 1990). The result of such attitudes was that prison officials felt little compunction about subjecting females to the most "abominable conditions including infestations of insects and rodents, filth, inadequate nutrition, disease, total idleness or meaningless labour, harsh punishments for prison infractions, and sexual abuses by male guards" (Faith 1993, 129).

The brutal treatment of inmates, particularly women and children, at Kingston Penitentiary was of such a magnitude that public concern led to the appointment of a royal commission in 1848 to investigate prison conditions (Beattie 1977). The **Brown Commission** documented a range of abuses perpetrated against female inmates including cruel and excessive discipline, starving, and sexual abuse by prison guards, and the warden was subsequently charged with numerous offences (see Chapter 1). Although some of the recommendations of the Brown Commission were implemented, such as the banning of the use of cat-o-nine-tails (leather-knotted whips) on women prisoners, the central recommendation that a suitable separate facility be built for the women was ignored. Indeed, throughout the 19th century, little changed for federal women prisoners at Kingston Penitentiary, and they continued to be housed in makeshift accommodations until well into the 20th century.

Separate Women's Prisons: The Mercer Reformatory

Nonetheless, the idea of separate prisons for women was gaining momentum among reformers, although it was Ontario provincial authorities who were the first to establish separate facilities for female offenders. A large part of the impetus for separate prisons were the deplorable conditions in the province's county and district jails, where most women offenders were sentenced for offences such as vagrancy, prostitution, and drunk and disorderly conduct. These jails typically lacked separate quarters for women, were overcrowded, and also served as asylums, hospitals, and shelters for the homeless where none existed within reasonable distance (Ruemper 1995).

The model for separate women's prisons throughout North America was based primarily on the work of the influential Englishwoman **Elizabeth Fry**, who was the first penal reformer to focus exclusively on the plight of women prisoners (Faith 1993; Morris 1987). Fry believed that complete segregation of the sexes would prevent the sexual abuse of women inmates by guards, and was necessary because the needs of women prisoners were different from those of men. As part of the movement for separate prisons, the image of the female offender was softened and reshaped from that of "a morally depraved monster to that of an errant child"; women offenders were seen as victims of a poor upbringing who lacked proper moral guidance and restraint (Rafter 1990, xxxii). Reformers envisioned separate prisons as places run by women administrators, and where women offenders would be resocialized into appropriate feminine behaviour and their traditional domestic roles in an atmosphere of "maternal care."

In Canada, the first official women's reformatory, the **Mercer Reformatory**, opened in Toronto in 1879 to house women serving sentences of between two months and two years. The reform program at Mercer combined basic education, religious, moral, and domestic training, and emphasized the importance of women knowing their place in society (Ruemper 1995, 372). For the most part, women inmates were treated as stubbornly disobedient children in need of strict supervision and severe restrictions on their autonomy. Instead of the more diversified programs available to male prisoners at this time, at Mercer there were only the traditional female prison tasks of laundering, sewing, and domestic work (Strange 1986). In this way, Mercer Reformatory established a correctional program for women that reinforced and perpetuated stereotypical sex roles for women.

Despite good intentions and the compassionate efforts of Mary Jane O'Reilly, early on it was apparent that the reality of life at Mercer fell short of reformers' objectives—much of the regimen was commonplace, and the programs limited to reflect prevailing attitudes about women's work and role in society. Moreover, the goal of rehabilitation was soon "overshadowed by an emphasis on work and privation" (Strange 1986, 13). Testifying before a commission on Ontario prisons in 1890, the deputy superintendent for Mercer Reformatory conceded that the institution was not reforming female inmates, but was "simply a place of detention" (Ontario 1891, 745).

The Prison for Women at Kingston

Despite the many shortcomings of the Mercer Reformatory, women inmates there fared considerably better than federal female prisoners at Kingston Penitentiary. It was not until 1913 that separate quarters for women were finally built within the existing penitentiary walls. However, by this time concern with female prisoners had shifted, and the prominent and controversial issue became the centralization of federal female inmates in one institution (Moffat 1991). As early as 1914, another royal commission, the **Macdonnell Commission**, recommended that the female unit be disbanded and the inmates be dispersed to provincial institutions. The Commission based its recommendation for decentralization on the small number of inmates, their low risk to public safety, and the special hardships endured by women who were geographically separated from their families and communities (Cooper 1993).

This recommendation was ignored and, following the recommendations of the 1921 **Nickle Commission**, a separate women's federal penitentiary, the **Prison for Women (P4W)**, was built across the road from the penitentiary in 1934. As the only federal prison for women, all federal female inmates served their sentence at Prison for Women under maximum security custody, regardless of their actual security classification.

Since the establishment of the Prison for Women, numerous government reports have attempted to resolve the same set of interrelated dilemmas: how to reduce geographic dislocation, inferior conditions, and limited programming for a small and diverse population distinguished by sentence length, type of offence, home community, race, and language (Task Force on Federally Sentenced Women 1990). In 1938, only four years after P4W opened, the **Archambault Commission**, whose members were appalled at the inferior conditions of the prison, concluded that the prison should be closed and the women returned to their home provinces (Cooper 1993). Some 50 years later, in 1977, the **MacGuigan Report** reiterated this conclusion, stating that the prison was "unfit for bears, much less women" (Task Force on Federally Sentenced Women 1990, 30). In all, since 1934, more than a dozen government reports have identified serious limitations, inadequacies, and inequities in the provision of services to federal female prisoners and all but one, the **Fauteux Report**, have concluded that the prison should be closed (see Box 10.1).

The recommendations in these many reports did lead to some minor improvements at the Prison for Women, but it was not until the 1970s that the problems began to receive serious and sustained attention (Arbour 1996). The renewed interest in female prisoners coincided with a strengthening of the women's movement that emphasized women's right to equal treatment with men in various spheres of life, including incarceration. One important reform in the mid 1970s, exchange of service agreements between federal and provincial governments, was designed to reduce the problem of geographic dislocation by allowing some federal female inmates to serve their sentences in their home provinces.

Legal Struggles for Equality

Beginning in the 1980s, feminist social reformers increasingly utilized litigation to obtain equal rights and treatment for female prisoners (Hannah-Moffat 1994). In this regard, a significant development occurred in 1981 when the Canadian Human Rights Commission declared that "federal female offenders were discriminated against on the basis of sex, and that in virtually all programs and facility areas, the treatment of federal women inmates was inferior to that of men" (Moffat 1991, 189). The development was in response to a complaint of sexual discrimination launched on behalf of women at the Prison for Women by the group called "Women for Justice."

The improvements in programs and services that followed were not enough to stem an alarmingly high incidence of suicide among women inmates at Prison for Women, particularly among Aboriginal women. In the years between 1989 to 1991, eight women inmates at Prison for Women committed or attempted suicide. It is in this context that a federally sentenced Aboriginal woman, **Carol Maureen Daniels**, launched a court case, *R v. Daniels* [1990], arguing that her rights under the Canadian Charter of Rights and Freedoms would be violated if she was incarcerated at the Prison for Women. The judge agreed, stating that her right to life and security protected under the Charter would be violated if she were incarcerated there because of "the high risk of death by suicide in a far away 'medieval, castle-like prison',", something that was "unacceptable in a free and democratic society" (Arbour 1996, 246).

BOX 10.1	Major Government Reports Identifying Problems in the Provision of Services to Federally Sentenced Women Prisoners

1848 Brown Commission: Report of the Royal Commission to Inquire and Then Report upon the Conduct, Economy, Discipline, and Management of the Provincial Penitentiary.

1913 Macdonnell Commission: Report of the Royal Commission on Penitentiaries.

1921 Nickle Commission: Report of the Committee Appointed by the Right Honourable J.C. Doherty, Minister of Justice to Advise Upon the Revision of the Penitentiary Regulations and the Penitentiary Act.

1938 Archambault Commission: Royal Commission to Investigate the Penal System in Canada.

1947 Gibson Report: Report of General R.B. Gibson Regarding the Penitentiary System in Canada.

1956 Fauteux Committee: Report of A Committee Appointed to Inquire into the Principles and Procedures Followed in the Remission Service of the Department of Justice.

1969 Ouimet Committee: Report of the Canadian Committee on Corrections.

1970 Royal Commission on Status of Women

1977 Clarke Report: National Advisory Committee on the Female Offender.

1977 MacGuigan Report: Sub-Committee on the Penitentiary System in Canada.

1978 Needham Report: National Planning Committee on the Female Offender.

1978 Chinnery Report: Joint Committee to Study the Alternatives for the Housing of the Federal Female.

1978 Berezins and Dunn: Progress Report on the Federal Female Offender Program.

1979 Canadian Advisory Council on the Status of Women

1981 Canadian Human Rights Commission

1988 Canadian Bar Association

1988 Daubney Committee: Standing Committee on Justice and Solicitor General on Its Review of Sentencing, Conditional Release, and Related Aspects of Corrections.

1990 Task Force on Federally Sentenced Women: Creating Choices: The Report of the Task Force on Federally Sentenced Women.

1996 Arbour Report: Commission of Inquiry into Certain Events at the Prison for Women in Kingston.

SOURCE: Adapted from Arbour 1996.

Substantive Equality versus Formal Equality: Creating Choices

By the late 1980s, it was becoming evident to many observers that the problems created by accommodating women in correctional systems oriented towards the male offender could not be rectified by simply extending the same programs and services available in men's prisons. Increasingly, reformers argued against striving for formal equality and advocated a fundamental shift in correctional philosophy towards female prisoners consistent with a model of substantive equality. This model stresses the idea that female prisoners share more in common with women not incarcerated than they do with male prisoners, and that meaningful reform must recognize the very different needs and life experiences of women prisoners (Arbour 1996; Shaw 1993).

This shift in philosophy underlies the most important catalyst for change in current correctional services for federal female inmates: the 1990 report *Creating Choices*, produced by the Task Force on Federally Sentenced Women. For the most part, the Task Force reiterated the findings of previous government reports on the Prison for Women: that it was over-secure, that it was erroneously based on a male model of corrections, that women prisoners were geographically dislocated and separated from their families, that the programs and services were inadequate, that the special needs of prisoners serving a life sentence as well as francophone or Aboriginal inmates were ignored, and that there were few community facilities or services for women prisoners. What primarily distinguishes this report from its many predecessors is its explicit feminist philosophy, its particular recognition of the unique problems of Aboriginal women offenders, and the fact that the report has had a significant impact in changing correctional policies and programs directed at federal female offenders.

The report advocates a new approach to reforming women's prisons based on the core feminist principles of empowerment, meaningful choices, respect and dignity, supportive environments, and shared responsibility for the welfare of women. Specifically, the report recommended that the Prison for Women should be closed and, in its place, five smaller, regional prisons, including a healing lodge for Aboriginal women, should be built across the country. In addition, the report urged the implementation of programs and services in the regional facilities that are responsive to women's needs and encourage the development of self-esteem and self-sufficiency. It further stresses the need for physical environments that are conducive to reintegration, highly interactive with the community, and reflective of the generally low security risk of federally sentenced women (Correctional Service of Canada 1992).

A few months after the release of *Creating Choices* in 1990, the Solicitor General formally endorsed the philosophy and recommendations of the Task Force by announcing that the Prison for Women would be closed and replaced by new regional facilities. By 1996, four new regional centres were operational in the following locations: Truro, Nova Scotia (Atlantic regional facility); Kitchener, Ontario (Ontario regional facility); Joliette, Quebec (Quebec regional facility). In addition, a healing lodge for Aboriginal women was built on the Nekaneet Reserve in Saskatchewan. Each of these new facilities is designed to house anywhere from 30 to 70 women. The Burnaby Correctional Centre for Women, a provincial facility already housing federal female inmates under an exchange of service agreement, was to serve as the Pacific regional facility. While there is little question that these developments represent a major landmark in transforming women's federal imprisonment, many of the longstanding inequities and problems facing women prisoners, especially provincial prisoners, remain unresolved.

A STATISTICAL PROFILE OF WOMEN PRISONERS IN CANADA

Incarceration Numbers and Trends

As is the case with men, women sentenced to periods of incarceration of two years or more serve their time in federal institutions, while those sentenced to less than two years are incarcerated in provincial facilities. Beyond this basic similarity, however, there are marked differences between men and women on a variety of factors, including the number of offenders sentenced to prison, the offences leading to incarceration, sentence length, criminal histories, and personal characteristics. An appreciation of these basic differences is a fundamental precondition for developing policies and programs that adequately meet the specific needs of imprisoned women.

As in the past, women constitute a small proportion of all incarcerated offenders. In 1996/97, women accounted for 4 percent of all sentenced admissions to federal custody (182 women versus 4,387 men). In provincial prisons, women accounted for 9 percent of all sentenced admissions (9,720 women versus 98,277 men). Across the different provinces, the percentage of female admissions is highest in Alberta (12 percent) and Saskatchewan (10 percent), and lowest in the Yukon, New Brunswick, and Nova Scotia (5 percent each) (Statistics Canada 1998). Overall, women constituted 8.8 percent of all adult sentenced admissions to federal and provincial/territorial prisons.

A one-day snapshot of all inmates in adult correctional institutions on October 5, 1996, reveals that women accounted for 5 percent of all prisoners (1,807 women out of 37,541 inmates). Women made up 7 percent (approximately 1,500) of the inmates in provincial/territorial facilities and about 2 percent (approximately 35) of inmates in federal facilities (Statistics Canada 1999, 3).

While many more men than women are admitted to prison in every year, the percentage increase in sentenced admissions has been far greater for women than men over the past two decades (see Table 10.1). Between 1983/84 and 1996/97, there was an 84 percent increase in the number of federal female admissions (from 99 to 182), compared with a 13 percent increase for men. However, percentage increases can be misleading because the numbers of federal female admissions are small and fluctuate considerably from year to year. In this regard, it is important to note that the relative proportion of women admitted to federal prisons has changed minimally during this period, ranging from between 2 and 4 percent. At the same time, the number of women admitted to provincial prisons from 1978/79 to 1996/97 has increased by 113 percent (from 4,555 to 9,720), compared with an increase of 14 percent for men during the same period. Here again, however, the relative proportion of women sentenced to provincial custody over the same time period has increased more modestly from 5 to 9 percent.

Offence Profiles of Female Prisoners

There are significant differences in the offence profiles of women and male prisoners at both the federal and provincial levels. Table 10.2 provides a breakdown of offences for female and male federal prisoners in 1996. Overall, a smaller proportion of women than men were imprisoned for violent offences (64 percent versus 73 percent). The largest proportion of women were convicted for homicide and attempted murder (37 percent) and drug-related offences (27 percent) as their most serious offence. Taken together, these crimes accounted for 64 percent of female prisoners, but only 32 percent of male prisoners.

TABLE 10.1	Women as Percentage of Adult Sentenced Admissions to Federal and Provincial/Territorial Custody, Canada		

Year and Type of Admissions	Total Number of Admission	Number of Female Admissions[a]	Females as Percent of All Admissions
Federal Custody			
1983–84	3,977	99	3
1984–85	3,804	85	2
1985–86	3,910	140	4
1986–87	3,966	97	2
1987–88	4,029	104	3
1988–89	3,977	114	3
1989–90	4,247	115	3
1990–91	4,296	141	3
1991–92	4,878	146	3
1992–93	5,583	167	3
1993–94	5,174	155	3
1994–95	4,758	143	3
1995–96	4,402	130	3
1996–97	4,569	182	4
Provincial Custody			
1978–79	91,102	4,555	5
1979–80	91,932	5,516	6
1980–81	102,614	6,157	6
1981–82	112,458	6,747	6
1982–83	131,291	7,877	6
1983–84	129,748	9,082	7
1984–85	123,776	7,427	6
1985–86	119,301	8,351	7
1986–87	116,269	6,976	6
1987–88	117,374	8,216	7
1988–89	116,092	9,126	7
1989–90	115,114	9,209	8
1990–91	114,834	9,855	8
1991–92	75,827	6,824	9
1992–93	79,883	7,189	9
1993–94	119,907	10,792	9
1994–95	117,938	10,614	9
1995–96	114,562	10,540	9
1996–97	107,997	9,720	9

[a] The actual numbers of female admissions for the years 1990/91 to 1996/97 were not reported by Statistics Canada. Numbers for 1990/91 and 1995/96 from Goff (1999, 10, 57). Numbers for 1992/93 to 1994/95 and 1996/97 calculated from reported data on total admissions and the percentage of female admissions in each year.

SOURCES: Adapted from Campbell 1990; Statistics Canada 1990/91–1996/97.

TABLE 10.2   Distribution of Male and Female Federal Inmates by Offence Type, 1996[a]

	Women %	Men %
Homicide/Attempted murder	37	24
Sexual assault	1	14
Serious assault	10	4
Robbery	13	24
Other violent offences	3	7
Break and enter	—	12
Theft	4	1
Fraud	1	—
Other property offences	2	2
Impaired driving	1	1
Drug offences	27	8
Percentages based on total of	210	13,619

[a] Only the most serious offence is recorded. Missing data for 33 inmates.
SOURCE: Adapted from Statistics Canada 1998, p. 10.

In provincial/territorial prisons, it is also the case that a smaller number of women than men are imprisoned for violent offences (28 percent versus 34 percent). As shown in Figure 10.1, the largest proportions of women are imprisoned for property offences (36 percent). In particular, women were most often imprisoned for theft, especially, shoplifting (12 percent), or drug-related offences (13 percent). Other common female offences include various public order offences, liquor-related offences, and traffic offences (Statistics Canada 1999).

A disproportionate number of female inmates in both the federal and provincial/territorial prisons are Aboriginal. Although Aboriginal women 18 years and older constitute approximately 1.3 percent of the total female population in Canada (LaPrairie 1989), they represent 20 percent of federal female inmates and 23 percent of provincial/territorial inmates. Moreover, Aboriginal women constitute a larger proportion of female than male inmates in both correctional systems. The over-representation of Aboriginal women is especially pronounced in the Prairie provinces and the territories, where Aboriginal women make up the majority of imprisoned women (Lipinski 1991).

Aboriginal women have somewhat different offender profiles than non-Aboriginal women. In particular, Aboriginal women are more often incarcerated for violent crimes than non-Aboriginal women. In 1995, 77 percent of female Aboriginal federal inmates were incarcerated for violent offences, compared with 44 percent of non-Aboriginal women (Correctional Service of Canada 1995). At the provincial/territorial level, the differences have typically been even more pronounced. In 1989, for example, 28 percent of Aboriginal women versus 8 percent of non-Aboriginal women were incarcerated for violent offences (LaPrairie 1989).

As a group, female prisoners have less extensive criminal histories than men, as evidenced by the number of current offences, past convictions, and prior terms of incarceration.

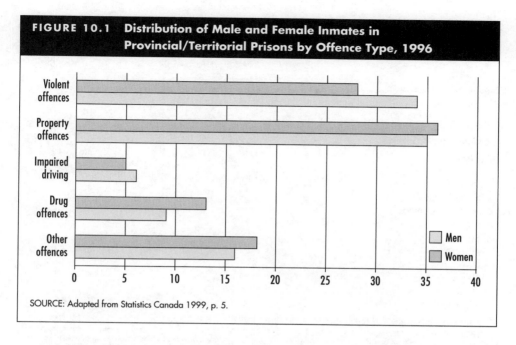

FIGURE 10.1   Distribution of Male and Female Inmates in Provincial/Territorial Prisons by Offence Type, 1996

SOURCE: Adapted from Statistics Canada 1999, p. 5.

At the federal level, 55 percent of women compared with 26 percent of men were imprisoned for only one offence (Statistics Canada 1999) (see Table 10.3). A much larger proportion of federal women (76 percent) than federal men (54 percent) had no previous term of incarceration. Moreover, federal male inmates are more serious recidivists than women; 10 percent of men compared with only 4 percent of women had more than three previous terms of incarceration. At the provincial level, 38 percent of women had only one current offence, compared with 33 percent of men. In addition, 50 percent of women had no or only one prior adult conviction, compared with 36 percent of men. Here again, men had more extensive criminal backgrounds: the proportion of males with five or more previous convictions was almost double that of female inmates (21 percent versus 12 percent) (Solicitor General of Canada 1997).

Beyond this, the level of recidivism generally is higher for women inmates in provincial/territorial prisons than for federal female inmates (see Table 10.3). Among federal female inmates, several factors appear to be related to the likelihood of recidivism, the most important of which are race, age, and original offence. In particular, female offenders who were Aboriginal, younger, and originally charged with robbery or manslaughter were most likely to be re-admitted to federal custody (Belcourt, Nouwens, and Lefebvre 1993).

Gender differences in sentence length at both the federal and provincial levels tend to reflect the fact that women are convicted of less serious offences, and have less serious criminal histories (see Table 10.3). For federal inmates, the average sentence length for women is 4.5 years compared with 4.9 years for men (Statistics Canada 1999). More specifically, 58 percent of women compared with 49 percent of men were serving a sentence of six years or less. A further 25 percent of women compared with 30 percent of men were serving sentences of 10 years or more, and roughly equal proportions of both men and women were serving life/indeterminate sentences (20 percent versus 18 percent).

TABLE 10.3	**Offence Profiles of Male and Female Federal Inmates, 1997**	
	Women %	**Men %**
Serving a sentence for [a]:		
Murder	19.9	15.5
Schedule I offence	45.7	62.4
Schedule II offence	23.5	8.8
Non-Schedule offence	10.9	13.2
Sentence Length:		
Under three years	22.7	16.7
Three to six years	35.3	32.8
Six to ten years	17.4	20.8
Ten years or more	4.2	12.1
Life/Indeterminate	20.4	17.7
Number of previous terms of federal incarceration:		
None	74.8	53.8
One	5.9	11.1
Two	12.3	17.4
Three	3.1	7.3
More than three	3.9	10.4
Percentages based on total of:	**357**	**14,091**

[a] Schedule I offences include sexual offences and other violent crimes. Schedule II offences include serious drug offences and conspiracy to commit serious drug offences.

SOURCE: Adapted from Solicitor General of Canada 1997.

At the provincial level, in 1996, the average sentence for women was 153 days compared with 184 days for men. More particularly, 51 percent of women compared with 44 percent of men were serving sentences of less than six months. Beyond this, the large numbers of women sentenced to very short terms is significant for two reasons. First, it would appear that the greater use of these short sentences accounts for the higher female imprisonment rate in Canada compared with other countries such as Australia, England, and Wales (Shaw 1994). Second, a significant proportion of women sentenced to short terms are imprisoned for failure to pay a court-ordered fine; in 1989/90, 30 percent of female admissions (2,746 women) to provincial prisons were for fine default. Many observers have questioned the appropriateness of incarcerating thousands of women each year because they lack the financial resources to pay a fine.

Social and Demographic Characteristics of Women Prisoners

Research consistently reveals that the lives of the overwhelming majority of women prisoners are characterized by social and economic disadvantages of every kind, and reflect the subordinate social and economic status of women generally in Canadian society (Johnson and Rodgers 1993). As shown in Table 10.4, the majority of women prisoners in both federal and provincial/territorial prisons are young, single, undereducated, and unemployed at the time of incarceration. More particularly, the majority of federal and provincial/territorial inmates are under the age of 34 and single. A larger proportion of federal prisoners than provincial/territorial prisoners have less than Grade 12 education, and were unemployed at the time of

TABLE 10.4   **Personal Profiles of Male and Female Federal and Provincial/Territorial Inmates, 1996**

	Federal		Provincial/Territorial	
	Women %	Men %	Women %	Men %
Age:				
18–24	17	13	18	26
25–34	40	38	43	37
35–44	30	29	27	25
45–54	10	13	8	8
55+	2	6	2	3
Aboriginal	20	14	23	18
Single[a]	69	58	76	76
Education:				
Less than Grade 12	76	75	55	73
Unemployed	80	54	64	43
Percentages based on totals[b] of:	210	13,619	1,484	20,537

a Includes separated, divorced, or widowed.

b Due to missing data on selected characteristics, actual totals vary for each category.

SOURCE: Adapted from Statistics Canada 1999, pp. 5, 7.

incarceration. On all these various dimensions, Aboriginal inmates tend to be even more disadvantaged than non-Aboriginal women (Task Force on Federally Sentenced Women 1990; Elizabeth Fry Society of Edmonton 1993a, 1993b).

In addition, approximately two thirds of women in prison have a serious problem with drugs or alcohol and this substance abuse is associated with their offending in some way (Shaw 1994). Although male prisoners also tend to have substance abuse problems, a recent study of federal inmates found that men more often abused alcohol, while women were twice as likely as men to report at least moderate drug abuse (Loucks and Zamble 1994). Aboriginal female inmates are even more likely than non-Aboriginal female inmates to have substance abuse problems (Elizabeth Fry Society of Edmonton 1993a).

Although there is considerable similarity in the personal backgrounds of male and female prisoners, certain aspects of women's life histories that tend to be unique. For example, women prisoners tend to have experienced more physical and sexual abuse either in childhood or adulthood, or both.[1] In addition, at least two thirds of women in prison have children, and up to two thirds of these mothers are likely to be single parents. Apart from the special economic and emotional burdens that single parenthood imposes on female offenders before imprisonment, women with children obviously face particular difficulties with respect to the care of their children upon incarceration (Shaw 1994).

Many of these problems overlap, such that women who have been physically or sexually abused are also likely to have substance abuse problems, low educational levels, few job skills, physical and mental health problems, and little community support. Moreover, while some of the basic needs of female prisoners are similar to those of male prisoners, they clearly also have very different and specific needs.

FACILITIES FOR FEMALE PRISONERS

Provincial Prisons

A significant part of the inequality experienced by women prisoners is related to the inferior facilities in which they are housed. The small number of women prisoners, together with the enormous size of the country, and the federal-provincial separation of responsibility for prisoners have created special problems for women prisoners including inadequate, antiquated accommodations, geographic isolation from families and homes, and significant disparities in programs and services across different facilities.

The vast majority of women prisoners in Canada are housed in a variety of provincial/territorial facilities. For example, in Ontario women may be housed in as many as 32 different jails or detention centres (Shaw 1994); in Alberta, in 1993, there were eight provincial facilities housing female offenders (MacDonald et al. 1993). Some facilities such as the Burnaby Correctional Centre for Women in British Columbia, which opened in 1990, are relatively new; others such as the Portage Correctional Centre in Manitoba were built in the last century for male prisoners (Comack 1996). While some of these provincial facilities house only women, many others are so-called co-ed prisons—a misleading term since these institutions were not built or designed to house women as well as men. Consequently, in many jurisdictions across Canada where there are too few women to justify building separate facilities, women offenders are housed in men's institutions. As in the past, women are often imprisoned in whatever space is available and convenient to the dominant male inmate population.

Exchange of Service Agreements

Because until recently, there was only one federal prison for women, as compared with more than 40 for men, it was much more difficult for women at the Prison for Women to maintain relationships with children, relatives, and friends. Such geographic dislocation and isolation were not only a major source of the additional emotional hardship experienced by female prisoners, but they also made the task of planning for their release and reintegration into society all the more difficult. The problem of geographic dislocations was partially addressed in the mid 1970s when federal-provincial exchange of service agreements allowed some female inmates to serve their sentences in provincial institutions so that they could remain closer to their families and communities. Faith (1993) observed that nearly one half of all federal female inmates have utilized this option.

However, such transfers were not equally available to all federal female prisoners: there was an uneven geographical distribution of these agreements, which put women from certain parts of the country at a disadvantage. In addition, eligibility was based on sentence length, severity of offence, and personality of the offender (Moffat 1991). Furthermore, provincial prisons were generally inadequate to meet the needs of federal prisoners because they were designed for short-term prisoners and offered fewer resources than the P4W with respect to vocational and education training, recreational facilities, and counselling support. As a result, federal female inmates were forced to choose between serving their sentences in their home provinces or accessing the more extensive programs and services at the P4W (Task Force on Federally Sentenced Women 1990). Moreover, according to a report by the Law Society of British Columbia (1992), the situation in provincial prisons was demoralizing and stressful for many federal female inmates because they were housed with women serving minimal sentences under less restrictive conditions.

Security and Classification Issues

One of longstanding inequities in the accommodation of women prisoners at both the provincial/territorial and federal levels is that women have not had access to the range of facilities with different security levels (see Chapter 6) available to men. This system of **cascading** allows men to earn, through good behaviour, transfers from more restrictive environments to less restrictive environments with more privileges and resources. However, the small number of women's prisons has meant that women from every security classification are imprisoned together in the same facility, and are generally subject to a single security system. Typically, this means that even though the majority of women prisoners are suitable for low security settings, all tend to be subject to the high levels of security designed for the minority of women perceived as high risk. This problem was most acute at the P4W but is also apparent in provincial facilities. For example, while many provincial prisons attempt to differentiate among inmates level of risk and their right to certain privileges, it is difficult to achieve such differentiation within the confines of a single institution (Faith 1993; Law Society of British Columbia 1992).

Federal Regional Facilities

The construction of the new regional facilities for federal female inmates has ameliorated the problems of geographic isolation and overclassification, but these problems are by no means resolved. Certainly, women residing in the new facilities are closer to their families and homes than they were before. However, some dislocation is inevitable, and practical and monetary considerations may still limit visits and contact with family and friends. In addition, depending on the location of her home province, an Aboriginal woman who wishes to serve her sentence at the Aboriginal healing lodge may have to choose between being housed in this unique facility or proximity to her family and community (Moffat 1991).

Classification and security concerns at the federal level are also still problematic. Originally, it was intended that each regional facility would accommodate all federally sentenced inmates from that region, and that the overall security model would reflect the generally low-risk/low-security needs of the majority of women, with some specialized accommodations for the 10 percent of women who were regarded as high risk (Correctional Services of Canada 1992). The emphasis was to be on "dynamic security"—a high level of staff-inmate interaction and staff support—rather than on the traditional physical barriers (e.g., fences, locks, and high-tech surveillance) or traditional discipline measures (e.g., segregation) (Shaw 1993). Replacing the fortress-like living conditions of the P4W, the new facilities would have cottage-style houses accommodating six to ten women each and were designed to promote wellness by providing "natural light, fresh air, colour, space, and privacy" (Task Force on Federally Sentenced Women 1990).

These plans, however, were modified as a result of several factors. First, concerns were expressed about the perceived risks to the public of situating female prisons within residential communities. Second, a series of events at Edmonton Institution in its first year of operation, including seven escapes, the murder of an inmate by another inmate, and an attack on a guard, generated a great deal of publicity, including calls to close the prison (see Box 10.2). As a result, security measures were enhanced in all of the regional facilities and correctional authorities decided that maximum security prisoners, and those who were considered high risk because of serious psychiatric problems would not be housed at the new regional facilities.

BOX 10.2   **Shut It Down—Smith**

Mayor Bill Smith called for the closure of the Edmonton women's prisons after three inmates, two of them killers, slipped through a door to freedom.

Tuesday night's escapade brought the number of escapees to seven in the last 18 days . . .

[Smith] wants the jail shut down until proper security measures are taken. "It's now obvious that the facility is not capable of maintaining the security the citizens of this city are entitled to."

Smith was only partly satisfied by news that Ottawa had ordered the medium and maximum security prisoners to be transferred to provincial jails. The move would leave only five minimum-security inmates in the women's prison.

"I'm still sticking with my original statement—close the facility," Smith said.

Smith has lost all confidence in what he called the "no-security" prison. "I'm sure everybody in the city has."

SOURCE: Tanner 1996. Reprinted with permission of the *Edmonton Journal*.

Consequently, although the P4W was scheduled to close by 1994 (later delayed to 1996), it remains open. In the interim, conditions at the P4W came to national attention as a result of incidents that occurred in April 1994. In response to a period of several days during which prisoners attacked guards, lit fires, and threw human waste, the warden called in a male riot squad, the Institutional Emergency Response Team (IERT), who shackled and strip-searched female inmates. Female inmates involved in these incidents were subjected to body-cavity searches, kept in segregation for many months, and denied access to lawyers, regular exercise, and basic necessities. In her 1996 report investigating these events, Justice Louise Arbour wrote a scathing indictment of the treatment of the women inmates, which led to the resignation of the head of Correctional Service of Canada and the announcement that a Deputy Commissioner of Women's Corrections would be appointed to prevent such violations of prisoners' rights in the future (see Box 10.3).

Cross-Gender Staffing in Women's Prisons

The deployment of an all-male riot squad at the Prison for Women raises the broader issue of the proper role of male correctional staff in women's prisons. The fact that the majority of female inmates report having been victims of sexual or physical abuse is one of the principle reasons that the Task Force on Federally Sentenced Women took the position that men should not be employed as primary workers in the day-to-day living situation of women inmates in the new regional facilities. This recommendation is based on the belief that the employment of men in positions of authority would recreate "the power imbalance, sense of insecurity, degradation and fear that are inherent in most abusive relationships," and, as a result, significantly retard the healing of a woman's emotional scars (Pollack 1994, 38). Moreover, there are those who believe that male staff could have a positive and "normalizing" effect in women's prisons since, once released back into the community, women will have to interact with men in many capacities. The issue is likely to remain controversial since the Correctional Service of Canada has recently lifted its restrictions on male employment in women's prisons. Currently, all of the regional facilities with the exception of the Edmonton facility and the healing lodge have male primary workers (Correctional Service of Canada 1995).

BOX 10.3	Excerpts from the Arbour Commission of Inquiry into Certain Events at the Prison for Women in Kingston

The society in which many women offenders live is neither peaceful nor safe. By the time they go to prison, they should be entitled to expect that it will be just.

In its Mission Statement, the Correctional Service of Canada commits itself to "openness", "integrity", and "accountability". An organization which was truly committed to these values would, it seems to me, be concerned about compliance with the law, and vigilant to correct any departures from the law; it would be responsive to outside criticism, and prepared to engage in honest self-criticism; it would be prepared to give a fair and honest account of its actions; and it would acknowledge error. In this case, the Correctional Service did little of this.

Too often, the approach was to deny error, defend against criticism, and to react without a proper investigation of the truth . . .

The deplorable defensive culture that manifested itself during this inquiry has old, established roots within the Correctional Service, and there is nothing to suggest that it emerged at the initiative of the present Commissioner or his senior staff. They are, it would seem, simply entrenched in it . . .

As for the [inmates'] treatment by the IERT [Institutional Emergency Response Team], their prolonged segregation, the inadequate segregation review and grievance process, I think that they should have received an apology. I also think that they are entitled to compensation.

SOURCE: Arbour 1996.

PROGRAMS AND SERVICES IN WOMEN'S PRISONS

Women, like men, enter prisons with many problems; however, by and large, correctional strategies for programming have been developed for a male inmate population and applied in women's prisons with little recognition of the special needs of women. Consequently, programs and services offered to female prisoners have been unresponsive to their needs, have been defined by traditional female stereotypes, and have failed to reach parity with the number and range of resources offered to male prisoners.

Provincial Prisons

The problem of inadequate programs and services is especially pronounced for women incarcerated in provincial facilities. Although a considerable amount of recent attention has focused on federal female inmates, comparatively little concern has been directed at improving programs and services for the vast majority of women imprisoned in provincial prisons. These women continue to be at a disadvantage not only in relation to male prisoners, but also in relation to federal female inmates.

Numerous factors make the task of improving programs and services for provincial female prisoners a difficult challenge. There are simply too few women, dispersed across a range of facilities, and sentenced to short periods to make it practical to implement meaningful vocational and educational programs. Consequently, many of the programs and services for women in provincial prisons are of short duration, and staffed by unqualified personnel or prison guards. Given these limitations, as well as the distrust that traditionally exists between prison staff and inmates, and the generally punitive atmosphere of prisons, it may be unrealistic to expect prisons alone to resolve the longstanding and diverse problems faced by women prisoners (Comack 1996).

In addition, programs in provincial facilities continue to be defined by traditional female stereotypes and provide women with few opportunities to gain truly marketable skills. For example, even in the newer provincial prisons such as the Burnaby Correctional Centre for Women in British Columbia, available work programs follow traditional gender-defined roles that perpetuate job segregation and female poverty upon release—e.g., beauty parlour training, a sewing shop to produce uniforms for male inmates, a five-week course in floral arrangement, and a dog-obedience training program. There are, in addition, educational upgrading programs but most women do not take advantage of them because they are the lowest paid of the institutional options. Consequently, the majority of women spend time in the higher paid and traditional tasks of cleaning, doing institutional laundry, or otherwise assisting with the maintenance of the institution (Law Society of British Columbia 1992).

Furthermore, prisoners at the Burnaby Correctional Centre maintain that men in both federal and provincial facilities in British Columbia still receive more choices in programming and more effective dental, medical, and counselling services. This point was underscored in 1991 when a federally sentenced inmate, Gayle Horii, successfully brought a legal injunction to block her transfer to Burnaby in order to remain as the only female prisoner in a male federal institution. She based her suit on the grounds that she would lose her right to university-level courses, as well as access to the psychologist of her choice, and would have fewer visiting privileges because of Burnaby's policies and higher levels of security (Law Society of British Columbia 1992).

Federal Prisons

The 1981 decision by the Canadian Human Rights Commission that women suffered from outright discrimination in the provision of programs and services led to a number of reforms for federal female prisoners at the Prison for Women. For example, educational and recreational programs were improved, and vocational choices were expanded from basic hairdressing to include woodworking, ceramics, upholstering, and word-processing. A few women were given permission to leave the prison during the day to attend local university classes. In addition, the administration also arranged for the construction of a private cottage on the grounds, which facilitated some women's opportunities for visits with family members (Faith 1993). Even so, as the Task Force on Federally Sentenced Women (1990) observed, the programs did not reach parity with the number and range of programs offered to male federal prisoners. Furthermore, long waiting lists for new services such as sexual abuse counselling meant that the existence of a program or service did not necessarily mean that it was readily available to female inmates.

In addition, existing programs for federally sentenced women did not go far enough in recognizing the diverse needs of different inmates, particularly Aboriginal women and long-term federally sentenced women. In addition, existing policies work to the detriment of women serving the longest sentences, who comprise a growing proportion of federal female prisoners; as of 1997, there were 88 women serving sentences of 10 years or more. The problem is that these women have access to fewer programs and privileges because eligibility is paced so that access increases as an inmate nears her parole eligibility date. Women serving long sentences, particularly life sentences, are disadvantaged because they are many more years away from parole eligibility than other inmates (Correctional Service of Canada 1994). Such policies contribute to lifers' feelings of being lost in the system and being powerless to improve their situation (Hattem 1994).

Given the short period in which the new regional facilities have been operational, the process of implementing programs and services is an ongoing one and far from complete. However, a number of programs that are seen as women-centred and responsive to the needs of federally sentenced women have been identified as ones to be implemented in all the facilities (Correctional Service of Canada 1995). These include:

- Women's Substance Abuse Treatment Program;
- Living Skills Program, including cognitive skills;
- Anger management, and parenting skills;
- Literacy and continuous learning skills;
- Survivors of Abuse and Trauma Programming;
- Mental Health Services;
- Vocational training; and
- A Residential Mother-Child Program.

Programs specifically designed to address the particular needs of long-term federally sentenced women are also planned and some preliminary steps have been taken, such as a staff-training component designed to increase awareness of the issues faced by women serving longer sentences (Correctional Service of Canada 1994).

In addition, of course, the establishment of the **healing lodge** for Aboriginal women is one of the most important programming reforms that resulted from *Creating Choices* (see Box 10.4). While there are many parallels between the Okimaw Ohci healing lodge and the regional facilities, there are also differences. One of these fundamental differences is that the operation and program strategy of the healing lodge is based on Aboriginal healing and Aboriginal teachings. This has resulted in a staff largely composed of Aboriginal people, a unique staff training plan, and a central role for elders in the healing lodge operation. In terms of programming, the central emphasis of the healing program is on survival of physical and sexual abuse and freedom from substance abuse through reconnection with Aboriginal culture in its broadest sense (Correctional Service of Canada 1995).

The Experience of Imprisonment

When the emotional, physical, and substance abuse problems that women bring into prison are combined with the longstanding lack of programs and services to deal with these problems, and the general pains associated with loss of freedom and confinement, it is not surprising that many observers believe that the experience of prison is worse for women than it is for men (Heidensohn 1985). Research has also shown that female inmates tend to have many more emotional and mental health problems than male prisoners. Compared with

| BOX 10.4 | Okimaw Ohci Healing Lodge |

Okimaw Ohci (Thunder Hills) Healing Lodge is a 30 bed treatment facility for Federally Sentenced Aboriginal Women, using traditional healing practices and operated by Aboriginal Staff. It is located in the sacred Cypress Hills, on Nekaneet Band Reserve land, approximately 30 kilometres from the town of Maple Creek, in the south-west corner of Saskatchewan.

Program Development

The central emphasis of the healing program is on survival of physical and sexual abuse and freedom from substance abuse through reconnection with Aboriginal culture in its broadest sense. As a preliminary step, the curricula or guidelines developed for the Core Programs for women inmates will be used at the Healing Lodge; however, delivery methods will be culturally appropriate and will involve the participation of the resident Elder(s).

Healing Lodge Vision

An opportunity exists through the Vision of the Healing Lodge to re-kindle the Spirit of Federally Sentenced Aboriginal Women as the Healing Lodge is central to the empowerment and healing of women.

The Healing Lodge will enable federally sentenced women to: restore their pride and dignity as women and mothers; restore a sense of worth, dignity and hope; rebuild their families and their communities; build bridges between Aboriginal and non-Aboriginal societies; promote the healing of the Earth and all her creatures.

More specifically, the Healing Lodge will be a place to:

1) Have seasonal gathering for the celebration of the Four Directions.

2) Conduct ceremonies including the Sweatlodge, Fasting, Pipe Ceremonies, Feasts, U-Wipi Ceremonies, Shaking Tent, Cedar Bath Ceremony, Give-A-Way Ceremonies, Sundances, Rain Dance Ceremonies, and all other ceremonies related to Spiritual and Cultural well-being.

3) Share the teachings of oral traditions where ceremonies can be protected, where rebirth of language, customs, beliefs and traditional methods of teachings and healing can take place in a natural way.

4) Redevelop relationships with all creatures who share the Earth.

5) Promote traditional methods of teaching and learning.

6) Provide on-site accommodation for children of parents who are residents of the Healing Lodge.

7) Provide a setting for shared learning experiences for Aboriginal and non-Aboriginal people.

8) Create an economic base that will provide for agriculture and self-sufficiency of the land.

9) Create an economic land base that will provide for self-sufficiency and encourage Aboriginal crafts such as hide tanning, etc., that would result in an authentic craft store.

SOURCE: Correctional Service of Canada 1995. Reproduced with the permission of the Minister of Public Works and Government Services Canada, 2000.

male inmates, female inmates are much more likely to suffer from depression and to have reported suicide attempts (Loucks and Zamble 1994). Other problems such as high-anxiety levels, eating disorders, and self-injury are also more prevalent among women prisoners (Shaw 1994). Within the female prison population, the range and severity of these problems are greatest for Aboriginal women and women serving the longest sentences. It has been suggested that the emotional reactions of women serving life sentences parallel the stages of grief experienced by terminally ill patients. However, while most terminally ill patients come to accept their situation, for women serving life sentences, grief and mourning at their separation from society is ongoing (Jose-Kampfner 1990).

One manifestation of the pains of imprisonment experienced by female inmates is self-injurious behaviour. The use of sharp-edged objects as a means of self-mutilation has been a longstanding problem in women's prisons. It is suggested that there is a link between self-injurious behaviour and prior sexual abuse (Shaw 1994). In particular, psychologists speculate that self-mutilation is a specific response to anxiety that offers temporary relief and distraction from emotional pain, tension, and anger (Task Force on Federally Sentenced Women 1990; Hoffman and Law 1995). As one women at the Prison for Women put it: "Prison is frustration and anger so intense that cutting into the arteries of my own arm only alleviates some of the pain" (6).

A longstanding practice in women's prisons has been to place women who injure themselves or attempt suicide in segregation—a practice that tends to increase their suicidal tendencies. The suicide rate among Aboriginal women is especially high. It is estimated that between 1977 and 1991, 12 women at P4W killed themselves; eight of these women were Aboriginal (Faith 1993). Another common response to women who engage in slashing, suicide attempts, or other behaviour deemed problematic by prison authorities is to prescribe psychotropic drugs of various kinds (Cookson 1977). Drugs have long been used as a means of controlling female prisoners and, as is the case in the general population, such medications are much more likely to be prescribed to women than men in prison (Dobash, Dobash, and Gutteridge 1986; Hattem 1994).

Of all the many factors that contribute to the pains of imprisonment, none compares with the separation of inmate mothers from their children. This is a source of pain and emotional hardship that affects the majority of women inmates, since two thirds of women prisoners are mothers and, of these mothers, two thirds are likely to be single mothers (Shaw 1994). Much more than is the case for men, women inmates suffer the stresses of worrying about the care and placement of their children, the risk of losing their children to child welfare authorities, and prison policies and rules that make it difficult to see their children (Faith 1993; Martin 1997; Wine 1992). Over the years, there have been isolated efforts by federal and provincial corrections officials to address the special needs of inmate mothers including increasing visitation privileges, and constructing special facilities for such visits, as well as inmate-staffed childcare programs that provide supervision during visitation hours, and annual camp retreats that allow women and their children to spend weekends together (Griffiths and Verdun-Jones 1994).

In recent years, there has been increased support for programs that allow female inmates to keep their children with them in prison (Hale 1988). This is a controversial issue and likely to remain so. While many believe that prison is no place for children, proponents of live-in mother-child programs argue that the trauma and long-term damage that result from separation far outweigh any disadvantages associated with the arrangement. In any event, efforts at implementing such programs continue to be limited. At the provincial level, two prisons have provided limited accommodations for inmates with children. The Burnaby Correctional Centre had accommodations for four children and children were allowed to stay until they reached two years of age. At the Portage Correctional Institution in Manitoba, over the past 12 years, more than 100 babies have been part of the infant live-in program where they were allowed to stay until they reached the age of 10 months. However, neither of these programs is currently operational due to overcrowding and other problems.

At the federal level, the recommendation from *Creating Choices* that women be allowed to live with their children was accepted by the government as an important programming component in the regional facilities (Labrecque 1995). Currently, the regional facilities at Kitchener and Joliette, as well as the Aboriginal healing lodge have live-in mother-child programs, and it is intended that these programs will eventually be available in all the facilities.

SUMMARY

A historical perspective reveals that the root causes of gender disparities in the treatment of male and female prisoners can be traced to two longstanding issues: the administrative problems resulting from the relatively small numbers of women prisoners, and correctional policies and programs heavily steeped in stereotypes of the female offender and traditional sex roles for women. Despite the fact that female prisoners are more socially and economically disadvantaged than men and have special and unique needs, programs and services for women prisoners have fallen far short of those available to male prisoners.

After decades of administrative neglect, vacillating policies, and inadequate resources, the task of reforming prison conditions for women has begun to receive serious attention from correctional authorities. Whether, and to what extent, this impetus for reform will continue to effect positive changes in accommodations, policies, and programs for women prisoners remains to be seen. While many significant changes have occurred in recent years to redress past inequities, there is no easy solution to the problems facing women prisoners, and reform is necessarily an ongoing process.

KEY TERMS AND CONCEPTS

Archambault Commission	Elizabeth Fry	MacGuigan Report
Brown Commission	Fauteux Report	Mercer Reformatory
Carol Maureen Daniels	healing lodge	Nickle Commission
cascading	Macdonnell Commission	Prison for Women (P4W)
Creating Choices		

STUDY AND DISCUSSION QUESTIONS

1. Do you think that female prisoners should be allowed to keep their children with them in prison? Why?

2. Do you think that men should be employed as guards and front-line correctional workers in women's prisons? Why?

3. Do you agree with the new correctional philosophy towards federal female prisoners embodied in *Creating Choices*? What do you think are the strengths and weaknesses of this new model of female corrections?

4. Do you think it is possible to significantly reduce the rate of female incarceration in Canada? If so, how?

WEBLINKS

Fact Sheet on Alternatives to Incarceration, Canadian Association of Elizabeth Fry Societies: **www.web.apc.org/~kpate/facts1_e.htm**

Text of the Commission of Inquiry into Certain Events at the Prison for Women in Kingston: **www.sgc.gc.ca/epub/corr/e199681/e199681.htm**

Women and Prison, Prison Activist Resource Center: **www.prisonactivist.org/women**

NOTE

1. *Creating Choices* reported that 78 percent of federal sentenced women were physically abused and 53 percent were sexually abused. The figures reported by Aboriginal women are even higher; 90 percent have experienced physical abuse and 61 percent have been victims of sexual abuse (Task Force on Federally Sentenced Women 1990).

REFERENCES

Adelberg, E., and **C. Currie** (Eds.). 1993. *In Conflict with the Law: Women and the Canadian Justice System*. Vancouver: Press Gang Publishers.

Arbour, L. 1996. *Commission of Inquiry into Certain Events at the Prison for Women in Kingston*. Ottawa: Public Works and Government Services Canada.

Beattie, J.M. 1977. *Attitudes towards Crime and Punishment in Upper Canada, 1830–1850: A Documentary Study*. Toronto: University of Toronto, Centre of Criminology.

Belcourt, R., T. Nouwens, and **L. Lefebvre**. 1993. Examining the Unexamined: Recidivism among Female Offenders. *Correctional Service of Canada Forum* 5(3): 10–14.

Campbell, G. 1990. Women and Crime. *Juristat Service Bulletin* 10(20): 1–14.

Carrigan, D.O. 1991. *Crime and Punishment in Canada: A History*. Toronto: McClelland and Stewart.

Comack, E. 1996. *Women in Trouble: Connecting Women's Law Violations to Their Histories of Abuse*. Halifax: Fernwood Publishing.

Cookson, H.M. 1977. A Survey of Self-Injury in a Closed Prison for Women. *British Journal of Criminology* 17(4): 332–347.

Cooper, S. 1993. The Evolution of the Federal Women's Prison. In E. Adelberg and Claudia Currie (Eds.), *In Conflict with the Law: Women and the Canadian Justice System*. Vancouver: Press Gang Publishers.

Correctional Service of Canada. 1992. *Regional Facilities for Federally Sentenced Women, Draft #4, Operational Plan*. Ottawa: Construction Policy and Services/National Implementation Committee.

———. 1994. *Long-Term Federally Sentenced Women: Literature Review.* Ottawa: Federally Sentenced Women Program.

———. 1995. *Overviews: Correctional Service of Canada Regional Facilities for Federally Sentenced Women.* Ottawa: Federally Sentenced Women Program.

Dobash, R.P., R.E. Dobash, and S. Gutteridge. 1986. *The Imprisonment of Women.* New York: Basil Blackwell.

Elizabeth Fry Society of Edmonton. 1993a. *Building Pathways: The Employment Needs of Provincially Sentenced Women.* Edmonton: Elizabeth Fry Society of Edmonton.

———. 1993b. *Building Pathways: The Employment Needs of Federally Sentenced Women.* Edmonton: Elizabeth Fry Society of Edmonton.

Faith, K. 1993. *Unruly Women: The Politics of Confinement and Resistance.* Vancouver: Press Gang Publishers.

Feinman, C. 1983. An Historical Overview of the Treatment of Incarcerated Women: Myths and Realities of Rehabilitation. *Prison Journal* 63: 12–26.

Goff, C. 1999. *Correction in Canada.* Cincinnati: Anderson.

Griffith, C.T., and S.N. Verdun-Jones. 1994. *Canadian Criminal Justice* (2nd ed.). Toronto: Harcourt Brace & Company.

Hale, D.C. (1988). The Impact of Mother's Incarceration on the Family System: Research and Recommendations. *Marriage and Family Review,* 12(1/2): 143–154.

Hannah-Moffat, K. 1994. Unintended Consequences of Feminism and Prison Reform. *Forum for Corrections Research* 6(1): 7–10.

Hattem, T. 1994. The Realities of Life Imprisonment for Women Convicted of Murder. *Forum for Corrections Research* 6(1): 42–45.

Heidensohn, F. 1985. *Women and Crime.* New York: New York University Press.

Hoffman, L.E., and M.A. Law. 1995. *Federally Sentenced Women on Conditional Release: A Survey of Community Supervisors.* Ottawa: Federally Sentenced Women Program.

Johnson, H., and K. Rodgers. 1993. Images and Realities: Profiles of Women Offenders. In E. Adelberg and C. Currie (Eds.), *In Conflict with the Law: Women and the Canadian Justice System.* Vancouver: Press Gang Publishers.

Jose-Kampfner, C. 1990. Coming to Terms with Existential Death: An Analysis of Women's Adaptation to Life in Prison. *Social Justice* 17(2): 110–124.

Labrecque, R. 1995. *Study of the Mother-Child Program.* Ottawa: Federally Sentenced Women Program.

LaPrairie, C. 1989. Some Issues in Aboriginal Justice Research: The Case of Aboriginal Women. *Women and Criminal Justice* 1(1): 81–91.

Law Society of British Columbia. 1992. *Gender Inequality in the Justice System.* Vancouver: Law Society of British Columbia.

Lipinski, S. 1991. Adult Female Offenders in the Provincial/Territorial Corrections Systems, 1989/90. *Juristat Service Bulletin* 11(6): 1–10.

Loucks, A., and **E. Zamble**. 1994. Some Comparisons of Male and Female Serious Offenders. *Forum for Corrections Research* 6(1): 22–25.

MacDonald, A., **S. Kushniruk**, **I. Martins**, and **P. Bennett**. 1993. *In Justice to Women.* Edmonton: Edmonton Social Planning Council.

Martin, M. 1997. Connected Mothers: A Follow-up Study of Incarcerated Women and Their Children. *Women and Criminal Justice* 8(4):1–23.

Moffat, K. 1991. Creating Choices of Repeating History: Canadian Female Offenders and Correctional Reform. *Social Justice* 18(3): 184–203.

Morris, A. 1987. *Women, Crime and Criminal Justice.* Oxford: Basil Blackwell.

Ontario. Prison Reform Commission. 1891. *Report of the Commissioners Appointed to Enquire into the Prison and Reformatory System of Ontario.* Toronto: Warwick and Sons.

Phillips, J. 1994. Women, Crime, and Criminal Justice in Early Halifax, 1750–1800. In J. Phillips, T. Loo, and S. Lewthwaite (Eds.), *Essays in the History of Canadian Law,* Vol. V. Toronto: Osgoode Society.

Pollack, S. 1994. Opening the Window on a Very Dark Day: A Program Evaluation of the Peer Support Team at the Kingston Prison for Women. *Forum for Corrections Research* 6(1): 36–38.

Rafter, N.H. 1990. *Partial Justice* (2nd ed.). New Brunswick, NJ: Northeastern University Press.

Ruemper, W. 1995. Locking Them Up: Incarcerating Women in Ontario, 1857–1931. In L.A. Knafla and S.W.S. Binnie (Eds.), *Law, Society, and the State: Essays in Modern Legal History.* Toronto: University of Toronto Press.

Shaw, M. 1993. Reforming Federal Women's Imprisonment. In E. Adelberg and C. Currie (Eds.), *In Conflict with the Law: Women and the Canadian Justice System.* Vancouver: Press Gang Publishers.

———. 1994. Women in Prison: A Literature Review. *Forum for Corrections Research* 6(1): 13–18.

Solicitor General of Canada. 1997. *Basic Facts About Corrections in Canada.* Ottawa: Public Works and Government Services Canada.

Statistics Canada. 1990/91 to 1996/97. *Adult Correctional Services in Canada.* Ottawa: Canadian Centre for Justice Statistics.

———. 1998. A One-Day Snapshot of Inmates in Canada's Adult Correctional Facilities. *Juristat* 18(8), Catalogue No. 85-002.

———. 1999. Female Inmates, Aboriginal Inmates, and Inmates Serving Life Sentences: A One Day snapshot. *Juristat* 19(5), Catalogue No. 85-002.

Strange, C. 1996. Unlocking the Doors on Women's Prisons. *Resources for Feminist Research* 14(4): 13–15.

Tanner, A. 1996. Shut It Down—Bill Smith. *Edmonton Journal* May 2, B1.

Task Force on Federally Sentenced Women. 1990. *Creating Choices: The Report of the Task Force on Federally Sentenced Women.* Ottawa: Task Force on Federally Sentenced Women.

Wine, S. 1992. *A Motherhood Issue: The Impact of Criminal Justice System Involvement on Women and their Children.* Report prepared for Corrections Branch, Ministry of the Solicitor General of Canada. Ottawa: Supply and Services Canada.

C h a p t e r

TREATMENT PROGRAMS IN CORRECTIONS

Paul Gendreau, Paula Smith,
and Claire Goggin
Centre for Criminal Justice Studies
University of New Brunswick
Saint John, New Brunswick

LEARNING OBJECTIVES

After reading this chapter, you should be able to:

- Discuss the evolution of the rehabilitative ideal in corrections;
- Discuss the contribution of meta-analysis to the study of offender rehabilitation; and
- Describe the principles of effective and ineffective treatment programs.

Facts do not cease to exist because they are ignored.

—Aldous Huxley

The purpose of this chapter is to review the evidence regarding the efficacy of correctional rehabilitation programs in preventing offenders from returning to a life of crime (i.e., recidivism). Many definitions of **correctional rehabilitation** exist (e.g., Sechrest, White, and Brown 1979, 20–21) but there tends to be concordance on three issues: 1) the treatment is planned; 2) the treatment targets malleable features of the offender's personality and life circumstances that contribute to his or her criminality; and 3) the treatment techniques employed (e.g., various counselling and behaviour modification modalities) are designed to positively reinforce pro-social attitudes, behaviours, and skills. We should note, however, that rehabilitation does not include specific deterrence interventions (e.g., incarceration, boot camps, or electronic monitoring) that are meant to suppress or punish future criminal behaviour by making the offender fearful of committing crimes.

The degree to which any approach, such as rehabilitation, gains acceptance among policy-makers depends not only on the amount and quality of the evidence generated, but also upon the social context of the times. The perceived value of the rehabilitative ideal, particularly in recent years, has come to be viewed with considerable suspicion in some quarters. Therefore, before undertaking a review and discussion of current evidence regarding the effectiveness of rehabilitation, a brief history of the rehabilitative movement, and the social realities that both encouraged and hindered its growth, is in order.

THE REHABILITATIVE IDEAL

For approximately one hundred years, until the 1970s, the rehabilitative ideal was, arguably, the pre-eminent philosophy in North American corrections (Cullen and Gendreau in press).

The belief that offenders should be reformed or rehabilitated dates back to the beginnings of the penitentiary system in North America in the early 1800s (de Beaumont and de Toqueville [1883] 1964). The penitentiary experience would "do good" things for offenders (McGee 1969); it was not to serve as punishment. The reformers of the 19th century were explicit on this matter. For example, Brockway (1871, 42) stated:

> If punishment, suffering, and degradation are deemed deterrent, if they are the best means to reform the criminal and prevent crime, then let prison reform go backward to the pillory, the whipping-post, the gallows, the stake: to corporal violence and extermination! But if the dawn of Christianity has reached us, if we have learned the lesson that evil is to be overcome with good, then let prisons and prison systems be lighted by this law of love. Let us leave, for the present, the thought of inflicting punishment upon prisoners to satisfy the so-called justice, and turn toward the two grand divisions of our subject, the real objects of the system, vis.: the protection of society by the prevention of crime and reformation of criminals.

At a seminal conference in Cincinnati in 1870, leading corrections experts arrived at a consensus that the treatment of criminals was to serve two purposes: to protect society and to reform offenders without being mean spirited (Wines 1871, 541). In fact, some of the language used by the conference participants—instilling hope, emphasizing reward over punishments—resonates with 20th-century learning and behaviour modification theory (see Mower 1960; Spiegler and Guevremont 1998), the precursor of many contemporary treatments.

Ascendancy of the Rehabilitative Ideal

The treatment paradigm that evolved from the work of these late 19th-century scholars, and one that was to remain unchallenged for many decades thereafter (Allen 1981), had several important implications for latter-day rehabilitative practices. It was presumed that the genesis of offender criminality lay in a variety of psychological and social factors. The rehabilitative enterprise should, therefore, involve identifying the unique factors that led each offender into crime. Once identified, the offender could be placed in a treatment program where his or her particular needs would be addressed. The professionals charged with treating the offender would carry out their duties in a manner akin to that of the **medical model**. For example, the offender would be diagnosed, a treatment regime would be prescribed and followed, and—this is crucial given the subsequent vilification of the rehabilitative ideal (Rothman 1980)—the change agent, or agency, would have a great deal of discretion in determining the course of action necessary to effect change in the offender.

It was not until the mid 1950s that further major reforms to the rehabilitative ideal were proposed. In 1954, the American Correctional Association was founded. Prisons became known as correctional institutions. For proponents of the rehabilitative ideal, the next two decades witnessed a number of exciting initiatives. Sophisticated classification systems were introduced (e.g., Warren 1969). Prison-based treatment programs ranging from individual and group counselling to therapeutic milieux, behaviour modification, and vocational and educational programming were initiated. With the emergence of community-based corrections in the 1960s, the granting of parole was often made contingent upon the offender progressing satisfactorily in institutional treatment programs. By 1975, when the American Probation and Parole Association was established, a number of parole/probation settings had developed innovative treatment programs reporting sizeable reductions in recidivism (see Ross and Gendreau 1980). It was felt that community reintegration strategies, even more so than prison-based programming, offered the greatest promise for the optimization of the rehabilitative ideal.

During this period, a few criminologists (e.g., Bailey 1966; Cressey 1958; Logan 1972) claimed that the evaluation literature provided little support for the claims of rehabilitation supporters. Approximately half of the treatment studies with control group comparisons reviewed by Bailey, Cressey, and Logan, among others, were found to have little effect on recidivism rates. These naysayers, however, were largely ignored. The prevailing viewpoint during this period, as evidenced by the popularity of such highly praised books as Karl Menninger's (1968) *The Crime of Punishment*, criminological articles publications in general (Toby 1964), and various task forces (e.g., Task Force on Corrections 1967), was that the only sensible and productive correctional policy was that of rehabilitation. Rehabilitation was unanimously supported among almost all of the players in the criminal justice field (American Friends Service Committee Working Party 1971).

Times Change: Rehabilitation in Decline

In 1974, Martinson published one of the most cited works in criminology, entitled "What Works? Questions and Answers about Prison Reform." This article was a précis of a more comprehensive review of several hundred pages in length that was published a year later (Lipton, Martinson, and Wilks 1975). Martinson based his conclusions on an analysis of 231 studies published between 1945 and 1967 that reported the effects of offender treatment programs on 286 outcome measures. Consistent with the conclusions reached by the skeptics, as noted previously, Martinson reasoned "that with few and isolated exceptions the rehabilitative efforts that have been reported so far have had no appreciable effect on recidivism" (25). Furthermore, Martinson sounded a note of despair when he stated that "we haven't the faintest clue about how to rehabilitate offenders and reduce recidivism" (48). In the words of Walker (1985, 168), Martinson's pronouncement, labelled "**nothing works**," became an instant cliché and exerted an enormous influence on both popular and professional thinking. Many scholars and policy-makers, Martinson included (Martinson 1976), began advocating that the punishment of offenders should be pursued much more vigorously.

Why was Martinson's edict so eagerly received when others who had earlier expressed similar views were ignored? Was Martinson's argument so brilliant and persuasive, or did he deliver a message that conveniently suited the times? Some academics side with the latter interpretation (Cullen and Gendreau 1989; Cullen and Gilbert 1982). Martinson's message was delivered at a time when, especially in the United States, social unrest was on the rise.[1] From the mid 1960s until about a decade later, events occurred in the U.S. (e.g., Kent State, Vietnam, Watergate, the Attica prison riots, campus unrest, civil disobedience in the streets) that led many observers to question the ethics, let alone the ability, of government to act as a competent, trustworthy civil administrator (Cullen and Gendreau 1989).

The more general question of the role of government in the lives of its citizens also had specific application in the criminal justice field. Prison unrest became commonplace and controversy arose over the sentencing and release decisions of judges and parole authorities (Cullen and Gendreau in press; Useem and Kimball 1991).

Neither side of the political spectrum was impressed with the status quo in criminal justice, which they felt was due, in part, to the pernicious policies emanating from the rehabilitative ideal. Conservative policy-makers viewed prison disturbances and the fact that courts and parole boards allowed offenders to serve only a fraction of their sentences as a sign of the system's weakness. One must also be mindful of concomitant increases in crime rates during the latter 1970s. As such, like parents wishing to punish disrespectful or wayward children, the conservative response was to "**get tough**" on criminals. Conservatives advocated abolishing parole, instituting mandatory minimum sentences, and implementing a fixed schedule of lengthier sentences, such as the "three strikes and out" laws (i.e., life sentences upon third convictions regardless of the crime), as well as making prison living conditions much harsher (see Gendreau, Goggin, and Cullen 1999; Shichor and Sechrest 1996). Only then would good order be returned to the criminal justice system.

In contrast, liberals felt the system was out of control because the rehabilitative model gave carte blanche to correctional officials who, presumably, exercised their discretion in an inequitable and coercive fashion. Prison officials were characterized as agents of social control who discriminated against the downtrodden. Moreover, treatment programs were scathingly described as degradation ceremonies that simply widened the net and did more harm than good (see Binder and Geis 1984).

Unlike the conservative "get tough" agenda, liberals championed the "**justice model**," which minimized the goal of crime control and lay greater emphasis upon ensuring that justice was administered fairly. In terms of policy, undue discretion would be reined in by imposing fixed sentences, abolishing parole, and by making rehabilitation—where it was available at all—strictly voluntary. Offenders would thereby be protected from the vagaries of a capricious system once appropriate protective legal mechanisms were established (Conrad 1981).

In conclusion, Martinson's message arrived at the precise moment to have maximal impact (see Box 11.1). Science had passed judgement; the rehabilitative model had no empirical support, its claims having been exposed as fraudulent. Both the conservative and liberal schools were revitalized by the task of bringing order to the chaos that resulted from rehabilitation's misguided policies.

We take pains to note that Martinson (1974) and Lipton, Martinson, and Wilks (1975) were not entirely wrong in their conclusions. On the heels of their publications, other reviewers (e.g., Greenberg 1977; Wright and Dixon 1977) confirmed the Lipton group's pessimistic findings, as did a special panel commissioned by the National Academy of Science

BOX 11.1   Martinson Revisited

The body of literature examined by Lipton, Martinson, and Wilks (1975) is deceptive in that, at first glance, it seems more than substantial. Cullen and Gendreau (in press) have taken another look at the data base and have found that in only 138 of 286 comparisons was recidivism measured as an outcome. Secondly, probation, parole, imprisonment, physical custody, and medical methods were categorized as treatments, which is most unorthodox. Eliminating these categories from the analysis leaves 73 recidivism outcome measures. Thirdly, the number of studies per treatment category was very limited, from a low of 7 for "counselling" to a high of 20 for "milieu therapy." There was also tremendous heterogeneity within each category. For example, "counselling" could mean anything from Rogerian to psychodynamic to directive counselling methodologies. Of note, there were no categories for "cognitive behavioural" or "behaviour modification" treatments, which have, since the early 1970s, constituted the treatments of choice in a substantial majority of offender treatment studies.

(Sechrest, White, and Brown 1979) that thoroughly re-evaluated the results of the review by Lipton, Martinson, and Wilks (1975). Indeed, challenges to the new orthodoxy of "nothing works" were met with scorn. As a case in point, witness the response to Palmer (1975) when he dared to suggest that some of Martinson's conclusions merited revaluation. Palmer noted that quite a few studies that reported data on recidivism outcomes—48 percent to be precise—were successful. Furthermore, those programs that were conducted in the community, with juveniles or with offenders who were at moderate risk, produced the best results. Obviously, some programs were effective. Palmer also raised another very important point. He predicted that meaningful gains in treatment success would be forthcoming once researchers learned more about program/offender interactions, in other words, "which methods work best for which type of offenders, and under what conditions or in what types of settings?" (150).

Martinson (1976) replied with a vicious personal attack. In his opinion, Palmer's research data were indecipherable rubbish, not worth the price of a cup of coffee. It was likely at this point, around 1976, that the credibility of the rehabilitative ideal was at its nadir. Shortly thereafter, the resuscitation of the movement gradually began to take shape.

Revivification of Rehabilitation: 1976 to the Mid 1980s

Rejuvenation of the rehabilitative ideal could only occur, however, when its proponents came to realize that they had been somewhat naive and overconfident in the 1950s and 1960s (Palmer 1992). Progress would be made if and when they abandoned their panacea mindset and took a sober look at the treatment literature, as Ross and McKay (1978) did in their review of the literature on behaviour modification with offenders.

In addition, rehabilitation's prospects took a modest turn for the better when Martinson (1979) updated his previous review to include studies published since 1972. He now distanced himself from his nothing-works stance and moved closer to Palmer's interactionist position when he concluded:

I have often said that treatment added to the networks of criminal justice is impotent . . . the conclusion is not correct . . . treatments will be found to be "impotent" under certain conditions, beneficial under others, and detrimental under still others (254).

Unfortunately Martinson was not able to elaborate upon his thinking in this area due to his untimely death. His recantation was also generally ignored, demonstrating once again the potent effect that social context can have in influencing a message's receptivity.

Another source of optimism originated from outside the field of criminology. Criminologists were quite comfortable with the nothing-works scenario. The empirical reality and their ideological preferences were congruent (Binder and Geis 1984; Cullen and Gendreau in press). Thus, there was no need to pursue what, in criminologists' minds, was a dead issue. Rather, the impetus for change came from psychology, a profession that had contrasting intellectual and practice predispositions. Most of the proponents of change were from the so-called "Canadian school" of rehabilitation (Logan et al. 1991).[2] Members of this group adhered to the scientist-practitioner model within their discipline (clinical/ community psychology) and, fortunately for them, most Canadian correctional and governmental jurisdictions were supportive of rehabilitation policies. Both parties took it for granted that an important part of the job was to implement, administer, and evaluate offender assessment and treatment programs. Well versed in learning theory and related behavioural treatments, they operated under the assumption that criminal behaviour, like almost all forms of social behaviour, was largely learned and, therefore, could be modified through the application of a schedule of ethical and appropriate rewards and punishments. Serious reservations were expressed about the assumption implicit within the nothing-works doctrine, suggesting as it did that criminal offenders, unlike others, were incapable of relearning or acquiring new behavioural repertoires (e.g., Gendreau and Ross 1979, 466).

Thus, they undertook a number of literature reviews and demonstration projects (e.g., Andrews 1980; Andrews and Kiessling 1980; Andrews et al. 1986; Gendreau and Andrews 1979; Gendreau and Ross 1979, 1981a, 1981b, 1983/1984, 1987; Ross and McKay 1978; Ross and Fabiano 1985) that they hoped would validate the utility of the rehabilitative ideal.

One crucial aspect of their work was to look into the "black box" of treatment programs, or as Gendreau (1996a, 118) stated:

> Unlike Martinson and his followers, we believe it is not sufficient just to sum across studies or file them into general categories. The salient question is what are the principles that distinguish between effective and ineffective programs?—what exactly was accomplished under the name of "employment"? As a result of endorsing the perspective of opening the "black box," we have been able to generate a number of principles of effective and ineffective intervention.

The first objective was to provide "bibliotherapy for cynics" (Gendreau and Ross 1979). These authors uncovered scores of studies that reported reductions in recidivism, in some cases of considerable magnitude (i.e., 20 to 50 percent). Reviews of this type (see also Andrews 1979) provided the foundation for developing some elementary **principles of effective intervention**. For example, it was discovered that a majority of the most effective programs were behavioural in nature.

Secondly, as psychologists, they were sensitive to individual differences, an idea that criminologists had long rejected (Andrews and Wormith 1989). Indeed, individual differences research—which offenders respond best to what types of treatments and therapies— underwent great advances in the late 1970s and early 1980s (for a detailed review see Gendreau and Ross 1987, 370–374).[3] Offender risk to re-offend was identified as a potentially important individual difference variable. That is, it was hypothesized that offenders rated as higher on risk (e.g., antisocial attitudes, substance abuse, criminal history) may benefit the most from intensive behavioural treatments (e.g., Andrews et al. 1986).

In addition to identifying what appeared to be effective program components, the Canadian group also shed light on aspects of programs that led to failure (i.e., increased offender recidivism). Particularly crucial was the concept of **therapeutic integrity**, or:

> To what extent do treatment personnel actually adhere to the principles and employ the techniques of the therapy they purport to provide? To what extent are the treatment staff competent? How hard do they work? How much is treatment diluted in the correctional environment so that it becomes treatment in name only? (Gendreau and Ross 1979, 467).

As testament to this unfortunate reality, which Gendreau and Ross (1979) felt was widespread, the reader is directed to Quay's (1977) reassessment of Kassebaum, Ward, and Wilner's (1971) famous prison counselling program. While the research by Kassebaum and colleagues was cited as a prime example of a methodologically rigorous evaluation that demonstrated that treatment was ineffective, Quay discovered that the program had little therapeutic integrity. In fact, the program had a weak conceptual base, used counselling groups that were unstable, and employed unqualified, poorly trained counsellors who did not believe in the efficacy of the program. A somewhat similar example came from an examination of 27 empirical investigations of applied behavioural programs for delinquency prevention (Emery and Marholin 1977). They found that in only 9 percent of cases were the behaviours targeted for change uniquely selected for each individual in the program. Furthermore, in only 30 percent of studies were the behaviours for which the youth was referred reflected in the behaviours targeted for treatment (e.g., one client was referred for stealing cars but was treated for tardiness).

Other aspects of unsuccessful programs appeared to be related to individual difference factors and types of treatment. Some evidence indicated that even high-quality treatment services had little impact upon the recidivism of low-risk offenders, and Rogerian nondirective and psychodynamic-oriented treatments were notably ineffective modalities (see Andrews 1979; Gendreau and Ross 1983/84).

CUMULATING KNOWLEDGE: WHAT WORKS IN OFFENDER REHABILITATION

From the latter 1980s to the present, the validity of the rehabilitative ideal has been revived. This has been due both to the generation of new knowledge and, in our opinion, to recent developments in how knowledge is cumulated. What, for example, should one make of this acrimonious debate about the effectiveness of correctional rehabilitation? Even though we have referenced a good number of review articles that are highly supportive of treatment, and that we find quite convincing, attacks against rehabilitation have continued since the 1980s (e.g., Clarke 1985; Gibbons 1986; Lab and Whitehead 1990; for a review see also Gendreau 1996b; Andrews and Bonta 1998). With some exceptions (Currie 1998; Latessa and Allen 1999), most criminology texts and criminologists still ignore or dismiss rehabilitation's usefulness (Andrews and Bonta 1998; Moon et al. 2000). Given this apparent lack of concordance, what is one to believe?

Part of the reason for such disparate interpretations lies in how literature is reviewed. So far in this chapter we have cited only narrative reviews of the offender treatment programs. At this point, we shall clarify what constitutes a narrative review. Typically, the author tries to establish the truth of an issue (e.g., does treatment work) by reading a few influential theoretical articles, sifting through some of the available evidence, and then choosing the results that substantiate a particular "take" on the matter. Critics of the narrative review (Glass, McGaw, and Smith 1981; Rosenthal 1991) have pointed out that crucial data are often omitted and the conclusions reached can be subject to the whims of prejudice and ideology (see Chapter 9). Narrative reviews are woefully imprecise.[4] They are also very difficult to replicate; after all, how does one replicate a reviewer's thinking, which is often covert? Finally, most contemporary literatures consist of at least dozens of studies (e.g., Gendreau and Ross 1987). There are limitations on how much information the mind can systematically process in dealing with myriad outcomes, methodologies, and study characteristics (e.g., type of subjects, quality of research design).

Fortunately, for the purpose of demonstrating the effectiveness of treatment programs in reducing recidivism, quantitative research synthesis has come into vogue in medicine and psychology in the last 20 years (Hunt 1997). The techniques used to quantify the results of studies are subsumed under the term meta-analysis. Although this is discussed in Chapter 9 as well, it is worthwhile to reiterate the rudiments of meta-analysis since it will be crucial to understanding any forthcoming advances regarding what works in correctional rehabilitation.

In contrast to **narrative reviews** or box-score tabulations (i.e., how many studies produce a significant effect versus how many do not), a **meta-analysis** computes an "effect size" between treatment and outcome (i.e., recidivism) for each study. The effect size can be negative (indicating that the treatment increases recidivism) or positive (indicating that the treatment reduces recidivism). Sometimes more than one effect size per study may be generated. The end result of a meta-analysis is a number—the average effect size—which is a precise point estimate of the relationship between treatment and outcome across all studies. Typically, the effect size statistic is reported as Pearson $\underline{r}$[5] with its corresponding confidence interval (Rosenthal 1991; Schmidt 1996).

Within a meta-analysis each study is also coded on a number of dimensions such as type of subjects, offender risk level, type and dosage of treatment, therapist qualifications, study setting, and quality of research design. These factors can then be correlated with overall treatment effect. For example, assuming an overall treatment effect size of $r = .20$ for a group of studies, which is equivalent to a 20 percent decrease in recidivism, it would not be unusual to find that this value may be somewhat modulated (i.e., increased or decreased) when its relationship with individual moderators is examined.

One should note, however, that meta-analysis is not foolproof. The quality of the literature and the accuracy of the coding of study characteristics can affect the results. Nevertheless, the consensus is that, for the purposes of summarizing large bodies of literature in order to generate rational policies, meta-analysis is a method far superior[6] to that of the narrative review (Gendreau, Goggin, and Smith 2000).

To illustrate, Beaman (1991) compared meta-analytic and narrative reviews on a variety of study characteristics (e.g., the nature of the literature under review, the magnitude and direction of effect size, the relationship between criterion and moderators) and found the former to be more informative than the latter by about 50 percent on average. Another limitation of narrative summaries is their tendency to underestimate the magnitude of an effect. This may be due, in part, to the necessarily prudent path taken by reviewers lacking exact quantitative effect size estimates. For example, Cooper and Rosenthal (1980) discovered that, in using both narrative and meta-analytic techniques in reviewing identical literatures, the former failed to identify a statistically significant effect about half the time (i.e., higher Type II error rates).

Finally, one of the most compelling features of any meta-analysis is its replicability. Unlike the narrative review, subject as it may be to the whimsy of its author, meta-analysis lends itself to independent re-examination. In this way, it makes an invaluable contribution to knowledge synthesis in a given area by clarifying not only what does work but, equally, what does not.

We now turn to the results from meta-analyses conducted on offender treatment programs and related matters such as recidivism prediction.

Meta-Analytic Reviews: Overall Effects

The first meta-analyses of offender rehabilitation programs began to appear in the mid 1980s (Davidson et al. 1984; Garrett 1985; for a review see Gendreau and Ross 1987, 391–394; Ross and Fabiano 1985). These pioneering quantitative syntheses presaged familiar themes that would be validated in future meta-analyses. They were mostly limited to juvenile samples and the studies surveyed did not overlap to a large extent. On average, a modest majority ($n \approx 55$ percent) of the effect sizes were found to produce positive results vis-à-vis recidivism.

Several years later Lipsey (1992) summarized the results of a huge database of juvenile interventions ($n = 443$ effect sizes). Sixty-four percent of these were positive (i.e., reduced recidivism)—a noticeable improvement over the 50 percent baseline reported by Martinson and Palmer almost 20 years previously. The average reduction in recidivism within the Lipsey sample varied from 5 percent to 9 percent depending on the statistical adjustments made to the effect sizes. Subsequently, Lösel (1995) provided a comprehensive assessment of 13 meta-analyses of juvenile and adult offenders treatment programs published between 1985 and 1995. He found that mean effect sizes ranged from .05 to .18 with an overall mean of about $r = .10$. Using Rosenthal's (1991) BESD statistic, this would mean that the recidivism rates for the treatment and control groups would be 45 percent and 55 percent, respectively. The results of further meta-analyses (Andrews, Dowden, and Gendreau 1999; Redondo, Sanchez-Meca, and Garrido 1999) concurred with those of Lösel's. It should also be noted that these positive results were not extenuated by methodological factors such as subject attrition, quality of research design, length of follow-up, or inclusion of published versus unpublished studies (Lipsey 1992; in press).

This robust replication of positive results is truly impressive given the variability among the sample of studies, coding schemes, and researchers. Even criminologists antagonistic to rehabilitation have produced positive results in their own meta-analyses (Whitehead and Lab 1989). Additionally, Lösel (1995) and Lipsey (1992) have suggested that the overall treatment effect size is likely underestimated as treatment studies, by design, do not often incorporate treatment-control group comparisons and tend to include dichotomous measures that are not overly sensitive to detecting differences in outcome (i.e., recidivism).

Cynics may counter that a 10 percent reduction in recidivism is of little practical value. Nothing could be further from the truth (see Lipsey and Wilson 1998). Lipsey and Wilson (1993) and Rosnow and Rosenthal (1993) noted that many medical treatments have proven to be cost effective when the incidence of serious illness is reduced by only a few percentage points. In this regard, Cohen (1998) calculated the cost effectiveness of saving high-risk juvenile offenders. Admittedly, crime cost-benefit analyses are imprecise as they are based on estimates of the rate of criminal participation and include categories such as "prison" and "suffering" along with "property loss" and "lost wages." Notwithstanding these caveats,

Cohen found that the criminal career of the average high-risk youth incurs costs of between $1.7 and $2.3 million. Depending on the point at which the intervention occurs and its attendant costs, treatment programs can be cost effective when even "small" reductions in recidivism result (see also Aos et al. 1999; Greenwood et al. 1996).

Meta-Analytic Reviews: The Search for Principles

The meta-analyses of the mid 1980s furnished the first quantitative confirmation of the results from earlier narrative reviews that examined the "black box" of treatment effectiveness. Even though the studies reviewed by the Davidson group (1984) and Garrett (1985) were fairly divergent and used somewhat different meta-analytic methods, the general trend in their results was that behaviourally oriented programs, or at least those with considerable structure (e.g., academics, vocational, family therapies), generally produced the largest reductions in recidivism. Although the mean effect sizes were not large in these instances (e.g., approximately 10 percent), they were greater than those of non-behavioural or relatively unfocused interventions (e.g., "group therapy," psychodynamic or milieu-type therapies), which sometimes produced slight increases in recidivism. The Ross and Fabiano (1985) study, which was more of a narrative analysis, further suggested that the greatest gains could be anticipated from cognitive-behavioural interventions. Special commendation should be made regarding the Davidson group's attempt to analyze the influence of a large number of moderators on effect size estimates. Worthy of note in their results is that professional training (e.g., psychology, education) and evaluator involvement in the design, implementation, and control of an intervention are positively correlated with program success.

We emphasize that it is not our intention to downplay all of the important meta-analyses (see Lösel 1995) conducted subsequently to the aforementioned, but it would be fair to say that the results of the first group of meta-analyses continued to be corroborated, obviously with further refinements, by later investigators (e.g., Izzo and Ross 1990; Lipsey 1992). We now turn to two meta-analyses that looked further into the "black box" in an attempt to confirm the principles of effective intervention. These meta-analyses came from researchers within the Canadian school (Andrews et al. 1990; Andrews et al. 1999).

The principles of effective intervention that Andrews et al. (1990) wished to test were grounded in their own narrative reviews, previous meta-analyses, as well as the clinical wisdom and insight of many years of field work and consultation with other experts in offender treatment. Essentially, the rationale underlying their meta-analysis could be described as follows (for a later and much more detailed exposition of the principles, see Andrews 1995; Andrews and Bonta 1998; Gendreau 1996a, 1996b; Gendreau, Cullen, and Bonta 1994):

1. Effective treatments are those that target attributes consistent with the most robust predictors of recidivism. There are two types of predictors: those classed as static (e.g., criminal history) and those that are dynamic (e.g., antisocial values), that is, changeable. The latter are typically referred to as criminogenic needs. Examples of these are antisocial attitudes and cognitions, pro-criminal associates, and personality factors such as impulsiveness and poor self-control. Recent meta-analyses have demonstrated that these types of criminogenic needs are powerful predictors of recidivism while others that were once thought to be useful (e.g., low self-esteem, depression, anxiety) are not (Gendreau, Little, and Goggin 1996). Targeting these latter factors for intervention, as has often been the case, will produce little change in offenders' rate of criminal behaviour.

2. Effective treatments are behavioural in nature. This is known as the general responsivity principle.[7] Central to any behavioural program is the principle of operant conditioning; that is, that a behaviour will be learned if it is contingently reinforced. Positive reinforcers, which are usually pleasant or desirable, increase or strengthen the likelihood of a behavioural response. There are four basic types of reinforcers: material (e.g., money, goods), activities (e.g., recreation), social (e.g., attention, praise, approval), and covert (e.g., thoughts, self-evaluation).

    The most prevalent type of behavioural program is known as "cognitive behavioural." There are several different types of strategies in this regard—some rather subtle in their differences—but basically all attempt to restructure the distorted or erroneous antisocial cognitions of an individual. Secondly, they try to assist the person in learning new adaptive cognitive and life skills. With practice, the offender's behaviour can be modified through "shaping."

3. High-risk offenders are the optimal target population for behavioural intervention (i.e., the risk-need principle) and tend to represent the greatest risk to the public (see Bonta 1996). In contrast, low-risk offenders require much less intervention. They have relatively few problem behaviours that require attention. Subjecting them to intensive services is not cost effective; moreover, it may actually increase their rates of recidivism (Andrews and Bonta 1998, 243).

4. Other factors, if addressed, can enhance treatment effectiveness. These include operating programs in the community as opposed to an institutional setting, ensuring that the program employs staff who are interpersonally sensitive, well trained, and clinically supervised, and providing structured relapse prevention (or "aftercare") whenever possible. Among the most important considerations is "specific responsivity." This concept refers to the practice of matching styles and modes of treatment service to the learning styles of offenders (Andrews and Bonta 1998, 245; Gendreau 1996a, 122–123). Factors that should be taken into account in service delivery are the offenders' lack of motivation to participate in the program, or their feelings of anxiety or depression. Cullen et al. (1997, 403) outlined a concrete example of how specific responsivity functions in the case of offenders with intellectual deficits:

    . . . offenders who have low IQs would perform more effectively than higher functioning offenders in an instructional format that requires less verbal and written fluency and less abstract conceptualizations. In addition, they would likely profit from a more extensive use of tangible reinforcers and from repeated, graduated behavioral rehearsal and shaping of skills. Moreover, therapists should be selected who relate optimally to offenders' styles of intellectual functioning and to the content of the treatment modality.

Examples of programs that follow many of the principles noted above, and which have demonstrated effectiveness, include the following:

1. Community: Multisystemic therapy based in four Ontario sites: a) Barrie-Orillia, Kinark Youth Services, Robert Thompson Centre, and Katalpua-Tamarack Centre; b) London-Craigwood Youth Services; c) Mississauga-Associated Youth Services; and d) Ottawa-Eastern Ontario Young Offender Services.

2. Prison: Integrated Service Delivery Model, Rideau Correctional and Treatment Centre, Merrickville, Ontario.

The Andrews et al. (1990) study examined 80 treatment program evaluations that generated 124 treatment-control group comparisons (effect sizes) in which they categorized treatment quality as follows: a) appropriate—consistent with the above-noted principles; b) inappropriate—inconsistent with those principles; and c) unspecified—programs whose treatment quality could not be determined due to a lack of information. Recall that this approach differs from previous meta-analyses and many subsequent ones (e.g., Wilson, Gallagher, and MacKenzie 1999) that tend to classify programs generically (e.g., vocational, counselling, family therapy).

The most striking result reported by Andrews et al. (1990) was that recidivism was reduced by 30 percent through appropriate interventions, 13 percent through unspecified interventions, and, of some concern, increased by 7 percent when inappropriate treatments were used.

One criticism of this meta-analysis, and others, made by opponents of rehabilitation, is that spurious significant relationships among variables may arise by chance alone and then be magically transformed into "principles" through tautological wizardry (Logan and Gaes 1993). In fact, there is nothing wrong with a purely inductive dust-bowl empirical approach (see Lipsey in press). As noted previously, one of the strengths of this form of analysis is its ease of replication. In fact, the Andrews et al. (1990) meta-analysis was predicated on a theoretical framework first espoused 10 years previously (see Cullen and Applegate 1997).

In regard to replicating the 1990 findings, Lipsey (1992, 159) found that in his meta-analysis the "larger order of effects are with few exceptions, those defined as the most clinically relevant (appropriate treatment) in the Andrews et al. (1990) review." Antonowicz and Ross (1994) reached similar conclusions, as did Pearson, Lipton, and Cleland (1996).

Finally, Andrews et al. (1999) extended their data base to 230 studies that produced 374 effect sizes. Again, upon analyzing this new data with a view to treatment quality, they reported an effect size of $r = .26$ or a 26 percent reduction in recidivism for appropriate treatments. Meanwhile, programs that were rated as inappropriate produced a 2 percent increase in recidivism. This meta-analysis also provided a major advance in extending the validity of some of the aforementioned "principles." Andrews et al. found a substantial correlation of $r = .55$ between the number of criminogenic needs targeted by a program and reductions in recidivism. Those criminogenic needs that had the strongest correlations with recidivism were antisocial cognitive and skill deficits, self-control deficits, and problems in the family, peers, school, and work domain. In contrast, the correlation between the number of non-criminogenic needs targeted and recidivism was negative $r = -.18$). Examples of non-criminogenic needs were low self-esteem, anxiety, physical activity, and fear of official punishment (specific deterrence).

The risk principle was confirmed. Unfortunately, few studies could be found where high-risk and low-risk offenders, assessed in the same way, were compared on similar treatments. In these instances, the correlation between targeting higher risk subjects for treatment and recidivism was $r = .46$.

Andrews et al. (1999) also reported that an involved, skilled evaluator contributed to program success, as did community-based intervention settings. Other moderating factors of note were attending to the integrity of program implementation and service delivery (for a review of a separate set of principles in this regard, see Gendreau, Goggin, and Smith 1999) and who sponsored the program. As to the latter, justice agencies and their staff tended to be associated with less effective programs, which may be due to their being overwhelmed by other "law and order" factors and lack of staff interest/training in treatment programming (see Box 11.2).

BOX 11.2   Treatment of a High-Risk Offender

File information indicates that Robert has two brothers and three sisters, two of whom had eventual problems with the law. His father had a substance abuse problem and both parents seemed to have little interest in their children. At school, Robert was frequently truant. His teachers reported that his verbal abilities were deficient, and that he shared little interest in school work. He was expelled on numerous occasions for various school misconducts, namely being disrespectful to staff, petty theft, and substance abuse.

During his adolescence, Robert's associates were almost exclusively pro-criminal. A pattern of minor law violations occurred that led to receiving two sentences of probation over the next six years. Robert dropped out of school after completing grade 10. He had a sporadic work history, mainly construction jobs.

At 19, Robert was charged with a theft of over $2,000 and assault, and was sentenced to 18 months' imprisonment in a provincial correctional institution. He has probation conditions after expiration of his sentence. At the time of his offence, Robert's associates continued to be pro-criminal.

Robert was administered several actuarial measures in the prison intake unit, and the results were as follows:

- Aggression Questionnaire: 15th percentile
- Level of Service Inventory, Revised: 40 (maximum possible 54; approximately 70 percent chance of recidivism)
- Minnesota Multiphasic Personality Inventory-2: 4–9 profile elevation, all other scales in "normal" range

- Pride in Delinquency: 7 (maximum possible 10)
- Psychopathy Check List: 50th percentile

While in the institution (two months), he has not received a misconduct and accepted whatever work details have been assigned him. He socializes with other offenders who have a lengthy criminal history. In his classification interview, Robert minimized the seriousness of his offence and claims the assault charge was provoked. He claimed he wants to do his time quietly. He has no objections to being assigned to treatment programs but offered the opinion he does not need much in the way of help from "shrinks." After reviewing all of the evidence, he appears to be quite manipulative in his personal interactions. The prison case management classification committee categorized him as moderate high risk.

He was immediately assigned to a high school equivalency program. At the mid-point of his sentence, about four months prior to his placement on probation, he will be scheduled to enroll in the six-week intensive substance abuse and criminal-thinking programs. Attendance at Alcoholics Anonymous will be mandatory. He will not be scheduled for the anger management program.

Because of his manipulativeness, it was noted that Robert's program should be individualized with as much structure as possible. It is recommended that he enter into a behavioural contract where tangible rewards will be made contingent upon his progress in the two treatment programs noted above. Suitable progress will be determined by documented improvement on staff-administered behavioural ratings, questionnaires on attitudes, substance abuse, and criminal thinking, and socialization patterns and activities (e.g., inmates he chooses to socialize with) in prison. In addition, since Robert seems to have the ability to learn quickly by observation, treatment staff have been advised to use vivid modelling exercises with him along with graduated practice and corrective feedback.

Meetings will be scheduled with his probation officer after Robert leaves prison. If his progress in treatment has been more than satisfactory—for example, a reduction in risk level from moderate high to low as assessed by several of the measures noted above—he will be a candidate for minimal-level supervision while on probation. If otherwise, the level of community supervision (e.g., surveillance, treatment) required will be adjusted accordingly.

Finally, before addressing the prospects for rehabilitation in the new century, we wish to make special note of one very significant aspect of what does not work as revealed by meta-analysis. We are referring here to specific deterrence strategies that, as the reader will recollect from the beginning of the chapter, are the opposite of rehabilitative programs in that they attempt to "get tough" or punish offenders by instilling fear. Such strategies, so highly esteemed in the minds of both politicians and the public, are not based on either a probative social science heuristic of criminal behaviour or documented prerequisite conditions for behaviour change, be that through persuasion or punishment (Gendreau 1996a, 128–129; Gendreau, Goggin, and Cullen 1999). Instead, the rationale is rooted in vague "common sense" beliefs that inducing psychological pain, increasing surveillance, and breaking down offenders by humiliation are effective punishing strategies.[8]

The two most common public policy examples of instilling fear in offenders is through incarceration or administering community-based sanctions. The former is assumed to be so aversive or stigmatizing that offenders will not want to return.[9] North Americans, notably in the U.S., have invested heavily in the construction of new prisons and have the highest incarceration rates among western countries (see Gilliard 1999). Gendreau, Goggin, and Cullen (1999) examined the effects of length of incarceration by meta-analyzing 325 risk-controlled comparison groups involving 336,052 offenders who either spent more time in prison (mean = 30 months) than their counterparts (mean = 13 months), or served a brief period in prison versus received a community sanction. The overall result across all comparisons was that time in prison is associated with slight increases in recidivism of between 2 to 4 percent.

The community-based sanction movement was born in the 1980s (see Chapter 13). As one champion of the movement remarked, "we are in the business of increasing the heat on probationers . . . satisfying the public's demand for just punishment . . . Criminals must be punished for their misdeeds" (Erwin 1986, 17). The main conduit for these sanctions was "intensive supervision probation (or parole)"—commonly referred to as "ISPs." By watching offenders closely and, presumably, increasing the certainty with which misdeeds would be detected, offenders were specifically deterred from re-offending. ISPs also often involved other means of detection, such as random drug testing, electronic monitoring, or house arrest. Restitution to victims was commonly part of a community-based sanction. Boot camps were sometimes used as adjuncts to programs for ISPs.

How well have these types of programs worked? The best experimental and quasi-experimental studies reveal virtually no influence of these programs on recidivism (Petersilia and Turner 1993). Narrative reviews, some quite extensive, have reached the same conclusion (Cullen, Wright, and Applegate 1996; Gendreau et al. 1993). Some of the earlier meta-analyses (Andrews et al. 1990; Lipsey 1992; Lipsey and Wilson 1998) examined small samples of studies that fell into the intermediate sanction category. They reported increases in recidivism ranging from 2 to 12 percent.

More recently, Gendreau, Goggin, and Fulton (2000) conducted a meta-analysis of 88 comparisons of ISP-type programs with control groups that received "lesser or no sanction." Only restitution was associated with a slight decrease in recidivism (4 percentage points versus controls). Three types of sanctions—intensive supervision probation, drug testing, and boot camps—had no effect on recidivism. The Scared Straight program and electronic monitoring produced a 5 to 7 percent increase in recidivism, respectively.[10] Subsequently, Gendreau et al. (1999) expanded the data base to include 150 comparisons involving 56,602 offenders. The overall effect size for all types of intermediate sanctions was found to be $r = .00$. The only condition under which community-based sanctions produced reliable reductions in recidivism was when they were administered in concert with some form of treatment (i.e., counselling, education, etc.).

Taken together, these results reveal that relying on punishment as a means of "correctional treatment" is unlikely to work and, thus, is an imprudent investment of resources.

REHABILITATIVE IDEAL: FUTURE PROSPECTS

Given the evidence in support of the rehabilitative ideal, can one anticipate that it will re-establish its preeminence on the correctional policy landscape? At times the barriers seem almost insurmountable.

For example, at present, there is not one major political party in North America that does not endorse at least some "get tough" policies with respect to crime and its perpetrators. Mandatory minimum sentences, such as "three strikes and you're out" are wildly popular throughout the United States and beginning to generate interest in Canada as well (Gendreau, Goggin, and Cullen 1999). We have already noted that some professions, such as criminology, are indifferent, if not hostile, to correctional rehabilitation (Moon et al. 2000). Note that only one criminal justice program in North America (at the University of Cincinnati) places any emphasis on offender rehabilitation in its curriculum. We predict that as criminal justice program graduates move into the system or become academics, they will continue to reflect such deficits in their training. That is, they will serve as poor advocates of rehabilitative policies and be even less likely to feel compelled to conduct research in the area. As well, ethnocentrism within and between disciplines exists in academia, preventing the free flow of information to the detriment of all concerned; moreover, there are only a minuscule number of university-based graduate clinical training programs that focus on offender assessment and treatment (Gendreau 1996b, 151–157).

There are also problems at the field level. Extensive surveys of the quality of treatment services offered in the field have revealed that as few as 10 percent to 20 percent of programs adhere to the guidelines of what we know to be effective treatment principles (Gendreau and Goggin 1997). Some of the problems outlined include a failure to assess offenders comprehensively using valid risk measures, targeting non-criminogenic needs for treatment, using treatments that lack empirical validity, and employing staff without appropriate credentials and training. In short, there has been a dearth of therapeutic integrity in too many correctional programs. Not surprisingly, when Lipsey (in press) compiled the results from 196 "real world" programs, he found that, on average, these correctional programs were only half as effective in reducing recidivism as were "demonstration" projects that usually have substantial external supports (e.g., informed evaluators, academic links).

Finally, there is a paucity of leadership in senior-level government policy positions because of the influx of content-free generic managers or government appointments via bald-faced nepotism (Gendreau 1999; Gendreau, Goggin, and Fulton 2000). Such managers have a greater tendency to be overly sensitive to political dynamics with a resultant susceptibility to quick-fix, "flavour of the month" policy decisions. It is our opinion that criminal justice systems have not been immune to this problem, as evidenced by so-called innovations as boot camps and three-strikes laws.

We hope to leave the reader, however, with some optimism regarding rehabilitation. Despite the political reality, there remains a remarkable amount of faith in rehabilitation among the general public. While the social climate is now more punitive than before, extensive surveys have confirmed that the public favours the delivery of *effective* rehabilitation services to offenders and—even more thought-provoking given the current political emphasis on tax reduction—people are quite willing to pay for them, in certain instances (Applegate, Cullen, and Fisher 1997; Cullen, Fisher, and Applegate in press). It would seem then that the ball is now in corrections' court; it behooves correctional systems to do a much better job of delivering rehabilitation services. Fortunately, in Canada, organizations such as the Correctional Service of Canada have stayed the course on rehabilitation over the years and have established comprehensive auditing and accountability systems to further develop treatment programs.

While the Andrews et al. (1999) meta-analysis revealed that the reported incidence of well-designed treatment programs in the research literature has declined in the last decade, there remain some excellent examples of effective rehabilitation services (for a review, see Gendreau and Goggin 1996, 40; Wexler et al. 1999). We now wish to direct attention to two such programs currently operating in Canada.

The first of these is a program for serious juvenile delinquents developed over a 15-year period by Henggeler and his colleagues (1998) at the Family Services Research Center at the Medical University of South Carolina. Their principal modality, multisystemic therapy (MST), has some innovative features (for a synopsis, see Cullen and Gendreau in press), the most important of which is its social-ecological orientation. It views delinquents as caught up in multiple systems—family, peers, school, and community. Thus interventions are focused not only on the individual but also on the context in which he or she is situated. Service is very intensive, often entailing daily contact, sometimes on a 24-hour basis, and can last up to five months. Therapists are held strictly accountable for the results of their efforts. MST staff provide frequent professional support and consultation. The program has expanded to about 25 sites (Henggeler 1999). Evaluations indicate reductions in recidivism of as high as 50 percent for serious juvenile delinquents (e.g., Bourduin et al. 1995). Multisystemic therapy has been expanded to Canada under the aegis of Leschied and colleagues (see Leschied and Cunningham 1999) and is now being evaluated in five sites in Ontario. Initial results indicate that the Canadian MST program is producing meaningful reductions in recidivism after six months, compared with other community-based or institutional services (Leschied 1999).

The second program is based at the Rideau Correctional and Treatment Centre (Ontario Ministry of Correctional Services) in Merrickville, Ontario. The setting has a long treatment history dating back to the 1970s. The current program as evaluated by Armstrong and her colleagues (1999) closely follows the principles of effective treatment as detailed by Andrews, Gendreau, and others. The Rideau's Integrated Service Delivery Model lasts up to 15 weeks (approximately 300 hours of direct service delivery). The program addresses anger management, substance abuse, and criminal thinking/lifestyle criminogenic needs.[11] The latest evaluation reports a reduction in recidivism of approximately 20 percent, depending on the outcome measure used (Armstrong et al. 1999). These are the best outcome results in the literature of which we are aware for a stand-alone prison-based program.

Programs such as these, as well as effective rehabilitative efforts reported elsewhere, are far more cost effective than the alternatives, such as incarceration or community-based sanctions (Aos et al. 1999; Leschied and Cunningham 1999). In the long-term, despite a present-day sociopolitical context that is somewhat inhospitable to rehabilitation, the continuing cumulation of knowledge will eventually have an impact on policy in the criminal justice field (see Gendreau 1999).

SUMMARY

For approximately one hundred years, the rehabilitative ideal was the dominant correctional philosophy in North America. This ideal, as described in greater detail in Chapter 2, coincided with the development of the penitentiary system of the early 19th century. Faith in the ability of correctional systems to reform offenders through rehabilitation (e.g., counselling and parole), however, began to erode in the mid 1970s in the aftermath of prevailing social unrest; also at that time a sizeable cohort of academics began to dismiss rehabilitation as morally flawed and practically ineffective. Subsequently, two perspectives on correctional treatment emerged to supplant rehabilitation. The "get tough" movement wanted to control crime through increasing incarceration and imposing community-based sanctions (see Chapter 13). In contrast, the "justice model" insisted that neither get-tough nor rehabilitation strategies were effective policies. Rather, the only constructive policy to pursue was to ensure that justice was administered fairly (e.g., determinant sentencing). Nevertheless, for the next quarter century a substantial body of literature was generated that provided increasing testament to the fact that rehabilitative services were effective in reducing recidivism. The conclusions in this regard have been further substantiated by the application of quantitative research synthesis methods (i.e., meta-analysis), which have determined that behavioural programs that target criminogenic needs (e.g., antisocial attitudes) of high-risk offenders can reduce recidivism by about 25 percent. This, in turn, means tremendous cost savings. On the other hand, meta-analyses of get-tough programs have demonstrated conclusively that they have very little effect in reducing recidivism. While it is unlikely that the rehabilitative ideal will ever return to its former status of almost unequivocal acceptance, our current knowledge as to what works in controlling offenders' criminal behaviour leaves no doubt that rehabilitative strategies will continue to play a central role in correctional policy, particularly in Canada. In fact, Canada continues to maintain a leading role in generating both the underlying theory of effective correctional treatment and the data necessary to support it.

KEY TERMS AND CONCEPTS

correctional rehabilitation   medical model   narrative review

"get tough"   meta-analysis   principles of effective intervention

"justice model"   "nothing works"   therapeutic integrity

STUDY AND DISCUSSION QUESTIONS

1. Compare and contrast the conservative "get tough" view of rehabilitation versus the liberal "justice model" view.

2. Explain why Martinson's 1974 message was so well received.

3. Identify and discuss five of the eight characteristics of ineffective rehabilitation programs in relationship to their impact on offender recidivism.

4. Discuss the contribution of meta-analysis to the assessment of offender treatment programs.

5. "A 10 percent reduction in recidivism is of little practical value." Indicate your agreement or disagreement with this statement and why.

6. Identify and discuss the four principles of effective intervention.

WEBLINKS

Correctional Service of Canada, overview of offender treatment programs:
www.csc-scc.gc.ca/text/programs_e.shtml

Correctional Service of Canada, Results of criminal justice research:
www.csc-scc.gc.ca/text/pblct/forum/index_e.shtml

U.S. National Criminal Justice Research Service: **www.ncjrs.org**

NOTES

1. Although social upheaval was considerably less common in Canada during the same period, the following were notable events: student protests at Sir George Williams University (now Concordia) in Montreal in 1969, resulting in $2,000,000 in damages; a prison riot at Kingston Penitentiary in 1971, leaving one prisoner dead and incurring $1,000,000 damage; and the death of a hostage during a hostage-taking and riot at the British Columbia Penitentiary in New Westminster in 1975.

2. Being a member of the "Canadian school" was not a compliment in the minds of those who strongly disagreed with the Canadian psychologists' promotion of rehabilitation and meta-analysis as an analytical tool (see Logan et al. 1991). Oddly enough, Francis Cullen, a sociologist, was also assigned membership in this school, although at last sighting he still holds his American passport and is living happily in Cincinnati. We must emphasize that, during this period, American psychologists Vicki Agee, William Davidson II, and Ted Palmer, in particular, also made major contributions to advancing knowledge about effective interventions.

3. Some of the most important reviews and studies in this regard are those of Arbuthnot and Gordon (1986); Lerner, Arling, and Baird (1986); Lukin (1981); Reitsma-Street and Zager (1986); and Wormith (1984).

4. To illustrate these points see Gendreau and Ross 1979, 1987. The only thing a policy-maker could reasonably conclude from these summaries is that some treatment programs reduce recidivism, but one would not know by exactly how much or which treatments were better than others.

5. Under most circumstances—where recidivism rates are not extremely high or low and the ratio of the treatment and control group sample sizes are within 3:1—the r value can be taken at face value (Cullen and Gendreau in press). An $r = .20$ means that the difference between the two groups in recidivism rates is 20 percent or very close to it. Another way to the convey the meaning of r is by Rosenthal's (1991) BESD statistic. The recidivism rate for the treatment and control groups is computed from a base rate of 50 percent. Thus, with a correlation of $r = .20$ between treatment and re-offending, it can be concluded that the recidivism rate in the treatment group is 40 percent (50 percent minus 10 percent) compared to 60 percent in the central group (50 percent plus 10 percent).

6. We take pains to note that narrative reviews may arrive at the general truth of the matter such as that "treatment works" and that some treatments appear to be "better" than others but these conclusions lack precision and important moderators may often be lost in the shuffle (see Gendreau and Andrews 1990).

7. Readers wishing to learn more about the nature of behavioural programs should consult general source material in psychology (Masters et al. 1987; Spiegler and Guevremont 1998) and works discussing the application of this approach to offenders (Andrews and Bonta 1998, 286–288; Gendreau 1996a, 120–122).

8. There is no empirical support in the psychological behavioural change literature, by the way, for any of the above-noted methodologies (Cullen and Gendreau in press).

9. There are other perspectives. One is that prisons are "schools of crime" and a third is that they are "psychological deep freezes" and have little effect on recidivism (see Gendreau, Goggin, and Cullen, 1999, for a detailed assessment of the various perspectives).

10. Electronic monitoring programs are popular in Canada and three of these programs have been recently evaluated. They are those run by the provincial departments of corrections in British Columbia, Saskatchewan, and Newfoundland. The conclusion reached by the evaluators (Bonta, Wallace-Capretta, and Rooney 2000) is that electronic monitoring has little effect on recidivism and its availability tends to result in a net-widening effect (also see Chapter 13).

11. Of all of the programs scored on a widely used measure of treatment quality (the Correctional Program Assessment Inventory, Gendreau and Andrews 1996; see also Gendreau and Goggin 1997), the Rideau program scored the highest.

REFERENCES

Allen, F.A. 1981. *The Decline of the Rehabilitative Ideal: Penal Policy and Social Purpose.* New Haven, CT: Yale University Press.

American Friends Service Committee Working Party. 1971. *Struggle for Justice: A Report on Crime and Punishment in America.* New York: Hill and Wang.

Andrews, D.A. 1979. *The Dimensions of Correctional Counseling and Supervision Process in Probation and Parole.* Toronto: Ontario Ministry of Correctional Services.

———. 1980. Some Experimental Investigations of the Principles of Differential Association through Deliberate Manipulations of the Structure of Service Systems. *American Sociological Review* 45: 448–462.

———. 1995. The Psychology of Criminal Conduct and Effective Treatment. In J. McGuire (Ed.), *What Works: Reducing Reoffending.* West Sussex, UK: John Wiley.

Andrews, D.A., and **J. Bonta**. 1998. *The Psychology of Criminal Conduct* (2nd ed.). Cincinnati: Anderson.

Andrews, D.A., and **J.J. Kiessling**. 1980. Program Structure and Effective Correctional Practices: A Summary of the CaVIC Research. In R.R. Ross and P. Gendreau (Eds.), *Effective Correctional Treatment.* Toronto: Butterworths.

Andrews, D.A., and **J.S. Wormith**. 1989. Personality and Crime: Knowledge Destruction and Construction in Criminology. *Justice Quarterly* 6: 289–309.

Andrews, D.A., C. Dowden, and **P. Gendreau**. 1999. Clinically Relevant and Psychologically Informed Approaches to Reduced Re-offending: A Meta-Analytic Study of Human Service, Risk, Need, Responsivity, and Other Concerns in Justice Contexts. Unpublished manuscript, Carleton University.

Andrews, D.A., J. Kiessling, D. Robinson, and **S. Mickus**. 1986. The Risk Principle of Case Classification: An Outcome Evaluation with Young Adult Probationers. *Canadian Journal of Criminology* 28: 377–384.

Andrews, D.A., I. Zinger, R.D. Hoge, J. Bonta, P. Gendreau, and **F.T. Cullen**. 1990. Does Correctional Treatment Work? A Clinically Relevant and Psychologically Informed Meta-Analysis. *Criminology* 28: 369–404.

Antonowicz, D.H., and **R.R. Ross**. 1994. Essential Components of Successful Rehabilitation Programs for Offenders. *International Journal of Offender and Comparative Criminology* 38: 97–104.

Aos, S., P. Phipps, R. Barnoski, and **R. Lieb**. 1999. *The Comparative Costs and Benefits of Programs to Reduce Crime: A Review of National Research Findings with Implications for Washington State.* Olympia, WA: Washington State Institute for Public Safety.

Applegate, B.K., F.T. Cullen, and **B.S Fisher**. 1997. Public Support for Correctional Treatment: The Continuing Appeal of the Rehabilitative Ideal. *Prison Journal* 77: 237–258.

Arbuthnot, J., and **D.A. Gordon**. 1986. Behavioral and Cognitive Effects of a Moral Reasoning Development Intervention for High-Risk Behavior-Disordered Adolescents. *Journal of Consulting and Clinical Psychology* 54: 208–216.

Armstrong, B., G. Bourgon, K. Ricciuti, E. Yates, S. Boudreau, J. Finn, B. Goguen, K. Morton, E. Rivera, O. Simonyi, K. McFarlane, V. Mowat-Leger, L. Robertson, and **C. Holmes**. 1999. *Report of an Integrated Service Delivery Model: Effective Correctional Treatment Based on Risk/Need Assessments, Motivational Levels, and Sentence Length.* Merrickville, Ontario: Ontario Ministry of Correctional Services.

Bailey, W.C. 1966. Correctional Outcome: An Evaluation of 100 Reports. *Journal of Criminal Law, Criminology, and Police Science* 57: 153–160.

Beaman, A.L. 1991. An Empirical Comparison of Meta-Analytic and Traditional Reviews. *Personality and Social Psychology Bulletin* 17: 252–257.

de Beaumont, G., and **A. de Toqueville**. [1883] 1964. *On the Penitentiary System in the United States and its Application in France*. Carbondale: Southern Illinois University Press.

Binder, A., and **G. Geis**. 1984. Ad Populum Argumentation in Criminology: Juvenile Diversion As Rhetoric. *Crime and Delinquency* 30: 624–647.

Bonta, J. 1996. Risk-Needs Assessment and Treatment. In A.T. Harland (Ed.), *Choosing Correctional Options That Work*. Thousand Oaks, CA: Sage.

Bonta, J., **S. Wallace-Capretta**, and **J. Rooney**. 2000. Can Electronic Monitoring Make A Difference? An Evaluation of Three Canadian Programs. *Crime and Delinquency* 46: 61–75.

Bourduin, C.M., **B.J. Mann**, **L.T. Cone**, **S.W. Henggeler**, **B.R. Fucci**, and **R.A. Williams**. 1995. Multisystemic Treatment of Serious Juvenile Offenders: Long-Term Prevention of Criminality and Violence. *Journal of Consulting and Clinical Psychology* 63: 569–578.

Brockway, Z.R. 1871. The Ideal of a True Prison System for a State. In E.C. Wines (Ed.), *Transactions of the National Congress on Penitentiary and Reformatory Discipline*. Albany, NY: Weed, Parsons.

Clarke, R.V.G. 1985. Jack Tizard Memorial Lecture: Delinquency, Environment, and Intervention. *Journal of Child Psychology and Psychiatry* 26: 505–523.

Cohen, M.A. 1998. The Monetary Value of Saving a High-Risk Youth. *Journal of Quantitative Criminology* 14: 5–32.

Conrad, J.P. 1981. Where There's Hope There's Life. In D. Fogel and J. Hudson Eds., *Justice As Fairness: Perspectives of the Justice Model*. Cincinnati: Anderson.

Cooper, H.M., and **R. Rosenthal**. 1980. Statistical Versus Traditional Procedures for Summarizing Research Findings. *Psychological Bulletin* 87: 442–449.

Cressey, D.R. 1958. The Nature and Effectiveness of Correctional Techniques. *Law and Contemporary Problems* 23: 754–771.

Cullen, F.T., and **B. Applegate**. 1997. *Offender Rehabilitation: Effective Correctional Intervention*. Aldershot, UK: Ashgate.

Cullen, F.T., and **P. Gendreau**. 1989. The Effectiveness of Correctional Treatment: Reconsidering The "Nothing Works" Debate. In L. Goodstein, and D.L. MacKenzie (Eds.), *The American Prison: Issues in Research and Policy*. New York: Plenum.

———. In press. Assessing Correctional Rehabilitation: Policy, Practice, and Prospects. In J. Horney (Ed.), *National Institute of Justice Criminal Justice 2000: Changes in Decision Making and Discretion in the Criminal Justice System*. Washington, DC: Department of Justice, National Institute of Justice.

Cullen, F.T., and **K.E. Gilbert**. 1982. *Reaffirming Rehabilitation*. Cincinnati: Anderson.

Cullen, F.T., **B.S. Fisher**, and **B.K. Applegate**. In press. Public Opinion about Punishment and Corrections. In M. Tonry (Ed.), *Crime and Justice: A Review of Research* (Vol. 2). Chicago: University of Chicago Press.

Cullen, F.T., **J.P. Wright**, and **B.K. Applegate**. 1996. Control in the Community: The Limits of Reform? In A.T. Harland (Ed.), *Choosing Correctional Interventions That Work: Defining the Demand and Evaluating the Supply*. Newbury Park, CA: Sage.

Cullen, F.T., **P. Gendreau**, **G.R. Jarjoura**, and **J.P. Wright**. 1997. Crime and the Bell Curve: Lessons from Intelligent Criminology. *Crime and Delinquency* 43: 387–411.

Currie, E. 1998. *Crime and Punishment in America.* New York: Metropolitan Books.

Davidson, W., R. Gottschalk, L. Gensheimer, and **J. Mayer**. 1984. *Interventions with Juvenile Delinquents: A Meta-Analysis of Treatment Efficacy.* Washington, DC: National Institute of Juvenile Justice and Delinquency Prevention.

Emery, R.E., and **D. Marholin**. 1977. An Applied Behavior Analysis of Delinquency: The Irrelevancy of Relevant Behavior. *American Psychologist* 32: 860–873.

Erwin, B.J. 1986. Turning Up the Heat on Probationers in Georgia. *Federal Probation* 50: 17–24.

Garrett, C.J. 1985. Effects of Residential Treatment of Adjudicated Delinquents: A Meta-Analysis. *Journal of Research in Crime and Delinquency* 22: 287–308.

Gendreau, P. 1989. Programs That Do Not Work: A Brief Comment on Brodeur and Doob. *Canadian Journal of Criminology* 31: 133–135.

———. 1996a. The Principles of Effective Intervention with Offenders. In A.T. Harland (Ed.), *Choosing Correctional Interventions That Work: Defining the Demand and Evaluating the Supply.* Newbury Park, CA: Sage.

———. 1996b. Offender Rehabilitation: What We Know and What Needs to Be Done. *Criminal Justice and Behavior* 23: 144–161.

———. 1999. Rational Policies for Reforming Offenders. *ICCA Journal of Community Corrections* 9: 16–20.

Gendreau, P., and **D.A. Andrews**. 1979. Psychological Consultation in Correctional Agencies: Case Studies and General Issues. In J.J. Platt and R. Wicks (Eds.), *The Psychological Consultant.* New York: Grune and Stratton.

———. 1990. Tertiary Prevention: What the Meta-Analyses of the Offender Treatment Literature Tell Us About What Works. *Canadian Journal of Criminology* 32: 173–184.

Gendreau, P., and **C. Goggin**. 1996. Principles of Effective Correctional Programming. *Forum on Corrections Research* 8: 38–41.

———. 1997. Correctional Treatment: Accomplishments and Realities. In P. Van Voorhis, M. Braswell, and D. Lester (Eds.), *Correctional Counseling and Rehabilitation.* Cincinnati: Anderson.

Gendreau, P., and **R.R. Ross**. 1979. Effective Correctional Treatment: Bibliotherapy for Cynics. *Crime and Delinquency* 25: 463–489.

———. 1981a. Offender Rehabilitation: The Appeal of Success. *Federal Probation* 45: 45–48.

———. 1981b. Correctional Potency: Treatment and Deterrence on Trial. In R. Roesch and R.R. Corrado (Eds.), *Evaluation and Criminal Justice Policy.* Beverly Hills: Sage.

———. 1983/84. Correctional Treatment: Some Recommendations for Successful Intervention. *Juvenile and Family Court* 34: 31–40.

———. 1987. Revivification of Rehabilitation: Evidence from 1980s. *Justice Quarterly* 4: 349–407.

Gendreau, P., F.T. Cullen, and **J. Bonta**. 1994. Intensive Rehabilitation Supervision: The Next Generation in Community Corrections? *Federal Probation* 58: 72–78.

Gendreau, P., C. Goggin, and **F. Cullen**. 1999. *The Effects of Prison Sentences on Recidivism.* Ottawa: Solicitor General of Canada.

Gendreau, P., C. Goggin, and **B. Fulton**. 2000. Intensive Supervision in Probation and Parole. In C.R. Hollin (Ed.), *Handbook of Offender Assessment and Treatment*. Chichester, UK: John Wiley.

Gendreau, P., C. Goggin, and **P. Smith**. 1999. The Forgotten Issue in Effective Correctional Treatment: Program Evaluation. *International Journal of Offender Therapy and Comparative Criminology* 43: 180–187.

———. 2000. Generating Rational Correctional Policies: An Introduction to Advances in Cumulating Knowledge. *Corrections Management Quarterly* 4: 52–60.

Gendreau, P., C. Goggin, F.T. Cullen, and **D.A. Andrews**. 1999. Getting Tough on Offenders: Does It Work? Unpublished manuscript, Centre for Criminal Justice Studies, University of New Brunswick.

Gendreau, P., T. Little, and **C Goggin**. 1996. A Meta-analysis of the Predictors of Adult Offender Recidivism: What Works! *Criminology* 34: 575–607.

Gendreau, P., M. Paparozzi, T. Little, and **M. Goddard**. 1993. Does Punishing Smarter Work? An Assessment of the New Generation of Alternative Sanctions in Probation. *Forum on Corrections Research,* 5: 31-34.

Gibbons, D.C. 1986. Breaking Out of Prisons. *Crime and Delinquency* 32: 503–514.

Gilliard, D.K. 1999. *Prison and Jail Inmates at Midyear 1998*. Washington, DC: U.S. Department of Justice, Bureau of Justice Statistics.

Glass, G., B. McGaw, and **M.L. Smith**. 1981. *Meta-analysis in Social Research*. Beverly Hills, CA: Sage.

Greenberg, D.F. 1977. The Correctional Effects of Corrections: A Survey of Evaluations. In D.F. Greenberg (Ed.), *Corrections and Punishment*. Beverly Hills, CA: Sage.

Greenwood, P.W., K.E. Model, C.P. Rydell, and **J. Chiesa**. 1996. *Diverting Children from a Life of Crime: Measuring Costs and Benefits*. Santa Monica, CA: RAND.

Henggeler, S.W. 1999. Multisystemic Therapy: An Overview of Clinical Procedures, Outcomes, and Policy Implications. *Child Psychology and Psychiatry* 4: 2–10.

Henggeler, S.W., S.W. Schoenwald, C.M. Bourduin, M.D. Rowland, and **P.B. Cunningham**. 1998. *Multisystemic Treatment of Antisocial Behaviour in Children and Adolescents*. New York: Guilford Press.

Hunt, M. 1997. *How Science Takes Stock: The Story of Meta-Analysis*. New York: Russell Sage Foundation.

Izzo, R.L., and **R.R. Ross**. 1990. Meta-analysis of Rehabilitation Programs for Juvenile Delinquents. *Criminal Justice and Behavior* 17: 134–142.

Kassebaum, G., D.A. Ward, and **D.M. Wilner**. 1971. *Prison Treatment and Parole survival: An Empirical Assessment*. New York: John Wiley.

Lab, S.P., and **J.T. Whitehead**. 1990. From "Nothing Works" to "The Appropriate Works": The Latest Stop on the Search for the Secular Grail. *Criminology* 28: 405–417.

Latessa, E.J., and **H.E. Allen**. 1999. *Corrections in the Community*. Cincinnati: Anderson.

Lerner, K., G. Arling, and **S.C. Baird**. 1986. Client Management Classification Strategies for Case Supervision. *Crime and Delinquency* 32: 254–271.

Leschied, A.W. 1999. Personal communication with authors.

Leschied, A.W., and **A. Cunningham**. 1999. A Community-Based Alternative for High-Risk Juvenile Offenders. *Forum on Corrections Research,* 11: 25–29.

Lipsey, M.W. 1992. Juvenile Delinquency Treatment: A Meta-Analytic Inquiry into the Variability of Effects. In T.D. Cook et al. (Eds.), *Meta-Analysis for Explanation: A Casebook.* New York: Russell Sage.

————. In press. Can Rehabilitative Programs Reduce the Recidivism of Juvenile Offenders? An Inquiry into the Effectiveness of Practical Programs. *Virginia Journal of Social Policy and Law.*

Lipsey, M.W., and **D.B. Wilson**. 1993. The Efficacy of Psychological, Educational and Behavioral Treatment. *American Psychologist* 48: 1181–1209.

————. 1998. Effective Interventions for Serious Juvenile Offenders: A Synthesis of Research. In R. Loeber and David P. Farrington (Eds.), *Serious and Violent Juvenile Offenders: Risk Factors and Successful Interventions.* Thousand Oaks, CA: Sage.

Lipton, D., **R. Martinson**, and **J. Wilks**. 1975. The Effectiveness of Correctional Treatment: A Survey of Treatment Evaluation Studies. New York: Praeger.

Logan, C. H. 1972. Evaluation Research in Crime and Delinquency: A Reappraisal. *Journal of Criminal Law, Criminology and Police Science* 63: 378–387.

Logan, C.H., and **G. Gaes**. 1993. Meta-Analysis and the Rehabilitation of Punishment. *Justice Quarterly,* 10: 245–263.

Logan, C.H., **G.G. Gaes**, **M. Harer**, **C.A. Innes**, **L. Karacki**, and **W.G. Saylor**. 1991. *Can Meta-Analysis Save Correctional Rehabilitation?* Washington, DC: Federal Bureau of Prisons, Department of Justice.

Lösel, F. 1995. The Efficacy of Correctional Treatment: A Review and Synthesis of Meta-Evaluations. In J. McGuire (Ed.), *What Works: Reducing Reoffending.* West Sussex, UK: John Wiley.

Lukin, P.R. 1981. Recidivism Changes Made by Delinquents during Residential Treatment. *Journal of Research in Crime and Delinquency,* 10: 101–111.

Martinson, R. 1974. What Works? Questions and Answers about Prison Reform. *Public Interest* 35: 22–54.

————. 1976. California and the Crossroads. In R. Martinson, T. Palmer, and S. Adams (Eds.), *Rehabilitation, Recidivism and Research.* Hackensack, NJ: National Council on Crime and Delinquency.

————. 1979. New Findings, New Views: A Note of Caution Regarding Sentencing Reform. *Hofstra Law Review* 7: 243–258.

Masters, J.C., **T.G. Burish**, **S.D. Hollon**, and **D.C. Rimm**. 1987. *Behavior Therapy: Techniques and Empirical Findings.* San Diego: Harcourt Brace Jovanovich.

McGee, R.A. 1969. What's Past Is Prologue. *Annals of the American Academy of Political and Social Science* 381: 1–10.

Menninger, K. 1968. *The Crime of Punishment.* New York: Penguin.

Moon, M.M., **J.L. Sundt**, **F.T. Cullen**, and **J.P. Wright**. 2000. Is Child Saving Dead? Public Support for Juvenile Rehabilitation. *Crime and Delinquency* 46: 38–60.

Mower, O.H. 1960. *Learning Theory and Behavior*. New York: Wiley.

Palmer, T. 1975. Martinson Revisited. *Journal of Research in Crime and Delinquency* 12: 133–152.

———. 1992. *The Re-Emergence of Correctional Intervention*. Newbury Park, CA: Sage.

Pearson, F.S., **D.S. Lipton**, and **C.M. Cleland**. 1996. *Some Preliminary Findings From The CDATE Project*. Paper presented at the annual meeting of the American Society of Criminology, 20 November, Chicago.

Petersilia, J., and **S. Turner**. 1993. Intensive Probation and Parole. In M. Tonry (Ed.), *Crime and Justice: An Annual Review of Research* (Vol. 17). Chicago: University of Chicago Press.

Quay, H.C. 1977. The Three Faces of Evaluation: What Can Be Expected to Work. *Criminal Justice and Behavior* 4 : 21–25.

Redondo, S., **J. Sanchez-Meca**, and **V. Garrido**. 1999. The Influence of Treatment Programmes on the Recidivism of Juvenile and Adult Offenders: A European Meta-Analytic Review. *Psychology, Crime, and Law* 5: 251–278.

Reitsma-Street, M., and **L. Zager**. 1986. *Information on Several Classification and Treatment Systems*. Philadelphia: International Differential Treatment Association.

Rosenthal, R. 1991. *Meta-Analytic Procedures for Social Research*. Beverly Hills: Sage.

Rosnow, R.L., and **R. Rosenthal**. 1993. *Beginning Behavioral Research*. New York: Macmillan.

Ross, R.R., and **E.A. Fabiano**. 1985. *Time to Think: A Cognitive Model of Delinquency Prevention and Offender Rehabilitation*. Johnson City, TN: Institute of Social Science and Arts.

Ross, R.R., and **P. Gendreau**. 1980. Effective Correctional Treatment. Toronto: Butterworths.

Ross, R.R., and **B. McKay**. 1978. Treatment in Corrections: Requiem for a Panacea. *Canadian Journal of Criminology* 20: 279–295.

Rothman, D.J. 1980. *Conscience and Convenience: The Asylum and its Alternatives in Progressive America*. Boston: Little, Brown.

Schmidt, F. 1996. Statistical Significance Testing and Cumulative Knowledge in Psychology: Implications for Training of Researchers. *Psychological Methods* 1: 115–129.

Sechrest, L., S.O. White, and E.D. Brown (Eds.), 1979. *The Rehabilitation of Criminal Offenders: Problems and Prospects*. Washington, DC: National Academy of Sciences.

Shichor, D., and **D.K. Sechrest**. (Eds.), 1996. *Three Strikes and You're Out: Vengeance as Public Policy*. Thousand Oaks, CA: Sage.

Spiegler, M.D., and **D.C. Guevremont**. 1998. *Contemporary Behavior Therapy* (3rd ed.). Pacific Grove, CA: Brooks Cole.

Task Force on Corrections, President's Commission on Law Enforcement and Administration of Justice. 1967. *Task Force Report: Corrections*. Washington, DC: U.S. Government Printing Office.

Toby, J. 1964. Is Punishment Necessary? *Journal of Criminal Law, Criminology and Police Science* 55: 332–337.

Useem, B., and **P. Kimball**. 1991. *States of Siege: U.S. Prison Riots, 1971–1986*. New York: Oxford University Press.

Walker, S. 1985. *Sense and Nonsense about Crime: A Policy Guide.* Monterey: Brooks/Cole.

Warren, M.Q. 1969. The Case for Differential Treatment of Delinquents. *Annals of the American Academy of Political and Social Science* 62: 239–258.

Wexler, H.K., **G. De Leon**, **G. Thomas**, **D. Kressel**, and **J. Peters**. 1999. The Amity Prison TC Evaluation: Reincarceration Outcomes. *Criminal Justice and Behavior* 26: 147–167.

Whitehead, J.T., and **S.P. Lab**. 1989. A Meta-Analysis of Juvenile Correctional Treatment. *Journal of Research in Crime and Delinquency* 26: 276–295.

Wilson, D.B., **C.A. Gallagher**, and **D.L. MacKenzie**. 1999. *A Meta-analysis of Corrections-Based Education, Vocation, and Work Programs for Adult Offenders.* Unpublished manuscript.

Wines, E.C. (Ed.). 1871. Declaration of Principles Adopted and Promulgated by the Congress. *Transactions of the National Congress on Penitentiary and Reformatory Discipline.* Albany, NY: Weed Parsons.

Wormith, J.S. 1984. Attitude and Behavior Change of Correctional Clientele: A Three-Year Follow-up. *Criminology* 22: 595–618.

Wright, W.F., and **M.C. Dixon**. 1977. Community Prevention and Treatment of Juvenile Delinquency. *Journal of Research in Crime and Delinquency* 14: 35–67.

12

CONDITIONAL RELEASE

Tim Segger and Darryl Plecas
University College of the Fraser Valley
Abbotsford, British Columbia

LEARNING OBJECTIVES

After reading this chapter, you should be able to:

- Describe the historical context from which conditional release in present-day Canada has emerged;

- Know the legal structure for authority and responsibility under which parole and other forms of conditional release are granted to incarcerated offenders in Canada;

- Understand the nature and purpose of conditional release in Canada as part of an overall strategy for correctional sentence administration aimed at reintegrating offenders into the community;

- Appreciate the roles of risk assessment and risk management as they apply to conditional release decision-making and offender supervision, and to cases involving special types of offenders;

- Recognize the differences among various forms of conditional release, how and when offenders become eligible for each of them, and how decisions are made by the releasing authority;

- Be aware of conditional release success rates and know what happens in cases of failure; and

- Describe the role for victims in the conditional release process.

Our greatest glory consists, not in never falling, but in rising every time we fall.

—Confucius

There is perhaps very little in corrections that is so misunderstood by Canadians as "conditional release"—the release of inmates back into the community, in one form or another, before the end of their prison sentences. Misconceptions abound about which inmates get released, at which point in their sentence they get released, the reasons for their release, and just who it is that decides upon the release (Conroy 1999; Roberts 1993; also see Chapter 3).

Just why these misconceptions exist is not clear. Part of the problem may be that usually only cases of failure of conditional release make the news; very little is reported about rates of success (see Chapter 3). This imbalance becomes more skewed because reported cases of failure are often those with very horrible consequences. Thus our view of conditional release becomes framed by the emotions aroused by, and particulars of, those consequences, rather than the particulars of conditional release overall.

Although one could dedicate a whole textbook or a complete course to the study of conditional release, this chapter presents a concise but comprehensive introduction to conditional release in Canada today. It is hoped that, in meeting the learning objectives listed above, readers will become well informed about this aspect of Canadian corrections, and will be critical consumers of information about conditional release presented in the mass media.

CONDITIONAL RELEASE: A BRIEF HISTORY

Although parole has existed in Canada for the last 100 years, having been established in 1899 under the *Ticket of Leave Act*, the possibility of attaining release from prison before serving one's full sentence dates back to the *Penitentiary Act* of 1868 (see Chapter 2). This legislation built upon earlier models in Ireland and in Australia where the Scottish-born Captain Alexander Maconachie (1787–1860) was among the first to tie early release of offenders to positive behaviour in prison. The notion of "earned remission" formed the basis for another form of conditional release in Canada, "mandatory supervision."[1] In 1901, "dominion parole officers" took up the tasks associated with pre-release assessment and, in 1905, the Salvation Army became involved in parole work, including assisting inmates in their reintegration into the community. This tradition continues to this day as such private agencies as the Salvation Army, the John Howard and Elizabeth Fry Societies, Catholic charities, and Native organizations such as the Native Clan Organization continue to provide parole services under contract to the Correctional Service of Canada.

Tickets of leave were granted by the Remission Service, created within the Department of Justice. In 1959, the *Ticket of Leave Act* was replaced by the *Parole Act*, under which the National Parole Board was established and the Remission Service dissolved. Parole officers were employed by the National Parole Service under the auspices of the Board. In 1966, the Board was removed from the Ministry of Justice and placed under the authority of the Ministry of the Solicitor General, along with Canadian Penitentiary Service and the RCMP. Based upon a recommendation of the Task Force on the Creation of an Integrated Canadian Corrections Service in 1977, the Parole Service was separated from the Parole Board and merged with the Canadian Penitentiary Service to create the Correctional Service of Canada within the Ministry of the Solicitor General.

The *Parole Act* provided the National Parole Board with the authority to grant day and full parole to offenders in federal, provincial, and territorial institutions across Canada. A 1977 amendment to the Act permitted provinces to create their own parole boards with jurisdiction over inmates serving sentences in provincial jails. There are currently three such boards in existence: the British Columbia Board of Parole, the Ontario Board of Parole, and the Commission québécoise des liberations conditionelles.

THE PURPOSE OF CONDITIONAL RELEASE

If all offenders sent to prison were sentenced to spend the remainder of their lives behind bars, there would be no need for any form of conditional release. The fact is, however, that all but a very few of those serving time in Canada can look forward to a specific date at which their sentences will end, which is the date the **warrant of committal** issued by the sentencing judge expires, at which point they return to the outside community.

Suppose for a moment that there were no such thing as parole or statutory release. How would things be different if inmates were to re-enter the community only at the very end of their sentences? Keep in mind that, as of the **warrant expiry date** ex-offenders are instantly free: they are free to go where they wish, associate with whomever they want, and generally do as they please. This is true even of ex-inmates who may still have obvious problems and those whom officials believe have a high potential for re-offending. There is nothing that correctional officials can do to monitor or help the person because, once the sentence is completed, they have no jurisdiction, no authority over, and no responsibility for the individual. In this sense, both the offender and the community are on their own.

Unless it can be assumed that newly released inmates pose no further threat to the community, or require no further assistance in making the transition from a society of captive offenders to society at large, then it would seem to be in the best interests of both the community and the offender to provide a program of supervised and assisted reintegration into that community. Such a period of reintegration, however, would have to occur prior to the end of the sentence since, after that, the legal authority to supervise no longer exists.

From this perspective, conditional release serves quite a different primary purpose than most people think. The primary purpose is not merely to provide opportunities for early release for incarcerated offenders who appear to be low security risks and who have otherwise shown themselves to be worthy. Rather, assuming that any prisoner reintegrating into the community is likely to have some untreated or transitional problems, and that many prisoners will be threats to the safety and security of ordinary citizens to some degree, the primary purpose of conditional release is to facilitate reintegration in a fashion that enhances ex-prisoners' likelihood of success and reduces both short- and long-term risk to the community.

There are also some secondary purposes that are served by the conditional release portion of an inmate's sentence:

- Conditional release provides an important enhancement to rehabilitation programs offered inside prison. For instance, an inmate who has participated in a drug, alcohol, cognitive skills, or parenting program in the institution will gain much greater benefit from such programs when they are supplemented by associated community-based programs of a follow-up and reinforcement nature.

- To the extent that conditional release is structured to provide inmates with the possibility of early release, it can motivate them to participate in rehabilitation programs in the first place. The more committed offenders are to engaging in such programs, the more productively their time is spent, and the more likely it is that their risk to public upon release is effectively diminished.

- Conditional release helps ensure that prison terms are used as our lawmakers intended—as a last resort, imposed only when it is felt that the goals of sentencing cannot be met safely through alternative measures. Remember that the primary role of incarceration in sentencing is not punishment, but public safety. Judges sentence individuals to prison largely because they have attributes *at the time of sentencing* that suggest they would pose an unacceptable risk to the public if not locked up. Inmates can, however, by participating in rehabilitation programs, change these attributes and begin to develop more positive ones that will enable them to live in the community without placing it at risk. Conditional release provides the means by which the possibility of such change is respected, while continuing to address concerns about public safety by providing post-release supervision by corrections officials with the power to return the offender to prison.

THE AUTHORITY TO GRANT CONDITIONAL RELEASE

As with the detention of offenders, the legal authority for their release is provided for in a general way by the Constitution and the Charter of Rights and Freedoms. More specific references to forms of conditional release are found in the *Corrections and Conditional Release Act* (CCRA) and, to a lesser extent, the Criminal Code of Canada. As an administrative tribunal constituted under the CCRA, the National Parole Board exercises the authority to grant, deny, or revoke parole, or to detain adult offenders otherwise eligible for statutory release (see Types of Conditional Release below). The Board has no jurisdiction over young offenders, except for those sentenced in adult court.

It is worth noting that in Canada, by law, all adult offenders must be considered for conditional release. While this does not mean that all will be released before their warrant expiry date, it does mean that policies, procedures, and agencies must be in place to ensure that the requirements of the law are met. In fulfilling these requirements, the National Parole Board and the Correctional Service of Canada are accountable to Parliament and thus, ultimately, to the Canadian people. Similarly, provincial and territorial correctional and releasing agencies are accountable, through their solicitors or attorneys general, to their respective legislatures.

The organizational structure of conditional release decision-making at the federal level is outlined in Figure 12.1. In general, the National Parole Board is responsible for decisions regarding day parole and full parole, while the Correctional Service has granting authority over forms of temporary absence (see Types of Release and also Special Cases below). The Board's national office is in Ottawa and each of the five federal administrative regions—Pacific (British Columbia and Yukon), Prairie (Alberta, Saskatchewan, Manitoba, Northwest Territories, and Nunavut), Ontario, Québec, and the Atlantic (Maritime provinces and Newfoundland)—has a Board office headed by a Senior Board Member. Note that while the Board operates autonomously of Correctional Service, the parole officers, whether based in correctional institutions or in the community, are part of the organization of the Correctional Service of Canada.

Parole board members, both federal and provincial, are appointed for fixed terms by order-in-council, that is, by Cabinet. Board members are selected to serve, on either a part-time or full-time basis, as representatives of their communities. Previous experience related to criminal justice is not required; however, extensive training for members is provided.

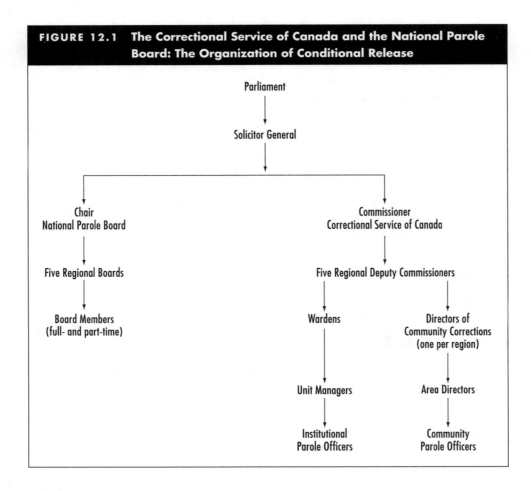

FIGURE 12.1   The Correctional Service of Canada and the National Parole Board: The Organization of Conditional Release

TYPES OF CONDITIONAL RELEASE

Conditional release is very deliberately a gradual process for most offenders; actually beginning the day the offender arrives in prison. Once the offender has been sentenced, the eligibility dates for various kinds of conditional release are set (see the list below), and the offender is encouraged to develop a plan of rehabilitation with activities focused on developing suitability for gradual reintegration into the community. Within this "correctional plan," offenders will take their first step back into the community in a very limited way. Actual releases would likely begin with escorted day passes. Assuming these are completed successfully, the offender would then move to unescorted passes and, with success in these, to releases allowing daily absences from prison on a regular basis for a limited period of time. These conditional releases are to be undertaken in concert with the inmate's involvement in rehabilitative programs available inside the prison. However, in cases such as Paul Bernardo and Clifford Olson, while these offenders have participated in rehabilitation programs, because of the severity of their offences and public outrage, it is unlikely that they will receive full parole.[2]

This process will be less gradual for some offenders than others and, in some cases, offenders are not suitable for passes of any kind, let alone any form of parole. Nonetheless, once such offenders as these have served two thirds of their sentences, they are usually placed on a form of conditional release known as statutory release.

Having a variety of forms of conditional release increases the likelihood that reintegration will be gradual, and enhances the ability to assess the offender's readiness for full conditional release. This is an important consideration in terms of both the offender's progress in the correctional plan and the assessment of risk to the community if he or she were to be released. The types of conditional release include:

- **Temporary Absences:** A *temporary pass* is what most people know as a "day pass," and authorizes an inmate to leave the prison to attend some nearby location for a specific purpose. These include:
  - *Medical temporary absences*, granted to allow inmates to get medical tests or receive medical treatment not available inside the prison;
  - *Administrative temporary absences*, allowing inmates to visit social agencies to help them prepare for release in accordance with their correctional plan;
  - *Compassionate temporary absences*, permitting inmates to attend funerals or visit seriously ill family members; and
  - *Reintegration temporary absences*, granted to aid in the inmate's personal development, allowing him or her to strengthen family relationships or participate in community service activities in keeping with the correctional plan. The majority of this type of pass is escorted "group temporary absences" in which the offender is part of a group of inmates out together under the supervision of an authorized escort.

While such passes are most commonly granted for a few hours during the day, they can also be granted for evening activities and for as long as 15 days (or an unlimited time if the pass is for medical reasons). Whatever the length of the pass or the reason it was given, it may be either escorted or unescorted. **Escorted temporary absences** are completed under the escort of a correctional employee or a trained volunteer authorized by the prison warden. Inmates on **unescorted temporary absences** are permitted to leave the prison on their own, without an escort of any kind. Unescorted passes are not available to maximum-security inmates.

Over the five-year period from 1991/92 to 1995/96, temporary absences were granted to approximately 7,400 inmates per year and, as Table 12.1 shows, 90 percent of the average annual number granted (46,691) were escorted. The number of federal prisoners receiving temporary absences over the period remained fairly stable; however, the penitentiary population in Canada rose by 14 percent during the same time. Thus, the grant rate has actually declined, due in most part to a decline in the use of reintegration temporary absences (Solicitor General of Canada 1998).

- **Work Releases:** A *work release* allows an inmate to leave the prison to participate in a community service or structured work program. Inmates normally leave in the morning and return to the institution in the evening. Although inmates need to be eligible for unescorted temporary absences before they can be granted a work release, all work releases are completed under the escort of a correctional officer. Work releases

TABLE 12.1 **Average Number of Temporary Absences Granted Per Year[a], 1991/92–1995/96**

Purpose of Absence	# Escorted	# Unescorted	Total Temporary Absences	% of Total
Medical	12,993	149	13,142	28%
Administrative	1,426	187	1,613	3%
Compassionate	740	59	797	2%
Reintegration	26,672	4,467	31,139	67%
Overall average	41,831	4,860	46,691	100%
% of total	90%	10%	100%	

[a] All figures rounded.

SOURCE: Adapted from Solicitor General of Canada 1998.

can be for as many as 60 days and are renewable, although a recent review of their use indicates that most offenders rarely work more than a few days (Grant and Beal 1998). Prior to the introduction of the CCRA in 1992, work releases were granted as a form of day parole to about 350 offenders per year. Since that time, about 300 per year have been granted specifically as work releases (Solicitor General of Canada 1998).

- **Day Parole:** *Day parole* is similar to work release in that it normally involves leaving the prison in the morning and returning in the evening. It differs, however, in that the inmate's activities on day parole must be specifically intended to prepare him or her for either full parole or statutory release. Although supervised by a parole officer, the inmates are not under escort. Day paroles are granted for periods of up to four months, although renewals are possible so as to extend the time to a maximum of one year.

As was the case with temporary absences, the number of day paroles granted declined over the five-year period from 1991/92 to 1995/96, although the grant rate actually increased. As Table 12.2 shows, while most offenders who applied for day parole received it, the number of applicants dropped substantially. In reviewing this decline, the CCRA Working Group (Solicitor General of Canada 1998) suggested that part of the reason may involve changes to day parole eligibility introduced with the CCRA, which moved the eligibility date from one sixth of the sentence to six months prior to full parole eligibility. The Working Group also cited the use of work releases, which were previously classed as day paroles, and the fact that many inmates eligible for accelerated parole review (see Full Parole below) would not bother to apply for day parole since they are within months of being granted full parole anyway.

In July 1997, with the passage of Bill C-55, an amendment to the CCRA provided for first time non-violent offenders to be eligible for day parole at one sixth of their sentence (as opposed to six months before full parole eligibility). As a result, it is reasonable to expect an increase in the number of day paroles applied for and granted.

- **Full Parole:** Once granted *full parole*, inmates can leave the institution and spend the remainder of their sentences in the community under the supervision of a community-based parole officer. They are required to comply with all instructions

TABLE 12.2   Number of Paroles Applied For and Granted Per Year, 1992/93–1996/97[a]

Fiscal Year	Day Paroles Applied For[b]	Day Paroles Granted	Grant Rate
1992/93	7891 (61%)	4129 (32%)	52%
1993/94	6779 (49%)	3544 (26%)	52%
1994/95	6537 (45%)	3143 (22%)	48%
1995/96	5385 (37%)	3164 (22%)	59%
1996/97	4055 (28%)	2693 (19%)	66%
Overall Average	6129 (44%)	3335 (24%)	54%

[a] All figures rounded.

[b] Percentage in brackets represents the percentage of all federal prisoners.

SOURCE: Adapted from Solicitor General of Canada 1998.

of that officer and to abide by all conditions set down by the National Parole Board. Such conditions will vary from case to case, depending on the history of the offender involved, and (as per section 133(3) of the *Corrections and Conditional Release Act*) may include any conditions the Board "considers reasonable and necessary in order to protect society and to facilitate the successful reintegration into society of the offender." In general, these conditions place restrictions on where the offender can live and travel, whom he or she can associate with, and which activities require special permission. They may also require, for example, that the parolee abstain from alcohol, attend a program, receive treatment, or report to the police on a regular basis.

Many federal offenders receive full parole as a result of **accelerated parole review**. This review, introduced in 1992 as part of the CCRA, is designed to expedite the conditional release process for non-violent offenders considered to be at low risk for re-offending. To qualify for accelerated parole review, inmates must be serving their first federal sentence (two years or more) and must not have been convicted of a Schedule I or a Schedule II offence; also, their parole eligibility date must not have been extended by judicial determination (see Special Cases below). The Board reviews each case prior to the eligibility date without a hearing (called a "paper decision"). Unless a risk assessment leads the Board to believe the inmate is likely to commit a violent offence before the sentence expires, release on full parole is authorized as of the eligibility date.

Table 12.3 shows the number of paroles granted over the five years from 1992/93 to 1996/97. Note that the number of regular paroles granted declined significantly over the period while the number of accelerated parole grants remained fairly stable. The overall decline in full paroles is interesting, especially since, as noted earlier, the federal prison population grew by 14 percent between 1991/92 and 1995/96. Furthermore, the decline is not related to Board decision-making; as Table 12.3 also shows, the overall grant rate was at its highest in 1996/97, when the actual number of full paroles granted was at its lowest for the period. It is likely that this difference is due to the drop in applications, due in turn to a declining proportion of eligible inmates in the Canadian penitentiary population.

| **TABLE 12.3** | **Number of Accelerated and Regular Full Paroles Granted Per Year[a], 1992/93–1996/97** | | | |

Fiscal Year	# Accelerated Full Paroles Granted	# Regular Full Paroles Granted	Total Full Paroles Granted	Accelerated Paroles as a % of all Full Paroles
1992/93	350 (89%)	2225 (34%)	2575 (37%)	14%
1993/94	1070 (86%)	1528 (27%)	2598 (38%)	41%
1994/95	1147 (80%)	1080 (20%)	2227 (33%)	52%
1995/96	1081 (83%)	917 (19%)	1998 (34%)	54%
1999/97	1052 (83%)	685 (23%)	1707 (40%)	62%
Overall Average	940	1287 (26%)	2227 (34%)	42%

[a] All figures rounded. Grant rate in parentheses.
SOURCE: Adapted from Solicitor General of Canada 1998.

- **Full Parole (Exceptional Cases):** Section 121 of the CCRA provides for inmates to be released for reasons other than those for which parole is normally granted. Specifically, the Act states that parole may be granted to an offender:

  a) who is terminally ill;

  b) whose physical or mental health is likely to suffer serious damage if the offender continues to be held in confinement;

  c) for whom continued confinement would constitute an excessive hardship that was not reasonably foreseeable at the time the offender was sentenced; or

  d) who is the subject of an order to be surrendered under the *Extradition Act* or the *Fugitive Offenders Act* and to be detained until surrendered.

  Offenders granted parole under this section of the CCRA must be eligible for full parole and, in the view of the National Parole Board, must not be individuals who would place the community at risk. Those inmates serving an indeterminate sentence, a life sentence, or life commuted from a death sentence are not eligible for full parole under these conditions.

- **Statutory Release:** *Statutory release* is similar to accelerated parole review in that inmates need not apply for it. If they are not already on full parole and they have served two thirds of their sentence, it is normally granted automatically. The only instance in which this is not the case is where the Correctional Service of Canada has reasonable grounds to believe that an offender, if released, is likely to commit a serious drug offence, a sex offence against a child, or an offence causing death or serious harm to another person. Such cases are referred to the National Parole Board, which may decide to detain the inmate, rendering him or her ineligible for statutory release. Offenders released on statutory release are under the supervision of a parole officer and must abide by the conditions of statutory release. In some cases, those conditions may include a **residency requirement** for the offender to reside in a community correctional centre or a psychiatric facility. In 1995/96, the first full year in which this requirement was in force, it was applied in 18 percent of the statutory releases granted by the Board (Solicitor General of Canada 1998).

TABLE 12.4	Number of Offenders Reaching Statutory Release Date and Percentage Actually Placed[a], 1992/92–1996/97	
Fiscal Year	**# Reaching Statutory Release Date**	**% of Offenders Actually Placed**
1992/93	3872	94%
1993/94	4183	84%
1994/95	4847	82%
1995/96	4920	92%
1997/98	5225	92%
Overall Average	4609	88%

[a] All figures rounded.

SOURCE: Adapted from Solicitor General of Canada 1998.

Table 12.4 shows the percentage of those reaching their statutory release date who were actually placed on this form of release between 1992/93 and 1996/97. Note that the number of offenders reaching statutory release date increased each year and that over the five-year period 12 percent of them were not released. Some offenders waive their right to statutory release, preferring to stay in prison until they can be released without any form of supervision. Most of the 12 percent, however, is made up of those offenders determined to be an undue risk to the community and thus deemed ineligible by the Board (Solicitor General of Canada 1998).

PROVINCIAL INMATES AND PAROLE

As mentioned above, besides the National Parole Board, there are three provincial boards of parole in Canada: The British Columbia Board of Parole, the Ontario Board of Parole, and the Commission québécoise des liberations conditionelles. Thus inmates in provincial prisons serving sentences of less than two years in these three provinces who wish to be considered for conditional release must apply to the provincial board with jurisdiction in their case. All other provincial or territorial inmates, like federal inmates, must apply to the National Parole Board.

For a number of reasons, as a form of conditional release for provincial inmates, parole is not utilized nearly as much as for their federal counterparts (Brunet 1998). One reason is that provincial inmates are able to earn remission; up to one day can be deducted from a provincial sentence for each two days served. If discharged at the two-thirds point, the sentence is considered to be over; there is no provision for supervision after release. In addition, provincially served prison sentences tend to be fairly short[3] and inmates must be serving over six months to be eligible to apply, and successful provincial parole applicants must forfeit their earned remission to be under supervision until their warrant expiry date. Furthermore, increasingly, provincial inmates are being released on forms of extended temporary absences, which can last until the discharge date (and thus still allowing the inmate to retain all remission earned) and which can be granted by correctional officials without requiring parole board involvement (Hatch-Cunningham and Griffiths 1997). Thus parole is more commonly a process involving federal as opposed to provincial offenders (see Box 12.1).

BOX 12.1   Conditional Release in a Global Context

Interview with Yvon Dandurand, who is the Director of Policy Development and Human Rights, International Centre for Criminal Law Reform and Criminal Justice Policy in Vancouver. Dr. Dandurand is also a professor in the Department of Criminology and Criminal Justice at University College of the Fraser Valley in Abbotsford, British Columbia.

How common are conditional release programs outside of Canada?

Imprisonment is the most widely used form of criminal sanction around the world, regardless of the type of legal system or level of development of a country. It is applied more than any other form of punishment. Therefore, you might expect conditional release programs to be quite common. In fact, however, parole is not widely used around the world. One finds it mostly in developed western countries.

In most other countries, there are various kinds of administrative mechanisms permitting the lawful release of offenders from prison for humanitarian reasons or for reasons relating to the management of the prison population. Such release decisions are made in some cases by some form of judicial authority; in other cases, correctional officials make them. In many instances, these decisions may be made quite arbitrarily. Most of the administrative regimes governing the release of offenders in other countries have little in common with parole, as we know it in Canada.

Do you think that parole is generally perceived as an important part of a modern criminal justice system?

During the past two decades, there has been a fair amount of activity promoting community sanctions in general. Parole systems have been developed recently in some Eastern European countries as part of efforts to modernize their criminal justice system. There also is the Association of Parole Authorities International, which promotes the concept and facilitates exchanges of ideas between jurisdictions. Other organizations, such as the United Nations Interregional Crime and Justice Research Institute, actively promote the use of probation and parole. If you add the fact that the inflation of prison population creates a serious challenge to policy-makers and governments, you may not be surprised to find out that the concept is gaining in popularity. When it does not do so as a means to facilitate the successful reintegration of offenders into the community, it certainly does as a means to reduce prison overcrowding. In September 1999, for instance, the Council of Europe Committee of Ministers adopted a recommendation inviting member states to make more frequent use of early parole to reduce the length of sentences actually served.

Are there any international standards concerning the release of offenders?

In international law, there are several human rights instruments pertaining to the rights of persons in conflict with law.

The most important ones are the Universal Declaration of Human Rights and the International Covenant on Civil and Political Rights. There are also the United Nations Standard Minimum Rules for the Treatment of Prisoners, adopted in 1957. All of those human rights instruments set limits on what the state can legally or legitimately do to people in conflict with the law. These instruments are meant to promote the rule of law in making decisions about offenders and to combat arbitrariness in such decisions.

Discretionary decisions are not necessarily arbitrary, but they can be. That is likely why human rights advocates often see them as particularly suspicious. Since parole decisions always involve some level of discretionary decision-making, they always represent a potential threat to the human, civil, and political rights of inmates. Parole authorities have had to address concerns regarding the equity, clarity, and predictability of their decisions. During the last decade or so, countries with a properly developed parole system have had to better articulate the nature of the process and the criteria, under the law, that must guide discretionary release decision-making.

During the 1980s there were various calls internationally for more noncustodial sentences. In 1985, the seventh United Nations Congress for the Prevention of Crime and the Treatment of Offenders recommended that countries take measures to decrease their reliance on prison as a form of punishment, to reduce their prison population, to develop alternatives to imprisonment, and to promote the successful reintegration of offenders into the community.

It was, and continues to be, widely believed that the increase in prison populations and prison overcrowding represent the most serious threats to the rights of inmates and the efficient management of prisons.

In 1990, the United Nations also adopted the Standard Minimum Rules for Non-Custodial Measures (also known as The Tokyo Rules). These are non-binding rules that recommend releasing offenders from an institution to a non-custodial program be considered at the earliest possible stage, and that post-sentencing dispositions be subject to review by a judicial or other competent independent authority, upon application by the offender.

The public view of conditional release in Canada is not very positive. Is that also the case elsewhere?

I would say that the credibility of criminal justice institutions is, in many countries, at an all-time low. In these countries, and at times also in Canada, the justice system is perceived by large segments of the population as unresponsive to its demand for safety. That often generates a public sense of frustration and leads to regrettable developments in criminal justice policy. Certain parole decisions or notorious cases of offender recidivism while on parole can quickly exacerbate the public's feeling of insecurity or its frustration with the criminal justice system.

Parole has been used in Canada for 100 years. Do you think that parole has a future?

So far, parole systems around the world have survived several attempts to abolish them. You may remember that not so long ago, in 1986, the Canadian Sentencing Commission adopted the view that the length of time an offender spends in custody should be fixed at the time of sentencing. The Commission recommended the abolition of full parole, except in cases of life sentences. The recommendation was well received by many sectors of Canadian society but was rejected by the Canadian government.

In the United States, 15 states have abolished their parole boards. Three other states have reinstituted parole boards after eliminating them. At the federal level, the role of parole has been severely limited. Many states, with the encouragement of federal Truth-In-Sentencing Incentive Grants, have adopted "truth in sentencing" laws, providing partial funding for prison construction in exchange for setting limits on the use of parole. Despite these initiatives, however, the number of adults on parole in the United States continues to grow.

The cynical view, of course, is that parole will survive because it is a partial cure to the chronic problem of prison overcrowding. Some would argue that the main argument in favour of parole is that it is cheaper than building new prisons and that, to some extent, it allows correctional authorities to regulate the size of the prison population.

Personally, I believe that parole has a future, at least in Canada. Whether it does or not will probably depend largely on whether the public better understands what the parole system is trying to achieve and how it contributes to the longer term protection of society. In that sense, I suppose that the survival of the parole system will also depend largely on the quality of the release decisions that are being made.

WHEN OFFENDERS ARE ELIGIBLE FOR RELEASE

The dates at which offenders are eligible for most types of conditional release are important because they provide calendar markers as offenders develop their correctional plan. At the very least, offenders will have the opportunity to be reviewed for conditional release at these times in their sentence—even if correctional authorities do not support any application they might make for release. At the same time, because these dates are staggered, they set the tone for conditional release being viewed as a process by which offenders would reintegrate into the community in a gradual fashion. The dates that most offenders are eligible for each type of release are shown by Table 12.5 (see also Special Cases below).

SPECIAL CASES

While the general criteria for conditional release eligibility apply to most cases, there are some special cases in which these criteria are modified. These modifications have been undertaken due to considerations of risk that relate to each type of case.

Life Sentences

As implied by the term, a life sentence ends with the death of the offender, as opposed to a set date. Since parole eligibility and statutory release dates are normally calculated as a fraction of the time to the warrant expiry date, statutory release does not apply, and the parole

| Table 12.5 | When Offenders Are Eligible for Conditional Release[a] | | |

Category of Offenders	For Unescorted Temporary Absences	For Day Parole	For Full Parole
Serving less than two years	not eligible	$1/6$ of prison sentence	$1/3$ of prison sentence
First-time federal sentence, non-violent offender	at the greater of 6 months or $1/2$ of PED[b]	at the greater of 6 months or $1/2$ of PED	directed release at $1/3$ of prison sentence
Serving 2 years or more, but not life or an indeterminate sentence	at the greater of 6 months or $1/2$ of PED (discretion of the Warden)	at the greater of 6 months or 6 months prior to PED	at the lesser of 7 years or $1/3$ of prison sentence
Sentenced as a Schedule I or Schedule II offender	at the greater of 6 months or $1/2$ of PED (discretion of the NPB)	at the greater of 6 months or 6 months prior to PED	at the lesser of 10 years or $1/2$ of prison sentence
Serving an indeterminate sentence	at 3 years	at 3 years	at 3 years
Serving life for an offence other than murder	at 4 years	at the greater of 6 months or 6 months prior to PED	at 7 years
Serving life for first-degree murder	at 22 years	at 22 years	at 25 years
Serving life for second-degree murder	at 3 years prior to PED	at 3 years prior to PED	at 10–15 years as determined by sentencing judge
Young offender sentenced to life in adult court for murder	at $1/2$ of time prior to PED	at $1/5$ of time prior to PED	at 5–10 years as determined by sentencing judge

[a] Eligibility dates are specified in the *Corrections and Conditional Release Act* and in the Criminal Code.

[b] PED refers to full parole eligibility date.

1. Offenders classified as maximum security are not eligible for unescorted temporary absences.

2. Offenders are eligible for escorted temporary absences the day they begin their sentences.

3. Offenders, except those serving life or indeterminate sentences, are eligible for statutory release after serving two thirds of their sentence (unless determined ineligible through a detention review conducted by the National Parole Board). Offenders serving life or indeterminate sentences are not eligible for statutory release.

eligibility date for those serving life sentences is determined differently. Some offenders convicted of first-degree murder are not eligible for full parole until they have served at least 25 years (as determined at time of sentencing). Others, sentenced to life for second-degree murder, will have their parole eligibility date set by the judge at somewhere between 10 and 25 years. Three years before that date, they become eligible for day parole (day parole eligibility date) and unescorted temporary absences, which require approval by the National Parole Board. While unescorted temporary absences can be approved at any time at the discretion of the Correctional Service, they are also subject to Board approval. Also, offenders who have served 15 years of a life sentence, with a minimum incarceration period of over 15 years set by the judge, can apply for a **judicial review** of their parole eligibility. If a review is allowed, a judge and jury in the jurisdiction in which the offender was convicted will decide whether to reduce the remaining time to be served before parole eligibility date (see section 745 of the Criminal Code). This is sometimes referred to as the "faint hope clause" (Roberts 2000). It is important to keep in mind that even if the jury decides to amend the parole eligibility date (and the decision must be unanimous), the offender must still apply to the National Parole Board and convince it that society will not be placed at risk if conditional release is granted.

In cases where offenders are sentenced to life with no stipulated minimum to be served, the parole eligibility date is automatically set at seven years and day parole eligibility date at six and a half years. These lifers are eligible for unescorted temporary absences at four years and escorted temporary absences at any time, at the discretion of the Correctional Service of Canada, with Board approval. For young offenders sentenced to life in prison in an adult court, eligibility for full parole will be set by the judge at some point between 5 and 10 years into the sentence with an eligibility date for day parole and unescorted temporary absences date set at four fifths of the time served. The Board must also approve escorted temporary absences for these offenders, and, as with all adult lifers, there is no statutory release date.

Indeterminate Sentences

Those designated by the courts as **dangerous offenders** (see Box 12.2) are sentenced to an **indeterminate sentence**, which has no set warrant expiry date. These inmates are not eligible for statutory release and are first eligible for parole after serving seven years. If they are denied parole at this time, the Board must review their case at least every two years thereafter. They must also apply to the National Parole Board for all forms of temporary absence.

Long-Term Offenders

Long-term offender is a special designation for sex offenders who, the courts have decided on the basis of a special hearing, are likely to re-offend after completing their sentences. For these inmates, the judge at such a hearing can specify a post-release period of up to 10 years of supervision by Correctional Service case management officers.

Judicial Determination

In some cases where the offences are deemed by the courts to be serious enough, the judge may extend the period of parole date eligibility as part of the sentence. Thus, for Schedule I

BOX 12.2	"Dangerous Offender"—1953

The 1953 Criminal Code used the term "habitual offender" to identify dangerous offenders. Section 660(2) of the Code stated: ". . . an accused is an habitual criminal if

a) he has previously, since attaining the age of eighteen years, on at least three separate and independent occasions been convicted of an indictable offence for which he was liable to imprisonment for five years or more and is leading persistently a criminal life, or

b) he has been previously sentenced to preventive detention."

(serious violent crime) and Schedule II (serious drug crime) offences, the parole eligibility date may be delayed by **judicial determination** until one half (as opposed to the usual one third) of the sentence has been served. Of 632 offenders sentenced to prison for Schedule I and Schedule II offences the four and a half years from 1992 to 1997, judicial determination was applied in only 3.5 percent of the cases (Solicitor General of Canada 1998).

DETERMINING SUITABILITY FOR RELEASE

Not everyone who is placed on conditional release is ready for reintegration. Indeed, most offenders placed on statutory release have not been assessed as being ready for release. If they had been viewed as good candidates for release, they likely would have been placed on parole. But even in the case of temporary absences and day parole, the release is not always granted under the premise that the offender is entirely ready for reintegration; rather, the release may be granted because it improves the offender's suitability for full parole.

The matter of deciding which offenders are suitable for conditional release begins with an assessment of the offender's needs and the level of risk identified when the individual first arrives in prison, and with the steps that he or she takes to address those needs while progressing through the sentence. The process of deciding always involves a team decision, based on information drawn from many sources, on the input and recommendations of several individuals, and with attention to many different issues. These issues include:

1. The offender's current offence and criminal history overall (e.g., What is the statistical likelihood of the offender committing further offences in light of what is known about previous offenders with similar criminal histories?);

2. The significance of drugs and alcohol in the offender's past and future (e.g., Does the offender have a drug or alcohol problem? In what ways, if any, are drugs and alcohol associated with the offender's criminal behaviour?);

3. The offender's history with respect to psychological, psychiatric, and physical problems (e.g., Have any apparent problems been sufficiently addressed?);

4. The offender's history and association with violence (e.g., Does the offender have a problem with managing anger or a tendency towards violence?);

5. The offender's social, family, employment, and educational history (e.g., Does the offender have a stable background or a dysfunctional one?);

6. The offender's history of non-compliance with the criminal justice system (e.g., Does the offender have a history of failing to appear in court, driving while under suspension, being unlawfully at large, breaching bail or probation supervision? Has the offender previously failed on conditional release?);

7. The offender's participation and progress in treatment and other programs (e.g., Has the offender benefited from treatment? Can any needed treatment be continued in the community?);

8. The offender's release plan (e.g., Is the plan realistic? Is it feasible?);

9. The offender's support network (e.g., Are there family, friends, and organizations in the community who are able and willing to help the offender reintegrate?);

10. The offender's understanding of his or her criminal history, problems, and risk factors (e.g., Does the offender understand what he or she needs to do to remain crime free?);

11. The offender's need for supervision and guidance (e.g., Is the offender willing to be, and capable of being, supervised in the community? Is it possible to provide the level of supervision deemed necessary?); and

12. The offender's likelihood of re-offending, and the consequences of re-offending (e.g., Is anyone likely to be harmed if the offender committed a new offence?).

In reviewing the above issues, prison and parole officials consider information provided through many sources. Box 12.3 lists a number of information sources available to the National Parole Board.

BOX 12.3 | **Primary Information Sources for National Parole Board Decision-Making**

- **RCMP FPS (Fingerprint Section) Sheet** provides a chronological listing of the offender's criminal record, including all charges, convictions, and dispositions.

- **Penitentiary Placement Report**, prepared by Correctional Service of Canada officials upon the offender's arrival in prison for the most current offence, provides some background history on the offender, and an assessment of risk, identifies needs, and recommends a plan to address those needs.

- **Progress Summary**, prepared by Correctional Service officials specifically for an offender's request for a specific release, provides a summary of the offender's institutional performance and progress. It also contains the case management team's assessment and recommendations regarding release.

- **Criminal Profile Report**, prepared by Correctional Service officials, provides a detailed description of the current offence and analysis of the causes, and a synopsis of the offender's criminality overall. In doing so, this report may include a summary of input from the police, courts, victims, and the offender's family and significant others.

- **Psychologist and Psychiatric Reports** provide professional assessments and recommendations regarding the offender's needs and suitability for various programs and releases.

- **Judge's Comments**, prepared by the sentencing judge, provide the judge's reasons for giving a specific offender a particular sentence.

- **Police Report**, prepared by the police, provides details of the crime(s), their knowledge and assessment of the offender and his or her criminality, and their concerns and opinions about the offender's reintegration.

- **Victim Statement** provides the victim's version of the crime(s), the personal impact of the crime(s), and any concerns the offender being released.

- **Community Assessments**, prepared by Correctional Service officials and based on interviews with individuals in the community, report on the quality and helpfulness of the relationships the offender expects to maintain upon release.

THE ROLE OF RISK MANAGEMENT

While it may be said that the whole Canadian criminal justice system is concerned with risk management, that is, making decisions about lawbreakers in a way that will maximize the protection of society, nowhere is this more obvious than in the decisions made about releasing incarcerated offenders back into the community. Even though the protection of society may be compromised at any point in the system (for example, by police mishandling of evidence, charge reduction due to plea bargaining, or inappropriate sentencing by a judge), it is much more likely the blame for re-offence will be placed squarely at the feet of conditional release decision-makers (Pepino 1993). It is perhaps for this reason that Correctional Service of Canada and National Parole Board go to great lengths to address the issue of risk to society directly in making decisions about releasing inmates prior to sentence expiration.

In a sense, the release process for a federal inmate begins the day of arrival at the regional reception centre for intake assessment, a process that may take up to eight weeks to complete. As a result of this concentrated format of testing, assessments (including psychological and psychiatric assessments), and interviews, the inmate's correctional plan is developed and provides an outline of how the offender's sentence can be undertaken so that successful community reintegration is the ultimate goal (Motiuk 1998a). The offender's progress in terms of this correctional plan becomes an important criterion for release decision-making as the inmate becomes eligible for various forms of conditional release (see classification and case management in Chapter 4). Because successful reintegration is unlikely to be realized immediately upon release, parole is an important latter phase of the offender's overall correctional plan.

National Parole Board policy requires risk to be determined on the basis of two primary considerations: whether the inmate is likely to re-offend and whether the risk to the public is considered undue in terms of the level of harm that may result from the type of offence a particular offender may be likely to commit. Part of the process of determining risk involves reviewing the offender's file, in particular information related to risk factors identified at the intake assessment and information about the inmate's behaviour up to conditional release eligibility. Also, part of the process is a review of the offender's release plan and how it addresses previously identified specific risk factors.

File documentation pertaining to risk factors and needs areas at the time of incarceration includes such intake assessment information as the offender's criminal history, offence severity, sex offence history, psychiatric reports, substance abuse history, and score on the Statistical Information on Recidivism (SIR) scale, which provides comparative information about the risk of re-offending for a category of statistically similar offenders. Relevant file information about the offender's institutional behaviour and performance is reviewed in order to determine how the inmate's level of risk may have changed since the time of intake. Indicators of beneficial interventions that may have reduced the level of risk include progress in the correctional plan and participation in programs designed to address the risk and need factors identified in the intake assessment. The National Parole Board is also interested in hearing directly from offenders about their insight into their criminal behaviour, their appreciation of the gravity of the offence and acceptance of responsibility for it, their understanding of precipitating factors, and their awareness of risk management skills.

In terms of assessing the release plan, the Board looks for evidence that the type of release, its purpose, and management strategy address the offender's identified needs and risk factors. Those involved in the decision also assess the potential for stressors or other factors in the release environment that may increase the risk of re-offence. Community input is obtained, where appropriate, from the police and victims in the releasing community, as well as from the offender's family or from sponsors. Once the Board has determined the risk based on an assessment of risk factors at the time of incarceration, institutional progress during incarceration, and factors pertaining to the release plan itself, it may impose specific additional conditions on the offender in granting a conditional release, in order to reduce the risk of recidivism.

Of course, no system is perfect; errors in risk prediction have occurred and will, no doubt, continue to occur (see Box 12.4). Sometimes the fault is with the system itself, such as in those instances where the Board has not been in possession of all available information upon which to base its decisions. But it should be kept in mind that even when decisions made are informed by the fullest, most deliberate, and most comprehensive review of the best information, such decisions are still based on the educated opinions by Board members about the level risk involved in each case (Sutton 1994). Infallibility can hardly be expected, particularly when we understand that the Parole Board's mandate is not limited to releasing offenders who will successfully complete their sentence in the community.

BOX 12.4	Inside the Fateful Decision to Free a Child-Killer: The Case of Francis Carl Roy

Inside the Fateful Decision to Free a Child-Killer

Eight months before Francis Carl Roy raped and murdered Alison Parrott, a National Parole Board member expressed grave concerns about letting him live outside prison without supervision—but was outvoted by two parole board colleagues.

The three-person panel decided to let Mr. Roy live unsupervised in the community five days out of seven with the specific condition that the convicted rapist was "not to run in parks unless accompanied." Alison's body was found in a park by the Humber River in west-end Toronto on July 27, 1986.

Mr. Roy was convicted of first-degree murder in April of this year and sentenced to life imprisonment with no parole for at least 25 years.

Documents obtained by *The Globe and Mail* under the *Access to Information* Act provide the first substantial picture of the behind-the-scenes decisions made by the parole board in dealing with Mr. Roy's long criminal career and his attempted rehabilitation.

Just two months before the murder, another parole board panel gave Mr. Roy a glowing report, while noting that budget constraints prevented him from receiving necessary psychological counselling.

SOURCE: Adapted from Barber 1999a.

Arrest Warrant Issued Hours before Alison Slain

The National Parole Board issued a warrant for the arrest of Francis Carl Roy hours before the convicted rapist abducted and killed Alison Parrott, according to a corrections official.

The board decided to issue the warrant after his assault on a woman, according to the source, who asked to remain anonymous.

The assault occurred on July 23, 1986; Alison disappeared on July 25; and Mr. Roy went to police and confessed to the July 23 assault two days after the abduction, on July 27.

But parole officials were aware of the assault before Mr. Roy's confession and issued a warrant suspending his day parole before the Parrott abduction, according to the official.

A suspension warrant authorizes police to arrest paroled offenders and hold them in jail until the matter that triggered the warrant is investigated by the parole board.

By the time the board reviewed his case again, Mr. Roy had been interviewed and cleared in connection with Alison's disappearance. Its review, dated August 26, 1986, concluded that his "drunk and disorderly" conduct on July 23 was not sufficiently severe to require further imprisonment.

"It is our feeling that the risks in this case are not unduly high given the bail conditions," a three-person panel, which included Max Stienburg, concluded in the August report. (Mr. Stienburg expressed reservations about granting Mr. Roy extended day parole in November 1985.)

SOURCE: Adapted from Barber 1999b.

Alison Abducted after Roy Tried to Turn Himself In

Convicted murderer Francis Carl Roy attempted to turn himself in to authorities the day before he lured Alison Parrott to her death, according to National Parole Board records.

The parole board issued a warrant for Mr. Roy's arrest on July 24, 1986, the day before Alison disappeared, spokesman John Vandoremalen said.

"He put in three calls to his parole officer," Mr. Vandoremalen said yesterday. Mr. Roy told the official he had violated his parole by drinking and "would likely be charged in an assault."

His parole officer then issued a suspension warrant, which cancelled Mr. Roy's parole and notified police that they should arrest and imprison him.

The warrant was not executed until three days after that, the day Alison's body was discovered, when Mr. Roy surrendered to Toronto police and was taken back into custody.

He remained in custody until mid-August, when the board reinstated his day parole.

The incident Mr. Roy called to report involved a July 23 attack on a woman whom he had lured to his apartment, punched and attempted to smother with a pillow. He pleaded guilty to assault in November of that year, was fined $200 and put on probation for two years.

Because parole officials depend on police to execute their warrants, the speed with which Mr. Roy was picked up "would have been a question of how fast police could have got hold of him," Mr. Vandoremalen said.

SOURCE: Adapted from Barber 1999c.
All extracts reprinted with permission from *The Globe and Mail.*

To be more specific, the Board could be said to fulfill its mandate most effectively when it correctly identifies and releases all parole applicants who complete their sentences outside the penitentiary walls without further incident, and also correctly identifies and denies release to all applicants who will be unsuccessful in completing their sentence in the community. Thus, an error can be said to have occurred each time an inmate on conditional release re-offends, and each time an offender who would have been successful is denied release. Since only the first type of error can actually be counted, one may well ask why the Board grants release to anyone at all, since this would result in no countable errors at all. The simple answer is, of course, that this would be unethical as well as against the law (see Authority to Grant Conditional Release above).

The more complicated answer has to do with the National Parole Board's responsibility to contribute to the protection of society. In this regard, one may well ask whether a system that releases inmates "cold turkey" rather than gradually, with no assistance, supervision, or power to revoke the release from an incarceration experience that has offered little or no reward for participating in rehabilitating (or risk-reducing) program opportunities truly holds the protection of the community as central to its mission. In other words, while choosing to release no one may be an effective short-term tactic, it is likely to be counterproductive as a long-term strategy for preventing further social harm by previous offenders.

Of course, risk management does not end with the Board's assessments of risk. Even if such probabilistic assessments of serious harm posed to the public were more accurate, it should be remembered that the dynamics of each case are subject to change after release. Furthermore, even a small risk is still a risk, and some proportion, however small, of a low-risk group is still expected to re-offend in some manner. Thus, risk management must continue with post-release supervision.

The community-based parole officer is critical to the Correctional Service of Canada's strategy to manage the risk of offenders on conditional release (see Box 12.5). The parole officer must be capable of providing the assistance needed for the offender to achieve successful reintegration into the community and must be prepared to provide the necessary degree of control required to prevent a violation of a condition of release or, even worse, re-offence. The risk assessments conducted at intake and by case management prior to release are important determinants of the type and level of supervision the parole officer will maintain, and help ensure that the factors identified in the offender's correctional plan continue to inform the efforts of both the Correctional Service and the offender to complete that plan (Motiuk and Serin 1998; Motiuk, Shelley, and Brown 1994).

Generally speaking there are three levels of supervision intensity: **periodic supervision**, requiring a minimum of one face-to-face contact between the parole officer and the offender each month, and **active supervision** and **intensive supervision**, which require a minimum of two and four face-to-face contacts per month respectively. Only those inmates assessed as low in terms of "criminal history risk" and "case needs risk" are placed on periodic supervision upon release. Those rated as low/medium, medium/low, or medium/medium on these two scales are assigned to active supervision, while all others (high on either scale) are supervised at the intensive level.

THE HEARING

In accordance with section 140 of the *Corrections and Conditional Release Act,* each inmate eligible for a form of conditional release authorized by the National Parole Board is entitled to a hearing in which a review of the individual's case is conducted. As an inmate's **parole eligibility date** approaches, he or she is advised of the right to apply for parole and a hearing is automatically scheduled. Those who, for whatever reason, do not wish to apply for parole must indicate this intention by signing a **waiver of the right to a hearing**. It is possible for the Board to make paper decisions without actually interviewing the offender, although this is fairly uncommon. In order for the inmate to prepare for an upcoming review, the Board is required to provide the parole applicant with all relevant information considered in decision-making at least 15 days prior to the hearing.

BOX 12.5 The Parole Officer

In the Correctional Service of Canada, there are two kinds of parole officer, the institutional parole officer and the community parole officer. While institutional parole officers are more concerned with pre-release parole planning and preparation, community parole officers are responsible for parole supervision and providing community-related information institutional staff involved in developing the offender's correctional plan.

The community parole officer's job is a demanding one, requiring a high level of skill, sound judgement, and personal commitment. Those providing parole supervision need to find the balance for each case between providing support and assistance and enforcing the terms and conditions imposed by law and by the National Parole Board. They visit with the offender regularly, maintain contact with others such as the offender's family and employer, and keep in touch with the police as well as sponsors or support workers who may be playing a role in the offender's correctional plan. They must be prepared to take appropriate disciplinary action if an offender breaches a condition of release. They also prepare regular reports on each case describing the offender's progress, and incident reports describing any violations or offences while the offender is on release. The average caseload for a community parole officer is 25 to 30 offenders, perhaps lower if the caseload has a large number of offenders requiring intensive supervision.

A university degree is required to become a parole officer, usually in a social science such as criminology or in social work. Those wishing a career in parole usually begin by applying to the Correctional Service of Canada for an entry-level position, such as a correctional officer.

Hearings are held at each institution, usually on a monthly basis. Usually two or three Board members comprise a **panel** before which the applicant appears (the more serious the case, the more Board member votes are required to render a decision to release, which often necessitates a case review by members not actually present at the hearing). Others present include the applicant's case management officer and the assigned parole officer, each of whom has helped prepare the case by organizing relevant file and interview information into a report format for panel members to review. While Board members prepare hearings by studying the case files for each applicant beforehand, the hearing provides a forum at which the relevant information is reviewed with the applicant, as well as an opportunity for that person to make an in-person presentation to the panel members.

Such hearings are administrative as opposed to judicial or quasi-judicial; formal rules of evidence are not required. Thus, while there is no provision for an offender to be represented by counsel, he or she is permitted to have an "assistant" present to provide support and advice and, if the offender wishes, to address the panel on his or her behalf. Such an assistant may be a family member, friend, lawyer, or spiritual advisor. In most cases, the applicant interview and information-sharing phase of the hearing is followed by a deliberation period during which the applicant is not present; at the end of its deliberations, the panel decides either to grant or deny conditional release. The decision and the reasoning behind it are then shared in person with the applicant.

Others present at a hearing may include uninvolved observers and interpreters. In cases where the parole applicant is not fully conversant in either of Canada's official languages, interpreters are provided to ensure that the applicant is fully aware of the information provided to the panel and understands the proceedings being conducted. Any member of the public over the age of 18 with an interest in the parole process, including victims of the applicant's crimes, can apply to be an observer at a hearing. Observers are not permitted to participate in the hearing itself, but may submit information prior to the hearing that may be considered in the Board's deliberations. Observers are also permitted to take notes during the proceedings.

The National Parole Board has an appeal division to which an applicant may appeal a decision to deny conditional release. Appeals cannot be frivolous, and must relate to such grounds as the fairness of the hearing process, the accuracy and completeness of information used by the Board, or whether the Board procedures were followed in accordance with the appropriate legislation (CCRA). Appeals are conducted by way of a file review, without an actual hearing.

The National Parole Board also maintains a registry of decisions. Each Board decision (including appeal decisions) made since proclamation of the CCRA and the reasons for it are archived. The registry allows individuals interested in a particular case access to the decision record in keeping with freedom of information legislation. In addition, researchers can gain access to groups of decision records after personal identifiers have been removed.

In 1996/97, the Board rendered a total of 27,036 decisions of which 16,811 were federal pre-release and 8,209 were federal post-release (e.g., parole revocation or termination). About 930 were pre- and post-release decisions involving provincial offenders. During the same year, there were 719 requests for access to the decision registry by victims, 586 by the media, and 344 others including researchers and offenders' family members (Solicitor General of Canada 1998).

THE CONDITIONAL RELEASE POPULATION

According to Motiuk (1998a), in 1997 there were 7,583 federal offenders on conditional release, 297 females and 7,286 males, with 57 percent of these on full parole, 32 percent on statutory release and 11 percent on day parole. The majority of these offenders (58 percent) were between the ages of 30 and 50 with approximately equal proportions above and below this group.

In terms of the length of time since release, three distinct time frames can be distinguished: phase one, the first six months after release, the most difficult with the highest proportion of failures; phase two, the second six months; and phase three, beginning after the first year on conditional release. Offenders in phase three are much more likely to succeed in the long term than those in the earlier stages of release. In 1997, 43.5 percent of the federal conditional release population were in phase three, with 22.5 percent and 19 percent in phases two and three respectively (Motiuk 1998b).

CONDITIONS OF RELEASE

Almost anyone working in corrections can tell you that there are some offenders who do not want conditional release. They refuse even to apply for it, often because they do not like the conditions that go with the release. These conditions will vary depending on the type of release and the offender involved, but they can be very restrictive.

In the case of temporary absences and work release, for example, the conditions are fitted to the specific purpose of the release. That is, offenders are expected to go directly to a specified location, fulfill the specific purpose of the release, and then return directly to the prison (all within a specified number of hours). They are not permitted to drink alcohol or do anything else that is not directly related to the stated purpose of the release. Furthermore, whenever under escort, they are required to remain in sight of the escorting official.

For parole and statutory release, there are conditions that apply to every offender, as well as additional conditions that may be set down by the National Parole Board as it sees fit. In this regard, the Board can set down *any* condition it feels is reasonable and necessary to facilitate the offender's reintegration. Moreover, the Board can add, reduce, and otherwise change conditions as the offender progresses through the conditional release period. Some of the conditions listed in the Board Member Orientation Manual that apply to all offenders on conditional release are the following:

- Upon release, the parolee must go directly to his or her place of residence, report immediately to the parole officer, and thereafter stay within a stated geographical area (within Canada);
- The parolee must report immediately to the parole officer any change that may affect his or her ability to comply with the conditions of release; these changes include those relating to a change of address, employment, family situation, and change in financial situation;
- The parolee must report to the police and parole officer as instructed and advise the parole officer any time he or she is questioned by police;
- The parolee must obey the law and keep the peace;
- The parolee must not have in his or her possession any weapon;
- The parolee must carry identification and a certificate of release and produce both when requested to do so by any peace officer; and
- The parolee must follow all lawful instructions given by their parole officer.

BREACH OF CONDITIONS

As noted above, conditional release implies that an inmate is released to serve a period of the sentence in the community under certain conditions imposed by the National Parole Board for reasons of risk management and facilitating offender reintegration. Releasees are expected to abide by all such conditions. What happens, then, when one or more of these conditions are breached or violated?

When parolees breach a condition of their release, it does not necessarily mean that they are returned to prison. The nature of the breach might be such that the parole officer determines that a warning or counselling is the most appropriate intervention. However, the breach may be serious enough that the parole officer recommends **parole suspension**, which results in the offender being returned to custody while the parole supervisor assesses the seriousness of the breach. If the parole supervisor feels that the violation does not constitute an undue risk to society and is not likely to lead to renewed criminal activity, he or she may choose not to proceed with suspension. Suspension, however, is only a temporary measure. A federal offender's suspension must be either cancelled (followed by re-release) or referred to the Board for possible **parole revocation** within 30 days. Table 12.6 presents the percentage of

TABLE 12.6   Percentage of Federal Conditional Releases Revoked per Year,[a] 1992/93–1996/97

Fiscal Year	% Revoked in Day Parole	% Revoked on Accelerated Parole[b]	% Revoked on Full Parole	% Revoked on Statutory Release
1992/93	34	(10) 100	30	46
1993/94	27	(216) 97	38	50
1994/95	25	(582) 67	31	42
1995/96	20	(841) 47	27	42
1996/97	17	(914) 44	28	44

[a] All figures rounded.
[b] Actual numbers of releases presented in parentheses for accelerated parole review, which was first initiated during 1992/93.
SOURCE: Solicitor General of Canada 1998.

cases per year in which conditional release was revoked. Note that the rates are consistently higher for accelerated parole release (in which the Board directs eligible inmates to be released at their parole eligibility date without a hearing provided they are deemed unlikely to commit a violent offence, as opposed to a breach of conditions or less serious criminal offence) and for statutory release (in which the Board can deny release only if it believes it likely the inmate will commit an offence involving death or serious harm to a person, a sexual offence involving a child, or a serious drug offence) than for day parole and regular full parole.

Once a suspension has been referred to the Board for review, the circumstances surrounding the breach are assessed. If the Board concludes that resumption of release would not constitute an undue risk, the suspension will be cancelled and the offender re-released. If, however, the Board feels that the risk of re-offending has risen to an unacceptable level, the conditional release will be revoked. If, in the opinion of the Board, the risk of re-offending has risen due to circumstances beyond the offender's control, the conditional release will merely be terminated. **Parole termination** an administrative action that involves the offender's return to custody but with no blame implied. It would appear that neither the National Parole Board nor individual parole officers take breaches of conditions lightly, as evidenced by the fact that most revocations are not the result of new crimes but occur as a consequence of "technical" violations of the terms of conditional release (Larocque 1998; Plecas and Segger 2000).

SUCCESS AND FAILURE ON CONDITIONAL RELEASE

We hear so much about individual cases of failure on conditional release that it often seems there are more failures than successes; however, if one looks at the statistics on conditional release, it becomes apparent that the success rates for all types of conditional release are actually very high. In the case of temporary absences, for instance, 99.7 percent of escorted temporary absences and 98.8 percent of unescorted temporary absences granted in 1996/97 were completed successfully (Solicitor General of Canada 1997a).

The rates of failure and success for day parole, full parole, and statutory release can be looked at in a number of ways, one of which is to consider the percentage of offenders on each type of release who commit a new offence before completion of their supervision period. From this perspective, as Table 12.7 shows, the failure rate is reasonably low for each type of release and has dropped substantially for each type of release from what it was in 1992/93. These figures are consistent with the authors' own review of re-offending among penitentiary inmates placed on conditional release in British Columbia from 1995 to 1997. That review, which allowed for an 18-month follow-up period, showed 8 percent of day parolees, 12 percent of full parolees, and 13 percent of those on statutory release re-offending (Plecas and Segger 2000).

Equally significant is the percentage of offenders who have committed violent crimes after release but before their warrant expiry date. The average percentages over the five-year period are less than 2 percent for day parole and accelerated parole, less than 3 percent for regular full parole, and just over 3 percent for statutory release (Solicitor General of Canada 1998). The five-year trend revealed in Table 12.7 is corroborated by the findings of a recent review by Larocque (1998) of re-offending by offenders on conditional release, which showed that the number of serious offences committed dropped by 14 percent between 1992/93 and 1996/97.

To put these failure rates in perspective, it is worth noting the results of a recent study of re-offending conducted in the United States. Langan and Cunniff (1992), examining re-offending among individuals sentenced to probation, found that of 79,000 offenders sentenced in 1986, over 40 percent of them were rearrested for a new crime while still on probation. Worse, one in five of those arrested were arrested for a violent offence (murder, rape, robbery, assault), and nearly as many were arrested for drug trafficking. Compared to these results then, failure rates among offenders on conditional release in Canada are impressively low.

VICTIM INVOLVEMENT IN CONDITIONAL RELEASE

Many victims do not want to have anything to do with the conditional release of the offender(s) who victimized them. On the other hand, although there is no legal requirement that they do, some victims do want to be connected to the process of conditional release, and the *Corrections and Criminal Release Act* provides for this in a number of ways.

To begin with, where the victim requests, and where the Chair of the National Parole Board is of the opinion that the interest of that victim outweighs any invasion of the offender's

TABLE 12.7 **Percentage of Conditional Releases Revoked Because Releasee Committed a New Offence, 1992/93–1996/97**

Fiscal Year	% Revoked on Day Parole	% Revoked on Accelerated Parole	% Revoked on Regular Full Parole	% Revoked on Statutory Release
1992/93	8	30	13	18
1993/94	7	37	14	19
1994/95	5	23	9	11
1995/96	4	16	6	12
1996/97	4	15	8	13

SOURCE: Solicitor General of Canada 1998.

privacy, the Board may disclose certain information about the offender. Specifically, the Board may disclose the offender's age, where the sentence is being served, any hearing or release dates, conditions of release, reasons for a release decision, the release status and destination of the offender upon release, and whether or not the offender has appealed a Board decision. The only information that the victim has an absolute right to, however, is the offender's name and offence, the length of the sentence, and the eligibility and review dates for unescorted temporary absences and parole.

Victims may also express their concerns directly and formally to the Board, or indirectly through communication with correctional officials who will convey their concerns to the Board in a written report. Statements made directly to the Board can be oral, written, or taped, and may include requests that certain conditions be applied to a release (e.g., that the offender not live near or have any contact with the victim). Unless there is reason to believe that the hearing would be disrupted or otherwise negatively affected, victims are permitted to attend as observers. It is important to remember though, that although the victim's concerns and requests are seriously considered, victims have no right to veto a Board decision.

ABORIGINAL OFFENDERS AND CONDITIONAL RELEASE

A review of the CCRA five years after its implementation entitled *Towards a Just, Peaceful and Safe Society* (Solicitor General of Canada 1998) provides a descriptive and statistical overview of the special problems and issues involving Native offenders in Canada's penitentiaries, with special regard to conditional release and the Board's response to them. In general, Aboriginal offenders are over-represented in the penitentiary population, comprising 3 percent of the Canadian population, but 12 percent of the population of federal offenders (15 percent of the incarcerated population). Aboriginal offenders are more likely than non-Aboriginal offenders to serve their sentences in institutions as opposed to in the community; they are less likely to be eligible for accelerated parole review and are more likely to waive their parole review. They are less likely than non-Aboriginal offenders to be released on full parole, more likely to be released on statutory release, and more likely to be referred for detention during the statutory release period. While Aboriginal offenders on full parole are more likely than non-Aboriginal offenders to be returned to prison for a technical violation, they are no more likely to be revoked for commission of a new criminal offence under any form of conditional release.

The Correctional Service of Canada and the National Parole Board has been aware of the special problems and apparent inequities involving Aboriginal offenders and has undertaken a number of initiatives in terms of treatment modalities, programs, and reintegration planning in an attempt to ameliorate the situation (Ellerby 1994; see Chapter 9). In 1992, the Board began the practice of Elder-assisted hearings based on restorative justice principles, with panels composed of Aboriginal and non-Aboriginal members. The Elder helps Board members to appreciate Native cultural nuances in the hearing process.

The Statistical Information on Recidivism scale has not been validated as an accurate risk prediction tool for the Aboriginal offender population.[4] Thus, where possible, the Board uses the services of professionals of Aboriginal ancestry for assessments of Aboriginal offenders. Board members also receive training in Aboriginal culture, including ceremonies, spirituality, and teachings, so they can gain a better understanding of a Native offender's healing through participation in institutional Aboriginal programs. These initiatives help the

Board members in their efforts to assess the risk level involved in each Aboriginal case more appropriately.

The National Parole Board has also made a concerted effort to increase the number of Aboriginal people who sit as Board members. As of February 1998, 14 percent of full-time members and 10 percent of part-time members were self-identified as being of Aboriginal ancestry. The Board now makes a special effort to recruit Aboriginal peoples to fill vacancies as they occur.

PARDONS

While technically speaking it is not a form of conditional release, an offender can be granted, upon application, a **pardon** by the National Parole Board after completing his or her sentence and a waiting period "of good conduct." That period varies from three to five years from the warrant expiry date, depending on the seriousness of the offence. In accordance with the *Criminal Records Act*, any federal agency with records of the convictions of a pardoned offender must keep them separate, and is not permitted to disclose the information to anyone without the permission of the Solicitor General.

For all intents and purposes, then, one's criminal record is "erased"; however, it does not erase the fact that one was convicted of a criminal offence. A pardon granted in Canada may not be recognized by a foreign government and does not guarantee entry privileges to another country. It is important to keep in mind that pardons, like parole, can be revoked. Conviction for an indictable offence automatically nullifies a pardon, and the National Parole Board may decide to revoke a pardon for a summary conviction. In 1996/97, the Board granted 17,529 pardons, an increase of about 14 percent over the previous year (Solicitor General of Canada 1997b).

Although they are rarely used, the Board also has the authority to grant **conditional pardons**, under which an inmate is released from imprisonment, subject to similar conditions and terms of supervision to those that apply to parolees. Conditional pardons can be granted in cases in which the offender is not yet eligible for parole and is not considered a risk to the community. In addition, it must be shown that the offender's incarceration results in a degree of inequity, injustice, or hardship out of proportion to the nature and seriousness of the offence committed.

ISSUES FOR THE FUTURE

According to Morgan-Sharp and Sigler (1999), throughout the known history of society, at least of so-called western society, the treatment of lawbreakers has repeatedly alternated between periods typified by punishment or retribution and those typified by rehabilitation or treatment. They identify the present dominant paradigm, in the United States in particular, as one of punishment and retribution. There is little doubt that this is fairly well reflected in much of Canadian public opinion today (Conroy 1999; Gibbs 1999; Solicitor General of Canada 1999; see Chapter 3). The justice system tends to be seen as less than effective in combating crime and there are frequent calls for more punitive approaches to crime control, including greater use of prisons, longer sentences, and more restricted access to (or even the abolition of) conditional release (Solicitor General of Canada 1999).

In the National Parole Board's strategic plan, published in 1999, the centennial anniversary of conditional release in Canada, the Board clearly recognizes the challenge presented by current public perceptions about crime, personal security, and justice, and recommends a proactive response: taking responsibility for educating the public about the role of conditional release in contributing to public safety (Solicitor General of Canada 1999). Clearly the Board realizes that, as the future unfolds, it must be part of the processes that shape public perceptions and opinions about Canadian public and social policy.

Part of this strategy includes greater transparency in the conditional release decision-making process for the public, the press, victims, and others with a specific interest. We can expect such increased openness and accountability to be accompanied by greater public involvement in National Parole Board policy development, citizen "engagement" as opposed to "consultation" (Solicitor General of Canada 1999).

Other sociopolitical trends and issues likely to influence conditional release policies and practices include the victim rights lobby, expanding popularity of the restorative justice model, increasing community responsibility for setting and attaining criminal justice goals (as evidenced in the continuing pressure to implement community policing in the place of traditional models), increasing recognition of Aboriginal peoples as a category of Canadians with a distinctive set of needs, problems, and entitlements, and a deepening appreciation of the cultural diversity that typifies Canadian society. In terms of conditional release, as we move into the first decade of the 21st century, we can expect to see changes in policy and procedure that reflect these dimensions of change in the sociopolitical landscape:

- Increased accommodation for victims in conditional release decision-making;
- More attention paid to restorative aspects of offender reintegration, with the process becoming less focused on the isolated needs of the offender as opposed to the well-being of all those involved in or affected by the release;
- Enhanced public access to information about release-related decisions and greater opportunity for public input into conditional release policy development;
- Greater flexibility in the ritual form attendant to decision-making; for example, using a hearing model that takes into account the unique culture, values, language, and traditions of Aboriginal offenders; and
- Membership of parole boards increasingly representative of the diverse communities and ethnic groups that make up Canadian society.

CONCLUSION

Conditional release is one of the most misunderstood aspects of corrections. As this chapter has suggested, part of the reason for this is the way parole and other forms of release are represented in the media and have thus come to shape much of the political agenda in Canada today. Another part of the reason is that process of conditional release is remarkably complex, beginning at the point of admission to prison and ending at expiry of the offender's warrant of committal. It is not a phenomenon that is easy to simplify; one cannot make general statements about it that accurately describe all cases. Readers who have mastered the material presented in this chapter, however, are well prepared to develop their own informed opinions about the role of conditional release in Canadian corrections and to critically evaluate information intended to influence those opinions.

KEY TERMS AND CONCEPTS

accelerated parole review
active supervision
conditional pardon
dangerous offender
day parole
escorted temporary absence
full parole
indeterminate sentence
intensive supervision
judicial determination

judicial review
long-term offender
panel
pardon
parole eligibility date
parole revocation
parole suspension
parole termination
periodic supervision
residency requirement

statutory release
temporary absence
unescorted temporary
    absence
waiver of the right to a
    hearing
warrant expiry date
warrant of committal
work release

STUDY AND DISCUSSION QUESTIONS

1. Part of the purpose of conditional release is to support incarcerated offenders' reintegration into the community. Who, besides the offender, should be taking responsibility for reintegration? His or her family? Prison authorities? The National Parole Board? Should society itself (you and I) take some responsibility for criminogenic factors associated with the structure and dynamics of Canadian society? Why?

2. Do provinces need their own parole boards? All provinces? Should provincial boards be dismantled, or should the National Parole Board be dissolved, giving provinces sole jurisdiction over the release of offenders in their own geographical area?

3. In terms of minimizing risk, many suggest that offenders should not be released prior to the end of their sentence and that parole should be abolished. Is this in the best interests of the criminal justice system, or of Canadian society? Why?

4. Imagine you are a community-based parole officer. What aspects of the job do you think would challenge you the most? What would provide you with the most job satisfaction?

WEBLINKS

National Parole Board of Canada: **www.npb-cnlc.gc.ca**
NPB fact sheets: Useful and up-to-date information about various NPB policies and procedures: **198.103.98.156**
Online version of the NPB Policy Manual: **198.103.98.156/mantoce.htm**

Online version of various documents related to the evaluation of the *Corrections and Conditional Release Act* five years after its proclamation: **www.sgc.gc.ca/eccra**

Ontario Board of Parole: **www.gov.on/sgc/english/parole/man.html**

Information (in English) about conditional release in the Province of Quebec: **www.secpub.gouv.qc.ca/anglais/detent/contrven/jail.htm#libcond**

News and information about Canada's Ministry of Justice: **canada.justice.gc.ca/news**

Publications available from Canada's Ministry of Justice: **canada.justice.gc.ca/publications**

NOTES

1. Mandatory supervision has since been replaced by statutory release, which is not tied to earned remission (see Types of Conditional Release later in this chapter).

2. Yet they are legally eligible to apply.

3. In 1995/96, the median prison length for all sentences handed down in Canada was 46 days; one half were for one month or less and only 3 percent were for periods in excess of two years (Du Wors 2000).

4. Over the years there have been a number of validation studies done on the SIR scale. And although not used for parole decision-making, based on its established predictive validity, the SIR scale has been used in research to assess risk of recidivism (see Cormier 1997).

REFERENCES

Barber, J. 1999a. Inside the Fateful Decision to Free a Child-Killer. *The Globe and Mail* 1 June, A1, A3.

———. 1999b. Arrest Warrant Issued Hours before Alison Slain. *The Globe and Mail* 1 June, A3.

———. 1999c. Alison Abducted after Roy Tried to Turn Himself In. *The Globe and Mail* 2 June, A3.

Brunet, L. 1998. Highlights in the History of Day Parole. *Forum on Corrections Research* 10(2): 7–10.

Conroy, J.W. 1999. *Re-framing Parole: The Perspective of Prisoners' Counsel.* Paper presented at Changing Punishment at the Turn of the Century: Finding a Common Ground. Conference of the Canadian Institute for the Administration of Justice. 26–29 September, Saskatoon.

Cormier, R.B. 1997. Yes, SIR! A Stable Risk Prediction Tool. *Forum on Corrections Research* 9(1): 3–7.

Du Wors, R. 2000. The Justice Data Factfinder. In J.V. Roberts (Ed.), *Criminal Justice in Canada: A Reader.* Toronto: Harcourt Brace.

Ellerby, L. 1994. Community-Based Treatment of Aboriginal Sex Offenders: Facing Realities and Exploring Possibilities. *Forum on Corrections Research* 6(3): 23–25.

Gibbs, W. 1999. Re-framing Parole. Paper presented at Changing Punishment at the Turn of the Century: Finding a Common Ground, a conference of the Canadian Institute for the Administration of Justice, 26–29 September, Saskatoon.

Grant, B. A., and **C. Beal**. 1998. Work Release Program: How It Is Used and For What Purposes. *Forum on Corrections Research* 10(2): 35–38.

Hatch-Cunningham, A., and **C.T. Griffiths**. 1997. *Canadian Criminal Justice: A Primer.* Toronto: Harcourt Brace.

Langan, P., and **M.A. Cunniff**. 1992. *Recidivism of Felons on Probation, 1988–89.* Washington, DC: U.S. Department of Justice, Office of Justice Programs.

Larocque, B. 1998. Federal Trends and Outcomes in Conditional Release. *Forum on Corrections Research* 10(2): 18–22.

Morgan-Sharp, E.F., and **R.T. Sigle**. 1999. Sentencing into the Twenty-First Century: Sentence Enhancement and Life without Parole. In R. Muraskin and R. Roberts (Eds.), *Visions for Change: Crime and Justice in the Twenty-First Century* (2nd ed.). Upper Saddle River, NJ: Prentice-Hall.

Motiuk, L. 1998a. Profiling Federal Offenders on Conditional Release. *Forum on Corrections Research* 10(2): 11–14.

———. 1998b. Situating Risk Assessment in the Reintegration Potential Framework. *Forum on Corrections Research* 10(1): 19–22.

Motiuk, L., and **R. Serin**. 1998. Situating Risk Assessment in the Reintegration Potential Framework. *Forum on Corrections Research* 59(2): 12–13.

Motiuk, L., **L. Shelley**, and **S.L. Brown**. 1994. Sex Offenders and Their Survival Time on Conditional Release. *Forum on Corrections Research* 6(3): 14–16.

Pepino, N.J. 1993. Managing Risk: Whose Problem Is It Anyway? *Forum on Corrections Research* 5(2):12–13

Plecas, D., and **T. Segger**. 2000. *Conditional Release Rates and Outcomes: A Comparison of Releases to the City of Abbotsford to Those within the Province of British Columbia Overall.* Report prepared for the Abbotsford Police Department. Abbotsford: University College of the Fraser Valley.

Roberts, J.V. 1993. Risk Management: The Views of the Public and the Challenge to Corrections. *Forum on Corrections Research* 5(2): 19–21.

———. 2000. Judicial Review of Parole Eligibility for Lifers. In J.V. Roberts (Ed.) *Criminal Justice in Canada: A Reader.* Toronto: Harcourt Brace.

Solicitor General of Canada. 1997a. *National Parole Board Pardon Application Booklet.* Ottawa: Ministry of the Solicitor General.

———. 1997b. *Basic Facts About Corrections in Canada.* Ottawa: Ministry of the Solicitor General.

———. 1998. *Towards a Just, Peaceful, and Safe Society: The Corrections and Conditional Release Act Five Years Later: Consolidated Report.* Ottawa: Ministry of the Solicitor General.

———. 1999. *The National Parole Board Vision and Strategic Plan: 2000 and Beyond.* Ottawa: Ministry of the Solicitor General.

Sutton, J. 1994. Learning to Better Predict the Future: National Parole Board Risk-Assessment Training. *Forum on Corrections Research* 6(3): 20–22.

COMMUNITY-BASED CORRECTIONS

Livy Visano
Department of Sociology
York University
Toronto, Ontario

LEARNING OBJECTIVES

After reading this chapter, you should be able to:

- Analyze the contexts (cultural, political, and economic) within which community corrections are articulated;
- Explain the nature and evolution of community-based corrections in Canada;
- Develop a critical appreciation of the relationship between community corrections and state-sponsored initiatives;
- Explain the limitations of current alternatives to incarceration;
- Critically analyze the relationship between corrections and community as a series of selective and cumulative judgements;
- Appreciate notions of liberalism and privatization in explaining community-based corrections; and
- Identify a set of remedies to enhance community action.

Not only do most people accept violence if it is perpetuated by legitimate authority, they also regard violence against certain kinds of people as inherently legitimate, no matter who commits it.

—Edgar Friedenberg

The study of community-based corrections enjoys a rich intellectual history. Traditional perspectives have succeeded in delineating different vantage points, various conceptual lenses through which we may learn to appreciate the phenomenon of community-based corrections. The concept of a community has always been a convenient and yet seductive instrument of control. Since the 1970s, Canadians have witnessed a proliferation of programs, strategies, and policies ostensibly designed to encourage a greater degree of community participation. This notion of a community, as a juridical invention and a controlled social artifact, has invited a painstaking return to apparently parochial values as well as a more passionate rediscovery of viable alternatives to supplement extant more formal state controls. Indeed, the concept of a community has been appropriated ideologically by the state to legitimate decisions, preserve privilege, and maintain authority relations (Visano 1994). Witness, for example, the current currency of common sense ideas about community legal aid clinics, community policing, criminal trials, community standards in jury deliberations, sentencing to community service orders in corrections—all of which have attained a heightened significance within the chatter of control (Foucault 1980). This shift towards community crime prevention, compensation, restitution, and victimization and the simple return of the bad or the mad to the sacred community echo a lingering pastoral nostalgia, a return to more "basic" familiar values. The social control industry has been busily promoting a normatively oriented community argument in an effort to capture the common sense of different publics, thereby ensuring greater degrees of cooperation, intelligence-gathering, and support. Community-based corrections, as an ambiguous term, invites problematic expectations, differential interpretations, and deference to state definitions.

The purpose of this chapter is to analyze the role of the community in corrections. Far too often the challenges of community corrections have been overlooked as a result of the pervasive rhetoric that conceals as much as it reveals about power imbalances. This chapter highlights the inherent contradictions of common sense assumptions about community corrections that have been ceremoniously paraded by various levels of government.

AN OVERVIEW OF COMMUNITY-BASED CORRECTIONS

Essentially, offenders in Canada serve only part of their sentence in prison (see Chapter 6). Almost all offenders (approximately 34,000 in 1996/97) eventually return to the wider community. Specifically, on any given day there may be about 14,000 offenders in prison and another 10,000 on some form of conditional release (see Box 13.1).

The notion of community-based corrections encompasses a wide variety of programs, including such options as diversion, probation, parole, community service, fine option programs, electronic monitoring, halfway houses, work camps, and work release programs. **Community-based corrections** is a program of supervised gradual release of offenders. This process of conditional release is designed to assist inmates with their respective reintegration into society transition from penal confinement. Accordingly, inmates enjoy a better chance of success if they receive supervision, opportunities, training, and support within the community to which they must readjust. According to the independent recommendations regarding quality conditional release of the National Parole Board, the protection of society is facilitated by the timely reintegration of offenders as law-abiding citizens (Correctional Service of Canada 1997b). For Charles Haskell (1994), Counsel for Correctional Service of Canada, the *Corrections and Conditional Release Act,* which came into force on November 1,

---

| BOX 13.1 | **Community-based Corrections and the Expansion of Sentencing Options** |

The twin forces of government cutbacks and prevailing ideology have contributed to the growth of sentencing options in order to reduce the number of offenders in correctional institutions. Intermediate or mid-range sentences are dispositions of the courts that fall between an absolute discharge and a sentence of imprisonment, involving the use of community programs. They are alternatives to incarceration that provide control and supervision that include intensive probation supervision, electronic monitoring, and intermittent sentencing. Intermittent sentencing permits the offender to stay at home and work or attend classes during the week while serving time on weekends. Intermediate sentences reflect the conviction that rehabilitation and reintegration can be more effectively achieved in the community.

1992 (see Chapter 12), enhanced both the institutional and community aspects of corrections. The *Corrections and Conditional Release Act* (CCRA) states that the purpose of the federal correctional system is to contribute to the maintenance of a just, peaceful, and safe society. Some of the measures include carrying out sentences imposed by courts through the safe and humane custody and supervision of offenders, and assisting the rehabilitation of offenders and their reintegration into the community as law-abiding citizens through the provision of programs in penitentiaries and in the community. Consistent with this act, the Correctional Service of Canada provides a range of programs designed to address the needs of offenders and contribute to their successful reintegration into the community.

The authority to grant parole and temporary absences is found in both federal and provincial correctional legislation and is exercised by correctional authorities in provincial and territorial systems. In accordance with the CCRA, upon release all offenders must abide by conditions set out in the release certificate. Conditions can include being required to travel directly to their homes and report regularly to their parole supervisor, curfews, prohibitions on drinking, and prohibitions on associating with certain people. Correctional Service of Canada staff may take action if they believe the offender is violating release conditions or may commit another crime. The Correctional Service may suspend the release and return the offender directly to prison until the risk is reassessed. An offender may be released again but under more severe restrictions and after more supervision or community support services are in place.

Clearly, community-based corrections consists of three interrelated activities—supervision, programming, and community involvement. Supervision is the direct monitoring of and communication with offenders by parole officers or by trained volunteers. Correctional Service of Canada staff rely on community contacts for important information on offenders to help the supervision process and deliver programs. In addition, community involvement means something larger—the community's willingness to accept back those offenders who reform themselves (Correctional Service of Canada 1997b). Some 20 percent of the 10,000 offenders under the jurisdiction of the Correctional Service are supervised through such contracts with organizations such as the John Howard Society, the Elizabeth Fry Society, and the Salvation Army. Community networks contribute to both supervision and support.

Community Residential Facilities: Halfway Houses

One of the earliest and most common forms of community-based corrections or intermediate sanctions involve the **community residential facility**. Such a facility is a halfway house, more specifically a type of post-incarceration program, owned and operated either by a non-governmental agency or by the Correctional Service of Canada. Each agency-owned facility contracts with Correctional Service to provide accommodation for and counselling and supervision of 15 to 30 offenders who are usually on day parole. The contract sets out detailed requirements regarding levels of control and assistance. There are 172 such centres under contract annually, preparing offenders for full parole—the least structured form of release to the community. In general, however, halfway houses provide accommodation to offenders who are on parole, statutory release, or temporary release. Hence they serve as transitional residential facilities and offer a humanitarian alternative to the harsh prison environment, providing a wider opportunity for offender reintegration.

Community correctional centres house primarily offenders on day parole and are designated as minimum security institutions and are run by Correctional Service staff. In 1996/97, the Correctional Service operated 16 such facilities. In these, the director, parole officers, and support staff work as a team, often in cooperation with community partners, to supervise and provide programs for offenders and prepare them for full parole. For the purpose of this chapter, no distinction is made between correctional residential facilities and community correctional centres (see Box 13.2).

BOX 13.2   Halfway Houses

Halfway houses are correctional facilities run by private agencies under contract to the government. They provide 24-hour supervision and are designed to assist in the reintegration of the offender into the community. Community residential facilities, or community corrections centres, are minimum security facilities operated by the federal government where inmates reside during a temporary absence or conditional release.

Non-state halfway houses flourished at the turn of the century and again in the 1950s. In Canada, the first such community supervision was undertaken by the Salvation Army at the turn of the 20th century. After World War II, other private interests were involved. In Quebec, probation was the preserve of non-state agencies until the 1967; in the 1970s, the John Howard Society and the Salvation Army, St. Leonard's Society (see Box 13.3) became heavily involved.

Successes:

According to Inciardi (1996), in the United States offenders who received 12 to 15 months of treatment in prison followed by an additional six months of drug treatment and job training were more than twice as likely to be drug-free than offenders who received only prison-based treatment. The Connecticut Alternatives to Incarceration Program (AIP) is very successful in terms of the ratios of new arrests; AIP is two to five times more effective than prison (State of Connecticut Judicial Branch Sanctions 1996). There is now ample proof, in many documented studies, that quality programs for reduction of recidivism work very well, are much more cost effective than simple incarceration, and should be substantially expanded. Drug treatments and education/training must be extensive. But cost-cutting these programs renders halfway houses relatively ineffective (Duguid 1997, 56–68; Batiuk, Moke, and Rounree 1997).

Failures:

Rouleau (1996), of the Université de Montréal, discussed the outcome data from her Montreal clinic for released sex offenders. She found that 37 (25 percent) had re-offended, and that 10 (25 percent) of these had committed new sexual offences. Child molesters accounted for most of the recidivists. Rouleau recommended better training for parole officers, more intensive community supervision, and more structure in the halfway houses and system. It was reported that almost one third of the 1135 prisoners being held in halfway houses prior to their trials had escaped, and that most of them still remained at large, many of them to be tried for murder.

BOX 13.3	St. Leonard's Society of Canada

Today, the St. Leonard's Society of Canada is a national voluntary criminal justice organization consisting of individuals and non-profit agencies who believe in community-based corrections and in society's role in working with people who come out of prison back into the community. Each affiliate is governed by a volunteer board of directors. The Society's national board is composed of a delegate from each affiliate and four members representing the community at large. The St. Leonard's Society is committed to the prevention of crime through programs that promote responsible community living and safer communities. The goals of the Society are to:

- Assist persons in conflict with the law and prevent recidivism by facilitating member agencies to provide educational programs, industrial workshops, community residential centres, and such other supportive programs as may be approved by the directors;

- Prevent crime by promoting, developing, and implementing improved policies, procedures, and service delivery within the criminal justice system;

- Promote acceptance of responsibility and accountability by persons in conflict with the law, in order to change behaviour that contributes to crime;

- Help the community understand its responsibility in both the incidence of crime and in the manner in which society responds to it.

These goals are achieved by operating halfway houses to help people make a successful transition from prison into the community, by running drug and alcohol treatment programs, by providing employment opportunities to develop job skills, by developing new programs to meet reintegration needs, by analyzing proposed legislative initiatives for their contribution to criminal justice and community safety, by publishing a newsletter called *Coast to Coast*, and by informing the community at large about criminal justice issues to increase awareness of the facts. Other types of day programs include after-school tutoring, family relationship, anger and emotions, violence, self-management, LifeLine (which helps those who have received long-term sentences to readjust to "life on the outside"), and victim-offender reconciliation.

History—St. Leonard's Society of Canada

The St. Leonard's Society was founded by the Reverend James G. Jones in Chicago in 1954, and named after St. Leonard of France, who has been the patron saint of prisoners since the sixth century. In 1962, the Reverend Neil Libby founded St. Leonard's House in Windsor, Ontario, and the organization expanded into a national group in 1967. By 1971, there were 10 homes affiliated with the St. Leonard's Society of Canada. The Society was contracted to initiate the Community Service Order Program in 1977, and again two years later to institute a Victim-Offender Reconciliation Program. In 1981, the Society created the Canadian Training Institute, which remains a national training body for residential staff. In 1988, the St. Leonard's Society became an affiliate-based organization, and by 1990 there were 16 affiliates operating more than 30 programs. Today there are 20 Society homes and affiliates across the country.

How Effective is the St. Leonard's Society?

The St. Leonard's Society of Metropolitan Toronto, seeking to meet the residential needs of recently released prisoners returning to the community, has developed a crime prevention centre.

Applying "what works" research to treatment, the agency strives to prevent such victimization in the first place. Crime prevention encompasses a vast array of interventions designed to prevent crime. Some crime prevention efforts

are focused on the community as a whole. These include programs such as Neighbourhood Watch, efforts to install better lighting in parks or alleys, the use of electronic or other surveillance in high-crime areas, and efforts to provide community support to families, children, and youth who are at the margins of society. These are often called "primary prevention" activities. "Secondary prevention" targets individuals or groups of people at risk of being involved in criminal activity. For example, failure to complete school is clearly linked to greater likelihood of involvement in the criminal justice system. Programs can be implemented to keep children in school or allow them to return to school. Other individuals or groups of groups that are at high risk of becoming engaged in the justice system can be targeted with appropriate services to reduce the risk, thereby ultimately reducing crime. "Tertiary prevention" comprises efforts to prevent further crimes by someone who has been charged or convicted. This includes everything from diversion programs for first-time offenders to rehabilitation efforts aimed at more persistent offenders.

The St. Leonard's Society makes materials and resources relating to crime prevention available to interested individuals, businesses, groups, and organizations in the community (victim resources referral and support, family violence prevention and intervention, attendance program, substance abuse program, and residential program).

The London affiliate of the Society deserves special note regarding its implementation of justice circles. Founded on the basic principles of accountability, and the role of the home community in dealing with incidents of crime, these circles effectively embody the community-based justice goals of the St. Leonard's Society. The Kingston Employment Project has offered continued work opportunities and support to clients. Program have been expanded to include life skills and job placement training, intermittent programs and LifeLine. St. Leonard's Pallet Company, a division of St. Leonard's Society of Brant, has served Brantford and the surrounding area for nearly 20 years. The Pallet Company operates a structured work program in a real industrial environment, all while competing in the marketplace.

In 1996/97, there were 4081 offenders on full parole, 912 offenders on day parole, and 2074 offenders on statutory release under the jurisdiction of the Correctional Service of Canada (1997a). These figures exclude provincial offenders on parole supervised by the Correctional Service where there were no provincial parole offices and also excludes federal offenders who had been deported, temporarily detained, or were unlawfully at large. Parole eligibility varies depending on the type of sentence received (see Chapter 12). For example, the majority of offenders are eligible to apply for full parole after serving either one third of their sentence or seven years, whichever occurs first. Offenders serving life sentences for first-degree murder are eligible after serving 25 years. As set out in the Criminal Code, most federal inmates are automatically released on statutory release after serving two thirds of their sentence if they have not already been released on parole. Whether on parole or statutory release, offenders are supervised in the community by the Correctional Service and will be returned to prison if they are believed to present an undue risk to the public (Correctional Service of Canada 1997a).

For the fiscal year of 1996/97, the Correctional Service had spent just over $1.1 billion. The average annual cost of incarcerating an offender in a federal institution during 1995/96 was $50,375. The average annual cost of supervising an offender on parole or statutory release during 1995/96 was $9,145 (National Parole Board 1997; Correctional Service of Canada 1997b). But the Correctional Service must rely on the cooperation of the community in opening a community residential facility (Castillo 1994). In terms of the sheer numbers of offenders under community supervision, community corrections represents a major component of the mandate of the Correctional Service. At any one time, approximately 43 percent of all offenders under federal jurisdiction are in the community on some form of conditional release (Correctional Service of Canada 1990).

There are other factors that point to the importance of community corrections. The primary goal of reintegrating offenders into the community, which is expressed in the mission statement of the Service, has drawn increasing attention to the significant role our community programs must play (Correctional Service of Canada 1990). Community residential facilities also form an important component of the community corrections operations of the Service. The supervision of offenders through parole offices and community residential facilities provides opportunities for parole officers to assist offenders in the process of adjusting to the community and support their efforts to maintain crime-free lifestyles. The community case management officer provides counselling and referral services, and generally performs the role of advocate broker in helping offenders gain access to community resources. To this end, there are also a number of programs funded by the Correctional Service designed to meet particular needs of conditionally released offenders. Such programs endeavour to use community resources such as education, religion, vocational, recreational, and medical services that are essential to reintegration. These include employment and skill-training programs, liaison programs for Native offenders, specialized psychological services for sex offenders, alcohol and drug abuse programming, and a wide variety of programs aimed at helping offenders acquire life skills. The majority of these programs are made available through contracts with community agencies that have expertise in addressing the specific needs and problems faced by offenders in the community.

In 1969, an amendment to the *Parole Act* led to what is today known as day parole. Under this type of parole, an offender must return to prison or a community residential facility each evening. Therefore, as the use of day parole use grew, so did the need for centres for offender accommodation and supervision (Brunet 1994). In 1973, Outerbridge conducted a study of community-based residential centres (cited in Brunet 1974). He predicted a stronger demand for these centres as a result of day parole and proposed that both levels of government work together with the private sector to reach agreements on the operation of community residential facilities in each region.

The halfway house phenomenon is not a new one. Attempts were made in the early part of the 19th century in North America to implement concepts and programs that today we would consider remarkably modern in tone and theory. Most of these attempts to establish community-based residential treatment programs were started by persons and groups with a strong religious orientation or by volunteers with a strong sense of social conscience from the mid 1850s to the early 1900s (Platt 1977; Smykla 1981; Scull 1977). In fact, the reintegration of offenders in the community dates back to ancient Greece and Rome, and to Renaissance Europe, where criminals were punished by the community alone (Benzvy-Miller 1990). Almost all original attempts were in the private sector and had no governmental support or involvement. More than a hundred years later, the same impulse began to manifest itself in different parts of the nation on behalf of different social disability groups. In the early 1950s, a few programs opened their doors; in the early 1960s, the tide began to swell into a torrent, with over 3000 programs listed in 1980s.

Citing Crawford (1988), Benzvy-Miller notes that approximately $25 million each year is spent to house 1200 federal prisoners a day in 170 halfway houses across Canada. For Evans (1990), however, there are three major challenges facing community corrections: ideology, demography, and resources. In terms of ideology, Evans contrasts a plethora of issues related to a justice model and a model of law and order (i.e., a shift towards surveillance and monitoring). In reference to demography, Evans draws attention to a new phenomenon—an increase in the number of elderly. Lastly, he predicts that the dearth of resources (e.g., fiscal problems of governments and the necessity to reduce deficits) will affect the ability to meet demands for service. Likewise, in the Report of the Federal, Provincial, and Territorial Deputy Ministers and Heads of Corrections (1996), the challenges of community-based corrections were identified in terms of available capacity and resources (cost-effective means) in dealing with escalating prison and penitentiary populations despite a decline in the reported crime rate.

Examples of community-based measures to offset escalating costs include bail verification and supervision programs; electronic monitoring and house arrest; fine option programs; enhanced probation and community-based treatment programs; temporary absences, including accelerated temporary absences, temporary release to offender's residence with or without electronic monitoring, temporary release to a community residence, and temporary release to treatment program in community, and temporary release with intensive community supervision by probation services; streamlined parole application procedures; capping capacity and the use of administrative temporary absences to relieve overcrowding; and an increased use of restorative justice and mediation approaches. For example, Saskatchewan uses intensive supervision electronic monitoring and parole and will expand administrative releases, electronic monitoring, and community supervision (see Box 13.4). Manitoba has had success in diverting some offenders to the restorative resolutions program and is examining intermediate sanctions such as electronic monitoring and mediation.

In Ontario, correctional facilities, projects to rationalize programs and services are under way to streamline correctional operations and meet deficit-reduction targets. Initiatives include electronic monitoring as a replacement for most community residences, video court pilot projects, development of strict discipline facilities for young offenders, stricter eligibility criteria for conditional release decisions, adult diversion and young offender alternative measures programs, and an in-depth review of the Ontario Board of Parole. The Ontario planning initiatives propose a strategically located network of highly efficient and cost-effective correctional facilities using advanced security and business technology (Progressive Conservative Party of Ontario 1999).

Prince Edward Island, meanwhile, in cooperation with the ministries of the Solicitor General, Justice, and Correctional Service of Canada, has undertaken a criminal justice/corrections review to assist with a long-range planning framework. The objectives include efforts to reduce costs, reassess, and rationalize responsibilities and resources, and improve administration and delivery of justice services consistent with government reform in the province.

ELECTRONIC MONITORING AS COMMUNITY-BASED CORRECTIONS

As is evident from the above initiatives, there is considerable discussion among senior government officials about the introduction of electronic monitors. As McCormick (1995) argues, electronic monitors physically limit the offender and simultaneously serve as visible reminders to offenders of their deference to an omnipresent process of social control. The monitor, as a new form of penal practice, extends the physical features of penal servitude to the reconstituted body of the released.

Deemed to be a cost-effective alternative to incarceration, **electronic monitoring** and **home confinements** are considered expressions of community corrections that have been met with mixed views. In utilizing these alternatives, the Correctional Service of Canada ensures a greater degree of safety to complement neighbourhood halfway houses. For non-violent

---

BOX 13.4   **Allaying Public Fears**

Canadians want a more punitive system to deal with crime but do not want the government to keep spending so much (Gomme 1992). Electronic monitoring is a partial response. Electronic monitoring is employed as a condition of probation for some low-risk offenders and can be used for those under house arrest. There is considerable popularity in Canada for this sanction, especially for impaired driving cases. Ostensibly the general purposes of electronic monitoring are a) the reduction of the incarcerated population; b) cutting of correctional costs; c) the provision of more humane control; and d) the protection of the public.

offenders, this alternative is even more cost efficient than halfway houses. Through a program of house arrest (Ball 1988), a criminal is required to wear an electronic monitoring device around his or her ankle or wrist. The device transmits signals to a monitoring base, where data are analyzed and recorded. That is, the monitor reports to a computer centre that determines whether the individual is present or absent. Interestingly, the offender usually pays all, or most, of the electronic monitoring cost as a condition of release. Such goals as crime deterrence, efficiency, punishment, prison overcrowding, and costs associated with incarceration are all shaping the use of electronic monitoring.

For Pacey (1983, 6), electronic monitoring has been employed, if not developed, as a result of a paradigm shift that places a great degree of emphasis on budget cutting and balancing, as well as an increased awareness of the need for rehabilitative models. In this manner, public confidence in community safety is also restored as a result of the belief that this device is "technically sound," built by qualified technicians, whose skill and knowledge are directed towards the personal safety concerns of the community and furthermore ensuring the personal safety of the community. The device details curfew violations and geographic movements. However, one may argue that electronic monitoring provides a more humane punishment while enabling rehabilitation—rehabilitation that traditional facilities fail to produce. With house arrest—electronic monitoring initiatives, correctional officers remain in full control over minor offenders serving time in their homes through telephone check-ups around the clock, periodically dropping by, and of course through electronic monitoring. Offenders are permitted to remain with their partners, maintain their employment, as well as perform community services. This transformation increases self-confidence, self-esteem, and aids the rehabilitative process.

During the 1960s, Dr. Ralph Schwitzgebel designed a primitive device for monitoring human behaviour (see Box 13.5). His original design was created on the basis for human manipulation as well, through chemical stimuli and tracking sensors. Schwitzgebel noted that "a remote radio-communications system using belt transceivers is presently undergoing prototype testing. Systems of this type can monitor geographical location and psycho-physiological variables, as well as permit two-way coded communication with people in their natural environment" (1973, 15). The development of the microchip allowed for the use of this prototype to be used by correctional officials.

BOX 13.5 Electronic Monitoring

Electronic monitoring programs were first established in the United States in the 1980s and their use has spread to other countries around the world. In Canada, electronic monitoring programs are in operation in four provinces. Many of the evaluations reported in the literature are plagued by the lack of adequate comparison groups and controls for offender risk and needs. As a result, there is evidence suggesting that many electronic monitoring programs widen the correctional net. That is, they target relatively low-risk offenders who would function well without the additional controls imposed by electronic monitoring; there was no relationship to program completion. Successful completion of electronic monitoring ranged from 86 to 89 percent across the three provinces. Comparisons with inmates and probationers, after controlling for offender risk and needs, found that electronic monitoring had no effect on recidivism (Bonta, Wallace-Capretta, and Rooney 1999). There are two general findings that have important implications for policy and practice. First, Bonta, Wallace-Capretta, and Rooney found no evidence that electronic monitoring has a more significant impact on recidivism than the less intrusive, and less costly, correctional measure of probation. Thus, the value added by electronic monitoring programs appears limited. Second, cognitive-behavioural treatment programming targeting high-risk offenders was associated with significant reductions in offender recidivism. Continued support of treatment programs for high-risk offenders, perhaps combined with electronic monitoring to increase treatment attendance, is suggested.

More recently, Ontario introduced an electronic monitoring program in 1996. Ontario had earlier experimented with electronic monitoring in 1989 but abandoned the program partly because an evaluation found it not to be cost effective. Gradually electronic monitoring became a community-based alternative to incarceration. That is, offenders who would normally be imprisoned could instead be placed into an electronic monitoring program.

Because many electronic monitoring programs appear to target low-risk offenders and run the risk of widening the correctional net, estimating the true cost savings is difficult. The cost-benefit analyses that have been reported in the literature have been equivocal (Bonta, Wallace-Capretta, and Rooney 1999).

At first glance, electronic monitoring appears to provide an effective alternative to prison. Although hardly a mature industry, electronic monitoring has attracted a growing number of manufacturers. Surveillance becomes capital intensive, rather than labour intensive. Technical developments drastically alter the economics of surveillance such that it becomes much less expensive per unit watched. Aided by technology, a few persons can monitor many people and factors. But electronic monitoring marks the government's move away from doing business with non-profit community groups that ran many of the halfway houses and towards corporate, commercial, and for-profit groups. Electronic monitoring signals a move away from humane, or at least human, forms of supervision in favour of a move towards technological forms of supervision, a move from human to technological control (Corbett and Marx 1991).[1]

Electronic monitoring costs about $10 per day per person wearing an ankle bracelet, compared with $62 a day per inmate in the city's prisons (Knights undated). For juveniles, the cost of electronic home monitoring is $10 a day, compared to $100 a day to keep them in a juvenile hall. For adults, the cost of a bed in jail is $40 a day. The cost of electronic home monitoring is almost nothing, because adults pay $12 a day to be in the program.

In general, electronic monitoring continues to raise legal and ethical questions concerning the privacy and dignity of those involved. Skeptics claim that surveillance of this kind effectively widens the net of penal control, extending the control measures of the prison to the community. And concerns are expressed that electronic monitoring does not always represent the least restrictive measure.

1. Of more than 3,000 defendants in Philadelphia who have worn ankle bracelets since 1988, only about two dozen have become fugitives. And, according to Probation Department data, only about 1 in 100 has been arrested for a new crime while on electronic monitoring (Ditzen 1996).

The use of tracking devices raises a plethora of ethical concerns. Ruebhausen and Brim note that "a concept of **privacy** is proposed that involves the right of a person to determine when and to what extent information about himself will be shared or withheld from others" (cited in Schwitzgebel and Kolb 1974, 249). As with incarceration, this control violates the rights and freedoms of offenders. Offenders and their families are subjected to intrusive telephone calls and disruptive visits by correctional staff. In addition, offenders wearing these devices often complain about irritating rashes and skin burns (A. Visano 1998).

In spite of these issues, deficit cutting, balanced budgets, and downsizing of governments throughout the 1990s have resulted in an increased interest in electronic monitoring. Issues of privacy and rehabilitation have been overshadowed by such central concerns as penal costs.

A CASE STUDY OF COMMUNITY-BASED CORRECTIONS: CITIZENS' ADVISORY COMMITTEES

The federal and provincial governments continue to highlight in their annual reports their respective government's commitment to effective community alternatives in responding to such criteria as the protection of society and the rehabilitation of offenders. The 1984 Annual Report of the Ontario Ministry of Correctional Services, which remains almost unchanged as we enter the new millennium, cites the following goals:

> To encourage and develop community-based work programs and to facilitate the participation of both individual citizens and the community at large in the criminal justice system (5).

As Commissioner of Corrections, Ingstrup (1987, 7–9) celebrates:

> Accepting that the community is the only environment in which the offender can fully demonstrate the ability to function as a law-abiding citizen, gradual release to the community, and quality community supervision and support are essential to achieve our Mission of protecting society by facilitating the timely reintegration of offenders . . . We will also strive to enhance public understanding and acceptance of our role through active, responsive and honest communication with the public.

What emerges from the plethora of government documents is the theme that the community plays an incredibly vital role in the criminal justice system, a critical element in forging new relationships with offenders and state agencies. The general public concurs, as indicated by Doob and Roberts (1988), who report that 70 percent of Canadians indicate that they would rather put money into the development of community sanctions than in building more prisons. Admittedly, the government sanctions directly and symbolically the processes of community participation. The notion of the community as a context, however, remains poorly operationalized within an illusory framework that masks any connotations of containment, politics, and struggle.

The purposes of this section is to explore the concept of community by providing a case study of a much celebrated exercise in federal corrections—the **citizens' advisory committee**—and to focus attention on the need to transform community inaction into "communities-in-action."

According to the Correctional Service of Canada (1984), the citizens' advisory committee benefits from a rich heritage of citizen participation. It has not only helped wardens become more aware of community concerns but has also encouraged citizens in a free society to offer valuable educational, cultural, and employment opportunities to offenders.

The citizens' advisory committee opens the operation of federal corrections to the public and is influential in bringing the offender and the community together in work projects that benefit both. In 1965, there were at least three formal committees: at Saskatchewan Penitentiary, Matsqui in British Columbia, and Beaver Creek Correctional Camp in Ontario. Throughout the 1970s, as federal corrections expanded centralized control, the committee evolved to become a more objective check on corrections within a "watchdog" orientation (Thorne and Detlefsen 1986, 6). In 1977, the Solicitor General accepted the recommendations of the MacGuigan Parliamentary Sub-committee, which fully supported the value of citizens' advisory committees. Recommendation 25 of the MacGuigan Report (1977) clearly stated that the Penitentiary Service should be open and accountable to the public. Recommendation 49 further declares that citizens' advisory committees should be established in all penal institutions, members should be recruited from a cross-section of society representing a wide variety of interests as well as ethno-cultural diversity, citizens' advisory committees should advise directors of local attitudes towards the institution and programs, and they should inform and educate the public—to name but a few recommendations. The Correctional Service of Canada (undated) requires these committees in every correctional institution and district parole office. Citizens' advisory committees have the following roles to:

1. Promote communication between inmates, Correctional Service staff and the public;
2. Participate in the overall development of the institution or district parole office;
3. Improve the local population's knowledge and understanding of these activities;
4. Provide conditions that will encourage public participation in correctional activities; and
5. Participate in developing community resources designed to support correctional programs (Correctional Service of Canada 1984).

The responsibilities of the citizens' advisory committee include advising the responsible local administrator or regional deputy commissioner on the overall development of the institution or district parole office and its programs, assisting in developing community resources, educating the local community, and providing continuing advice to the local administrator or regional deputy commissioner regarding the sensitivities, problems, needs, and pulse of the community. The Correctional Service of Canada (1987) details the policy objective as follows:

> To contribute to the functioning of the Service and humane treatment of offenders by involving citizens in the overall development of Service installations and by strengthening the ties between the field units and the local communities through the establishment of Citizen Advisory Committees.

This directive stipulates that members are appointed by the local director with the consent of the Deputy Commissioner of the region. Citizens' advisory committees would consist of no fewer than five members, appointed for no less than two years. Disagreements about the role and responsibilities of the committee that cannot be resolved locally may be referred to the Deputy Commissioner of the region, or if necessary to the Commissioner (Correctional Service of Canada 1987). The Report of the Standing Committee on Justice and Solicitor General (Solicitor General of Canada 1988, 205) recommends that the Correctional Service of Canada allocate more resources to the citizens' advisory committees "so that community participation in their activities may be more widespread."

The Central Ontario Citizens' Advisory Committee, which operated in Metropolitan Toronto, was unilaterally disbanded on October 7, 1988 (*The Globe and Mail*, 19 October

1988). The District Director of the Correctional Service, the most senior official in the Toronto area, sent letters to committee members informing them that as a result of "emotional crises," the Citizens' Advisory Committee was disbanded, and he indicated that new members would be appointed. The Toronto area had been a hotbed of controversy since the Correctional Service had begun to issue contracts to private agencies. The matter surfaced in early 1988 with the murder of Tema Conter. For months the local committee had been critical of the government's move to privatize halfway houses. Although the monthly meetings were congenial, the Chair and the Vice-Chair echoed numerous concerns about the levels of supervision, the "for profit" contracts, and the failure of local officials to keep committee members informed of pressing cases. On several occasions, for example, the acting Chair, like many other committee members, learned much about events not from local Correctional Service officials but from the media. As result of too many thorny questions about privatization asked by the Chair, Vice-Chair, Secretary, and several members, the District Director moved quickly to muzzle any complaints.

Just hours after disbanding this public advisory group, the Correctional Service reversed its decision and restored the committee. In a news release, the Deputy Commissioner noted that the dismissal was the result of a "misunderstanding" (*The Globe and Mail,* 20 October 1988, A21). According to this senior official:

> The real problem arises when you are into the land of policy . . . There are ambiguities here and there . . . [they] are not a watchdog or an ombudsman. They do not have authority to legislate change in the service. Their role is an advisory one, nudging here and there, or pushing here and there.

The Chair of this citizens' advisory committee commented: "We should be part of the fabric of the correctional service. The role we have played in the past is a very important one . . . We have no vested interests" (*The Globe and Mail*, 20 October 1998).

In the above case study, members of the Citizens' Advisory Committee had been working productively for years. But they mistakenly believed that the committee was a legitimate mechanism for genuine public input into the operations of the Correctional Service of Canada.

Clearly, the citizens' advisory committee can provide a valuable contribution to the Correctional Service. But, long- and short-term interrelated changes at the organizational, inter-organizational, systemic, and societal levels are warranted. Immediately, the Correctional Service must confront numerous barriers at the local level that include:

- The denial of a problem, the refusal to recognize the significance of community input;
- A self-arrogated sense of professionalism that fears change and is suspicious of critical inquiry;
- A lack of commitment to change;
- A dysfunctional public accountability; and
- A displacement of responsibility.

The following changes could easily be implemented; the Correctional Service of Canada, for instance, needs to:

1. Develop an understanding of community interests that moves beyond trite public statements;
2. Increase the flow of information;
3. Permit the citizens' advisory committee to distance itself from the Correctional Service;

4. Field questions from all community groups;

5. Encourage the proactive consultation of the citizens' advisory committee;

6. Utilize community resources;

7. Invite participation in the program planning and development stages;

8. Select members of the citizens' advisory committee from a cross-section of the community who will articulate issues of inequality, rampant in the criminal justice system, such as the treatment of the First Nations people, race, gender, class, and biases against people with disabilities; and

9. Use volunteers effectively.

In other words, it is now necessary to move from a posture of reflection to one of action. Individual citizens' advisory committees need to implement initiatives that confront traditional barriers. During the initial stages of involving community groups, the committees would be well advised to:

1. Provide information to prospective volunteers from labour, police, business, tenant/ ratepayer associations, advocacy groups, academics, service providers, and inmate committees;

2. Develop a brokerage role that would help volunteers become aware of the responsibilities of senior administrative officials;

3. Publicize in a culturally sensitive manner the activities of the Correctional Service and the committee;

4. Reach out to identify and encourage community or neighbourhood-based organizations;

5. Develop a capacity for inter-organizational collaboration not just with the police alone but with a wider representation of perspectives;

6. Organize resources so that they have the maximum impact on volunteers;

7. Evaluate the services of the committee and adjust policies to accommodate to the community rather than strictly to the Correctional Service;

8. Develop and implement explicit policies to improve community participation with appropriate protections against unilateral dismissals;

9. Emphasize more modern management approaches with an emphasis on human resource development and human relations skills;

10. Coordinate community events and workshops with other agencies to avoid confusion and enhance resource sharing;

11. Encourage joint ventures with other voluntary organizations;

12. Integrate linkages with service providers in health, education, employment, social assistance, etc.;

13. Assist in joint funding, joint personnel exchanges, and joint planning and support services;

14. Collaborate with service providers and advocacy groups that work with the socially disadvantaged;

15. Monitor the activities of the local Correctional Service branch;

16. Evaluate the objectives of the mission statement; and

17. Provide referrals to community agencies.

Access is a central dynamic that influences interplay between the community and the state agencies. Access refers not only to voluntary participation but also, more significantly, to the level of involvement in policy formulation, advising senior bureaucrats, setting directions for change in the Correctional Service of Canada and the citizens' advisory committee, ongoing consultations with both community leaders and Correctional Service officials. Furthermore, access refers to the ownership of the agenda that to date has been exclusively controlled by the Correctional Service.

CONCEPTUALIZING THE COMMUNITY

How then do we define community and what is the relationship between the community and crime? For Durkheim ([1897] 1951, 241), writing in 1897, the community shapes and protects individuals from criminal pursuits by providing a pervasive belief system that preserves social harmony, integrates, and constrains deviance. Specifically, Durkheim contrasted two types of integrating communities—mechanical and organic solidarities. **Mechanical solidarity** is the moral and social integration associated with life in simple societies, in which a collective dominant conscience based on similar social circumstances, feelings, and interests directs individuals to internalize these collective sentiments. **Organic solidarity**, evident in contemporary Canadian society, is the natural outcome of relationships grounded in highly organized divisions of labour. Highly specialized roles and the diversity of functions result in a weakening of the collective moral conscience and a general decline in social integration. In organic societies like Canada, laws regulate interactions of various social parts and provide restitution to aggrieved parties.

Community as a Social Construct

The concept of the community is far too frequently "decontextualized and too readily extricated from the larger processes of competition and changing property relations or the transformation of space, which loom large in structures of social relations" (Kahne and Schwartz 1978, 474). In contrast to the above "**community lost**" thesis, a "**community saved**" perspective has also emerged. The latter approach discovered persisting, vigorous kinship and friendship involvements that provide vitality, sociability, and support (Whyte 1955; Liebow 1967; Suttles 1972). But in their haste to rediscover well-established rich, complicated social relations within different communities/urban villages, studies of the community-saved tradition concentrate on self-contained personalized social environments. Others have argued that the community-saved argument remains grossly inadequate for it unduly isolates the community from larger social structures such as the national land market, labour, capital, and product (Greer 1972, 7)—that is, the whole economic and social order.

The above overview suggests that social order and its attendant controls exist within certain relational environments—notably the community. But the concept of community has been subject to endless and confusing debates (Gibbs 1967). In his review of the many meanings attributed to community, Hillery (1955) highlights three generally agreed-upon characteristics: the community as a spatially defined unit-geographic area; the community as common ties or modes of relationships where a prevailing normative value system characterizes a sense of belongingness, cooperation, or distinctiveness (Dank 1971); and the community as a social interaction (Siegal 1977). According to Gross (1967) and Effrat (1974) many studies have failed analytically to move beyond the social and physical boundaries of this "multi-dimensional ordinal variable."

The community, therefore, is characterized neither by the withering away of primary relationships nor by the triumph of secondary relationships. More appropriately, a growth of specialized networks of social relations extending across wide areas that interact in various complicated ways accompany urbanization. That is, the lowering of spatial barriers and the increased freedom to choose social relations have led to a proliferation of personal communities consisting of networks of personal ties, each more compatible and more supportive (Fischer 1976). Today, cities contain many subcommunities with identifiable patterns of relationships both locally and non-locally based. Meanwhile, personal communities are based on interest, rather than residential proximity; they usually entail manipulations of several networks simultaneously (Craven and Wellman 1973). As Suttles (1972) observed, these communities are not immune from outside pressures or impingements from larger societal environments.

Briefly, a sense of community is not necessarily linked to a particular time and space. A place may no longer contain social linkages but it can still strongly constitute community and identity. Thus, definitions of community are multifaceted—an important component of identity and emotional attachment about places.

Liberalism, Neoliberalism, and the Community

The community has become the basis of the social, that is, it is what binds us together as cognizant social beings involved in common projects. For the earliest liberal thinkers such as Thomas Hobbes (1588–1679), John Locke (1632–1704), and Jean Jacques Rousseau (1712–1778), the concept of community invoked a set of contractual obligations. **Liberalism** integrates the somewhat nebulous notion of community with contractual duties and obligations. Control is legitimated by institutions that promote a particular peace that protects privacy and property. For instance, in our society, privacy and property are articulated within a well-respected utilitarian framework of contact.

Although the father of liberalism, John Stuart Mill (1632–1704), stressed the importance of acting in ways that advance the greatest good for the greatest number, the foundations of liberalism consist of an unquestioned acceptance of the compatibility of capitalism

BOX 13.6	Liberalism and Neoliberalism

Liberalism is a doctrine that maintains the significance of the state, as an association of private interests, to facilitate the common good. Early liberalism favoured an increased responsibility of the state. The state was a trust set up by individuals to form a society to secure order. Despite the emphasis on the state, liberalism celebrated the centrality of the individual rights. The neoliberalism of the 1990s strives to link rights and utilities. Accordingly, the growth of private interests, rational choice models, and priority of rights over the good are all well respected. Critics argue that rights and freedoms in liberalism are illusory, especially since the interests of liberalism are consistent with the bases of capitalism. Neoliberalism in Canada is moving towards minimal state involvement, as well as state protection of a framework within which market forces can operate according to its own logic.

with democracy (Simon 1988). The fabric of order as envisioned by liberalism is woven together by a wide assortment of different but equal fibres constituting the liberal democratic quilt. As Locke argued, society as a patchwork is loosely formed by the unanimous agreements (contracts) of its members who make up the community. The right to property is seen as sacred, a right closely linked to notions of liberty and freedom. Accordingly, this right implies that each individual has an equal chance or opportunity to accumulate as much as he or she wishes or is able (White 1986).

The concept of community has never been adequately defined. There is much disagreement among criminologists as to what exactly constitutes community corrections. On the one hand, community corrections presupposes some agreement about the conceptual and empirical validity of community as an identifiable and viable concept. While ideologically appealing, the image of community used in much of the literature is often nostalgic, consensual, geographically limited, and value laden. This chapter, however, argues for a more precise conception of community that moves beyond the ideological banners of liberalism that legitimate decisions, preserve privilege, and maintain authority relations. Current appropriation of the concept of community standardize a discourse that privileges some voices and violates many "other" voices and histories. More recently, it has become more fashionable in both academic and government research to implicate the concept of community with neoliberal discourses about citizenship, private and public domains, and a restored faith in market conditions (Clarke 1999; Rose 1996). However, the concept of citizenship as currently employed by state functionaries is considerably flawed given that equal citizenship does not exist in an economically stratified society.

To appreciate community-based corrections fully, we argue that the notion of "community of interests" is a more appropriate term that encompasses the differential distribution of rights and duties. Membership and participation in community corrections vary considerably, and are influenced by the level of societal, economic, and political interests as these are perceived in terms of contractual responsibility.

Throughout the 1990s neoliberalism has succeeded in promoting a "responsibilization strategy" (Garland 1997). Responsibilization reflects both the diminishing ability of the state to provide full service and a process of downloading responsibility to the community. By linking **responsibilization** to community empowerment and governance, the community has become an effective tool in corrections. In downloading responsibility, the state has restructured corrections according to a partnership (see Box 13.7). This realignment is shaped by the politics of financial exigencies and neoliberal principles of private sector responsibility. It is this author's opinion that this realignment enables certain elements of the community to engage in a discourse of criminalization that continues to privilege the dominant ethos by connecting privacy and community. Responsibilization confers the "entitlements" of citizenship to those who are deemed responsible in carrying out their duties as citizens. This contrived community, according to Henry and Milovanovic (1991), reproduces social structures of crime and its control. As will be argued, neoliberalism publicly parades the community as an expression of state-supreme practices while simultaneously adhering to the inviolability of possessive individualism. What community is developed? Who are the participants? There is no simple answer to these loaded questions. The notion of community as reflected in the discussion above represents a set of complex oppositional contexts whose meaning depend on one's frame of reference.

BOX 13.7	Restorative Justice Movement

The restorative justice movement emphasizes problem-solving instead of just deserts. Crime is seen less as an act against the state, and primarily as an act against another person or the immediate community. The practice of restorative justice seeks to actively engage the offender, victim, and community into positive and healing action. Restorative justice is fundamentally concerned with restoring social relationships, and establishing or re-establishing social equality in relationships. Restorative justice inherently demands that one attend to the nature of relationships between individuals, groups, and communities (Llewellyn and Howse 1999).

Although Eglash is generally credited with coining the term restorative justice in 1977, the conception of justice to which he referred was not new. Restorative justice is not a new movement. Such conceptions of justice have been more or less prominent through most of history. In fact, restorative conceptions of justice claim their roots in both western and non-western traditions (Llewellyn and Howse 1999). Justice practices in pre-modern societies may have contained elements of restorative principles (such as restitution and compensation). Current applications of the idea began to develop and proliferate in the 1970s in North America, beginning with a victim-offender reconciliation program in Ontario in 1974. Hundreds of similar programs subsequently emerged in other North American sites and in Europe. A somewhat different model of restorative justice emerged in the Antipodes, one based on family group decision-making. That model was first introduced in New Zealand in 1989, incorporating Maori approaches to the handling of child protection and juvenile justice cases. The conferencing idea was subsequently borrowed and adapted by jurisdictions in Australia, the United States, Canada, the United Kingdom, Ireland, Singapore, and South Africa. Conferences can differ from victim-offender mediation schemes in that they bring more community people into the discussion, acknowledge a wider range of victimized people, and emphasize participation by the family members of offenders. Thus, a move towards a restorative model of justice is perhaps best understood as a return to the roots of community justice that predates modern criminal law.

Interestingly, pre-colonial African societies employed sanctions that were compensatory rather than punitive. Pre-colonial law sought to restore the disturbed social equilibrium within the community and sense of humanity, of the natural connectedness of people (Llewellyn and Howse 1999). The Japanese culture emphasizes not only the attitude of the offender in acknowledging guilt, expressing remorse, and compensating any victim, but also the victims' response in expressing willingness to pardon as determinative elements in the decision whether to report, to prosecute, and to sentence the offender.

In the Canadian context, the restorative justice movement has been characteristic of Aboriginal cultures. Ross (1996) speaks of an ancient conviction that the best way to respond to the criminal is not by punishing solitary offenders but by focusing on processes of teaching and healing all the parties involved, with an eye on the past to understand how things have come to be, and an eye on the future to design measures that show the greatest promise of making it healthier for all concerned (Llewellyn and Howse 1999). The Quaker and Mennonite traditions as with other aboriginal (Maori) customs have guided this movement.

Restorative justice theory owes much to recent movements aimed at addressing the failures of the existing justice system and developing new ways of doing justice. Van Ness (1990) identify several such movements (see Llewellyn and Howse 1999):

1. The informal justice movement emphasized informal procedures with a view to increasing access to and participation in the legal process.

It focused on delegalization in an effort to minimize the stigmatization and coercion resulting from existing practices;

2. Restitution as a response to crime was rediscovered in the 1960s. The movement focused on the needs of victims, maintaining that meeting the needs of victims would serve the interests of society more generally;

3. The victim's rights movement works to have the right of victims to participate in the legal process recognized; and

4. Reconciliation/conferencing movement (a victim/offender mediation, family group conferencing movement).

COMMUNITY-BASED CORRECTIONS AS PRIVATE INTERESTS

Throughout North America, beginning in the early 1980s, a profit-oriented community of private interests have entered the penal industry. According to the Report of Federal, Provincial, and Territorial Deputy Ministers and Heads of Corrections (1996), Alberta is exploring the possibility of **privatization**. Meanwhile, Nova Scotia will pursue not only a "cooperative business solutions approach" with the private sector but is also considering privatizing an adult male facility for the first time. By contrast, private correctional services have increased over 415 percent between 1990 and 1995 in the United States (Allen and Simonsen 1998).

Private corrections is nothing new in U.S. history. In the mid 1800s, penny-pinching state legislatures awarded contracts to private entrepreneurs to operate and manage Louisiana's first state prison, and New York's Auburn and Sing Sing penitentiaries (Smith 1993). As with anti-trust legislation and the progressive reforms that followed, public pressure impelled government regulation of private sector abuse. By the turn of the century, concerted opposition from labour, business, and reformers forced the state to take direct responsibility for prisons, thus bringing the first era of private prisons to an end. But within the last two decades, there has been a resurgence of the ideological imperatives of the free market, as well as huge increases in the number of prisoners and the concomitant increase in imprisonment costs. In an age of rising deficits and a growing disbelief in the welfare state, solutions are found in the interests of private capital. **Neoliberalism** maintains that the private sector can do it not only more cheaply given extant cash-strapped public resources and but also more efficiently in terms of "law and order." The converging trends of free-marketism, higher prison population, and escalating costs are part of the solution to run more than $20 billion a year corrections industry in the U.S. The Corrections Corporation of America, Wackenhut Corrections Corporation, U.S. Corrections Corporation, Pricor, among others, are all ready to turn a quick profit from the traffic in convicts. However, recent evidence indicates that private prisons do not experience any more control problems than public-run facilities (Thomas 1998).

There are two fundamental interrelated issues that warrant analysis: efficiency and accountability. Can private operators be trusted to run prisons for less without sacrificing "quality of service"? Efficiency in the delivery of human services means much more than the ability to house bodies cheaply while complying with minimal standards such as providing general deterrence, rehabilitation, and ensuring the safety of society. The reduction of recidivism means a reduction of the supply of profit producing "customers." As Smith (1993) notes, it is in the material interest of these companies, therefore, to produce not prisoners who have "paid their debt to society," but ones who will continue to pay and pay on the installment plan. The profit motive could cause private operations to cut corners, leading to poor or unsafe conditions—a more dangerous class of released inmates.

In terms of accountability, what oversight mechanisms ensure the primacy of society's interests? In law, the agencies of the government are subject to constitutional restraints that do not always apply to private entities. Typically, private interests have resisted compliance, especially if regulation erodes in any way the profit margin. Repressive apparatuses such as prisons that are run for profit cannot attend to the rights of inmates. To profit from crime, it is imperative for corporations to distort levels of crime, the need for more private prisons. Cheaper is not necessarily better when it particularly applies to public safety and rehabilitation.

Historically, private non-profit agencies in the business of aftercare operate with a considerable degree of accountability but such industries are not well regulated; staff are of dubious value; and such facilities tend to offer inferior services, hence undermining any rehabilitative initiatives. To reiterate, privatization offers different kinds of services and lower levels of accountability. Privatization responds all too easily to a credulous and ill-informed public moved by distorted media images and political propaganda about crime, as was evident in the 1999 Ontario provincial election. The community herein consists of only a certain set of "private interests," motivated not by fundamental principles of due process nor by correctional mandates of rehabilitation, but rather animated by the crass opportunism for a "fast buck."

SUMMARY

Within the correctional marketplace of rhetoric, jargon, and clichés, the concept of community has become a negotiable commodity, whose value is conveniently determined by the state. The community concept provides more than ideological legitimacy. Rather, as currently manipulated by sophisticated cadres of state bureaucrats committed to public relations campaigns, the community concept is designed to discipline "outside" participation, pre-empt criticism, and discourage much needed critical dialogue.

The "community" is an elusive concept that has been too easily appropriated by the state to engineer support for limited initiatives that fail to grapple with fundamental inequalities in corrections. This term is contextually determined and discursively constructed to satisfy organizational interests. Without reference to the context of power, the community concept has become a pretext for intervention and exclusion. A commitment to local contests, for example, is perceived as counter hegemonic and subject to coercive measures.

Given the proliferation of chatter about increased community participation, readers are further asked to reconsider the relationship between state machinations and democratic accountability. Interestingly, one wonders curiously what price will be paid by those who dare to question authority not from the outside community but from well behind its bars.

The normative notion of the community is related to the concept of hegemony, leadership based on the consent of the ruled, consent secured by the diffusion and popularization of ruling-class views. Hegemony, achieved through institutions of civil society, is the predominance of one class over other classes through consent rather than force. This consent is manifested through a generic loyalty to the ruling class by virtue of their position in society. Hegemony is based on economic, ethical, social, philosophical, and political interests.

The ideology of a community, as a system of ideas manifested in all aspects of social life, performs powerful correcting functions. As a cultural form, this ideology legitimates social control by directing cognition, evaluations, and ideals. With its links to political economy and the state, ideology encapsulates by distorting material conditions and privileges. For example, the dominant cultural ideologies incorporate features from other ideologies: neo-liberal myths about community have also become powerful instruments of domination.

Neoliberalism is a signifying system that manipulates and creates new discourses. As an ideology that popularizes freedom from government regulation, the primacy of market forces, privatization, fiscal reform, the reduction of state spending, and decentralization, neoliberalism disseminates information to satisfy elementary levels of popular curiosity.

Community initiatives such as restorative justice initiatives are of dubious value when unaccompanied by meaningful programs that embrace universal entitlements. Historically, state-sponsored community-based activities have been characterized by attractive legal palliatives replete with convenient mythologies. We need to journey beyond a reflexive celebration of a liberal rhetoric towards a more critical appraisal of the general implications of community activism. A prudent response to this pressing agenda warrants a detailed audit of accountability, independence, and control.

A community is embedded within many contexts: social, political, economic, and legal. Despite the niceties about the "sanctity of the community" that remains enshrined in lofty, nostalgic, and tantalizing mythologies, the community as envisaged in Canadian society is a product of orthodox liberalism and the ethos of convenient accommodation. But what community and whose community interests are we discussing? How do state-contrived communities respond to the challenges of social justice? Likewise, as Foucault (1980, 1) admonished, "one should start with popular justice, with acts of justice by the people." Does the community, therefore, appropriately reflect the dynamics, dialectics, and diversity of Canadian society? Community participation as currently manifested does not facilitate the resolution of social disputes on its own.

Communities-in-action, and not community inaction, should govern community-based corrections. Inequalities in corrections are ubiquitous. Victims feel ignored by an alienating system of justice; inmates, parolees, and their families suffer deprivation; correctional officers complain about the insensitivities of management, stress, and poor working conditions; and the general public remains ignorant and fearful of "alarming" crime rates, statistics that are often advanced to secure support for state practices.

An examination of advocacy and community-based empowerment provides a conceptually more comprehensive appreciation of community action in corrections. From a public policy perspective, however, a focus on communities-in-action is threatening. This commitment to meaningful action does not suffer from the vagueness and vulnerability of state-sponsored "community" constructions. Changes in legislation and administrative rules and regulations that protect independent community input are long overdue. Moreover, vigilance on the part of community-based organizations groups in reclaiming from both state and private corporations that which more appropriately belongs to them—corrections.

KEY TERMS AND CONCEPTS

citizens' advisory
    committee
community-based
    corrections
community correctional
    centres
"community lost"

"community saved"
community residential
    facility
electronic monitoring
halfway house
home confinement
liberalism

mechanical solidarity
neoliberalism
organic solidarity
privacy
privatization
responsibilization

STUDY AND DISCUSSION QUESTIONS

1. Assess the following claim: "Corrections, as an expression of power, can only be understood by interrogating structures of politics and privilege."

2. Define the phenomenon of community-based corrections. How is an analysis of the community central to a more comprehensive appreciation of the structures and processes of corrections?

3. Assess the concept of community-based corrections in terms of prevailing crime control ideologies, effectiveness, and the "blurring and reshaping of institutional boundaries." Highlight the relevant institutions, processes, and interests in community corrections.

4. Moving beyond and beyond the rhetoric of efficiency, discuss the issue of accountability.

5. Privatization, as a social accomplishment, shapes and is shaped by the nature of society. How does the study of community corrections invite a commitment to challenge normative assumptions such as responsibilization?

6. Discuss the "community of interests" in reference to the preference of neoliberalism to private sector responsibility.

7. Define the concept of halfway houses. How is an analysis of the community central to a more comprehensive appreciation of the structures and processes of rehabilitation?

8. "Privatization is derivative of the needs and demands of the wider political economy." Evaluate.

9. What are the strengths and limitations of community corrections?

10. What changes are required to facilitate better understanding of community interests?

11. Identify the impediments to effective community participation.

12. What role can be played by the community in reducing crime?

13. What are the dangers of privatizing corrections?

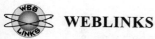

WEBLINKS

SHARE Incorporated (electronic monitoring services):
sharemonitoring.com/whatis.html

House Arrest Services: **www.housearrest.com**

Electronic Monitoring: **www.sgc.gc.ca/Epub/Corr/e199905/e199905.htm**

St. Leonard's Society: **www.stleonards.ca**

Australian Institute of Criminology, Restorative Justice Information:
www.aic.gov.au/rjustice/international.html

NOTE

1. A special note of gratitude is extended to Professor John Winterdyk; his suggestions were extremely helpful. I am grateful to Professor Brenda Spotton Visano for her insightful analysis of private sector economics as well as for her engaging support for this and other projects.

REFERENCES

Allen, H.E., and **C.E. Simonsen**. 1998. *Corrections in America: An Introduction* (8th ed.). Upper Saddle River, NJ: Prentice-Hall.

Ball, R.A. 1988. *House Arrest and Correctional Policy: Doing Time at Home*. Newbury Park, CA: Sage.

Batiuk, M.E., **P. Moke**, and **P.W. Rounree**. 1997. Crime and Rehabilitation: Correctional Education as an Agent of Change—A Research Note. *Justice Quarterly* 14(1).

Benzvy-Miller, S. 1990. Community Corrections and the NIMBY Syndrome. *Forum for Corrections Research* 2(2).

Bonta, J., **S. Wallace-Capretta**, and **J. Rooney**. 1999. *Electronic Monitoring in Canada*. Solicitor General Canada Public Works and Government Service of Canada. www.sgc.gc.ca/epub/corr/eem/eem.htm (April 2000).

Brunet, L. 1994. Community Residential Centres in Quebec: A Tripartite Agreement. *Forum for Corrections Research* 6(3).

Castillo, P. 1994. Putting the "Community" into Community Corrections. *Forum for Corrections Research* 6(3).

Clarke, C. 1999. *Motivation, Justification and Innovation*. Unpublished paper, doctoral candidate. Department of Sociology, York University.

Corbett, R., and **G.T. Marx**. 1991. Critique, No Souls in the New Machine: Technofallacies in the Electronic Monitoring Movement. *Justice Quarterly* 8(3).

Correctional Service of Canada. Undated. Commissioner's Directive 600-4-08.1. Ottawa: Solicitor General of Canada.

———. 1984. *Working Together: Citizens' Advisory Committees and the Correctional Service of Canada*. Ottawa: Solicitor General of Canada.

————. 1987. *Commissioner's Directive.* Citizens' Advisory Committee #023, January 1. Ottawa: Solicitor General of Canada.

————. 1990. A Profile of Federal Community Corrections. *Forum for Corrections Research* (2)2.

————. 1997a. *Facts, Offender Management System.* Ottawa: Supply and Services.

————. 1997b. *Basic Facts about Corrections in Canada.* Ottawa: Public Works and Government Services.

Craven, P., and **B. Wellman**. 1973. *The Network City.* Research Paper #59. Toronto: Centre for Urban and Community Studies, University of Toronto.

Crawford, T. 1988. Halfway Houses: Pleading a Case with Society. *Toronto Star*, 20 February. Quoted in S. Benzvy-Miller, Community Corrections and the NIMBY Syndrome. *Forum for Corrections Research* 1990 2(2).

Dank, B. 1971. Coming Out in the Gay World. *Psychiatry* 34, 182.

Ditzen, L.S. 1996. City to Extend Its Monitoring of Those under House Arrest. *Philadelphia Inquirer* 6 March, 1.

Doob, A., and **J. Roberts**. 1988. Public Punitiveness and Public Knowledge of the Facts: Some Canadian Surveys. In N. Walker and M. Hough (Eds.), *Public Attitudes to Sentencing: Surveys from Five Counties.* Aldershot, UK: Gower.

Duguid, S. 1997. Cognitive Dissidents Bite the Dust: The Demise of University Education in Canada's Prisons. *Journal of Correctional Education* 48(2): 56–68.

Durkheim, E. [1897] 1951. *Suicide.* G. Simpson (Trans.). New York: Free Press.

Eglash, A. 1977. Beyond Restitution. In J. Hudson and B. Galaway (Eds.), *Restitution in Criminal Justice.* Lexington, MA: Lexington Books.

Effrat, M. (Ed.). 1974. *The Community: Approaches and Perspectives.* New York: Free Press.

Evans, D. 1990. Challenges Facing Community Corrections in the Nineties. *Forum for Corrections Research* 2(2).

Federal/Provincial/Territorial Deputy Ministers and Heads of Corrections. 1996. *Bases of Community Corrections: Identifying the Problem: Corrections Population Growth.* Report for Federal/Provincial/Territorial Ministers Responsible for Justice, Ottawa.

Fischer, C. 1976. *The Urban Experience.* New York: Harcourt, Brace, and Jovanovich.

Foucault, M. 1980. *Discipline and Punish.* New York: Pantheon Books.

Garland, D. 1997. Governmentality and the Problem of Crime: Foucault, Criminology, Sociology. *Theoretical Criminology: An International Journal* 1(2): 173–214.

Gibbs, J. 1967. *Urban Research Methods.* Princeton: Van Nostrand.

The Globe and Mail. 1988. Ottawa Fires Watchdog Group Critical of Halfway House Plans. 19 October, A1–A2.

————. 1988. Corrections Official Reinstates Group. 20 October, A21.

Gomme, I. 1992. From Big House to Big Brother: Confinement in the Future. In K. McCormick and L. Visano (Eds.), *Canadian Penology.* Toronto: Canadian Scholars' Press.

Greer, S. 1972. *Urbane View.* London: Oxford University Press.

Gross, B. 1967. The City of Man: A Social System Reckoning. In W.E. Wald (Ed.), *Environment for Man.* Bloomington: Indiana University Press.

Haskell, C. 1994. The Impact of the Corrections and Conditional Release Act on Community Corrections. *Forum* 6(3).

Henry, S., and **D. Milovanovic.** 1991. A Constitutive Criminology: The Maturation of Critical Theory, *Criminology* 29(2): 293–315.

Hillery, G. 1955. Definitions of Community: Areas of Agreement. *Rural Sociology* 20, 111–123.

Inciardi, J. 1996. A Corrections-Based Continuum of Effective Drug Abuse Treatment. *National Institute of Justice Research Preview.* Washington, DC.

Ingstrup, O. 1987. *Mission Statement of the National Parole Board.* Ottawa: National Parole Board.

Kahne, M., and **C. Schwartz.** 1978. Negotiating Trouble: The Social Construction and Management of Trouble in a College Psychiatric Context. *Social Problems* 25, 5.

Knights, R. Undated. *Electronic Tagging in Practice.* Global Ideas Bank. www.globalideasbank.org/BI/BI-88.HTML (April 2000).

Liebow, E. 1967. *Tally's Corner.* Boston: Little, Brown.

Llewellyn, J.J., and **R. Howse.** 1999. *Restorative Justice: A Conceptual Framework.* Ottawa: Law Commission of Canada. www.lcc.gc.ca/en/papers/howse.html (April 2000).

MacGuigan, M. 1977. *Report to Parliament by the Sub-Committee on the Penitentiary System in Canada* (MacGuigan Report). Ottawa: Supply and Services.

McCormick, C. 1995. *Prisoners of Own Design.* Doctoral dissertation. Department of Sociology, York University.

National Parole Board. 1997. *Facts: Offender Management System.* Ottawa: Solicitor General of Canada.

Ontario Ministry of Correctional Services. 1984. *Annual Report.* Toronto: Government Services.

Pacey, A. 1983. *Culture of Technology.* Cambridge: MIT Press.

Platt, A. 1977. *Child Savers: The Invention of Delinquency.* Chicago: University of Chicago Press.

Progressive Conservative Party of Ontario. 1999. *Blueprint: Mike Harris' Plan to Keep Ontario on the Right Track.* Toronto: The Party.

Rose, N. 1996. Governing Advanced Liberal Democracies. In A. Barry, T. Osbourne, and N. Rose (Eds.), *Foucault and Political Reason: Liberalism, Neo-Liberalism, and Rationalities of Government.* Chicago: University of Chicago.

Ross, R. 1996. *Returning to the Teachings: Exploring Aboriginal Justice.* Toronto: Penguin Books.

Rouleau, J. 1996. *Towards a National Strategy.* Paper presented at the Conference with Sex Offenders, Montreal, 28–30 March.

Schwitzgebel, R. 1973. *Psychotechnology.* New York: Holt, Rinehart, and Winston.

Schwitzgebel, R., and **D. Knob.** 1974. *Changing Human Behavior: Principles of Planned Intervention.* New York: McGraw-Hill.

Scull, A. 1977. *Decarceration*. Englewood Cliffs, NJ: Prentice-Hall.

Siegal, H. 1977. Getting it Together: Some Theoretical Considerations of Urban Ethnography among Underclass Peoples. In R. Weppner (Ed.), *Street Ethnography*. Beverly Hills, CA: Sage.

Simon, D. 1988. Liberalism and White Collar Crime: Toward Resolving a Crisis. *Quarterly Journal of Ideology* 12(1): 19–30.

Smith, P. 1993. Private Prisons Are A Symptom, A Response by Private Capital to the "Opportunities" Created by Society's Temper Tantrum Approach to the Problem of Criminality, *Covert Action* Quarterly (Fall).

Smykla, J.O. 1981. *Community-based Corrections: Principles and Practices*. New York: Macmillan.

Solicitor General of Canada. 1988. *Taking Responsibility*. Standing Committee on Justice and Solicitor General on Its Review of the Sentencing, Correctional Release, and Related Aspects of Corrections. Ottawa: Supply and Services.

State of Connecticut Judicial Branch Sanctions. 1996. Longitudinal Study Finds Lower Re-Arrest Rates in AIP. In Criminal Justice Policy: A Review from the Research Community, Special issue. *National Institute of Justice Journal*.

Suttles, G. 1972. *The Social Construction of Communities*. Chicago: University of Chicago Press.

Thomas, C.W. 1998. Issues and Evidence from the United States. In S.T. Easton (Ed.), *Privatizing Correctional Services*. Vancouver: The Fraser Institute.

Thorne, B., and **M. Detlefsen**. 1986. *Advisory Citizen Participation in the Correctional Systems of Canada, The United Kingdom and Ireland*. Unpublished monograph. York University.

Van Ness, D. 1990. Restorative Justice. In B. Galaway and J. Hudson (Eds.), *Criminal Justice, Restitution, and Reconciliation*. Monsey, NY: Criminal Justice Press.

Visano, A.F. 1998. Electronic Monitors: A Question of Priorities. In Roots of Western Culture, an unpublished paper. Toronto: Atkinson College, York University.

Visano, L.A. 1998. *Crime and Culture*. Toronto: Canadian Scholars' Press.

———. 1994. The Culture of Capital as Carceral: Conditions and Contradictions. In K. McCormick (Ed.), *Carceral Contexts: Readings in Control*. Toronto: Canadian Scholars' Press.

White, R.D. 1986. *Law, Capitalism and the Right to Work*. Toronto: Garamond.

Whyte, W.F. 1955. *Street Corner Society*. Chicago: University of Chicago Press.

THE FUTURE OF CORRECTIONS IN CANADA

J. Oliver Doyle[1]
Sir Sandford Fleming College
Peterborough, Ontario

LEARNING OBJECTIVES

After reading this chapter, you should be able to:

- Identify some of the external variables that have an impact on the correctional system;
- Identify some of the internal variables that can affect the correctional system;
- Understand the realities of recent trends in areas, such as incarceration statistics;
- Be aware how these statistics compare with other jurisdictions, such as the U.S.; and
- Be aware of some possible future trends and directions in Canadian corrections.

The time is always right to do what is right.

—Martin Luther King Jr.

The correctional system can be viewed in simplistic terms: we will always have law-breaking members in any given community, and to think otherwise is utopian. Lawbreakers need to be taken to task, using a range of solutions. One sanction that is quickly supported and indeed expected by the public is incarceration. While this approach serves various needs of society and can be supported by different theorists (Cusson 1983; Allen and Simonsen 1998), the business of corrections has evolved into a very complex and expensive industry.

323

To understand possible future trends requires one to view the system holistically. Corrections is a link in the justice system chain—an extremely complicated one that carries an enormous burden of economic, political, and social responsibility.

Once an offender has been apprehended, properly charged, admits responsibility, or is found guilty by the judge, the available sanctions are many and varied. It becomes the responsibility of the correctional system to carry out these sanctions of the court.

The solutions to crime can, in theory and depending upon the severity of the offence, vary from **radical non-intervention**, as proposed by Edwin Schur (1973), to those supporting capital punishment. At present in Canada, corrections operates within these two ends of the spectrum (see Figure 14.1).

As reflected in Chapter 3, the public's knowledge of corrections is very limited. A random questioning of students among the hundreds who have completed the College Correctional Worker Program at Sir Sandford Fleming College over the years reveals that each one admits to having learned far more than he or she expected. Many graduates admitted they had no idea how complex the field of corrections was until their involvement in the training. The average member of the public is unaware of the extreme complexities and public perceptions seem to be restricted to "There has been a crime committed, so what is the punishment going to be? It better be tough!"

Another way to view the system is similar to a kaleidoscope image. On a micro level, inside an institution, changing a procedure or program can have an impact on the internal operations of different areas. This can also occur on a macro level of society as well, where for example a new law passed by the legislature can affect operations inside an institution.

Any attempt to predict what will and what must be addressed in order to ensure that corrections can provide the services it needs is a perilous challenge. There are a variety of different approaches that can be taken. For the purpose of this chapter, we will focus on a variety of variables. These variables can be clustered into external factors (see Figure 14.2) and internal factors.

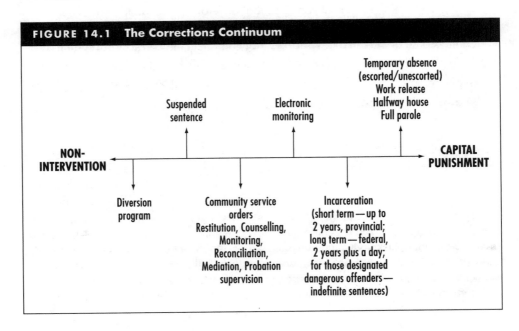

FIGURE 14.1   The Corrections Continuum

NON-INTERVENTION ← → CAPITAL PUNISHMENT

Suspended sentence

Electronic monitoring

Temporary absence (escorted/unescorted)
Work release
Halfway house
Full parole

Diversion program

Community service orders
Restitution, Counselling, Monitoring, Reconciliation, Mediation, Probation supervision

Incarceration (short term — up to 2 years, provincial; long term — federal, 2 years plus a day; for those designated dangerous offenders — indefinite sentences)

FIGURE 14.2   External Factors Affecting the Future of Corrections

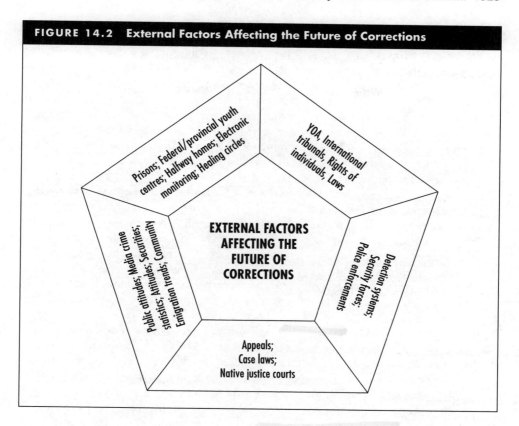

PUBLIC ATTITUDES AND AWARENESS

In the field of criminal justice, the public is commonly referred to as the **hidden element**. The public's views can have a significant impact on correctional policy and practice. However, people's interest and knowledge in the field of corrections is limited unless someone known to them becomes immersed in the system either as a victim or perpetrator of a crime. Few members of the public could be expected to explain the difference between the provincial and federal systems of corrections. Yet most have strong opinions about what should happen to young offenders or adults involved in these systems.

There is continuous pressure on the system to move in each direction as depicted in Figure 14.1. The issue of capital punishment was voted on in Parliament in 1976 when the Liberal government passed Bill C-84 and the death penalty was abolished (Correctional Service of Canada 1998). In 1987, the Progressive Conservatives revisited this decision when a motion to reintroduce the death penalty was defeated during a free vote. Hence, "the pressure to move in this direction seems to be off for now" (Correctional Service of Canada 1998, 16). However, public attitudes about corrections are fuelled by a complex interaction of social, economic, and political factors. In the future, we can expect periodic calls for reinstatement of the death penalty when the public experiences, usually though the media, a series of heinous murders or other serious indictable acts.

The Media

As discussed in Chapter 3, the media influence much of public opinion. Observational experience suggests there is a lot of interest in reporting negative and skewed news. When the concepts of temporary absence and early release were first introduced in Ontario in the early 1970s, for example, at one provincial institution it was the one inmate who failed to return and became involved in further conflict with the law who became the focus of the media's attention, not the dozens of successful cases reviewed by the institution's Temporary Absence Program Board. As such programs continue today, both at provincial and federal levels, the focus of the media remains on the failures rather than the successes.

Good news does not seem capable of retaining our interest, which appears whetted by the bizarre. We live vicariously through the media reports and for some years now news has been altered and shaped to become entertainment. There is a saying in Ireland to never let the truth interfere with reporting the facts. In North America, the public's perceptions can be shaped to reflect concern about safety. Undoubtedly, in some urban areas communities must cope with ongoing concerns with public safety issues. It has been argued that the press has fabricated crime waves. When something is reported, such as a home invasion, it increases people's anxieties. The person trying to sell us the latest sophisticated and expensive security system will use fear tactics if necessary. As the Commissioner of Corrections, Ole Ingstrup noted at an international symposium, the media are unlikely to tell us that between 1991 and 1996 there was a 13 percent decrease in crime in Canada (Coates 1998). This skewed representation of official facts fuels a prevailing concern amongst the public that security is somehow at risk. This feeling is constantly reinforced by negative reports of the relatively infrequent drive-by shootings, acts of racial hatred, home invasion, and such. This bombardment occurs through the various forms of media— radio, television, and the press. Statistics indicate that in Canada we watch, on average, 22.8 hours (Canadian children watch 17.9 hours) of television per week (compared to 50.8 hours in the U.S.) (Pungente and O'Malley 1999). While the number of viewing hours is lower than in the U.S., it is still an influencing factor as even the casual viewer cannot but notice the constant "newsbreaks." The objective appears to be to lure the viewer with some sensationalized morsel of news, often focused on a crime, a court decision, a public encounter, to watch "the full report on the 6 o'clock news." This must, over time, have an influence on the public's perceptions.

Even in the newspaper, the approach is similar. As one of many examples, a large, bold-type, half-inch high headline in the World Section of the *Peterborough Examiner* (1999) declares "8.1 Million Crimes Reported in the U.S. in '98." Someone scanning the newspaper may well recall this figure, yet a reading of the subsequent article reveals, "a seven per cent drop from 1997 and the lowest number [of violent crimes] reported since the Justice Department began tracking the figure in 1973."

While we might want to point an accusing finger at the media for fostering the public misconceptions about corrections, in the future senior correctional staff will need to play a more visible and aggressive role in educating the public about the operations, complications, and realities of the system.

Immigration and Cultural Diversity

The arrival of several boatloads of illegal immigrants in the summer of 1999 focused intense interest in the area of immigration into Canada. In a country known for its liberal attitudes, allegations by an RCMP officer about what might have occurred towards new immigrants reawakened earlier concerns about who may have gained admittance to Canada.

There continues to be a change in the **cultural diversity** of people living in Canada (see Figure 14.3). For example, in 1996, Canada was home to about 5 million immigrants—a 14.5 percent increase since 1991. This increase was slightly more than three times the growth rate (4 percent) of the Canadian-born population. Immigrants represent 17.4 percent of the population, the largest share in more than 50 years. This share had remained at around 15 to 16 percent between 1951 and 1991 (Statistics Canada 1997a, 1). Between 1971 and 1996, the proportion of people with a mother tongue other than English or French (allophones) increased from 13 percent of the overall population to nearly 17 percent. Mother tongue is defined as the first language a person learned at home in childhood and still understood at the time of the census (Statistics Canada 1997b, 1).

Any change in the population as a whole will be reflected in the population of those involved in the correctional system. For example, there is a higher percentage of culturally diverse inmates living in some of the institutions in the Kingston area whose mother tongue is neither English nor French.

This trend has implications for the Correctional Service of Canada staff and will no doubt have an impact on staff in provincial institutions. In the future, there will be a need to hire new staff from a broader cultural base and with wider language abilities, plus an increased training and sensitivity in matters of cultural diversity will be necessary.

Demographics

Just as the population in society is aging (see Table 14.1), so is the population of inmates in federal corrections. The average age of inmates was 33 in 1997/98, a decrease from 36 the previous year. The median of provincial/territorial inmates was 32, up from 31 in 1996/97

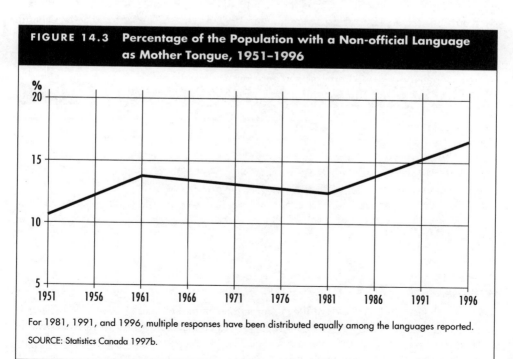

FIGURE 14.3   Percentage of the Population with a Non-official Language as Mother Tongue, 1951–1996

For 1981, 1991, and 1996, multiple responses have been distributed equally among the languages reported.

SOURCE: Statistics Canada 1997b.

(Reed and Roberts 1999). In addition, about 20 percent of those incarcerated are in for murder, which in Canadian terms is 25 years, not natural life, although they will be under supervision for life. Early in the new millennium a substantial numbers of "lifers" who are in their 50s will become eligible for community placement.

The data in Table 14.1 suggest, based on demographics alone, that the number of young offenders is likely to increase by 5 to 10 percent by 2016. The adult population in institutions may, in fact, be reduced considerably as the population ages. On the other hand, in society there will be a far greater target population of potential victims for con artists and such. This may offset possible gains for an aging population associated with reduced crime rates. It is possible that, as the population ages, the size of the high at-risk young adult population will shrink as the baby boomers begin to move out of the labour force. The range of economic opportunities available to young people should improve (Boe and Muirhead 1998). Changes in the demographic composition of the population will need to be addressed by all levels of corrections in the future.

Enhanced Security

There appears to be a growth in secured "gated" communities. The number of people employed in the security field is definitely increasing. On the positive side, one hopes this will deter and prevent crime. On the negative side, the sheer numbers may detect and capture more criminals, which may increase the possible numbers of those incarcerated.

In the area of police officers, if we use the city of Peterborough, Ontario, as a snapshot of trends, the crime rate in 1997 was 9.2 percent lower than it was the year before. Ironically, in response, police chief Terry McLaren suggested that "a decreasing crime rate is no reason not to have more police officers, especially since the province is willing to help pay for them." In fact, six new officers were hired in 1997. There is a similar trend at the Ontario Provincial Police (OPP), which plans to increase class sizes to hold an extra 1,000 recruits over the years 1999 and 2000 (*Peterborough Examiner* 1998b).

TABLE 14.1	Projected Population Growth between 1996 and 2016		
	1996	**2001**	**2016**
10–14 years	2,020,000	2,124,800	2,105,700
15–19 years	2,003,700	2,124,500	2,194,800
20–49 years	2,037,400	2,111,200	2,378,200
Total	6,061,100	6,360,500	6,698,700
Percentage increase or decrease		5% per increase over 1996	9.38 % increase over 1996
50–54 years	1,672,600	2,140,100	2,791,400
55–59 years	1,333,100	1,651,400	2,688,700
60–64 years	1,214,600	1,300,900	2,308,200
Total	4,220,300	6,092,400	7,788,300
Percentage increase or decrease		20.66 % increase over 1996	84% adapted increase over 1996

SOURCE: Adapted from Statistics Canada 1996.

It may be that the increased presence of a greater number of police officers partially accounts for the drop in the crime rate throughout most of the 1990s. It may be that more victims from crimes committed long ago are feeling more confident in reporting those assaults, especially sexual assaults; these are referred to as "historic cases" (McLaren 1999). Alternatively, police who are frustrated by the lack of court response to other crimes are concentrating on repugnant crimes, those to which courts respond more punitively. This could lead to more discriminating policing. Such an approach would undoubtedly gain public support. This could result in changing the composition of populations in correctional facilities, which in turn would require new programs and strategies for handling offenders.

Technological advances pose both threats and opportunities for corrections. This area of development has had an impact on the detection of crime and resulted in more precise evidence and a subsequently increased conviction and possible incarceration rate. Video cameras used by employers, banks, and stores have captured criminal activity such as child abuse, robbery, assault, and even murder. Some of the detected perpetrators of robbery and assault have turned out to be police officers. So the widening of the detection now, by using technology, will not be biased in anyway.

In many major European cities, downtown areas are monitored by police who can use cameras to zoom in to get evidence while alerting police patrols to focus on given a geographic area where a crime is taking place, resulting in a higher rate of arrests and convictions.

In some major cities, computers can be used to track crime patterns so that staff can be more selectively and effectively applied, in order to prevent crimes and reduce incarceration rates, admittedly at the price of our "right to privacy" (Pron 1999).

By the use of on-board computers, haulage trucks can be traced by satellite tracking systems. This, too, can act as a deterrent to prevent crime, as well as lower insurance and transportation costs. Unfortunately, if history is any indication, all this technology will probably give rise to more sophisticated criminals and crime. To paraphrase an old saying: "the criminal is always one step ahead of technology."

The use of DNA as evidence was made possible by legislation passed in the fall of 1995. Bill C-104 amended the Criminal Code and the *Young Offenders Act* to permit provincial court judges to issue warrants so that police may obtain body samples for forensic DNA analysis (Adams 1995). This can work in favour of the police by enhancing their methods and approach. The use of DNA evidence, in general, can also help to clear innocent parties who may be accused of serious crimes such as murder, as it did in the cases of David Milgaard, Donald Marshall, Benoit Proulx, Guy Paul Morin, and, most recently, Thomas Sophonow.

Policing will make greater use of these technologies, including helicopters for high-speed chases and assisting with night searches, video cameras mounted on police cruisers to record behaviour during "traffic stops," better equipment and methods to detect counterfeit money. As a result, the ability of police in the detection of crime will grow.

Technology is a double-edged sword, or as Franklin (1990, 23) describes it, technologies come with an enormous "social mortgage" (see Box 14.1). On the one hand, it may draw more people into the **correctional net** by increasing the number detected, apprehended, and successfully charged, rather than the more desirable effect of being a deterrent and helping reduce incidents of crime. On the other hand, technology will also be used by the criminal element to avoid detection and apprehension. This may affect the composition of who ends up in the correctional system. Currently, the majority of offenders tend to be less well educated than the public. Hence, we might see a bipolar distribution among the correctional

---

BOX 14.1 **Are We Going "Soft" On Prisoners?**

In late 1999, a federal task force report fuelled debate that corrections may be going soft on crime. Some of the more controversial recommendations included removing razor wire around the prisons, giving inmates keys for their rooms, and allowing inmates to prepare their own meals in facilities other than minimum security settings. The report also calls for the eventual removal of weapons by prison guards (*Crime and Justice International 2000*). While issues of public safety have been identified as one of the public concerns, it remains to be seen as to whether the public will "allow" the recommendations to be legislated.

---

population of tomorrow whereby there are the break-and-enter, assaultive types and the far more of those educated, technologically sophisticated scam artists or offenders involved in corporate computer crimes.

THE IMPACT OF THE COURTS

Court decisions can, and do, have an impact on the public's opinion that, in turn, is considered by the government at different levels in its decision-making. In recent elections in some provinces, such as Alberta and Ontario, the platforms and supporters of the Conservative and Reform parties focused on **law and order**[2] (Winterdyk 2000). Some critics claim the parties are being influenced by ideas borrowed from the United States. It may, in fact, be politicians responding to what the voting public wants. It is interesting to note the sentiments based on the General Social Survey (GSS) conducted by Statistics Canada:

> Looking at crime generally, the report said Canadians tend to have a favourable perception of the police, but aren't as happy with the courts.
> It suggests that politicians who propose longer sentences and tougher rules for parolees and other offenders are tapping into a sentiment shared by both city and rural dwellers.
> "Few residents of either area viewed the courts as doing a good job quickly providing justice and determining the guilt of offenders," the report said.
> There was also a strong perception that courts do more to protect the rights of the accused than of the victim.
> Logically, the survey found urban residents had a greater fear of crime than rural people and that most people felt crime rates had risen over the previous five years.
> While the rural areas were generally safer, the bucolic countryside wasn't so safe for young men (Hoy 1994).

In their successful re-election rhetoric during the 1999 campaign, the Ontario Conservatives perpetuated this theme of law and order. The focus was on the *Young Offenders Act* and the need to change it. While any provincial government can and does put pressure on the federal government, it is only within the latter's power to exact any such changes. The response of the electorate in re-electing the Conservatives suggests that this support of a law-and-order platform, with many other factors, reflected the needs and desires of the public to be more active, especially with young offenders and those on welfare rolls.

Of course, one of the great advantages of the political structure of Canada is that we can afford to be "two-pronged" in our voting. We can help install a law-and-order party at a provincial level and a liberal approach at the federal level or vice versa. Others might analyze this as simply the "needed checks and balances" within the system.

Decisions by courts can certainly raise the ire of the public from time to time. As recently as September 1999, the court handed down a sentence of four years to a drunken driver who had killed four people and badly injured others. This decision, elicited a response not only from the victims but also from the legal spokespersons for MADD (Mothers Against Drunk Driving) (Canadian Broadcasting Corporation 2000). Although such a case can have indirect effects on the attitudes and receptiveness of the public towards treatment of offenders, there are other court decisions that have had a direct influence on the daily working of corrections.

At a criminal court level, the experience has been, on occasion, that sentences given by judges do not allow enough time for the offender to take advantage of certain treatment programs, which may be of benefit to the individual. As the composition of our correctional population changes, the courts will need to address these changes and corrections must be prepared to handle them.

The Canadian Charter of Rights and Freedoms grants the right to freedom of religion. The first time a Native Elder entered a federal prison to conduct a ceremony was in 1972 in Alberta's Drumheller Institution. In 1992, with the enactment of the *Correctional and Conditional Release Act* (CCRA), the right of Aboriginal offenders to have access to traditional spirituality was entrenched in law, as per section 38. Moreover, section 80 of the CCRA provides that the Correctional Service of Canada shall provide programs designed particularly to address Aboriginal offenders (Correctional Service of Canada 1998, 8).

Native Justice

There is a process involving Elders, respected because of their knowledge and experience, who hear the circumstance of the offence from the victim(s). The community members can, and indeed are encouraged, to attend. The offender is listened to. Input from the community members is welcomed. The position of each party in the circle has significance.

The approach is one of transgression against the community as well as the individual. Therefore, a remedy is sought from the collective committee if the peace of the community is threatened. The approach is one of mediation and negotiation rather than an adversarial approach. The process focuses on the healing of wounds by restoring peace and equilibrium within the community—a **restorative process**.

Legislated Justice

Since the first Canadian Criminal Code was legislated in 1892 we have seen it continue to grow in size—today there are nearly 850 sections. The legislation of law is generally seen as a formal means of trying to maintain social order, although many argue that this is an erroneous assumption and point to countries such as the United States, which has more laws than other any western country but also has the highest crime rate. Nevertheless, the proliferation of laws at the different levels of government and their maintenance, application, and appeals seem destined in time to create an impossible task of administration due to the sheer volume and time involved.

It has been claimed there were 35,000 pages of new legislation produced each week by the four levels of government in the U.S. (Ruff 1983). Allowing for even one twentieth of that in Canada would be a sizeable amount. This can result in excessive stress and frustration by administrators of the system, with some uneven application.

> Tim Lipson (acting on behalf of the Criminal Lawyers Association during the Guy Paul Morin inquiry) had few kind words for the system which put Morin behind bars, saying it had a troubling "obsession" for pushing people through quickly rather than taking time to pursue quality investigations. The ailing Ontario Legal Aid Plan, he said is run "according to the financial bottom line and not the interests of justice" (Driscoll 1998).

Criminologists and legal scholars have long debated the effectiveness of creating new legislation. Yet the momentum appears unavoidable. In response, correctional systems develop new programs to **widen the net** and build new prisons— to paraphrase W.P. Kinsella, "build it and they will come." Similarly, we manage to fill these new programs and institutions. So the options continue to expand, which leads to even more new legislation being created in order to regulate new situations. Maybury (1993), among others, observes that we have drifted from natural laws to human-made or scientific laws. It is the latter that continually pose new challenges to corrections, and the criminal justice system in general, since such laws are subject to changes as a result of economic, political, and social shifts.

Community Corrections

As discussed in Chapter 13, community corrections encompasses a number of aspects including probation and parole, halfway houses, group homes for youth, electronic monitoring, and release circles for offenders. As the concept of community corrections continues to grow it will require additional resources at the provincial and federal levels. However, given the limited resources available at the different jurisdictional levels, it is likely that some correctional-based options may be deferred for economic reasons rather than for their effectiveness. Correctional decision-makers will need to be vigilant that this does not happen.

Canadian corrections will need to consider such pragmatic issues as caseloads, community responses, staffing, and community support in the future. In addition, it will be necessary to consider whether certain services could or should be better operated by government agencies or given over to the private sector.

Needless to say, there are different schools of thought as to the benefits and disadvantages of how community corrections should be administered and to what level this approach should be used. Certainly, for low cost, it does reduce the numbers of people who would otherwise possibly be incarcerated. Community programs options act as a definite deterrent to a large number of offenders who will be locked up if they fail to take full advantage of these alternatives. Such programs can also prevent institutionalization and "contamination" through exposure to "hardened" criminals inside by keeping people from entering youth centres and prisons in the first place.

Young Offenders

The *Young Offenders Act* (YOA) came into effect on April 1st, 1984. Even before its enactment, it was the subject of much controversy, which continues to this day. In fact, "it comes as no surprise to the reader that our juvenile justice system is the subject of considerable critical debate" (Winterdyk 2000, xi). As reflected in the media, the public is growing increasingly less tolerant of young offenders in the aftermath of such sensationalized cases as Ryan Garrioch, Reena Virk, Clayton McGloan, among others.

The shooting of a family in Toronto that resulted in the death of the mother and daughter plus the paralysis of the father or the home invasion and fatal beating with a baseball bat of an elderly couple in Ottawa demanded people's attention in view of the limited sanction applicable. Even the recent single fatal gang beating of Reena Virk in British Columbia, as well as others, repulsed the public, who voiced a strong need for more serious consequences. After a lengthy federal and provincial debate, a federal report entitled *Renewing Youth Justice Strategy* (Standing Committee on Justice and Legal Affairs 1997) produced a number of significant recommendations. The recommendations of the report focused on three main areas: prevention, meaningful consequences, and measures for violent and repeat young offenders.

As a result, the federal government has committed $32 million for crime prevention initiatives to develop programs and partnerships across Canada aimed at crime prevention and support of youth at risk (Department of Justice 1998, 1–2). In addition, the year 2000 is targeted for replacement of the YOA with a new and improved version that will be called the *Youth Criminal Justice Act* (YCJA).

Critics in the past have pointed out the loss of alternative measures and flexibility afforded by the 1908 *Juvenile Delinquency Act.* The lack of follow-up or aftercare supervision in the community following incarceration is seen as problematic (see Winterdyk 2000 for a comprehensive review). The result was a loss of job satisfaction compounded by the incarceration of more youth, ironically for longer periods. This was the very problem that advocates of the YOA suggested would be eradicated by the removal of the *Juvenile Delinquency Act.* They wanted rid of the old Act because of its indefinite sentencing and the need to earn one's way out of incarceration by showing appropriately acceptable behaviour.

The YOA in its present form has no provision for early release, with the exception of a review in court by a judge. Consequently, in the absence of parole, as an incentive to reinforce altered behaviour, we are left with the shock of incarceration and loss of freedom as motivators. The proposed changes aimed at providing a host of fine options and alternatives will, one hopes, address the current shortcomings. In preparation for these changes , six pilot diversion programs are being supported in Ontario, and pilot programs similar to Ontario's Youth Justice Committee are underway in Alberta, Manitoba, Newfoundland, Nova Scotia, and the Northwest Territories (Ministry of the Attorney General, 1999).

The implication for the youth justice system, in particular the area of corrections, remains unclear. Although intended to reduce custody rates, diversion and other measures may increase the number of youths involved in the justice system through its net-widening options.

The intention of holding the violent young offender more responsible will meet the needs of the public, who have been affected recently by the constant barrage of violent offences by youth. It will also act as a deterrent for a segment of youth. However, it would be naive to expect that such a policy would eliminate, or even dramatically reduce, the incidents of violent crimes by youth. As reflected in Table 14.1, it is anticipated the youth population will remain relatively stable with a possible slight increase.

Through various forms of media, we will continue to experience varying impacts on occurrences of crime such as alienation of youth, copycat incidents, need for notoriety and fame, and the proliferation of gangs. Many of us will continue to remember 1999 for the horrors of the W.R. Meyers High School in Taber, Alberta, and Columbine High School in Littleton, Colorado. However, the public needs to be reminded that although these were serious incidents, they are fortunately still very rare.

Delinquent youth have always been a source of consternation throughout the millennia. Yet research has consistently shown that the majority of youth outgrow of their delinquent behaviours. In fact, various studies have report that only about 6 percent of young offenders display chronic delinquent behaviour (Winterdyk 1996). Therefore, in spite of public pressure, the provinces will need to carefully consider the merits of constructing and maintaining detention centres over the expansion of alternative measure initiatives that could better serve those youth who have "lost their way." **Crime prevention** would represent not only a more humane approach but also a cost-effective strategy.

Having examined some of the major external factors that are likely to affect the future direction of corrections, we will now shift our attention a range of internal factors.

INTERNAL FACTORS AFFECTING THE FUTURE OF CORRECTIONS

Corrections have passed through several stages of development over the past century. In the past few years, there has been a renewed emphasis on changing the attitudes and behaviours of offenders so that upon their release there would be an increased security for society. (See Figure 14.4.) The initial momentum began with the development and declaration of the core values by the Correctional Service of Canada in 1989 (Correctional Service of Canada 1997, 8). They include:

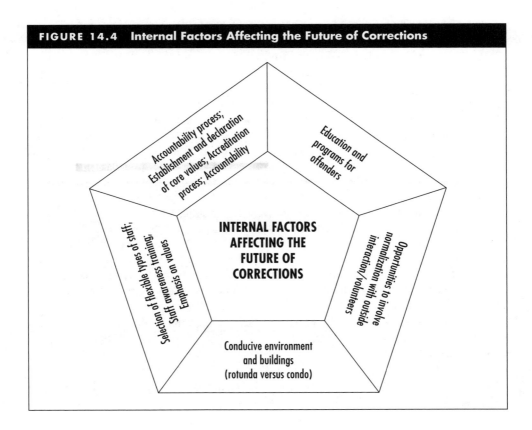

FIGURE 14.4   Internal Factors Affecting the Future of Corrections

Accountability process; Establishment and declaration of core values; Accreditation process; Accountability

Education and programs for offenders

Selection of flexible types of staff; Staff awareness training; Emphasis on values

INTERNAL FACTORS AFFECTING THE FUTURE OF CORRECTIONS

Opportunities to involve normalization with outside interaction/volunteers

Conducive environment and buildings (rotunda versus condo)

Core Value #1: We respect the dignity of individuals, the rights of all members of society and the potential for human growth and development.

Core Value #2: We recognize that the offender has the potential to live as a law-abiding citizen.

Core Value #3: We believe that our strength and our major resource in achieving our objectives is our staff and that human relationships are the cornerstone of our endeavour.

Core Value #4: We believe that the sharing of ideas, knowledge, values, and experience, nationally and internationally, is essential to the achievement of our mission.

Core Value #5: We believe in managing the Service with openness and integrity and we are accountable to the Solicitor General.

Concerns were raised by the Auditor General of Canada, the Office of the Correctional Investigator, and the Correctional Service's Taskforce on Offender Reintegration. In the fall of 1997 in Quebec City, management and staff representatives from Correctional Programs, Performance Assurance Sectors, the Commissioner, Senior Deputy Commissioner, Women Offenders Area, Director General of Aboriginal Issues, and the Wardens reaffirmed the importance of programs for offenders and the introduction of an accreditation process (Correctional Service of Canada 1999, 3).

The mandate of Correctional Service of Canada is clearly outlined in section 3 of the CCRA. It states: "The purpose of the federal correctional system is to contribute to the maintenance of a just, peaceful and safe society by assisting the Rehabilitation of Offenders and their reintegration into the community of law-abiding citizens through the provision of programs in penitentiaries and in the community" (Correctional Service of Canada 1998, 25).

The Accountability Process

The transition from an emphasis on the provision of programs to the accountability for the efficacy of such programs saw its roots at Quebec in 1997. The purpose of **accreditation** is to monitor the theoretical basis of a correctional program in order to prevent the program from becoming outdated and to prevent the program's delivery from drifting from the original effective model. The term accreditation is used to refer to a process by which the Correctional Service can:

- Objectively establish that its programs reflect valid scientific theory on personal development; and
- Monitor the delivery of these programs at its various program delivery sites to ensure the integrity of the program is maintained (Correctional Service of Canada 1999, 5).

Programming

The programs in question include Cognitive Skills, Anger and Emotions, Offender Substance Abuse Prevention Program, and Substance Abuse for Long-Term Offenders (Correctional Service of Canada 1999). Currently, these programs are offered to participants based on the detailed assessment of individual offenders' needs and completed by the assigned parole officers inside various penitentiaries (see Chapter 11). It is necessary for all offenders to have completed a Grade 10 education before participating in any of the core program(s). This condition has a two-fold advantage of better equipping the offender to cope with the world of work upon release and increasing the offender's capability to understand the readings, concepts, and tasks while participating in a program. Over 60 percent of offenders have below a Grade 10 education. It is anticipated this educational level will be increased to Grade 12 to be more realistic in keeping with job requirements in the community.

The Impact of Cognitive Skills Training on Post Release Recidivism among Canadian Federal Offenders (Robinson 1996), published by the Correctional Service, is very encouraging. As Robinson stated: "the current data also allows us to provide evidence that programming works with some groups of offenders who are the greatest source of fear among members of the public (e.g., violent offenders and sex offenders). Not surprisingly, the data also suggests that the program is not a panacea and that some groups derive few benefits in terms of recidivism reduction" (50).

Along with the recent changes in programming, it is reasonable to anticipate that there will be ongoing programming for offenders in the future. It is also expected that programs that are effective will be extended to young offenders possible through the enactment of the new YCJA.

One group of offenders apparently not positively affected by the Cognitive Skills Training are Native people. They only represent about 2.8 percent of the Canadian population in general, yet 14.5 percent of the male inmate population and 28.5 percent of the female are Aboriginal offenders (Correctional Service of Canada 1997, 20).

In a *Globe and Mail* article on a Supreme Court decision to leave a three-year sentence intact for manslaughter, the court said Aboriginal offenders are imprisoned in grossly disproportionate numbers (Makin 1999, A1 and A4).[3] This concern warrants even more attention in view of the fact that "the population of aboriginals aged 15 to 24 is projected to increase 26 percent by 2006, aged 35 to 54 is expected to grow 41 percent by 2006 and 62 percent by 2016" (Statistics Canada 1996).

As observed in Chapter 6, Canada's overall rate of incarceration is very high in comparison to other countries, and it has increased in spite of a declining crime rate throughout the 1990s. Furthermore, proposals put forth by the abolitionists and advocates of social crime prevention appear to receive only lip service among correctional policy-makers.

Concern on a number of levels has been recognized by the various jurisdictions with periodic meetings of federal, provincial, and territorial Ministers Responsible for Justice. The Deputy Ministers and Heads of Corrections have also been involved in a coordinated manner, having developed and presented their first major report in May 1996, which focused on reversing the growing incarceration rate. "Between 1989/90 and 1994/95 the federal penitentiary population grew by 22 percent and the provincial prison population, on average by 12 percent" (Federal/Provincial/Territorial Ministers of Justice 1998, 1). All this at a time when Canada's overall crime rate fell in 1998 for the seventh consecutive year.

Despite the drop in crime rate, Canadians fear of crime has grown: "Recent surveys/polls/focus groups (e.g., Angus Reid, September 1997; Goldfarb, March 1997) have indicated that the public views crime as increasing, as more violent in nature and the criminal justice system as too lenient and inconsistent" (Federal/Provincial/Territorial Ministers of Justice 1998, 3). These same surveys, supported subsequently by Environics (March 1998) and Springboard (May 1998), did go on to recognize that Canadians show public support for alternative sanctions. The government report on correctional population growth states: "When told the country's prisons are full, 54 percent of the Canadian sampled favour the use of non-prison sentences such as probation or community service. Support for alternative sentencing was highest in Alberta and Saskatchewan and lowest in Toronto" (3).

Chapter 14: The Future of Corrections in Canada   337

Based on the external factors and the demand for greater accountability of resources, it appears likely that there will be a reduction in institutional populations in Canada. However, the direction depends somewhat on social and political factors. For example, a recent newspaper headline announced "1.82 million inmates jam U.S. prisons," although "declining crime rates have helped reduce the rate of growth to the lowest level since 1979 (*Toronto Star* 1999).

In the Canadian corrections magazine *Let's Talk*, Coates (1998, 5) notes that "longer sentences increased the number of inmates in England, lengthening the average sentence from 21 to 23 months, adding 4,000 people to the prison population." Meanwhile, the Director General of the Correctional Service's Research Branch, Larry Motiuk (see Chapter 4), presented encouraging correctional statistics. The average federal sentence decreased from 44.8 to 43.1 months and offenders with sentences from two to five years spent approximately 25 months in federal custody. The success rates for parole and statutory release are the highest they have ever been; of the almost 3 million new offences known to police in 1997, 2,404 were committed by federal offenders (Coates 1999).

Although the concept of programming within the correctional area is often at the whim of external factors, in the future we are likely to witness a concerted effort by correctional officials to expand programming initiatives that are also accompanied by an evaluation component. Evidence of a more formalized approach to correctional practices can be found in such publications as *Forum on Correctional Research*, which began publication in 1989.

Normalization by Involvement of Volunteers

How the subject of high incarceration rates will be addressed in the future will include aspects we have already covered, including educating the public. This can take as number of forms.

The Environment

There is an interesting history of structures as applied to prisons over the centuries. Many of the public's images are constructed from the media's dark dungeon, from the approach of the *Man in the Iron Mask* to the frequent westerns depicting the barred cells of the "local lockup."

In reality, and as described in Chapter 2, correctional practices have evolved considerably throughout the centuries. This was especially true during the Enlightenment Period (1790–1830), which led to the modern penitentiary. Throughout the 1800s and early 1900s, corrections saw the emergence of the Pennsylvania model, which was based on the use of a separate and silent system where prisoners were kept out of sight from other offenders. The other dominant model was the Auburn system. This system emphasized a strict "silent system" and forbade prisoners from communicating or even gesturing to one another (see Chapter 6).

In Kingston's Prison Museum, it was noted on the Keepers log (a page that is turned in daily) that an 11-year-old prisoner had been given 10 lashes for speaking to another prisoner in French. The punishment was based on the assumption that a) he broke silence, and b) he was planning to escape. On a recent visit to the museum, a guide quipped that now we pay people to speak French.

Just as the notion of justice and corrections has evolved over the years, so has the actual physical structure of prisons. The structures certainly became modernized, with the opening of such a flagship as the Ontario Correctional Institute in Brampton in the early 1970s (soon to be closed). Like the secure care and treatment facility of Syl Apps Youth Centre in Oakville, this has inner open air courtyards with a limited view on exterior walls. Modifications to the original designs and usage had to be made for each because of security issues.

The designs of the new "super jails" perpetuate the old inwardly focused design. In fact, what is presently being proposed appears to revert to the rotunda, not unlike that of the Kingston Penitentiary vintage the mid 1800s. Although the buildings will be only two storeys high, some are intended to house 1,200 inmates, and one will have in excess of 1,500 people. They would cost $67 million and $87 million respectively. The building of such super-jails is contrary to the declaration made some 25 years ago by the then Minister of Corrections, Alan Grossman, namely that no new institutions built would have a capacity of greater than 120 people! Such a decision would have a big impact on the provincial systems. With the planned closure of dozens of institutions in Ontario, should a serious riot occur then the costs and implications could be grave. Added to this is the possibility of privatization. This idea is not a new one, having been done in Kentucky in the 19th century. In fact, the Auburn system was meant to have inmates produce enough to pay for the expense of crime (Fox 1983). In contrast, the Correctional Service's approach began with townhouse-type accommodations at William Head Institution in British Columbia and Bath, near Kingston, Ontario.

This style has now advanced from usage at a minimum security level to the newly opened Fenbrook Federal Institution in Ontario, with a condo/university-like campus approach at a cost of $65 million. Former warden at William Head, Fraser McVee was chosen to spearhead the Fenbrook concept, which took many years to bring to fruition (McVee 1999). There is no mass dining room. Inmates cluster in small groups to eat, having made their own dinner with groceries purchased from the IGA grocery store located within the perimeter. They are also responsible for their own clean-up and laundry. Many of the buildings are multipurpose, deliberately causing staff and offenders to intermingle at many points. The concept is very open and airy, congruent with the reintegration, which attempts to have life inside parallel the outside as much as possible (Centen 1999). The Bracebridge Library staffs a branch inside Fenbrook Institution, and a Mr. Subway operates engaging offenders as paid staff.

PRIVATIZATION OF CORRECTIONS

The **privatization** of corrections is a complex issue that easily requires an entire chapter. There is the question of institutional corrections versus community corrections. As well, the practical operational issues verses the philosophical aspects come into play. The motivation at any government level in privatizing a system is to save money. On paper this can appear so. However, many hidden, apparently unconnected costs arise, such as the cost of monitoring standards, or the cost of checking the qualifications of operators and staff for a possible parallel system, which would have to be paid by the taxpayers.

For many years, correctional systems have survived on the basis of "divide and conquer." Disgruntled inmates are sent from institution to institution. The move to "super" jails can results in two things.

1. There are fewer or no jails in which to manage these individuals or groups, following a disturbance, and
2. The costs of a major riot in an institution include the costs of bringing the riot under control, managing the aftermath, and rebuilding; these costs can be so high that any initial cost saving is quickly exceeded.

One does not require expertise in corrections to figure out that to make a profit while selling any government on cutting costs can only be achieved in one of two ways.

1. Engage fewer professional staff because they cost so much, hence dispense with rehabilitative programs. This has the effect of releasing more angry and damaged individuals on a unsuspecting public, with the potential of disastrous results. (Witness the history of the recent deinstitutionalizing of the mentally ill and the increased number of homeless on the streets, even though deinstitutionalization is one of many factors involved.)
2. Pay custodial staff less salary so they are less qualified and more prone to bribes and possible corruption within the system.

An alternative solution is to design the institution so as to require fewer staff. This too has a two-fold cost implications:

1. Less security is required for those incarcerated, which is a concern for administrators and can easily result in a far more dangerous environment in which to work or live.
2. An inwardly focused building, which facilitates easier monitoring and reverts to an approach of the 19th century, can have a negative psychological impact on the incarcerated. It provides a fish-bowl effect, which is stressful for both the watched and the watchers. Compare this with an open-concept facility such as Fenbrook Institution, with its refreshingly open, outwardly, community-focused structure, thus complementing reintegration goals and direction and providing a more psychologically positive environment.

As a whole, the public needs to decide, in an informed manner, the kind of society in which it wishes to live. If the decision is based on economic issues alone, while privatization may be easy to sell, it will prove to be a case of "pay now" (by continuing to support effective programming that focuses on successfully reintegrating as many as is safely possible) or "pay later" (by introducing a far more aggressive, dangerous criminal element in society where many more are disenfranchised). While as Canadians we pride ourselves on reaching out to many people in other countries with our aid, perhaps it is time to revisit the concept that "charity begins at home."

Special consideration and supports are provided to meet the unique needs of Native offenders and the newly integrated Inuit offenders. Provision of a sweat lodge, special areas for Inuit crafts and tools, involvement of Elders, liaison officers, and respecting Native foods and feasts all contribute to normalization.

Future trends, once they have successfully become entrenched at this level of security, could be extended to higher levels. In addition, the concept of restorative justice and reintegration will be introduced over a broader spectrum both within institutions and the community.

There exists a considerable number of offenders (in the thousands) who can be considered in need of circles of support. While these circles of support may be dismissed by many, their potential impact should not be underestimated; past history can attest to the strength and endurance of churches when they were in the forefront of change in correctional systems. It appears that the Correctional Service of Canada is taking notice and supporting this concept. Certainly, everyone has a vested interest, insofar as there are many individuals currently in the system who will soon reach their warrant expiry dates. Many of these were deemed too dangerous to be released earlier on parole. If they re-enter society without support, it can be a recipe for disaster.

Chiefs of police have the discretionary power, subject to meeting clearly defined criteria, to make known to the public the name and arrival date of such individuals (Beauchesne,

Fazackerley, and Vechter 1998). Although the police can and have exercised this power from the *Community Safety Act*, which came into force on June 4, 1998, it can be a double-edged sword.

Should the public become reactionary in a vigilante manner, the police must also protect the individual ex-offender who has "paid his or her dues" for the original offence. Such protection, of course, is paid for out of taxpayers' money and has reportedly exceeded a quarter of a million dollars for one individual in a 30-day period for police overtime (Cayley 1998).

The sheer economics of the situation will force all parties to reconsider their reactions very carefully. Meanwhile, the recidivism rate for offenders is very low, dipping to about 11 percent, and according to the Commissioner of Corrections, offenders involved in the first programs for Native people are lower, "only it is far too early to tell which variables are involved. Yet the signs are extremely encouraging" (Ingstrup 1999).

Therefore, it seems that both externally and internally, the programs in place for sex offenders and for Native people have the support of the Correctional Service and can realistically be expected to expand and grow. However, as Cayley (1998) observes, some of our notions of traditional practices of social control for Native people may not be relevant in today's culture. Therefore, as with any aspect for change, programs in the future should be carefully evaluated.

The Staff

The final one of the key internal factors is staffing. Historically, correctional staff was not required to more than a high school education and received minimal training for the job. Today, the standards and expectations of correctional personnel have changed significantly. One obvious example is the number of college-based correctional programs and professional workshops available to employees in the field.

While in many situations there is a clear division between custodial and treatment staff, the Correctional Service of Canada has been making a concentrated effort to train all levels and categories of staff about the information and objectives of all its core programs. Indeed, it is a requirement of the accreditation process to assess the awareness level of staff in this regard. It is also imperative that all staff, especially custodial staff, become and see themselves as change agents in reinforcing and reporting upon the conduct of those offenders participating in these core programs. After all, it is not the program specialists or the professional staff who are most exposed to offenders; it is the custodial staff and work supervisors. This, one hopes, will continue to happen.

This requires a different type of correctional officer—one who is well educated, dedicated, has good values, and is ethical and very flexible in her or his thinking. Initially, a target staff with 32 percent females was the aim. Although some institutions have surpassed the quota, in most institutes women represent approximately 20 percent of the staff.

The Correctional Service, meanwhile, is supporting and surveying the values of existing staff with a view to adapting its recruitment and hiring practices. However, the public needs to be aware of the daily stresses of work for correctional staff. On the one hand, the staff is responsible for the custody, safety, and control of individuals while they are incarcerated, and on the other hand, the staff has the additional role as modifier of behaviour. It is not an easy task. Indeed, a survey of provincial correctional staff in Ontario undertaken at York University in the mid 1970s indicated a life expectancy of 57 years for such staff, due to the stress of the job. When this is matched to the recently revised 75 years for males and 78 for females in the population at large, it is cause for concern. The system may need to consider what happens in jurisdictions such as Britain, where the retirement age is 50 years old after 25 years of working in corrections. If the intention is to incarcerate only the most violent people, then the effects on staff need to be monitored.

SUMMARY

The purpose of this chapter was to offer some observations about the future of corrections in Canada. To accomplish this task, we focused on a variety of external and internal correctional factors. As a result, we can pinpoint a number of directions in which we can reasonably predict corrections to develop and expand. We can expect corrections to:

- Focus on the most violent offenders, both young and old;
- Refine programs to be even more effective for a broader number of people;
- Expand involvement of Native leaders and others from the community;
- Educate the public on a continued "open book" approach to the facts and realities of the system;
- Continue to hire more female staff and people who can meet the many demands of the system;
- Expand accountability for the effectiveness of both community and institutional corrections;
- Increase training and consideration of special job conditions for staff; and
- Continue to focus on reducing incarceration by use of many effective programs.

These predictions are general in nature. Since it is not possible to predict anything without some degree of error, we have attempted to identify a variety of external and internal factors that relate directly or indirectly to the operation and practice of corrections. Perhaps the most important factor in whether any of the predictions will come true is public attitude. As we enter a new millennium, the public mood tends to be conservative in spite of initiatives to move towards restorative and rehabilitative programs. Other major unknowns are the criminogenic economic, political, and social conditions that will continue to affect crime trends and patterns.

In addition, correctional trends will be constrained by the sentencing policies of tomorrow. As Branham (1992) has suggested, sentencing guidelines will need to adjust to correctional system capacities; as reflected in other contributions to this text, corrections will need to find a balance between strengthening community-based correctional services (Chapter 13) and protecting society by incarcerating at-risk offenders (Chapter 6) versus offering proper supervision of released offenders (Chapters 11 and 12), recognizing the diversity and needs of "special" populations (Chapters 9 and 10), and addressing the issue of private-sector involvement.

In this chapter, it was also illustrated how corrections is never static. As evidenced in many of the chapters throughout this book, corrections is continuously evolving; with improved, ongoing, long-term research, the programs being offered will become more individualized and effective. It must also be recognized that corrections does not operate in a vacuum, and as the world "outside" changes at a rapid rate, so too will there be "new" crimes and new laws to define those perpetrators. Furthermore, as each evolves, the solutions will demand changes in the treatment and control of new classes of criminal behaviour. All this will occur against a media feeding the public more sensational and horrific detailed coverage. The responses by the justice system, especially corrections, may not be as rapid or as effective as the public may desire. This will always create a constant tension and dichotomy. For example, it must be remembered that while corrections represents the last stage of the criminal justice process, it also represents the first stage of potential re-entry into society for a majority of offenders.

Finally, it is imperative that correctional staff become more transparent while informing and educating the public as to the inner workings of the criminal justice system. There is a need to facilitate ongoing partnerships and the involvement of the public, segments of which have demonstrated for many years a willingness to engage in meaningful solutions to reintegrate law-breaking members of society. As Allen and Simonsen (1999, 593) note: "Corrections is at a crossroads and this generation of leaders and students can make a real impact if they decide to commit to excellence."

KEY TERMS AND CONCEPTS

accreditation

correctional net

crime prevention

cultural diversity

hidden element

law and order

privatization

restorative process

radical non-intervention

widen the net

STUDY AND DISCUSSION QUESTIONS

1. Sound correctional policy depends on a clear understanding of past and current factors. How do economic, political, and social factors complement correctional policy decision-making?

2. Social control is a major notion in criminology (and other social sciences) and has policy implications. In the context of this chapter, and acknowledging the other contributions to this text, how should corrections define control?

3. How do the external and internal factors relate to understanding the future directions and issues that corrections is likely to go in?

4. How might correctional policy prevent impulsive reactions and ensure that the external and internal factors can be addressed in a progressive manner?

WEBLINKS

Canadian Criminal Justice Association: **www.home.istar.ca/~ccja/angl/index.shtml**

Department of Justice Canada: **www.canada.justice.gc.ca/en/index.html**

Mothers Against Drunk Driving: **www.madd.ca**

Real Justice: **www.realjustice.org**

Statistics Canada: **www.statscan.ca**

NOTES

1. The author wishes to acknowledge the contributions of Hugh Kierkegaard and Daren Dougall.

2. At its National Convention in January 2000, the Reform Party renamed itself the Canadian Conservative Reform Alliance Party (CCRAP—yes, the brunt of numerous jokes by the opposition parties over the following days).

3. A male Treaty Indian is 25 times as likely to be admitted to a provincial jail than a non-Native male, and a female Treaty Indian is 131 times as likely (Makin 1999).

REFERENCES

Adams, P. 1995. Working for You. *MP Booklet*. Peterborough.

Allen, H.E., and **C.E. Simonsen**. 1999. *Corrections in America* (8th ed.). New York: Prentice-Hall.

Beauchesne, R., B. Fazackerley, and **L. Vechter**. 1998. *Commentary on the Community Safety Act.*

Blaskovic, M. 1998. New Officers Needed Even with Dropping Crime: Chief. *Peterborough Examiner,* 26 November, B2.

Boe, R., and **M. Muirhead**. 1998. Have Falling Crime Rate and Increased Use of Probation Reduced in Corrections? Some Trends and Comparisons. *Forum for Corrections Research* 10(2): 7.

Branham, L.S. 1992. *The Use of Incarceration in the United States: A Look at the Present and the Future.* Chicago: American Bar Association.

Canadian Broadcasting Corporation. 2000. *Ontario Morning* (radio broadcast), 27 January.

Cayley, D. 1998. *Prison and Its Alternative.* CBC Radio Series Toronto.

Centen, G. 1999. Personal interview with author.

Coates, L. 1998. Canada Hosts International "Beyond Prison" Symposium. *Let's Talk* June, 4

———. 1999. *Let's Talk,* March, 17

Correctional Service of Canada. 1997. *Basic Facts Booklet.* Ottawa: Queens Printer.

———. 1998. *50 Years of Human Rights: Milestones in Federal Correction.* Ottawa: Correction Service of Canada, Human Rights Division.

———. 1999. *Manual for Accreditation Process.* Ottawa: Queen's Printer.

Crime and Justice International. 2000. Proposed Prison Freedom. January, 13.

Cusson, M. 1983. *Why Delinquency?* (translated by Dorothy Crelinston). Toronto: University of Toronto Press.

Department of Justice. 1998. Minister of Justice Announces Youth Justice Strategy. News Release. Ottawa: Government of Canada.

Driscoll, J. 1998. Woman Asks for Term in Penitentiary. *Peterborough Examiner*, 30 January, A6.

Federal/Provincial/Territorial Ministers Responsible for Justice. 1998. *Corrections Population Growth.* Regina: Federal/Provincial/Territorial Ministers Responsible for Justice.

Fox, V. 1983. *Correctional Institutions.* Englewood Cliffs, NJ: Prentice-Hall.

Franklin, U. 1990. *The Real World of Technology.* Toronto: CBC Enterprises.

Hoy, T. 1994. *Peterborough Examiner.* Crime Hits City Dwellers Harder Than Country Cousins. 22 December, A4.

Ingstrup, O. 1999. Personal interview with author.

Makin, K. 1999. Top Court Appalled As Natives Fill Canada's Jails. *The Globe and Mail* 24 April, A1, A4.

Maybury, R. 1993. *Whatever Happened to Justice?* Placerville, CA: Bluestocking Press.

McLaren, T. 1999. Personal interview with author.

McVee, F. 1999. Personal interview with author.

Ministry of Attorney General. 1999. Fax to author. 15 September.

Peterborough Examiner. 1998. 1,000 New Police Around Ontario. 26 November, B2.

———. 1999. 8.1 Million Crimes Reported in the U.S. in '98. 19 July, A2.

Pron, N. 1999. Computer Gets Credit for Arrest. *Toronto Star* 29 September, A1.

Pungente, J.J., and **M. O'Malley**. 1999. *More Than Meets the Eye, Watching Television Watching Me.* Toronto: McClelland and Stewart.

Reed, M., and **J. Roberts**. 1999. Adult Correctional Services in Canada 1997/98. *Juristat* 7.

Robinson, D. 1995. *The Impact of Cognitive Skills Training on Post-Release Recidivism among Canadian Federal Offenders.* Ottawa: Correctional Service of Canada, Correctional Research and Development.

Ruff, H. 1983. *Ruff Times.* Alamo, CA: Target Books.

Schur, E.M. 1973. *Radical Non-Intervention.* Englewood Cliffs, NJ: Prentice-Hall.

Statistics Canada. 1996. Population Estimates for 1996 and Projections for the Years 2001, 2006, 2011, and 2016. *1996 Census.* Ottawa: Statistics Canada.

———. 1997a. *The Daily.* 4 November.

———. 1997b. *The Daily.* 2 December.

Standing Committee on Justice and Legal Affairs. 1997. *Renewing Youth Justice.* 13th Report of the Standing Committee on Justice and Legal Affairs. Ottawa: Queen's Printer for Canada.

Toronto Star. 1999. 1.82 Million Inmates Jam U.S. Prisons. 16 August, 3.

Winterdyk, J. (Ed.). 1996. *Issues and Perspectives on Young Offenders in Canada.* Toronto: Harcourt Brace.

———. (Ed.) 2000. *Issues and Perspectives on Young Offenders in Canada* (2nd ed.). Toronto: Harcourt Brace.

Index